Will and World

Will and World

A Study in Metaphysics

N. M. L. NATHAN

CLARENDON PRESS · OXFORD

1992

Oxford University Press, Walton Street, Oxford OX2 6DP

Oxford New York Toronto
Delhi Bombay Calcutta Madras Karachi
Petaling Jaya Singapore Hong Kong Tokyo
Nairobi Dar es Salaam Cape Town
Melbourne Auckland

and associated companies in
Berlin Ibadan

Oxford is a trade mark of Oxford University Press

Published in the United States
by Oxford University Press, New York

British Library Cataloguing in Publication Data
Data available

Library of Congress Cataloging in Publication Data
Nathan, N. M. L.
Will and world: a study in metaphysics/N. M. L. Nathan.
p.   cm.
Includes bibliographical references and index.
1. Will.   2. Free will and determinism.   I. Title.
BJ1461.N37   1992   123'.5—dc20   91-24031
ISBN 0-19-823954-8

Typeset by Best-set Typesetter Ltd
Printed in Great Britain by Bookcraft Ltd
Midsomer Norton, Bath

To A., M., and I.

Preface

THIS book is about the freedom and reality of the will, considered as objects of various oppositions between what we want to be true and what we believe to be the case. It is also about method. Similar oppositions are to be found throughout metaphysics, and everywhere they are amenable to the mode of treatment which I try both to use and to justify.

I am grateful to Paul Snowdon, John Heil, and anonymous readers of the Oxford University Press for criticisms and encouragement. My thanks go to the Leverhulme Trust for a research grant, and to the Universities of East Anglia and Liverpool for terms of leave and much other help. The Editor of *Ratio* gave kind permission for me to incorporate parts of my article 'Three Philosophical Research Programmes', which appeared in vol. 2 (new series), and Howard Robinson generously allowed me to use parts of my contribution to his forthcoming collection *Objections to Physicalism*.

N.M.L.N.

Liverpool
July 1991

Contents

I

Introduction

In a want and belief conflict, you want something to be true, but believe it to be false. In a positive solution, the world changes. In a negative solution, the change is only in your attitudes. In a positive solution your belief is abolished by that very change in the world by virtue of which it was always false. So for example you want something to happen and believe that it never will, but it does happen and that very event abolishes your belief. In a negative solution, you lose your want, or your belief in the falsity of what you want to be true. One or both of your two conflicting attitudes may even be deliberately destroyed. But what changes your attitudes does nothing to determine the truth-value of what you believed.

Some want and belief conflicts have no positive solution. There is in particular no positive solution to conflicts in which what you want is that some purely metaphysical proposition is true. Maybe there are spiritual substances, naturally necessary connections between events, non-natural moral properties, real objects with colour qualities. Among those who reject this relatively rich world-picture, some would like it to be true. But its truth-value is independent of any change in the world which could abolish a belief in its falsity.

All want and belief conflicts, metaphysical or otherwise, have on the other hand some negative solution. Maybe the victim will simply discover that what he wants to be true is true. Maybe he will lose his desire by discovering that it has an incoherent content or depends on a false belief about means and ends. Even if these easy ways out are not available, there are other methods, Pascalian, chemical, autohypnotic, by which it is possible, perhaps at very great cost, to destroy the belief, or, usually at less cost, the desire. It may also be possible, by a gentler method, to diminish the force of one at least of the two conflicting attitudes. If you want p to be true but believe it false then maybe you can diminish the force of the want, without eliminating it altogether, by reflecting that if *p* were true then something else would be false which you also want to be true. The principle applies as much to metaphysical attitudes as it does in everyday life. Suppose that, disliking perpetual illusion, but accepting a Lockean theory of perception, you want it to be true but believe it false that the physical world is pretty much as it appears to the senses. But with a physical world of that kind, you may also think, all physicalist theories of mind would be false. There would be some consolation in the thought if physicalism were something that you independently wanted to be true.

One aim of this book is to say something general about how the philosopher can help to resolve or mitigate metaphysical want and belief conflicts. But most of the book is an application of these generalities to a single, central, and I think testingly dark topic: the will, its existence and its freedom.

To talk here of conflicts and solutions, victims and consolations, may seem too strong. When do I not want this or that, and how can I want anything unless I believe that I do not have it? What follows, however, from wanting something to be the case is not that one believes that it isn't, but only that one does not believe that it is. There is an extra irksomeness when, as in a want and belief conflict, desire is accompanied by positive disbelief. And irksomeness is too weak a word when the contents of the attitudes are metaphysical.

Why, though, should desire-induced conflicts be the philosopher's concern? Why should he have any interest in our mere desires about the nature of things? Why should he have any aim but to discover what is in fact the case? The harmonization of beliefs and desires may have been a tacit objective in some philosophies of the past. If Berkeley was right, we should believe that there is no mind-independent visible world. He would not have been so anxious to claim that only a philosopher would believe otherwise if he had not hoped that nothing we need want to exist would be absent from a world purely of spirits and 'ideas'. If Kant was right, we have no knowledge of a transcendentally real world. But we still have knowledge of appearances, and Kant would not have tendentiously labelled that knowledge of empirical reality if he had not hoped to discredit our desire for something more. There are then precedents of a kind. But why are they precedents to be followed?

We can think of it in this way. Belief precedes philosophy, and belief poses a practical question if, as we can assume, it lies at least indirectly within the believer's control. The question it poses is: Should I or should I not continue to believe? To this question the pure search for truth may not reveal any obvious answer. Suppose it reveals only that there is no evidence either for or against the proposition believed. Should I in that case keep the belief, or is it wrong to continue to believe any proposition for whose truth one has no evidence? Or suppose that evidence does emerge for the falsity of the proposition I believe, and better evidence than any for its truth. Is it good enough evidence to outweigh the adverse consequences of my abandoning my belief? Equally, the pure search for truth may fail to reveal an answer to the practical question of whether I should go on wanting what I want. Now these practical questions about our attitudes are especially pressing when there is strife between the attitudes themselves, and in particular when the proposition which I believe is the negation of that whose truth I desire. In the latter situation, wishful thinking threatens to pre-empt a more reasonable solution. The study of want and belief conflicts can thus be seen just as a study of some relatively pressing practical problems about keeping or abolishing attitudes, problems to whose solution the pure search for truth makes only an incomplete contribution.

There would of course be less of a recommendation here if all philosophical knowledge were valuable for its own sake. But it will be agreed that not *all* knowledge has intrinsic value. We cannot, for instance, find an intrinsic value in just any heap of knowledge that somebody happens to pile up about the economic influence of the development in shipbuilding techniques, 1450–1485. And if nevertheless some knowledge has intrinsic value, it is hard to think of characteristics on which this value might supervene. Is knowledge valuable for its own sake when there is formal or structural beauty in the proposition or system of propositions known? But then why is it for its own sake rather than for the sake of that beauty or the contemplation of that beauty that the knowledge is valuable? Is knowledge intrinsically valuable when there is intrinsic value in the real object known to exist? But then why is it not merely that our knowledge is valuable as a means to preserving the real object, or for the sake of the knower's contemplation of it or its representation?

I will come back to questions about philosophical objectives in the final chapter. Assuming that metaphysical want and belief conflict resolution is indeed something to which the philosopher should contribute, I look in the next chapter at the general form which his contribution can take. Of the seven subsequent chapters, in which these generalities are applied or illustrated, the first five are on conflicts about the freedom of the will, and the last two on conflicts about volition as such.

2

Want and Belief Conflicts

THERE are two stages in the negative resolution of a want and belief conflict. At the deliberative stage, the victim or some alien helper tries to decide which if either of the two conflicting attitudes should be abolished. At the executive stage, the victim or somebody else carries the decision out. The philosopher has help to offer at both these stages. But before I go into the precise nature of what he has to offer, let me elaborate a little on my initial description of want and belief conflicts themselves.

1. FIRST- AND SECOND-ORDER CONFLICTS

The conflicts in my initial examples were between wanting a metaphysical proposition to be true and believing it false. But oppositions occur also between wanting to have a true belief in a metaphysical proposition and believing that one lacks this true belief. There is no reason why the philosopher should not also help in the resolution of these second-order conflicts, and no reason either why they too should not be called metaphysical.

It is easy to see how one and the same person can progress from a first- to a second-order conflict, easy to see how a conflict in which what the victim wants is not even partly that he has a certain attitude can be replaced by one in which his desideratum is at least partly that. Suppose you want it to be true but believe it false that there is an objective good, something which 'would be sought by anyone who was acquainted with it, not because of any contingent fact that this person or every person is so constructed that he desires this end, but just because the end has to-be-pursuedness somehow built into it'.[1] You want this to be true because you think that then there would be more

---

[1] Mackie (1977), 40.

practical agreement; you believe it to be false because you think that 'variations in moral codes are more readily explained by the hypothesis that they reflect ways of life than by the hypothesis that they express perceptions, most of them seriously inadequate and badly distorted, of objective values'.[2] But then you stop believing that there is no objective good. The argument about the two hypotheses suddenly seems unconvincing. It seems to rely on the principle that if p's truth is more simply explained by a hypothesis which does not entail q than by a hypothesis which does entail q, then that is evidence that q is false. The correct principle, you think, is that if p's truth is more simply explained by a hypothesis which entails not-q than by a hypothesis which does not entail not-q then that is evidence that q is false. And in the present case this latter principle seems not to apply: it is consistent with the hypothesis that the variations 'reflect ways of life' that some or even all of those who hold conflicting codes have an unexercised power to perceive a real objective good. But all the same, and even though you do not stop wanting there to be an objective good, in the inherent to-be-pursuedness sense, you are unable quite to believe that there is; there seems in fact to be no adequate argument either way. At this point a new conflict is liable to afflict you. It is not, I think, that your continuing desire for there to be an objective good will make you want just to believe that there is such a thing, so that the new conflict is just between wanting to believe this and believing that you do not. If you want it to be true that there is an objective good, this desire will make you want to have a true belief that there is, so that the new conflict is between wanting to have a true belief that there is, and believing that you lack this true belief. And of course someone else, who has never positively believed that there is no objective good, may have been afflicted from the outset by a conflict between wanting to have a true belief in an objective good and believing that he lacks that true belief.

Does wanting p to be true always generate the desire to have a true belief that p? Are there not cases in which you want p to be true while positively wanting not to believe it? You want to have done well but then you start worrying that you will become complacent if you believe as much. You want her to be happy

---

[2] Ibid. 37.

but think that if you believe that she is then you will not be able to resist telling someone who will then immmediately make sure that she is not. In each of these cases, you want p to be true but believe that p would be false if you believed it true. But I have not been able to imagine a case like this in which p is metaphysical.

I suggest, then, that our oppositions are liable to occur in pairs. The first member of such a pair is a first-order conflict between wanting a metaphysical proposition to be true and believing it false. The second member of the pair is a second-order conflict: the same person or someone else wants to have a true belief in that same metaphysical proposition but believes he lacks that true belief.

If metaphysical want and belief conflicts did occur in these pairs, that would make for economy in a general programme aimed at their resolution. Suppose you want p to be true and believe not-p, and you decide that although this conflict should be resolved by abolishing your belief, it would be wrong to resolve it by destroying your want. After you abolish your belief that not-p you are still afflicted by a conflict between wanting to have a true belief that p and believing that you lack this true belief. But whatever makes it wrong to resolve the first-order conflict by destroying your desire for p to be true will presumably also make it wrong to resolve the second-order conflict by destroying your desire to have a true belief that p. Or again, a piece of information, the victim's acceptance of which would help to dislodge the belief element in a first-order conflict, may also help to dislodge the belief element in a second-order conflict. Suppose there is good evidence for p which is better evidence than any evidence for not-p. Acceptance by a first-order victim of this proposition about evidence would make it easier for him to dislodge his belief that not-p. And since acceptance by a second-order victim of this information would make it easier for him to acquire a belief that p, it would also make it easier for him to dislodge his belief that he lacks a true belief that p.

According to the Introduction, metaphysical want and belief conflicts have no positive solutions, and one aim of philosophy is to help negatively to resolve them. The distinction I have now introduced between first- and second-order metaphysical want and belief conflicts does not oblige me to take this back. In a positive solution to a want and belief conflict the belief is abolished by that very change in the world thanks to which it was always false. In a negative solution the victim loses either his want or his belief in the falsity of what he wants to be true, but the truth-value of what he wants to be true and believes to be false owes nothing to what changes his attitudes. Obviously second-order conflicts have negative solutions: the victim can lose his desire to have a true belief that p or lose his belief that he lacks such a belief. But do second-order conflicts lack positive solutions? The victim's desire, in a second-order conflict, is to have a true belief that p. He may indeed do what results in his believing that p. Is his belief that he lacks a true belief that p then abolished by the very change in the world thanks to which it is false that he lacks a true belief that p? Not quite. His doing what results in his believing p is a change in the world which abolishes his belief that he lacks a true belief that p, and it is a change thanks to which it is false that he lacks a belief that p. But it is not a change thanks to which it is false that he lacks a *true* belief that p. For if p is a metaphysical proposition, its truth-value is independent of any change in the world which could produce a belief in its truth. Neither first- nor second-order conflicts have positive solutions if they are metaphysical.

2. EXECUTION

I distinguished between help in reaching a decision about what if anything of a negative kind to do about a want and belief conflict, and help in carrying that decision out. The decision—about which if either of the two conflicting attitudes to abolish—may be reached either by the victim or by someone who has been wondering how if at all he should intervene in a conflict which afflicts someone else. But whoever reaches the decision, the philosopher can help in its execution by supplying information whose acceptance by the victim makes a doomed attitude easier to dislodge.

I have already mentioned information whose acceptance by the victim will make the belief element easier to dislodge. In a first-order conflict the victim wants p to be true and believes not-p, where p is not even partly to the effect that he has a certain attitude. If the victim comes to believe that some proposition is good evidence for p and better evidence than any proposition is for not-p, then that will make his belief that not-p easier to dislodge. In a second-order conflict, the victim wants to have a true belief that p but believes that he lacks this true belief. If he comes to believe that some proposition is good evidence for p and better evidence than any proposition is for not-p, then that will make it easier for him to acquire a belief that p, and hence to dislodge his belief that he lacks the true belief that p.

What information is there whose acceptance by the victim will make it easier for him to abolish or diminish the want element in his conflict? Consider a first-order conflict, in which he wants p to be true but believes that not-p. His desire for p to be true will, I think, vanish if he comes to believe that its content is incoherent. Sometimes his want will then split into two wants with incompatible contents. But not always. Wanting to square the circle, he is finally convinced that this is logically impossible. There will not necessarily be any non-jointly satisfiable successor desires. The true thesis that your want does not survive your conviction that its content is incoherent is easy to confuse with the false thesis that your want does not survive your conviction that its actual satisfaction is logically impossible. Suppose you believe that x has happened and you want it not to have happened. You can believe that necessarily it is now too late for your want to be satisfied without believing that 'x did not happen' is incoherent. If you can cry over spilt milk, why can't you want to have your cake and eat it? There are two things which people are apt to mean by that, and neither is having a want with a content you believe to be incoherent. One of them is failing to have the true belief that what you want is logically impossible. The other is having two wants, whose objects, as you may perfectly well realize, are incompatible: you want to have your cake and you also want to eat it.

If you want x then you may want it either wholly or partly for its own sake or wholly or partly for the sake of something else. In the case where you want x at least partly for the sake of something else you believe a proposition about the relation between x and this something else. That proposition I will refer to as the internal proposition of your desire for x, and I will say that when you want x wholly or partly for the sake of something else your desire for x is wholly or partly based on your belief in the internal proposition of your desire for x. Anything that makes it easier to dislodge your belief in the internal proposition of your desire makes it easier to dislodge or at least diminish the strength of that desire itself. And, as we have seen, there are propositions about evidence whose acceptance by a believer will make it easier to dislodge his belief. So if, in a conflict between wanting p to be true but believing it to be false, the victim wants p to be true at least partly for the sake of something else, and he or someone else has decided to abolish or diminish his desire, there may be information about evidence against the internal proposition of his desire for p to be true whose acceptance by him will make it easier to carry this decision out. The same goes for the execution of decisions to abolish or diminish the desire in a second-order conflict. For, as we are assuming, no-one wants to have a true belief that p unless he wants p to be true.

What is the general difference between wanting something for its own sake and wanting it for the sake of something else? There is a difference between wanting something for its own sake and just wanting it without thinking at all about how it is related to anything else that you want. In order to want something for its own sake it is necessary to have a certain belief about your wanting it. A first hypothesis would be that N wants x for its own sake if and only if (i) he wants x, and (ii) he believes that there is no y and no relation such that he wants y and is caused to want x by his belief that x stands in that relation to y. Correspondingly, N wants x for the sake of y if and only if (i) he wants x, (ii) he wants y, (iii) he believes that x stands in a certain relation to y, and (iv) he believes that he is caused to want x by his belief that x stands in this relation to y. The relation here could be causal, as when he wants a curtain to keep the light out, or it could be logical, as when he wants this woman on the Board for the sake of there being at least one woman on the Board.

A paradoxical consequence of this first analysis is that if you want something both for its own sake and for the sake of something else then you believe two incompatible propositions about the causation of your want. A minor revision meets the objection. We can say that N wants x for its own sake if and only if (i) he wants x, and (iia) he believes that there is no y and no relation such that he wants y and is caused to want x as much as he does by his belief that x stands in that relation to y. And we can say that N wants x for the sake of y if and only if (i) he wants x, (ii) he wants y, (iii) he believes that x stands in a certain relation to y, and (iva) either he believes that he is caused to want x by his belief that x stands in this relation to y, or he believes both this and that he is not caused to want x as much as he does by his belief that x stands in this relation to y. What the first hypothesis in fact defines is wanting something purely for its own sake, and wanting something purely for the sake of something else.

Even when the victim of a want and belief conflict wants p's truth for its own sake, there is information his acceptance of which will at least help to diminish his desire. It is difficult to go on wanting p to be true as much as before if one comes to accept that if p then, probably at least, not-q, where q is something else that one wants to be true. The victim's desire will not of course be diminished if he believes that q is false anyway: he must either think that, actually, q is true, or have no belief as to q's truth-value. If I want to be a great composer, and believe that this is indeed my future, it will be a comfort for my not being an expert statistician if I believe that this would have prevented my musical greatness. Maybe there is still some consolation here if, wanting to be a great composer, I cannot quite believe that I never will be. But if I positively believe that I will never be a great composer then it is no comfort at all for my not being an expert statistician, that if I had been then musical greatness would not have been my destiny. If you want q to be true, then, and do not believe it false, your desire for p's truth will be diminished if you come to believe that if p then, probably at least, not-q. It is a principle constantly applied by friends, parents, psychotherapists. So too is the principle that if you want q to be false, and do not believe it to be true, your desire for p's truth will be diminished if you come to believe that probably q would have been true if something relevantly similar to p had been true.

Once, an elderly general practitioner consulted me because of his severe depression. He could not overcome the loss of his wife who had died two years before and whom he had loved above all else. Now how could I help him? What should I tell him? Well, I refrained from telling him anything but instead confronted him with the question, 'What would have happened, Doctor, if you had died first, and your wife would have had to survive you?' 'Oh', he said, 'for her this would have been terrible; how she would have suffered.' Whereupon I replied, 'You see, Doctor, such a suffering has been spared her, and it was you who have spared her this suffering; but now, you have to pay for it by surviving and mourning her.' He said no word but shook my hand and calmly left my office.[3]

3. DELIBERATION

I now turn from the execution of decisions about want and belief conflicts to the deliberations by means of which these decisions are reached. Since we are confining ourselves to negative solutions, these deliberations will be about which if either of the two attitudes is to be abolished. And as already noted, the deliberator may be either a victim, who wonders what if anything to do about his own conflict, or some helper or busybody who contemplates intervention in a conflict which afflicts someone other than himself. Let me now consider these two kinds of deliberation in turn.

In a first-order want and belief conflict, the victim wants p to be true, but believes that not-p. First let us consider his deliberations about whether he should abolish his belief that not-p. His conclusion will depend on his views about when in general believing is good or bad, or, as I shall say, on his value theory about belief. Here are some examples of such theories:

(1) It is better to believe a proposition than not to believe it if and only if believing it produces more happiness than not believing it.

(2) It is better to believe a proposition than not to believe it if and only if that proposition is true.

(3) It is better to believe a proposition than not to believe it if and only if either the proposition is true and believing it does not produce vastly less happiness than not believing it or the proposition is false and believing it produces vastly more happiness than not believing it.

Value theories do not by themselves yield decisions. Before he can decide what to do the deliberator still needs to determine which of the particular alternatives open to him would, by the standard of his own value theory, actually be for the best. But without a value theory he would not be able to deliberate at all.

[3] Frankl (1964), 14–15.

It is important not to become entangled at this point in controversies about the epistemic justification of belief. Even if 'Is my present belief that not-p epistemically justified?' means the same as 'Would it be best from an epistemic point of view for me to keep rather than abolish my belief that not-p?', still our deliberator is asking a different question. He is asking whether it would be best overall, best all things considered, for him to keep rather than to abolish his belief. I agree that if he accepts value theory (2) then there may be no difference between the actual course of his deliberations and the course they would have taken if he had considered things from a purely epistemic point of view. Whether there is such a difference depends on how 'epistemic' is defined, and on this there is no general agreement among epistemologists.[4] But, however 'epistemic' is defined, 'better', in (2), does still mean better overall; to think that only the 'epistemic' matters is not the same as to abstract from everything but the 'epistemic'. And (2) itself is just one of the many value theories which the victim, wondering whether he should abolish or keep his belief that not-p, might conceivably try to apply.

Let us begin by supposing that the victim does indeed accept (2). In this case he will have no difficulty at all in immediately concluding that he should not abolish his belief that not-p. If he accepts (2), then he thinks that it is better to keep on believing not-p if and only if not-p is true. But if he then accordingly asks whether not-p is in fact true, he will of course answer that it is. If he did not answer the question in this way, then that would be a sign that he did not actually believe not-p after all, in which case there would be no want and belief conflict to resolve.

But unfortunately the victim's deliberation about the belief element is unlikely to be as simple as this. Most people will think that even if the value of believing is largely determined by whether the proposition believed is true, the consequences of believing are also relevant. Believing the truth can have bad consquences, and occasionally it will have such bad consequences that not believing the truth is better. Equally, believing what is false will occasionally have consequences good enough to outweigh its intrinsic

---

[4] According to one recent survey, most epistemologists have in fact 'remained mute' on what exactly epistemic justification is supposed to be. See Pollock (1987), 81.

badness. Even on the fantastic view that nothing at all has any value for its own sake but believing the truth, it is conceivable that believing the truth has an instrumental disvalue which outweighs its intrinsic value. It is conceivable that your believing the truth today prevents many other people from believing the truth tomorrow. We must ask then how a victim can decide whether or not he should abolish his belief that not-*p*, if he thinks that in general the value of believing depends at least partly on the consequences of that believing.

No victim will seriously think that he can work out the probabilities of all the possible good and bad consequences of keeping and of abolishing his belief that not-*p*. And there is in any case a regressive difficulty about such calculations. Suppose he does try to work it all out and eventually reaches the conclusion that it would be best for him to abolish his belief that not-*p*. At least part of his reason for this conclusion will be a proposition of the form

(P1) there is a probability x that abolishing his belief that not-*p* will have consequences C.

Is it right for him to decide to abolish his belief that not-*p* without first having come to the rational decision that he should keep his belief in this form (P1) proposition? It seems not. But suppose he does come to such a decision. At least part of his reason for this decision will be a proposition of the form

(P2) there is a probability x that keeping his belief in the form (P1) proposition will have consequences C_1.

But surely he should not have decided to keep his belief in the form (P1) proposition without first having come to the rational decision that he should keep his belief in the form (P2) proposition. And so on *ad infinitum*. It looks then as if the victim, if he is to take the consequences of abolishing his belief that not-*p* into account at all, must be prepared to assume that what he judges to be best relative to those of its possible good and bad consequences which he is aware of and whose probability he has the time and ability to estimate will also be best relative to all of its possible good and bad consequences. And it looks as if he must be prepared to have a belief in a proposition of form (P1) or form (P2) or form (P3) or ..., the value of keeping which he does not try to estimate before relying on it in his calculations about the value of keeping his belief that not-*p*.

If its scope is correspondingly restricted, decision theory provides a perfectly good framework for deliberation. Jeffrey's decision theory enjoins us to maximize conditional expected desirability.[5] If $(Q_1, \ldots, Q_n)$ is a partition, a set of mutually exclusive and jointly exhaustive propositions, the conditional expected desirability of an action x is the sum of a series of products, each product corresponding to a different element of the partition. The first product is got by multiplying $P(Q_1/x)$, the probability of Q_1 given x, by $D(Q_1$ and $x)$, the desirability of the situation which the deliberator expects to arise if he takes the action x when Q_1 is true. The other products are got by doing the same for each other element in the partition.

The actions between which the victim is to decide are abolishing his belief that not-p (A) and leaving that belief alone (B). If we take as the partition (p and not-p), then the conditional expected desirability of A will be $D(p$ and A$)P(p/A) + D($not-p and A$)P($not-$p/A)$, and the conditional expected desirability of B will be $D(p$ and B$)P(p/B) + D($not-p and B$)P($not-$p/B)$. Since the victim already believes that not-p, he will assign a value of 1 to $P($not-$p/A)$ and to $P($not-$p/B)$, and a value of 0 to $P(p/A)$ and to $P(p/B)$. So A will have a higher conditional expected desirability than B if $D(p$ and A$)$ is greater than $D(p$ and B$)$. One state of affairs certainly produced by A when p is true is that the victim loses a false belief that not-p, and one state of affairs certainly produced by B when p is true is that he continues to have a false belief that not-p. If, on the victim's value theory about belief, true belief is intrinsically good and false belief intrinsically bad, then he will think that (p and A) produces a kind of intrinsic goodness which (p and B) does not produce, and that (p and B) produces a kind of intrinsic badness that (p and A) does not produce. But we are assuming that the victim thinks that the value of a belief state is determined not only by whether the proposition believed is true, but by the consequences of that belief state. So he will think that the overall value of (p and A) depends not only on the intrinsic goodness of the certain consequence that he himself loses a false belief, but also on the probability of its having all the other intrinsically good and bad consequences which it is possible for it to have. And he will think that the overall value of (p and B) will depend not only on the intrinsic bad-

[5] Jeffrey (1983).

ness of the certain consequence that he himself continues to have
a false belief, but also on the probability of its having all the other
intrinsically good and bad consequences which it is possible for
it to have. He knows that he is aware of only some of these other
possibilities, and he knows that, of those he is aware of, there
are few whose probabilities he can even roughly estimate. He can
only hope that the verdict which he would have reached on the
comparative value of (p and A) and (p and B) if he had had perfect knowledge will be no different from the verdict he reaches
on the basis of his rough estimates of the probabilities of the
relatively few possible intrinsically good and bad consequences
which he is able to take into account. He will also have to post-
pone until after these limited calculations any consideration of
questions about whether he should keep the beliefs about the
probabilities of these possible consequences on which he relies
in these calculations themselves. Or at least he will have to post-
pone consideration of questions about whether he should keep
his beliefs about the probabilities of the possible consequences of
keeping his beliefs about the possible consequences of A and B
when p is true. Or at least . . . And so on.

It may perhaps be easier for the victim to reconcile himself to
his relative ignorance of possible consequences and their probabilities if he reflects that it will be easier for him to prevent at
least some possible bad consequences of keeping his own belief
that not-p than it would be for him to prevent the similar results
of somebody else's keeping a belief that not-p. If for example he
is afraid of what may happen if he broadcasts his own belief that
not-p to a hysterical public, then he has the option of staying
silent. But if it were somebody else's belief that not-p which he
was wondering whether to abolish, discretion might be less easy
for him to secure.

But whether or not the victim has a partly consequentialist
theory of the value of belief, there does not seem to be any specific
help that the philosopher can offer the victim in his deliberations
about whether to abolish his belief that not-p. So long as the
victim is indeed a victim, he will already believe that not-p is
true, and will not therefore be interested in evidence for and
against p. And there is no reason to suppose that the philosopher
will have any more knowledge than the victim of the consequences
of keeping or abolishing the victim's belief.

Is there more scope for the philosopher to help in the victim's deliberations about whether or not to abolish his want? Certainly most people will think that the value of wanting is at least partly determined by the consequences of this wanting. And judgements about the consequences of wanting are as difficult to make and as remote from any specially philosophical competence as judgements about the consequences of believing. But it would not be at all surprising if the victim thought that, in general, the value of wanting something to be the case is also partly determined by the value of its actually being the case. If p's truth would be good, he may think, then it is also good to want p to be true, and if p's truth would be bad then it is bad to want p to be true. Suppose then that the victim wants p to be true without already thinking that p's truth would be good. Then if the question arises of whether he should abolish his desire for p to be true, he will be interested in evidence for and against p's truth being good. And even if we assume that no arguments are available which will influence the victim's views either on whether or not p's truth is good for its own sake or on whether or not p's truth is bad for its own sake, the victim may still look for evidence as to whether or not p's truth is conducive to other things that he thinks good or bad, and the philosopher may supply him with this evidence.

Now let me turn to second-order conflicts, in which the victim does not believe that not-p, but nevertheless wants, but believes he lacks, a true belief that p. These conflicts can be resolved by abolishing either the want or the belief. Since, as we are assuming, the victim wants a true belief that p only because he wants p to be true, his deliberations about the want element in the second-order conflict will simply be deliberations about whether to abolish his desire for p to be true. We have already considered deliberations of this type. As for abolition of the belief element, this can be done by acquiring a true belief that p. Suppose he has satisfied himself that having a true belief that p is better, even when the consequences of his having that belief are taken into account, than not having a true belief that p. What should he do? Should he just do whatever will result in his believing that p, on the grounds that once he believes that p, he will not himself think that p is anything but true? Obviously not, for he will know, before undertaking this action, that it may result in his having a false belief that p. What he wants is somehow to discover that

p is true. And here the philosopher can help in the victim's deliberations. Evidence for and against p is what the victim wants, and since p is a metaphysical proposition, the philosopher may be able to tell the victim what the balance of evidence is.

I turn finally to the deliberations of a person wondering what if anything to do about a conflict which afflicts someone other than himself. Consider a first-order conflict: the victim wants p to be true but believes not-p, where p is not a proposition about any of his own attitudes. How will the alien deliberator approach the question of whether he should abolish the victim's belief that not-p? Even if the deliberator believes that

(2) It is better to believe a proposition than not to believe it if and only if that proposition is true,

he cannot necessarily conclude straight away that the victim's belief that not-p should be preserved. For the deliberator is not the victim, and may not himself believe that not-p. The deliberator may have no initial belief as to the truth-value of p, and may welcome the philosopher's offer to discuss the balance of evidence. If this helps the deliberator to make up his mind whether or not p is true, it will help him to make up his mind about whether or not it is better to abolish the victim's belief that not-p. The same goes even if the deliberator thinks that in general the value of belief depends on its consequences as well as on the truth or falsity of the proposition believed. So long as the value of belief depends even partly on the truth-value of the proposition believed, the deliberator, if he has no initial belief as to the truth-value of p, will welcome a discussion of evidence for and against p.

How will the alien deliberator approach the question of whether to abolish the victim's desire for p to be true? He will not necessarily share this desire, and may have no initial view as to how good it would be if p were true. So, if the deliberator thinks that in general the value of wanting something to be the case depends on the value of its being the case, he may well be interested in whatever the philosopher has to say about the value of p's truth. In particular, he will be interested to hear whether there is some subtle incoherence in the content of the victim's desire, and in what evidence there is that p's truth is conducive to other things that he, the deliberator, values.

In alien deliberation about second-order conflicts, deliberation about the want element follows the same course as deliberation about the want element in first-order conflicts. The new question is whether the victim should be induced to believe that p. The alien deliberator, like the victim, may initially believe neither p nor not-p, and he may think that the value of belief depends at least partly on the truth-value of the proposition believed. In this case he will be as interested in the evidence for and against p as he would have been if he had himself been the victim. On the other hand, he may himself already believe that p is true, in which case his deliberation will concentrate on the consequences of the victim's gaining what he, the deliberator, takes to be a true belief.

4. A PROGRAMME

There are then various ways in which a philosopher can help to resolve metaphysical want and belief conflicts, various questions about the conflicting attitudes which he can usefully try to answer. The questions that I try to answer when I turn to want and belief conflicts about the will are of just four kinds. With p as the proposition which the victim of a first-order conflict wants to be true but believes to be false, I shall ask:

(1) Does the desire for p to be true have an incoherent content?

(2) When the victim wants p to be true for the sake of something else, is there good evidence for the falsity of what he then believes, which is better evidence than any for its truth? (In the jargon of Section 3 above, does the desire for p to be true have a doubtful internal proposition?)

(3) Is there good evidence for p which is better evidence than any evidence for not-p?

(4) Is there a proposition q such that (i) if p then probably at least not-q, (ii) the victim wants q to be true, (iii) the victim does not already believe that not-q?

Questions of form (1) are worth asking because, as we have seen, a desire does not survive its owner's recognition that its content is incoherent. One might conceivably think that it is better for the victim of a conflict by which one is not oneself afflicted to have a want with an incoherent content than not to have it. But if it has somehow been decided that a conflict should be resolved by abolition of the want, a revelation of incoherence is one means of putting that decision into effect. Questions of forms (2) and (3) are worth asking for a similar reason. There are conceivable circumstances in which someone might think that it is better for an alien victim to have a desire with a doubtful internal proposition, or to believe a proposition for which there is no good evidence or whose negation has better evidential support. But revelation of such facts will at least help to dislodge the attitude in question, once it has somehow been decided that this ought to be done. Positive answers to questions of form (4) signal the existence of palliatives. If it has somehow been decided that the conflict should not be resolved, then the victim's awareness that there are disadvantages in things being as he wants may at least diminish the force of his desire.

Nominally, questions of all four forms are about first-order conflicts. But their answers are also relevant to the resolution of the second-order conflicts by which, as I earlier suggested, first-order conflicts are liable to be accompanied. The suggestion (see Section 1 above) was that want and belief conflicts are liable to occur in pairs, whose first member is a first-order conflict in which the victim wants p to be true but believes not-p, and whose second member is a second-order conflict in which the same or another victim wants, but believes he lacks, a true belief in this same proposition p. Since, as I assume, the victim of this second-order conflict will not want a true belief that p unless he wants p to be true, answers to questions of forms (1), (2), and (4) are as relevant to the resolution of his conflict as to that of the first-order member of the pair. Questions of form (3) also have a bearing on second-order conflicts. The second-order victim, wondering whether to resolve matters by doing what will give him the belief that p which he thinks he lacks, will not be totally incurious about whether there is good evidence for not-p which is better than any evidence for p.

In the next four chapters (3–6) I describe want and belief conflicts about free decisions, and put to these conflicts questions of the four kinds just distinguished. In Chapter 7 I try to relate conflicts about free decisions to conflicts about free action more generally. In Chapters 8 and 9 I put questions of some of my four kinds to want and belief conflicts not about freedom but about volition as such.

3

Free Will

WANTING to make free decisions, people have for centuries thought some doctrine or other about regularity in the world both true and incompatible with the thesis that we do freely decide. If old and extreme determinisms like 'Every event has a cause' or 'Every event falls under a universal law of nature' are nowadays less popular than they were, other seemingly freedom-excluding theses about regularity in the world are still likely to be believed: that every mental event has a neurophysiological cause, for example, or that every event falls under either a universal or a statistical law of nature. First-order conflicts about freedom of decision are still endemic. Those, moreover, who positively believe determinisms or other theses about regularity in the world which they take to exclude our freedom are liable to have more cautious counterparts: there are those who, though they do not positively believe in any such seemingly freedom-excluding thesis, still cannot quite believe that every such thesis is false. On the argument of the last chapter, such people are threatened by second-order conflicts. Wanting there to be free decisions, they will want, but believe they lack, a true belief in their existence.

It is indeed difficult to see how the stock question of freedom and determinism can be given any definite non-arbitrary interpretation except as a problem of want and belief conflict resolution. Is freedom compatible with determinism? It depends on how 'freedom' and 'determinism' are interpreted. How then do we select our interpretations? Do we take the ordinary meanings of the two terms? There is no reason to suppose that either has just one ordinary meaning. A natural move would be to limit the discussion to those freedoms which we want to possess and to those determinisms for which it looks as if there might be good evidence. But the question of whether, in a determinism-generated conflict between wanting to be free and believing that one is not, the belief has good evidential support is already, on commonsense evidentialist assumptions, a question about whether the belief ought to be abolished. And once that question is posed, it is natural also to ask whether it is not the want rather than the belief that the victim would be better without. Maybe there is some hidden incoherence in the content of the want, or maybe the want is based on a false belief about means and ends, or maybe the belief should be maintained even though it has no evidential support. It does in fact become natural to pose the quite general question of which of the two conflicting attitudes ought to go.

If all philosophical knowledge is valuable for its own sake then of course the stock question *can* reasonably be interpreted in any way one fancies, and there is less reason to replace it by problems of want and belief conflict resolution. However we define 'freedom' and 'determinism', it may still in that case be possible to produce intrinsically valuable knowledge about their logical relations. But, as I noted in the Introduction, this doctrine about the value of philosophy is not easy to defend. And it is, I think, a fault in some recent philosophy of freedom that it presupposes the contrary. In his *Essay on Free Will* Peter van Inwagen tries to show that 'He could have done otherwise' is incompatible with a certain version of determinism. It is not clear why van Inwagen selects that particular version. If it were a version that people are in fact likely to believe, and to believe incompatible with a capacity for alternative action which they want to possess, then van Inwagen's arguments for the incompatibility would, if successful, block one escape from a want and belief conflict. If it were a version that we ought to believe, and if his incompatibilist arguments were successful, and if we want a capacity for alternative action, then a want and belief conflict would threaten us which ought not to be resolved except by abolition of the want. But there is no evidence that van Inwagen is at all interested in either of these trains of thought. He makes no effort to show that his version of determinism, which employs a rather strong concept of laws of nature, is any more popular than a weaker, 'Humean' thesis. And he positively denies that it ought to be believed. To believe it would, he says, be 'wholly unjustified', at least 'at the present time'.[1] As for the future, 'moral responsibility requires free will',[2] and he thinks that, quite independently of any argument for or against incompatibilism or

---

[1] Van Inwagen (1983), 204.
[2] Ibid. 180.

determinism, we cannot help believing that we know we have moral responsibility.[3] However arbitrary his interpretation of 'determinism', his incompatibilist arguments, if valid, would of course give us new knowledge of logical relations. And if such knowledge had an intrinsic value, then his project would have a point. But what if there is no intrinsic value in such knowledge? Van Inwagen's findings may of course still turn out to be very useful to the conflict-resolving philosopher. If free will as van Inwagen defines it is an object of desire, and if, contrary to what he himself thinks, his determinism is true, then his incompatibilism will be of great interest from a conflict-resolving point of view. Even if his determinism is not true, his arguments may still be adaptable to support incompatibilism with respect to some weaker but true thesis about regularity in the world. Or, if his determinism is not true, we may still want it to be true, and if it is incompatible with a freedom we want, that might help to console us when, for quite other reasons, we believe that we lack this freedom, or fail to believe that we possess it. The point is that these benefits would be quite fortuitous.

I have, anyway, chosen a direct approach to want and belief conflict resolution, and turn now to the first part of the programme which, with that goal in mind, I set out at the end of the last chapter. In the first section of this chapter, I distinguish various things we might mean by calling a decision free. In the second section, I argue that the important senses of 'free decision', from a conflict-resolving point of view, are those, or some of them, on which 'N freely decided to A' entails that his decision to A was not his only possibility. In the third section I consider which particular species of this extra possibility freedom the victims of want and belief conflicts are liable to want. With the central conflicts about free decisions properly identified, I can then turn in the next chapter to the questions proposed about internal propositions and coherence, and in subsequent chapters to the questions about evidence and palliatives.

1. VARIETIES OF FREE DECISION

One thing we might mean by calling an action free is simply that in acting the agent does as he wills or does what he wants, with

[3] Ibid. 209.

the willing or wanting conceived of as an actual member of the causal sequence in which the action consists. Decisions cannot be called free in this sense, for they are themselves willings, rather than sequences of events of which willings or wantings are members. But there are other senses in which actions or intentional actions can be called free whether or not they are decisions.

(1) 'N freely Aed' can be taken in a *negative extra possibility* sense. It then entails that N was able not to A.

(2) 'N freely Aed' can also be taken in a *positive extra possibility* sense, in which case it entails that N was able to do something other than Aing.

(3) N's Aing may have been free in the sense of *autonomous*, from which it would follow that (i) he wanted to A or wanted something to which he believed that Aing was conducive; (ii) the want here was one which he had himself chosen either to acquire or to go on having.

(4) N's Aing may have been free in the sense of *hierarchically coherent*, in which case (i) he wanted to A or wanted something to which he believed that Aing was conducive; (ii) the want here was one that he wanted to have; and (iii) he did not want not to have this second-level want.

(5) 'N freely Aed' may be taken in a *sole authorship* sense. It then entails that N originated his own Aing, was not caused to A.

(6) N's Aing may have been free in the sense of *unconstrained*. In this case he did not believe he would have suffered as a result of not Aing. We could say that the more difficult it is for N not to A, the less negative extra possibility freedom there is in his Aing. Constraint would then tend to reduce negative extra possibility freedom: believing that you will suffer by not Aing makes it more difficult for you not to A.

Autonomy, as I defined it, has various species. We could for example distinguish between those which do, and those which do not, require that N's choice, with respect to the want mentioned in (i), should itself exhibit the same species of autonomy. Galen Strawson's 'true responsibility' is an autonomy in which this is required: an action is 'truly responsible' only if (*a*) it is made according to a set of principles ('preferences, values, pro-attitudes, ideals, whatever') which the decider has already chosen according to some further set of principles, and (*b*) the choice of this further set of principles is also 'truly responsible'.[4]

Extra possibility freedoms also have several species, and I will now look in some detail at various species of positive extra possibility freedom, so far as it applies to decisions. To simplify the discussion, I will take it that in '*N* was able to do something at *t* other than deciding to *A*', which is entailed by '*N*'s decision at *t* to *A* was free in a positive extra possibility sense', the extra possibility is always a decision not to *A*. And in fact from now onwards, 'extra possibility freedom of decision' will unless I say otherwise always stand for a positive extra possibility freedom in which this is the extra possibility.

Even on this restricted interpretation, extra possibility freedom of decision has several species. For various things could be meant by the general formula '*N* was able to decide to *t* not to *A*'. The first species is conditional or C-freedom of decision. *N*'s decision at *t* to *A* was C-free only if the entailed statement about his ability to decide not to *A* is equivalent either to a single conditional of the form 'If *X* had been the case *N* would have decided at *t* not to *A*', or to a series of conditionals in which such a conditional is the first member and in which each subsequent member is about the conditions under which the antecedent of its immediate predecessor would be true.

One way of multiplying C-senses of 'free decision' is by assigning different values to the variables in the antecedents of the conditionals. Thus the antecedent of the conditional 'If *X* had been the case *N* would have decided at *t* not to *A*' might become 'If *N* had wanted not to *A*', or 'If *N* had wanted to decide at *t* not to *A*', or something of the form 'If *N*'s environment had been ...' For any one of these interpretations we can generate a further range of interpretations by specifying different relations between the time at which *X* would have been the case and the time *t* at which *N* in fact decided to *A*. The conditional might for example read 'If *X* had been the case at *t*, then *N* would have decided at *t* not to *A*', or 'If *X* had been the case before *t*, then *N* would have decided at *t* not to *A*'.

We can also ask this question: Given that *N* decided at *t* to *A* and that

---

[4] Strawson (1986), 29.

(A) If X had been the case, N would have decided at t not to A,

how would things have been just beforehand if N had decided at t not to A? Would they have been, in all other respects, just the same? Or would they have been different in some other respects as well? It will be easier to explore the possibilities here if we introduce a special concept of the *state* of the world at an instant. I borrow it from van Inwagen:

Our concept of *state* must be such that, given that the world is in a certain state at a certain instant, nothing *follows* about its state at any other instant: if x and y are any 'states' and some possible world is in x at t_1 and y at t_2, there is a world that is in x at t_1 and *not* in y at t_2. For example, we must not choose a concept of *state* that would allow, as a part of the description of the momentary state of the world, the clause, '... and, at T, the world is such that someone's left hand will be raised 10 seconds later than T'.[5]

Using this concept of the state of the world at an instant, suppose that

(B) If N had decided at t not to A, then the state of the world just before t would have been just as it actually was.

Then if (A) means, more specifically, 'if X had been the case just before t, N would have decided at t not to A', the conjunction of (A) and (B) yields the self-contradictory

(C) If X had been the case just before t, then the state of the world just before t would have been just as it actually was.

But there are other more specific interpretations of (A), which can be consistently conjoined with (B), e.g. 'If X had been the case well before t, N would have decided at t not to A'. And we can also consistently conjoin 'If X had been the case just before t, N would have decided at t not to A' with 'If N had decided at t not to A, then the state of the world just before t would have been different from what it actually was'.

Finally, we get different particular C-senses of 'free decision' according to how in general we interpret counterfactual conditionals. Suppose we interpret them on the lines suggested by David Lewis. 'If X had been the case, then N would have decided at t not to A', will then mean something like 'Either it is im-

---

[5] Van Inwagen (1983), 59.

possible that X was the case, or any possible world in which X is the case and N does not decide at t not to A is less similar to the actual world than some possible world in which X is the case and N decides at t not to A'. The alternative is to take the putting forward of a counterfactual as nothing more than a convenient way of asserting or conversationally implying various propositions purely about the actual world, one at least of the propositions asserted being a generalization about the topics of antecedent and consequent which is indispensible in the deduction of the latter from the former. Suppose for example you say this: 'If it had been one of my books it would have had my name in it'. Putting it thus would just be a convenient way of suggesting that the book does not have your name in it and of asserting that all your books have your name in them. Or take Quine's example: 'If Julius Caesar had been in command in Korea, he would have used the atom bomb'. Maybe this is just a convenient allusion to a portrait of Caesar's character, a description of the military situation in Korea, a generalization about what people with that kind of character do in that kind of situation, and a reminder that Caesar was born in the wrong century. On this kind of demystified interpretation, 'If X had been the case, N would have decided at t not to A' will entail that when things like X are the case, decisions like N's not to A are always made.

In debates about Moore's treatment of freedom it used to be argued that since 'N was able not to A' is incompatible with something with which 'If X had been the case then N would not have Aed' is compatible, the latter cannot be equivalent to the former.[6] A similar argument can be constructed for the conclusion that there is nothing which can naturally be called a conditional species of extra possibility freedom of decision. The issue is purely taxonomic: what I am taking as a species of extra possibility freedom may still figure in want and belief conflicts even if it should not be put in that particular category or indeed regarded as a freedom of any kind. But I may as well try briefly to clarify the issue.

Consider then the hypothesis that

(1) If X had been the case then N would have decided at t not to A

---

[6] See for example Lehrer (1966), 196.

is an interpretation of

(2) N was able to decide at *t* not to *A*.

The objection is that every natural interpretation of (2) is incompatible with the conjunction of

(3) Only if *X* had been the case just before *t* would *N* have been able to decide at *t* not to *A*

and

(4) *X* was not the case just before *t*.

But this conjunction *is* compatible with (1). So (1) is not a natural interpretation of (2). I think the objection is question-begging. Anyone who thinks that (2) might mean something of form (1) will wonder what 'able' means in (3), and naturally he will think it might mean something conditional, and more particularly something which makes the whole of (3) equivalent to

(3a) Only if *X* had been the case is it true that if *X* had occurred then *N* would have decided at *t* not to *A*.

But obviously the conjunction of (4) and (3a) is *not* compatible with (1). So the claim that we have in (3) and (4) a conjunction compatible with (1) but not with (2) depends on assuming the truth of something far too close for comfort to the actual conclusion to be proved. A further difficulty is that even if (3) is not taken as equivalent to (3a), its actual meaning is unclear, at least when it is possible that *X* was the case just before *t*. And someone who interprets (2) in terms of conditionals may well concede that he should include in his analysis a conditional which represents that possibility. We can see this by reverting to the old dispute about conditional analyses of the freedom of actions other than decisions. Here, (3)'s analogue is

(3)* Only if *X* had been the case would *N* have been able to do something at *t* other than *A*ing.

Lehrer provides an example of the sort of thing which might make sense of (3)*.[7] Only if I had chosen to eat a red sweet (and therefore not had the pathological aversion to red sweets which in fact makes me unable to eat them), would I have been able to eat one. But then the analogue of (1) will be

---

[7] Lehrer (1968), 32.

(1)* If just before t N had chosen to eat a red sweet at t, he would
have done so at t.

But if (3)* is true, then presumably N was unable to choose to eat
a red sweet, as well as unable actually to eat one. And so we do
not have a case in which it is true both that (1)* is compatible
with the conjunction of (3)* and (4)*, and that the antecedent of
(1)* is possible.

As a species of extra possibility freedom of decision, C-freedom
can be contrasted with freedom of decision in nomological possibility senses. Suppose that N decided at t to A. Then his decision
to A was free in an extra possibility sense only if he was able to
decide at t not to A. It was free in an nomological possibility sense
only if this ability statement is taken as equivalent to 'There is
no set of laws of nature whose conjunction with a complete
description of the world just before t entails that N did not decide
at t not to A'. There are as many different nomological possibility
senses as there are different ways of interpreting 'law of nature'.
So for instance some nomological possibility senses are determined
by a demodalized, 'Humean' interpretation of 'law of nature',
others by an interpretation which takes laws to be about naturally
necessary connections between events.

The third species of extra possibility freedom of decision which
I distinguish is simple or S-freedom. Someone might say that just
as visual experience acquaints us with colour-qualities, so introspection reveals experiences as of a power to decide. Maybe one
has experiences as of being simultaneously able to decide at t to A,
and able to decide at t not to A. 'Able to decide', in addition
to functioning as a conditional, may be usable, like 'red', as the
label for a content of experience. There would then be two
possibilities. Either you yourself, considered as an entity that
exists independently of being experienced, really do sometimes
have the quality of freedom of decision which you have experiences
as of having. Or it is merely that something has the power to
produce experiences in you as of your having this quality of
freedom of decision. In the first case, you have S-freedom of
decision. I am very uncertain whether there really are experiences
as of having a power to decide, as distinct from experiences as
of deciding. But I will assume, for the sake of argument, that
such experiences do exist. On that assumption, a further question

suggests itself. In a veridical experience as of being simultaneously able to decide at *t* to A, and able to decide at *t* not to A, what is the relation between the time at which one has these abilities, and the time *t* of the decisions that they are abilities to take? The time at which one has the abilities will I assume be the time just before *t*.

So far as I can see, there is nothing to prevent one and the same decision from being S-free and C-free and free in a nomological possibility sense.

The final distinction I draw between senses of 'free decision' is one which I will use a lot from now onwards. It is between *- and non-*-senses. N's decision at *t* to A was *-free if and only if (i) it was either C-free or S-free, and (ii) had N decided not to A, the state of the world just before that decision would have been exactly as it actually was. There is obviously no inconsistency in conjoining 'N's decision at *t* to A was S-free' with condition (ii). 'N's decision at *t* to A was C-free' will be inconsistent with (ii) if the time referred to in the antecedent of the conditional is itself the time just before *t*. But as we saw earlier, it is not part of the definition of C-freedom that this should be so.

A word on the relation between *-freedom and freedom in the nomological possibility sense. 'N's decision at *t* to A was free in the nomological possibility sense' entails

(1) There is no set of laws of nature whose conjunction with a complete description of the world just before *t* entails that N did not decide not to A.

And 'N's decision at *t* to A was *-free' entails

(2) If N had decided at *t* not to A then the state of the world just before *t* would have been exactly as it was.

The meaning of (2) depends on whether we adopt a demystified or a Lewis-style conception of counterfactuals. And (1) has as many interpretations as there are interpretations of 'law of nature'. I cannot think of any interpretation of counterfactuals and of 'law of nature' on which (1) entails (2), but, as we will see in Chapters 4 and 5, there are interpretations of counterfactuals and of 'law of nature' on which (2) entails (1), and hence the negation of the general determinist thesis

(3) For any true propositions *p* and *q* which respectively describe the state of the world at an instant and at an earlier instant,

there is a set of laws of nature whose conjunction with q entails p.

The question arises of whether there are also interpretations of counterfactuals and of 'law of nature' on which (2) entails the negation of

(4) For any true propositions p and q which respectively describe the state of the world at an instant and at a later instant, there is a set of laws of nature whose conjunction with q entails p.

I think that there are not, though it is not altogether easy to find a consistent interpretation of 'N's decision to A was both C-free and *-free' which is compatible with (4). We saw that 'N's decision at t to A was both C-free and *-free' will not be consistent unless 'N's decision at t to A was C-free' entails a conditional of the form 'If X had been the case at t_n then N would have decided not to A', where t_n is a time other than the time just before t which is referred to in the conditional entailed by 'N's decision at t to A was *-free'. But then if N's decision at t to A was both C-free and *-free and t_n is earlier than just before t, things at t_n would have been exactly the same, even though at some earlier time they would have been different. And counterfactuals and 'law of nature' can no doubt be interpreted so that this last consequence is incompatible with (4). To avoid the incompatibility it would be necessary to insist that t_n, in the antecedent of the C-freedom conditional, was later than just before t. But I shall not limit my subsequent discussion to *-free decisions which are also C-free, and we shall see that the logical relations between *-freedom and the negation of (4) remain the same whether the *-freedom is of the C-free or of the S-free kind.

2. AUTONOMY AND SOLE AUTHORSHIP

Various kinds of free decisions have now been distinguished. Which of these kinds of free decisions do victims of want and belief conflicts want there to be?

I shall limit the discussion in this and the next three chapters to those conflicts in which the desire is simply that there are free decisions, or that one has the true belief that there are free decisions, as distinct from conflicts in which the desire is only that there are more free decisions, or that this is truly believed. I shall limit it also to those conflicts in which doubts about the existence of free actions are not derived, as we will later see that they could be, from more radical doubts about the very existence of certain kinds of decisions, free or unfree. These conditions exclude conflicts in which the freedom wanted is of the hierarchical coherence or lack of constraint kind. Everyone wants to be less constrained and maybe some of us want more of our decisions to be hierarchically coherent. But, short of suspecting that nobody ever takes any decisions, you are not likely to suspect that nobody ever takes hierachically coherent or unconstrained decisions. Also excluded by these conditions are at least some conflicts in which autonomy is the object of desire. Suppose autonomy is taken in a sense on which it is sufficient for N's decision to A to be autonomous that (i) he wanted to make that decision or wanted something to which he believed that decision would be conducive, and (ii) the want here was one which he had himself chosen to acquire. Then, short of disbelieving in any decisions, we are not seriously liable to believe that nobody takes decisions which are autonomous.

But, as I noted in the previous section, autonomy can also be taken in stronger senses. And one of these senses is so strong that it obviously makes autonomous decision impossible. I am thinking of Galen Strawson's 'true responsibility'. A decision is 'truly responsible' only if (i) it is made according to a set of principles ('preferences, values, pro-attitudes, ideals, whatever') which the chooser has already chosen according to some further set of principles, and (ii) the choice of this further set of principles is also truly responsible. According to Strawson, 'true responsibility' is 'the freedom that most people think matters most to them'.[8] But it is impossible to make a 'truly responsible' decision because this would require 'the actual completion of an infinite regress of choices of principles of choice'.[9] It may seem that if we do indeed want there to be 'truly responsible ' decisions then our realization of their impossibility will plunge us into a want and belief conflict.

I think, though, that if there is in fact a conflict here then either it is quite easily resolved or it is not distinct from conflicts about

[8] Strawson (1986), p. v.
[9] Ibid. 29.

extra possibility freedom. If, as I argued in the previous chapter, no desire survives its owner's recognition that it has an incoherent content, then we cannot be plunged into a conflict about 'true responsibility' by believing that 'true responsibility' is excluded by an actual incoherence in the notion of someone's making an infinite number of choices of principles of choice. A desire for 'true responsibility' could not survive that belief. You might of course still be afflicted by a conflict about 'true responsibility' if you thought that it was only 'medically' impossible to make an infinite number of choices of principles of choice. Suppose then that you are thus afflicted and there is in fact no stronger impossibility here which you can be brought to recognize. Then to resolve your conflict it would be necessary to show that you want 'true responsibility' not for its own sake but for the sake of something else, and that your desire rests on a doubtful internal proposition. But there are, I think, only two things for the sake of which you might want 'true responsibility'. You might want it for the sake of being a genuine agent with extra possibility freedom, or you might want it for the sake of a certain intellectual satisfaction. In the second case it is easy to show that your desire has a doubtful internal proposition. In the first case, our assessment of the internal proposition of your desire can be virtually read off from our treatment of conflicts explicitly about extra possibility freedom.

How might you want 'true responsibility' for the sake of being a genuine agent with extra possibility freedom? This might be your thought. Unless my decision to A is in some way caused, then it is random, not genuinely mine. But if it is caused, then prima facie I was not able to have decided not to A. And that extra possibility freedom is something I want to have. I would, however, have been able to decide not to A, even if my decision to A had been caused, if I had chosen the causes themselves and had been able to choose different causes. So I want to be able to choose the causes of my decision to A, and the causes I choose might as well be my principles. But prima facie I would not have been able to choose different causes if my actual choice of causes was itself caused. I would, however, have been able to choose different causes, if I had chosen the causes of my actual choice of causes, and had been able to choose different causes. So I want to be able to choose the causes of my actual choice of causes of my decision to A, and again the causes that I choose might as well be my principles. And so on. Reasoning thus, you want 'true responsibility' for the sake of being a genuine agent with extra possibility freedom of decision. One internal proposition of your desire would then be that the causation of a desire excludes its extra possibility freedom. Whether that proposition is true depends on which particular species of extra possibility freedom we take. But another internal proposition of your desire would be that if, in deciding, you are a genuine agent then your decision must be caused. And that proposition, which I shall in any case have to consider when I turn to conflicts about extra possibility freedom, can, I think, be shown to be false without much preliminary disambiguation. An argument for this will be given in Chapter 4, Section 1.

How might you want 'true responsibility' for the sake of intellectual satisfaction? Your thought might be this. Unless I decide to A for a reason, my decision is irrational. But even if I do decide for a reason, that is not enough to make it really rational. For the principle which constitutes my reason for deciding to A may itself have been non-rationally come by. So I must also have acquired that principle by a rational decision. And so on. Reasoning in this way, you want 'true responsibility' for the sake of an infinitely regressive rationality. The internal proposition of the desire would then be that intellectual satisfaction requires this exorbitant rationality, and the falsity of the proposition could be demonstrated by producing something more modestly attractive. You decide to A for a reason, and the reason is that you want x. Your decision to A is 'truly responsible' only if, having wondered beforehand about going on wanting x, it was for a reason that you decided to go on wanting it. Suppose further that your reason for deciding to go on wanting x was that you wanted y and believed that x was conducive to y. Then it is also true that your decision to A is 'truly responsible' only if, having wondered beforehand about going on wanting y, it was for a reason that you decided to go on wanting y. But now suppose instead that your reason for deciding to go on wanting x was that you thought that your wanting x was conducive to x itself. It is the very fact that you already want x that makes you decide to go on wanting it. Is your decision to A 'truly responsible'? No, for 'true responsibility' requires each choice of principle to be made according to some *further* principle. But then why want 'true responsibility'? If you want x purely for its own sake and not for the sake of anything else that you want, what better reason could there be for deciding to go on wanting x than that wanting it is conducive to x itself? There is a parallel here with a case about belief which I considered in Section 3 of the previous chapter. A man thinks that in general it is better to believe p than not to believe p if and only if p is true, and then, wondering whether to go on believing some particular proposition, is induced by the mere fact that he does indeed then believe it to think that it is true and that therefore, according to his general value theory about belief, he should go on believing it.

I now turn briefly to conflicts about sole authorship. Why should anyone believe that he lacks it? The most likely reason is that he accepts one of those same theses about order in nature which appear to conflict with extra possibility freedom. Why should anyone want sole authorship? Perhaps, again, for the sake of extra possibility freedom. Certainly it is easy to believe that only if the agent is sole author, is not caused to decide, will he be able not to make this decision or able to decide otherwise. If this is the situation, the philosopher's contribution to the resolution to conflicts about sole authorship follows in an obvious way from his treatment of conflicts about extra possibility freedom.

Some writers would resist this diagnosis. Nozick has suggested that events can have a value over and above the intrinsic value that they lead to, simply by virtue of originating the causal process which leads to that intrinsic value. If an uncaused decision caused some intrinsically good state of affairs then the decision would have 'originative value' over and above the intrinsic value of the state of affairs which it caused.[10] I find this difficult to believe. If, as I will later suggest, extra possibility freedom is liable to be wanted for its own sake, then it is not necessary to postulate a special originative value in order to explain why sole authorship is liable to be valued by those who believe that causation excludes extra possibility freedom.

A different explanation of why people want sole authorship has been offered by Robert Kane.[11] He distinguishes between constraining control, in which A makes B take a decision which B

[10] Nozick (1981), 310–13.
[11] Kane (1985), 33–7.

prefers not to take, and non-constraining control, in which *B* takes the decisions he prefers to take, but *A*'s decision is the ultimate cause of *B*'s preferences. According to Kane we want our decisions to be free of both constraining and non-constraining control, and have a certain fear of covert non-constraining control. We want sole authorship because we realize that it is a logically sufficient condition for the absence of covert non-constraining control over our decisions. I doubt, however, that this really emancipates conflicts about sole authorship from conflicts about extra possibility freedom. For why do we want the absence of even overt non-constraining control? The answer seems to be that, wanting sometimes to take decisions as to whether or not to acquire new wants or allow old ones to continue, and wanting these decisions to have extra possibility freedom, we believe that they would not have this freedom if caused, and, *a fortiori*, if caused by the decisions of other agents. A treatment of conflicts about extra possibility freedom will enable us to see whether there is truth in this internal proposition of the desire not to be subject to non-constraining control. It is to these conflicts that I now finally turn.[12]

3. EXTRA POSSIBILITY FREEDOM

Which particular species of extra possibility freedom do victims of conflicts about it really want?

---

[12] There is a rhetoric of sole authorship which makes me uneasy about this rapid subsumption. Consider for instance this passage from William James: "'*Will you or won't you have it so?*' is the most probing question we are ever asked; we are asked it every hour of the day, and about the largest as well as about the smallest, the most theoretical as well as the most practical, things. What wonder that these dumb responses should seem our deepest organs of communication with the nature of things! What wonder if the effort demanded of them be the measure of our worth as men! What wonder if the amount which we accord of it be *the one strictly underived and original contribution we can make to the word!*' (*Principles of Psychology*, ii. 579, last italics mine) Perhaps then the thought is that your decision, if you are not its sole author, is not qualitatively unique, and nor, then, if you are constituted by your volitions, are you. The uniqueness of your decision is incompatible with its causation, because *x* causes *y* only if there are other events like *y* to which other events like *x* stand in some relation. A confused thought, which the conflict-resolver could easily pull from under the desire for sole authorship and origination, but less bald than the simple belief that sole authorship is a necessary condition for freedom of the extra possibility kind.

S-free decisions are certainly an object of desire. Whether or not there really are experiences as of S-freely deciding, some people think that they have such experiences. But if there were only such experiences, and no real S-decisions, then we would be under repeated illusions. Realizing this, and disliking the prospect of being constantly deceived, believers in experiences as of S-freely deciding want there to be real S-free decisions.

There is an equally simple thought which could prompt a desire for there to be decisions which are conditionally or C-free. N C-freely decided at t to A only if he was able to decide at t not to A, and only if, more specifically, there is some X such that had X been the case N would have decided at t not to A. And 'If X had been the case N would have decided at t not to A' is at least some evidence that on future occasions when something like X is the case N will make a decision like his time t decision not to A. Since we are liable to want to be able to predict human decisions, we are liable to want those conditionals to be true, knowledge of which helps us to make such predictions. And since no C-free decision can be taken unless some such conditional is true, we are liable to want there to be C-free decisions.

The most heavily discussed reason or seeming reason for wanting there to be decisions free in some extra possibility sense is that without them there would be no moral responsibility. What does it mean to say that someone is morally responsible for an action or decision? Presumably, that the action or decision has the freedom necessary for it to be morally good or bad. Saying that we want freedom for the sake of moral responsibility is simply a rather clumsy way of saying that we want freedom for the sake of there being morally good actions or decisions, or at least for the sake of its being possible that there are morally good actions or decisions. But morally good actions or decisions, in the mind of the person who wants freedom for this reason, are not likely just to be ones which he favours. Ordinary moral judgements include a claim to objectivity. Morally good actions will be seen by this person as ones with a special property of moral goodness, a non-relational property such that *necessarily* anyone who believes that something has that property will want this something to exist. But I am not sure which particular kind of extra possibility freedom is supposed to be necessary for the possession of such a property. As a non-believer in such properties, I certainly have no intuitions of my own about the kinds of freedom which they require in the actions to which they attach themselves.

Imagine, however, that, grateful for a decision, you subsequently come to believe that the decider could not have decided otherwise. This makes a difference to your attitude. You are less glad than before that the decision was made, and would still be less glad even if you did not suspect that the decider had an experience as of being S-free which has now sadly turned out to be illusory, and even if you did not suspect that his decisions are generally less easy to predict or manipulate than you originally thought. This suggests that the existence of decisions which are free in some extra possibility sense, or at least the existence of otherwise favoured decisions free in such a sense, is something that you are liable to want for its own sake, and not just for the sake of reducing the amount of illusion in the world, or for the sake of predictive knowledge. And the thought-experiment here does not require you to imagine that the decision for which you are initially grateful is one which possesses any special property of moral goodness.

But there is a difficulty. According to Frankfurt, a case can be constructed in which we would be prepared to hold someone morally responsible for an action even though we think that he could not have acted otherwise:

Suppose someone—Black let us say—wants Jones to perform a certain action. Black . . . waits until Jones is about to make up his mind what to do, and he does nothing unless it is clear to him (Black is an excellent judge of such things) that Jones is going to decide to do something *other* than what he wants him to do. If it does become clear to him that Jones is going to decide to do something else, Black takes effective steps to ensure that Jones decides to do, and that he does do, what he wants him to do. Whatever Jones's initial preferences and inclinations, then, Black will have his way.

Now suppose that Black never has to show his hand because Jones, for reasons of his own, decides to perform and does perform the very action Black wants him to perform. In that case, it seems clear, Jones will bear precisely the same moral responsibility for what he does as he would have borne if Black had not been ready to take steps to ensure that he do it . . . everything happened just as it would have happened without Black's presence in the situation and without his readiness to intrude into it.[13]

[13] Frankfurt (1986), 148–9.

The thought is that if, in a normal case, we deny that some man unable not to _A_ was morally responsible for _A_ing, this is not because moral responsibility is actually inconsistent with such an inability. It is because in this, as in all other normal cases of inability, there happens to be some further factor which genuinely does logically exclude moral responsibility. An abnormal and if necessary fictional case, in which there is inability without the presence of this further factor, helps us to see the real logical situation. According to Frankfurt, the further factor, missing in the case of Jones and Black, is that the agent, who could not have done otherwise, acted _only because_ he could not have done otherwise. The reader may suspect that, whether or not Frankfurt is right about the requirements of 'moral responsibility', he does in effect undermine the idea that, in my thought experiment about gratitude, extra possibility freedom emerges as an object of desire. It seemed that our attitude to a decision for which we are initially grateful would be changed by the discovery that the decider could not have decided otherwise. But does it not now appear that although, in a normal case, we are less pleased about a decision for which we were grateful when we discover that it lacked extra possibility freedom, what makes us less pleased is not the absence of this freedom, but the presence of some other factor, normally present when this freedom is lacking, but absent in cases like Frankfurt's?

It is not quite plain whether Frankfurt himself thinks that, in addition to not being required for 'moral responsibility', extra possibility freedom is not something we want. Idiosyncratically defining a will as a desire which causes an action, he presents us with this situation: 'a person has done what he wanted to do ... he did it because he wanted to do it, and the will by which he was moved when he did it was his will because it was the will he wanted.' According to Frankfurt, this person would have done what he did 'freely and of his own free will'.[14] And earlier, Frankfurt has claimed that a person who enjoys both freedom of action and freedom of the will ' ... has ... all the freedom it is possible to desire or to conceive. There are many good things in life, and he may not possess some of them. But there is nothing in the way of freedom that he lacks.'[15] This suggests that extra

[14] Frankfurt (1982), 94.
[15] Frankfurt (1982), 92–3.

possibility freedom is not something that we even desire. For one can do what one wants to do and do it because one wants to do it without being able not to do it or to do anything else. And one can have the will one wants to have and have it because one wants to have it without being able not to have it or to have a different will. But on the other hand, Frankfurt insists that it is 'a mistake ... to believe that someone ... acts of his own free will only if his will is free.' A person acts of his own will if he does what he wants to do and does it because he wants to do it, and the will by which he is moved is his will because it is the will he wants. But

A person's will is free only if he is free to have the will he wants. This means that, with regard to any of his first-order desires, he is free either to make that desire his will or to make some other first-order desire his will instead. Whatever his will, then, the will of the person whose will is free could have been otherwise; he could have done otherwise than to constitute his will as he did.[16]

Do we then want our wills to be free, and hence to have extra possibility freedom in the constitution of our wills, as well as wanting to act of our own free wills? Frankfurt does not say. And he stresses that the question of how, when it comes to the constitution of a person's will, 'he could have done otherwise' is to be understood 'has no bearing on the theory of moral responsibility'. He does, however, say that this question 'is important to the theory of freedom', which seems to suggest that we do after all want some kind of extra possibility freedom at least in the constitution of our wills.

But whatever exactly it is that Frankfurt himself thinks, we still need to consider whether Frankfurt-style cases undermine the thought experiment about gratitude. Imagine then that N decides to A. You are grateful to him for this, but ignorant of the circumstances of his decision. Actually, there is someone, Black, who, unknown to N, wanted N to decide to A. Black waited until it was clear to him that N was going to decide to A, and then did nothing. If, however, Black had known that without his own intervention N would have decided not to A, then Black would have intervened, and made N decide to A. And if it had been true that without Black's intervention N would have decided not to A, then Black would have known, in time for his own intervention,

[16] Frankfurt (1982), 94.

that this was true. Suppose you discover all this. Since, as you know, Black did not actually intervene, it seems that you will be just as pleased about N's decision to A as you were before and also that what pleases you in his decision will be the same as before. But since, as you now know, his decision to A lacked extra possibility freedom, this freedom cannot have been even part of what you were previously pleased about. And if, in a normal case, with no Black waiting in the wings, you *are* less pleased than before about N's decision to A when you discover that it lacked extra possibility freedom, the explanation must be, not that this freedom was part of what you were previously pleased about, but that something you do not like, which does not go with lack of extra possibility in the Frankfurt-style case, does go with this lack in the normal case.

One possible reply would be to insist that even in the Frankfurt-style case there are *some* kinds of extra possibility freedom which, Black notwithstanding, N's decision to A may still have possessed, and that it is one or more of these kinds of extra possibility freedom that we want. If we would still be just as pleased about N's decision, even after discovering about Black, it is because we still believe that the decision had freedom of one or more of these kinds. So it does not follow that when, in a normal or non-Frankfurt-style case, we discover that such a freedom is missing and are then less pleased than before, it is really something other than the absence of such a freedom that displeases us. What then are the kinds of extra possibility freedom which N's decision to A could still have even in a Frankfurt-style case? Clearly, his decision to A could still have been S-free. He could still have had that unanalysable property his possession of which would make his experience veridical if it were an experience as of being simultaneously able to decide to A and able to decide not to A. Also, N's decision to A could still have had a certain C-freedom. Your decision to A was C-free if and only if you were able to decide not to A, and part or the whole of what that means is something of the form 'If X had been the case, you would have decided not to A'. Substitute for 'If X had been the case' something of the form 'If Y had been the case and if Black had not existed' and you have a species of C-freedom which N could still have possessed even though Black did exist.

I agree that there are also some kinds of extra possibility freedom which N could not have possessed, given the nature and existence of Black. N's decision to A could not have been C-free in any sense governed by a conditional of the form 'If X had been the case, N would have decided not to A' in which the antecedent does not exclude Black's existence or curtail his powers. Nor could N's decision to A have been *-free, i.e. either C-free or S-free and such that had N decided not to A the state of the world just before that decision would have been exactly as it actually was. For if N had decided not to A, then either Black would not have existed or he would have lost his powers, and in either case the state of the world would not have been as it actually was when N decided to A. Can we then reply in a way which does not thus restrict the kinds of extra possibility freedom which we are still able to want?

Suppose we concede that for any kind of extra possibility freedom, discovery, in a Frankfurt-style case, that N's decision to A lacked freedom of that kind leaves you just as pleased about his decision as you were before. It is still not clear that what pleases you in his decision is the same as before. It could be that what now pleases you in N's decision to A is that it helps to constitute evidence that if Black had not existed then N would have made a decision to A which would have had just the extra possibility freedom which Black's existence in fact ruled out. If, in the Frankfurt-style case, you can know that N's decision to A lacks extra possibility freedom only because of Black's existence, then you can know that if Black had not existed, and if N had still decided to A, his decision to A would have had the extra possibility freedom which Black's existence rules out. And since Black in fact does nothing, and N does not know of his existence, the fact that N did decide to A is evidence that he would indeed still have decided to A even if Black had not existed. If you know all this, then it is perfectly possible that what pleases you about N's decision after you have discovered its circumstances, is not the same as what pleased you about it before this discovery. And since this is possible, the fact that you are just as pleased about N's decision to A after discovering that it lacks extra possibility freedom is perfectly consistent with the supposition that, in a normal case, your displeasure in the discovery that a decision you were grateful for lacks extra possibility freedom is indeed a sign that extra possibility freedom is something that you want. It will now be objected that this reply works only if we make it part of the Frankfurt-style case that you know that N's decision to A

lacked extra possibility freedom *only because of* Black's existence. There would be nothing different for you to be pleased about in *N*'s decision if you knew that it lacked this freedom quite independently of Black. For then *N*'s decision would not help to constitute evidence that he would have made it freely if Black had not existed. But the answer to this is that if part of what you discovered about the circumstances of *N*'s decision was that it lacked extra possibility freedom quite independently of Black's existence, then you would *not* be as pleased about his decision as you were before. If you are grateful for a decision but then discover that, for reasons which have nothing to do with any Black-like creature, the decision lacked extra possibility freedom, you are less pleased about the decision. And your displeasure will not vanish if you subsequently discover that there is an additional reason for the absence of extra possibility freedom, namely the existence of Black. Why then should your simultaneous discovery of both a Black-related and a 'normal' reason for the absence of extra possibility freedom in *N*'s decision to *A* leave you as pleased about it as you were before you know about the circumstances in which it was made?

I take it then that so far as concerns our desire for extra possibility freedom, Frankfurt-style cases leave things as they were. Reflections on gratitude do, then, show that we want there to be decisions free in some extra possibility sense, or at least that we want there to be otherwise favoured decisions free in such a sense, and that what we want is in neither case wanted just for the sake of less illusion or more predictive power, or indeed just for the sake of anything else.

There are other routes to the same general conclusion. In discussions of the theological problem of evil some such question as this is often posed. If God had made a world in which all decisions and actions were both good and unfree, and in which nobody even had experiences as of being free, then would not this world have been worse than at least some world in which there are both free good and free bad decisions and actions, worse perhaps even than our actual world? Some religious apologists seem to think that when 'free' is taken in an extra possibility sense this other world would certainly have been worse even than our actual world. They must then be attaching an intrinsic value either to free actions or decisions or to free good actions or decisions. *Ex hypothesi*, the world without freedom contains no illusions of freedom to make it worse, and neither can it be worse because of the unpredictability or uncontrollability of what is decided or done. Every goal, for the achievement of which this prediction or control might have been necessary, will be achieved in any case, because all actions are good.

Perhaps it will seem that what makes the world without freedom worse is not that it cannot have the intrinsic value of freedom, or the extra intrinsic value which freedom gives to a good action or decision, but rather that it cannot contain the extra intrinsic value represented by justice or giving people what they deserve, a value realized only in the treatment of free actions or decisions but realized as much in the punishment of free bad actions or decisions as in the rewarding of free good ones. Certainly only free actions or decisions deserve to be punished or rewarded. But surely what the believer in justice for its own sake really values is that justice should be done if the occasion of free action arises, rather than that the occasion should actually arise.

My conclusion is still indeterminate: either we want for its own sake the existence of decisions free in an extra possibility sense, or we want for its own sake the existence of otherwise favoured decisions free in such a sense. But which of these do we want for its own sake? (The question is more easily put in the terms of an objectivist theory of value: if free good decisions have an intrinsic value over and above the goodness, intrinsic or instrumental, which they would have had if they had not been free, is it also true that they would have had this additional value if they had not been good?) Suppose someone decides to harm you, and initially you believe that he was unable to decide not to do this. But then you change your mind. Even if this makes things seem better from a purely instrumental point of view, they may still seem worse overall. Maybe you have thought all along and continue to think that your enemy believed he was free: at least you can now be glad that this belief of his was not mistaken. If the freedom you now think he has is of the conditional kind, then at least you can now be glad that something is true, knowledge of which may help you to predict his future decisions. But even if things seem better in these and all other instrumental respects, you may still, on discovering his freedom, feel more hostile to his decision. How can that be so, if you want free decision for its own sake? One possible explanation is that you do indeed value free decision for its own sake, and dislike the juxtaposition, which you now think you find, of an intrinsically valuable freedom and a decision bad because it is a decision to do harm.[17] And that, I shall assume, is indeed the way it strikes us.

Which particular kind of extra possibility freedom is it that we thus want? Perhaps a further thought-experiment will help. Suppose that, full of gratitude for *N*'s decision to *A*, you then come to believe that although he could in some sense have decided not to *A*, he could not, *as things were just before his decision to A*, have decided not to *A*. And suppose that you do not come to believe this for any Frankfurt-style reason. Then your attitude alters. You are less glad that the decision has been taken. Now suppose that you ask yourself whether you would still be less glad if the qualification *as things were just before his decision to A* were missing. I am inclined to think that your answer will be that you would not still be less glad. If this is right then the sense of 'free' in question seems to be one on which the decider could, *as things were just before his decision*, have decided otherwise. And perhaps it will now emerge that not every kind of extra possibility freedom of decision can be coherently qualified in this way.

The formula '*N* could, as things were just before *t*, have decided otherwise at *t*' is ambiguous. It can mean either '*N* could, in the particular circumstances which obtained just before *t*, have decided otherwise at *t*' or 'In circumstances similar to those which obtained just before *t*, *N* could have made a decision of a kind different from that which he made at *t*'. Suppose we interpret the formula in the second or generalizing way. Then, given that no other circumstances are likely to be exactly similar to those which obtained just before *t*, it will be a puzzle why we should care about what could happen if such similar circumstances were to occur. This, or something very like it, is what puzzles Dennett,

---

[17] The desire that justice should be done for its own sake is sometimes attacked as a misplaced preoccupation with symmetry, a perversely aestheticizing interest in the juxtaposition of like with like. As H. L. A. Hart asks somewhere, what is the mysterious piece of moral alchemy in which the combination of the two evils of moral wickedness and suffering are transmuted into good? If the freedom which justice requires in an act punished or rewarded is valued for its own sake, and if we do want an intrinsically valuable freedom to be juxtaposed only with acts whose content is good, then punishment and reward, as objects of aversion and desire, could resemble not only the content of the act punished or rewarded but also the relation between the freedom of the act and its content.

when he discusses ability to act otherwise in chapter 6 of his recent book *Elbow Room*:

Although people are physical objects which, like atoms or ballbearings or bridges, obey the laws of physics, they are not only more complicated than anything else we know in the universe, they are also designed to be so sensitive to the passing show that they never can be in the same microstate twice...

There is some point in determining how a bridge is caused to react to some very accurately specified circumstances, since those may be circumstances it will actually encounter *in its present state* on a future occasion. But there would be no payoff in understanding to be gained by determining the micro-causation of the behaviour of a human being in some particular circumstance, since he will certainly never confront that microcircumstance again, and even if he did, he would certainly be in a significantly different reactive state at the time.

So if anyone is interested at all in the question of whether or not one could have done otherwise in *exactly* the same circumstances (and internal state), this will have to be a particularly pure metaphysical curiosity—that is to say, a curiosity so pure as to be utterly lacking in any ulterior motive, since the answer could not conceivably make a noticeable difference to the way the world went.[18]

Building on this, Dennett goes on to argue that in the case of a good action what we want is precisely that it is *not* the case that the agent could have done otherwise. We want the agent to be a person totally immune to temptation, a person to whom horrible courses of action are completely unthinkable.[19] And although in the case of a bad action we do want it to be true that the agent could have acted otherwise, this is like wanting that a machine which broke down on some particular occasion could have worked perfectly well. We hope that the fault is unlikely to be repeated, was an unlucky accident rather than the outcome of some basic defect in the design. Provided we think that the exact circumstances are utterly unlikely to recur, we do not mind whether or not, if they were to recur, the agent would have done the same thing again.[20]

But even if Dennett had been talking of decisions rather than of actions in general or actions other than decisions, none of what he

[18] Dennett (1984), 137–8.
[19] Ibid. 134–5.
[20] Ibid. 139–44.

says would have shown that we do not count a good decision taken at t as better if the decider was able, as things actually were just before t, to decide otherwise at t. The formula 'He could, as things were just before t, have decided otherwise at t' is only used in these contexts because one thing it can mean is 'He could, in the particular circumstances which obtained just before t, have decided otherwise at t'. Ignoring this particularizing meaning, Dennett pours justified scorn on an interest in the other, generalizing thing that the formula can mean.

.   Let us take it, then, that the formula is to be interpreted in the particularizing way. We still do not know how exactly to understand the 'as things were just before t' qualification. There seem to be three possibilities. (1) The point may be to suggest that if things had not been as they actually were just before N's time t decision to A, then he would not have had the ability to decide at t not to A. (2) The whole sentence may mean the same as 'N was able to do this: decide at t not to A with things as they actually were just before his time t decision to A'. (3) The whole sentence may mean the same as 'It is nomologically possible that with things as they actually were just before his time t decision to A, N decided at t not to A'.

The ability referred to in interpretation (1) could be that entailed either by the S-freedom of N's decision to A, or by its C-freedom, or even by its nomological possibility freedom. If interpretation (2) is to be distinct from interpretation (3), then 'N was able to do this', in (2), must not mean 'It was nomologically possible for N to do this'. But the ability referred to by interpretation (2) could again be either S-freedom or some C-freedom. If the ability referred to by interpretation (2) is that entailed by S-freedom, then interpretation (2) gives us: N had that property his possession of which would have made his experience veridical if it had been an experience as of being able to decide at t not to A with things as they were just before t. And if the ability referred to by interpretation (1) is that entailed by S-freedom, then interpretation (1) gives us: If things had not been as they actually were just before t then N would not have had that property his possession of which would have made his experience veridical if it had been an experience as of being able to decide at t not to A. On the C-interpretation, (1) gives us something of the form

(1a) If things had not been as they actually were just before N's time *t* decision to A, it would not have been true that if X had been the case then N would have decided at *t* not to A,

and (2) gives us something of the form

(2a) If X had been the case then it would have been true both that things would have been as they actually were just before N's time *t* decision to A and that N would have decided at *t* not to A.

(1a) and (2a) are not equivalent, because (2a) unlike (1a) entails that if X had been the case things would have been as they actually were just before N's decision to A. It has been claimed that there is no coherent conditional or hypothetical analysis of the 'able' in 'N was able, at the time and on the occasion in question, to act differently'. For it would follow from such an analysis 'that he would have acted differently in different circumstances in these circumstances, which means either that he would have acted differently in different circumstances—which is not equivalent to the claim that he would have acted differently in *these* circumstances—or means nothing very clear at all'.[21] But this argument is mistaken. (1a) does not entail 'If things had not been as they actually were just before N's time *t* decision to A, it would not have been true that if things had been different just before N's time *t* decision to A then N would have decided at *t* not to A'. For (1a) is consistent with 'If things had not been as they actually were just before N's time *t* decision to A it would not have been true that if things had been different long before *t*, then N would have decided at *t* not to A'. 'If things had not been as they actually were at *all* times up to N's time *t* decision to A, it would not have been true that if X had been the case then N would have decided at *t* not to A' may not mean anything very clear. But it is not equivalent to (1a).[22]

---

[21] Locke (1975), 107.

[22] Although there need not be any incoherence in C-interpretations of 'N was able, as things were just before his time *t* decision, to decide at *t* not to A', it is not easy to see what X might stand for in (1a) or (2a). So, for example, it will not do to take 'If X had been the case then N would have decided at *t* not to A', in (1a), as 'If N had wanted not to A more than he wanted to A then he would have decided not to A'. On that interpretation, you cannot make a C-free decision to A if you are indifferent between Aing and not Aing.

If interpretation (3) is correct, then the thought-experiment with gratitude shows that we want there to be decisions which are free in a nomological possibility sense. But if either (1) or (2) is the correct interpretation then the upshot, I think, is that we want there to be decisions which are *-free, decisions to A which are not only such that the person who took them was able to decide not to A, but also such that if he had decided not to A then things just beforehand would have been exactly as they actually were. On interpretation (1), whatever kind of ability to decide at t not to A it is that N has, he would not have had this ability in the first place, and therefore would not have been able to exercise it, if things just before his exercising it had been different. On interpretation (2) the ability is an ability precisely to decide at t not to A with things as they actually were just before the time t decision to A. So of course if *that* ability had been exercised things just beforehand would have been exactly as they actually were.

I see no way to decide between these three interpretations. Despite this, I will assume from now onwards that *-freedom is the kind of extra possibility freedom of decision that thought-experiments with gratitude reveal that we want. The reason for this assumption is as follows. In a conflict-resolving programme one should allow for the worst possibility. And if *-freedom were what we wanted, the want and belief conflicts which would then afflict us would be more difficult to resolve than those which would afflict us if nomological possibility freedom were what we wanted.

Why is there this difference in ease of treatment? Suppose that although you want there to be freedom of decision of a nomological possibility kind, your deterministic convictions initially lead you to believe that there is no such thing. The object of your desire, in this case, just is that there are decisions which do not fall under laws of nature. And there is a good hope that merely by disambiguating the notion of a law of nature, or contrasting the existing notion with some healthy or demystified part of itself, we can convince you that there is no interpretation of that notion such that both (i) you want there to be decisions which do not fall under laws of nature, and (ii) there is good evidence that all decisions do fall under such laws. There is an excellent example of this tactic in an early and famous essay by Ayer. The notion of laws as regularities is contrasted by Ayer with the notion of constraining laws, or laws conceived under the influence of 'an imaginative picture of an unhappy effect trying vainly to escape from the clutches of an overmastering cause'.[23] Whatever evidence we may have for the prevalence of laws of the first kind, we have no evidence whatever that all our decisions fall under those of the second. Whatever reason we may have for wanting our decisions not to fall under laws of the second kind, we have no reason whatever for wanting them not to fall under those of the first. But matters are more complicated if *-freedom is what we want. It is far from obvious that there is no interpretation of 'If he had decided not to A the state of the world just beforehand would have been exactly as it actually was' on which both (i) we want such counterfactuals to be true, and (ii) there is good evidence that all such counterfactuals are false. As I noted earlier, there is a demystified interpretation of such counterfactuals, and there is a Lewis-style interpretation. But as we will see in Chapter 5, it is not obvious which if either interpretation makes the existence of *-free decisions compatible with this or that deterministic or other thesis about order in the world.

There are, I know, writers who, though they think that we want freedom of a nomological possibility kind, see no prospect of resolving the consequent tensions by a disambiguation of determinism. Honderich is an example. He thinks that we want a freedom which we tend to express in 'could have done otherwise' terms, and part of whose very definition is that determinism is false. We want our futures to be open, alterable, unfixed, to be products not wholly of our environments and our own characters but of ourselves, conceived of as distinct from our dispositions. But '... *no sense* can possibly be attached to the idea of an unfixed future, or a future which somehow escapes or is released from environment and dispositions, other than that of a future not subject to the nomic connections asserted in a deterministic theory, but somehow subject to the person.'[24] Honderich also thinks that a certain determinism *is* true, and that partly because of this we should force ourselves to abandon the desire for an open future, a course made only a little easier by the fact that we sometimes also have the contrary attitude of not minding whether determinism is true, so long as our future actions will be the

[23] Ayer (1954), 283.
[24] Honderich (1988), 391.

consequences of our 'embraced desires'. But if, as well as stressing that 'free' and related terms are 'systematically ambiguous',[25] he had been more suspicious of 'fixed', 'unalterable', and 'nomic connection', this painful recommendation would not have been necessary. Certainly I hope that my future decisions will not be fixed by or forced to occur by the events which precede them. But why should I ever mind if my future decision to A is caused by an event E if it is only because I do not make a decision not to A that this causal relation holds, only because I do not make a decision not to A that whenever an E-type event occurs people make decisions like my decision to A? And what evidence is there for the prevalence of fixing or forcing by events as distinct from the prevalence of mere regularities in their succession? Maybe it is eccentric to call a relation causal, if it amounts to no more than a regularity which holds only by grace of human decisions. But even if that is so, it does not follow that there is any good evidence for the prevalence of those stronger and more alarming relations for which 'causal' is the currently proper label. Arguments on these lines also have their place in the treatment of want and belief conflicts consequent on a desire for there to be *-free decisions. They will be further developed in Chapter 5. The present point is only that with *-freedom conflicts they are rather more difficult to use.

This, then, is the position we have now reached. Want and belief conflicts about free decisions are either first- or second-order conflicts. Victims of first-order conflicts want there to be free decisions and believe that there are none. Victims of second-order conflicts want but believe they lack the true belief that there are free decisions. But victims of second-order conflicts want to have this true belief only because they too want there to be free decisions. And so their conflicts would, like first-order conflicts, be resolved by the abolition of this desire. What then is the actual content of the fundamental desire? Which kinds of free decisions do the victims want there to be? Concentrating, as I argued that we could, on conflicts about extra possibility freedom, we can say this. Enemies of illusion want there to be S-free decisions. Friends of prediction want there to be C-free decisions. And reflections on gratitude suggest either that we want there to be decisions free in a

[25] Ibid. 477.

nomological possibility sense or that we want there to be *-free decisions. The worst outcome, from a conflict-resolving point of view is that *-freedom is an object of desire. So that is the outcome I assume, leaving open the question of whether this *-freedom is S−freedom, or some kind of conditional freedom.

4

Coherence and Internal Propositions

WITH the central want and belief conflicts about free decisions now more definitely identified, I move to the questions proposed at the end of Chapter 2. I was to ask, of the desires in the first-order conflicts I had identified, whether they had incoherent contents and whether they had doubtful internal propositions. I was to ask about the evidential status of the propositions believed false in first-order conflicts. And I was to ask about palliatives. In this chapter I take up the first two questions. Victims of the conflicts which now concern us want there to be C-free, S-free, and *-free decisions. And, when they want there to be free decisions for the sake of moral responsibility, they also want there to be decisions which are free in an extra possibility sense which I am unable to specify. In the first two sections of this chapter I ask whether any of these desires has an incoherent content. And in the third section I ask whether any of them has a doubtful internal proposition.

1. RANDOMNESS AND RATIONALITY

Suppose that among the extra possibility senses of 'free decision' which figure in want and belief conflicts there are some on which it is necessarily true that a free decision is uncaused. *-senses are plausible candidates. N *-freely decided at t to A if and only if he was able to decide at t not to A and had he decided at t not to A the state of the world just before that decision would have been exactly as it actually was. It could be argued that necessarily the state of the world just before a *-free decision is not a sufficient condition for that decision, and that therefore it is necessarily true that a *-free decision is uncaused. This is a vulnerable argument, more so even than the arguments I shall consider in the next chapter for the conclusion that *-free decisions must be free in a nomological possibility sense. But let us grant for the moment that there is an extra possibility sense of 'free decision' such that (i) we want there to be free decisions, and (ii) it is necessarily true that free decisions are uncaused. The suspicion is that this sense is incoherent. In no sense of 'free decision' can it be true that a free decision is random or accidental or a purely chance event. But necessarily, if a decision is uncaused, then it is indeed random, accidental, something that happens purely by chance.

Obviously there is a danger of equivocation. One thing you might mean by saying that a decision is random is simply that it is uncaused. Another thing you might mean is that it is not within anyone's control, that it is a decision of a particular person only in the sense that it spontaneously happens in or to that person. Let 'random decision' be understood in the first, causation-excluding way. Then free decisions, if uncaused, are random. But it still has to be shown that free decisions must also be non-random. Now let 'random decision' be understood in the second, control-excluding way. Certainly free decisions will then be non-random. The taking of a decision, free or otherwise, is more than a matter of something's happening in or to the decider. If that were all it amounted to, deciding would be a purely passive affair. But it still has to be shown that free decisions must also be random. Perhaps the suspicion should be reformulated, as follows. No-one can actually take a decision, free or otherwise, nothing can actually be the decision *of* some paricular person, unless this decision is caused either by himself or by some element of the person himself. So if 'free' is understood in a sense which requires free decisions to be uncaused, it is necessarily true that no decisions are free in that sense.

But now we can reply that for a person to take a decision is not for him to cause that decision, but for him to cause or bring about something such that his bringing it about *is* his deciding. Just as raising one's arm is bringing it about that one's arm rises, so deciding to raise one's arm is bringing it about that one is in a state of intending to raise one's arm. Maybe, if the decision itself is free, then it is not caused; but the decision itself does not have to be caused by the person merely in order to be taken. It is necessary only that the person causes that state of intending to come about, his causation of which is identical to his deciding.

This, however, is to assume that, in the argument for incoherence, 'causation by the person himself' really was meant to be 'agent causation' rather than the causation of an event by an event. Whereas in fact the idea of agent causation itself seems to be incoherent. Broad asked the crucial question, and to the best of my knowledge no proponent of 'agent causation' has ever succeeded in answering it. 'How could an event possibly be determined to happen at a certain date if its total cause contained no factor to which the notion of date has any application? And how can the notion of date have any application to anything that is not an event?'[1] Let me then reformulate the argument once again. No decision, free or otherwise, can actually belong to a person except by being caused by a change in that same person. So if free decisions have to be uncaused, it is necessarily true that no decisions are free.

But now one will naturally reply that the freedom of a decision, if it requires that decision not to have causes, can hardly require it not to have the very causes which have to be postulated in order for it to have an owner. It must be causes of some other kind that its freedom would exclude. Alternatively, one may be willing to suppose that the self actually consists of a series of mental events which includes decisions, and which is unified in a way which does not require each member of the series to be caused. For a person to take a decision, on this theory, could simply be for the decision to belong to the series of which that person consists. We might even say that the series contains nothing but volitions. We would then begin to approach Berkeley's view. In his *Philosophical Commentaries* Berkeley found the whole notion of a being *which* wills unintelligible: 'Substance of a Spirit is that it acts, causes, wills, operates, or if you please (to avoid the quibble yt may be made on ye word it) to act, cause, will, operate.'[2] He seems, however, to have regarded a Spirit as a continuous willing, rather than as a series of volitions.[3] At the end of Chapter 9 I will offer some support for a purely volitional and non-substantial doctrine of the self, or at least for the serial form of this doctrine.

Someone may now say that we want there to be decisions free in a sense which is compatible with their rationality, as well as

---

[1] Broad (1952), 215.
[2] 829.
[3] See Lloyd (1985), 194.

cause-excluding. But necessarily, if a decision is in the relevant sense rational, then it is caused. So in wanting there to be free decisions we do after all want something incoherent. I agree that there is one sense of 'N's decision to A was rational' which makes that entail that his decision was caused. The formula can mean either 'N decided to A and there was a reason for him to decide to A', or 'N decided to A and he believed that there was a reason for him to decide to A', or 'N decided to A for a reason'. And the latter does indeed mean something on the lines of 'N was caused to decide to A by his belief that his deciding to A would be conducive to what he wanted'. Let us further grant for the sake of argument that we want there to be decisions made for reasons, as well as decisions for which there are reasons, and decisions for which the decider believes that there are reasons. It still does not follow that a desire for a cause-excluding freedom of decision would have an incoherent content. We want there to be free decisions; we want there to be rational decisions; these rational decisions cannot be free. But why represent this state of affairs by saying that our desire for freedom has an incoherent content, rather than simply by saying that there would be incoherence in the content of a desire for there to be decisions which are both rational and free? Whether we really are liable to have this latter desire is a question which I will have to consider later on, when I come to discuss palliatives for want and belief conflicts about freedom. But even if we do want there to be decisions both rational and free, and even if the content of the desire is incoherent, nothing follows about the coherence of our desire for freedom as such.

2. REGRESSION AND INDEPENDENCE

Of the two remaining suspicions of incoherence that I want to consider, the first is about C-interpretations of freedom of decision, those on which 'N was able to decide at t not to A' entails either a single conditional of the form 'If X had been the case N would have decided at t not to A' or a series of conditionals in which such a conditional is the first member and in which subsequent members are about the conditions under which the antecedents of their immediate predecessors would be true. Why do we need to allow here for a series of conditionals? Suppose one wants it to be true that if *X* had been the case, then *N* would have decided at *t* not to *A*. Then it seems that one is also liable to want it to be possible that *X* was the case. But if 'possible' here is itself given a conditional interpretation, then one will also want the antecedent of this second conditional to be possible, and so on *ad infinitum*. And the suspicion that I now want to consider is in fact that this infinite regress is vicious, and that incoherence is therefore liable to be found in the content of a desire for there to be C-free decisions.

One answer is that it is not clear that we are liable to want the antecedent of the first conditional to be possible in a conditional sense. Suppose one wants it to be true that if at $t - n$ *N* had wanted not to *A* then he would have decided at *t* not to *A*. Why should one additionally want it to be true that if some further set of conditions had obtained at or before $t - n$ then at $t - n$ *N* would have wanted not to *A*, as distinct from just want it to be true that it was empirically possible that at $t - n$ *N* wanted not to *A*, i.e. that there is no law of nature or set of laws of nature whose conjunction with a complete description of the state of the world just before $t - n$ entails that at $t - n$ *N* did not want not to *A*?

Another answer is that even if one does want the truth of an infinite series of conditionals, each member of which after the first is an interpretation of the proposition that the antecedent of its predecessor describes a possible state of affairs, it still does not follow that there is anything incoherent in the content of this desire. Certainly it would not take long to reach a conditional too complex to be the object of a separate conscious desire. I might want it to be true that if at $t - n$ *N* had wanted not to *A*, he would have decided at *t* not to *A*, and that if at $t - n$ *N* had wanted to want not to *A*, he would have wanted not to *A*, and perhaps even that if at $t - n$ *N* had wanted to want to want not to *A*, he would have wanted to want not to *A*. And that seems to be about the limit. But even so, I can want the truth of a series which goes on longer than this, so long as I do not try to contemplate the whole of a series which goes on longer than this. I can even want the truth of a series which goes on infinitely long.

The final suspicion of incoherence that I want to consider is about our seeming desire for there to be not just free decisions, but decisions whose freedom has a certain independence of what other decisions are made. If this is what we want, then again it looks as if we may want something with an incoherent content. Suppose you want it to be true that someone, *N*, who decides to *A*, could in the circumstances have decided not to *A*. You might want *N*'s actual decision to be independent in the sense that '*N* could have decided not to *A*' neither entails nor is entailed by any proposition to the effect that somebody makes a decision not to *A*, and neither entails nor is entailed by the proposition that nobody makes a decision not to *A*. Any decision independent in this sense satisfies what I will refer to as the Independence Condition. Now on certain interpretations, '*N* decided to *A* and could in the circumstances have decided not to *A*' entails a counterfactual conditional or a negative proposition about laws of nature. On *-interpretations it entails 'If *N* had decided not to *A*, the state of the world just beforehand would have been exactly as it actually was'. And on nomological possibility interpretations it entails 'There is no law of nature whose conjunction with a complete description of the state of the world just before *N* decided to *A* entails that *N* did not decide not to *A*'. But there are certain interpretations of counterfactuals in general on which the entailed counterfactual will mean something which prevents the Independence Condition from being satisfied. And there are certain interpretations of laws of nature in general on which the negative proposition about laws of nature will mean something which prevents the Independence Condition from being satisfied. So if, as you may well think, counterfactuals in general and laws of nature in general have to be interpreted in these ways if they are to be intelligible at all, then there is no intelligible or coherent interpretation of *-freedom of decision which satisfies the Independence Condition.

The menacing and perhaps uniquely intelligible interpretation of counterfactuals is the one I earlier called demystified and contrasted with a Lewis-style interpretation (see Chapter 3, Section 1). On this demystified interpretation, the counterfactual 'If *N* had decided at *t* not to *A*, the state of the world just beforehand would have been exactly the same', which is entailed by '*N* *-freely decided to *A*', entails 'Whenever something like *N*'s deciding at *t* not to *A* occurs, it is immediately preceded by a state of the world like the actual state of the world before *t*'. And the latter entails 'Sometimes a state of the world like the actual state of the world

just before t is immediately followed by something like N's deciding at t not to A'. But suppose, as seems reasonable, that 'something like N's deciding at t not to A' is taken to mean a decision
not to A. Then, on the demystified interpretation, the counterfactual to which we are committed when we say that N's decision
to A was *-free, entails that N's freedom violates the Independence
Condition. For this condition says that N can still have freely
decided to A even though in fact nobody decides not to A in
similar circumstances.

It is also worth noting that nomological possibility freedom of
decision cannot meet the Independence Condition, at least if, on
pain of unintelligibility, we must take laws of nature to be, in
part, spatio-temporally unrestricted generalizations about what
actually happens. Suppose then that laws of nature are generalizations of that kind with some extra property P. 'N was able
to decide at t not to A' will on the nomological possibility interpretation then mean 'It is false that both

(1) Whenever N or somebody like him is in circumstances like
N's just before t he will not make a decision like a decision at
t by N not to A

and

(2) (1) possesses property P'.

But this is equivalent to 'Either

(3) Once at least somebody in circumstances like N's at t makes
a decision like a decision at t by N not to A

or

(4) (1) does not possess P'.

And if the disjunction of (3) and (4) entails 'N was able to decide
at t not to A', then the latter is also entailed by (3). But it is part
of the Independence Condition that 'N could have decided not
to A' is *not* entailed by the proposition that somebody or other
makes a decision not to A. So freedom of decision in the nomological possibility sense does not satisfy the Independence Condition, on a certain demystified conception of laws of nature.

Nor for that matter could any coherent C-freedom satisfy the
Independence Condition, even a C-freedom not governed by an
'as things actually were' clause. For 'N C-freely decided at t to A'
entails something of the form 'If X had been the case, N would

have decided not to *A*'. On the demystified interpretation of counterfactuals, this entails 'Whenever something like *X* is the case, there is a decision not to *A*', which entails that somebody or other actually makes a decision not to *A*, so that the Independence Condition is once again broken.

The main point, however, is that the Independence Condition cannot be satisfied by *-freedom of decision. Suppose that our desire for the Independence Condition to be satisfied is so strong that we would not even faintly want a freedom of decision which could not meet it. Then all of our want and belief conflicts about *-freedom of decision could be resolved, if it were also true that the only coherent interpretations of counterfactuals and laws of nature were the ones I called demystified. I support this demystification, but I still think that we would on reflection want *-freedom, even on the understanding that it cannot satisfy the Independence Condition. This at any rate is what I shall assume from now on.

3. INTERNAL PROPOSITIONS

The internal proposition of your desire for *x* is the proposition which you believe about *x*'s relation to something else when you want *x* for the sake of that other thing (see Chapter 2, Section 2). If what I said in the last chapter is correct then it is at least sometimes for the sake of other things that victims of want and belief conflicts want there to be decisions free in extra possibility senses. And the internal propositions of these desires may still be doubtful even if, as now appears, the desires themselves do not have incoherent contents. What then are the internal propositions of the desires?

The desire revealed by reflections on gratitude was a desire that freedom should exist for its own sake. *-freedom, we assumed, was the freedom in question, and this *-freedom could be either S- or C-freedom.

But S-freedom of decision was also wanted for the sake of not being under a repeated illusion. The internal proposition believed by people who want S-freedom for this reason is that only if there really are S-free decisions will their repeated experiences as of S-freely deciding not be illusory. Obviously this is true if there are such experiences. But whether there are is a matter on which I have nothing to say: we must all make our own introspective efforts.

C-freedom was wanted for the sake of there being evidence as to what decisions people will make in the future. The internal proposition believed by those who want C-freedom for this reason is that the conditionals which are true if there are C-free decisions constitute such evidence. This is obviously true.

Finally, there was the desire of the person who wants there to be free decisions for the sake of moral responsibility. As already noted, it is difficult to determine what in this context 'free' actually means. One might well, however, still think that the whole desire has a false internal proposition. If my earlier analysis is correct, the internal proposition is that morally good decisions would not have their special property of moral goodness if they were not free. The property here is a non-relational property such that, necessarily, if you believe that something has it then you want this something to exist. And one might well think that nothing has such a property. How could one argue for this? If we leave aside Mackie's over-discussed and unconvincing critique of moral objectivism, in which properties of moral goodness are in any case slightly differently understood,[4] just one argument is current which might seem to serve. I criticize it, and then suggest something simpler.

The anti-objectivist argument that I want to criticize has been developed by Blackburn from what was, he says, a suggestion of Casimir Lewy's.[5] We are invited to consider these two theses. (i) Necessarily, if something has a moral property M, and a natural property S which underlies M, then anything else which has S has M as well. (ii) Given any natural property S which underlies a moral property M, it is possible for something to have S but not M. The argument then runs as follows. Either both of the modal terms in these two theses are given a 'conceptual' interpretation,

---

[4] According to Mackie ((1977), 40), the objective good whose existence is assumed in ordinary moral judgements 'would be sought by anyone who was acquainted with it, not because of any contingent fact that this person, or every person, is so constituted that he desires this end, but just because the end has to-be-pursuedness somehow built into it.' It is not that necessarily, if you believe that an action would be good then you want to take it, but rather that necessarily if you know that it would be good then you will take it.

[5] See Blackburn (1971), 101–24; (1984), 182–9; (1985), 46–67.

or both are interpreted 'metaphysically'. But, either way, the conjunction of (i) and (ii) would be so mysterious that it would be better not to believe that anything has moral properties. And although (ii) is false, on a 'metaphysical' interpretation of the two modal terms, both (i) and (ii) are true on a 'conceptual' interpretation.[6] I can see how someone might find it mysterious that even though there is no necessity in the world guaranteeing that if *x* is *F* then *x* is *G*, there is a necessity in the world guaranteeing that if *x* is *F* and *G* and *y* is *F*, then *y* is *G*:

consider the thought that B must be virtuous because he has the same natural properties as A, and A is virtuous: if we now ask what makes B virtuous, the answer must surely be his (B's) natural properties, and not any of A's natural properties. Yet if this is the case, then there must be a necessary connection between B's natural properties and his virtue. To suppose otherwise requires one to suppose that the way in which a moral property depends on natural properties in one case depends on the way in which the former is contingently associated with the latter in another case. If there is no necessary connection between B's natural properties and his virtue, then B could be as he is in all natural respects but not be virtuous. Yet if this is possible, why is it not possible once one takes account of the features of someone else, A, in whom virtue happens to be conjoined with the natural features that A possesses?[7]

If it is part of our current concept of a moral judgement that these 'metaphysical' necessities and possibilities govern the relations between moral and natural properties, then those who believe that the world is unmysterious will not believe that anything has a moral property, as currently understood. But Blackburn denies thesis (ii), on a 'metaphysical' interpretation of 'possible':

someone who holds that a particular natural state of affairs . . . underlies a moral judgement is very likely to hold that this is true as a matter of metaphysical necessity . . . if I hold that the fact that someone enjoys the misery of others underlies the judgement that he is evil, I should also hold that in any possible world, the fact that someone is like this is enough to make him evil.[8]

The claim is rather that because (i) and (ii) are both true on a 'conceptual' interpretation of their modal terms, and because on

---

[6] See Blackburn (1985).
[7] Baldwin (1985), 39.
[8] Blackburn (1985), 55.

this interpretation their joint truth is mysterious, we should not believe that anything has a property which it is correct to call a moral property. Now Blackburn cannot be claiming that the actual concept of a moral property is too mysterious for us even to have. And yet if we do have it, why should the mere fact that it is mysterious that we should have the concept make it unreasonable to suppose that anything has the property? Suppose that the modalities in (i) and (ii) are conceptual. Then (i) says that it is part of our concept of a moral property that F is a moral property only on condition that if x is S, and x's being S underlies x's being F, and y is S, then y is F. And (ii) says that it is not part of our concept of a moral property that F is a moral property only on condition that if x is S, and x's being S underlies x's being F, then if x were not F it would not be S. However mysterious it is that we have a concept partially describable as the concept of a property whose instantiations conform to the condition mentioned in (i) and may not conform to the condition mentioned in (ii), it is hard to see why there needs to be anything mysterious about there being a property whose instantiations always meet the one condition but do not always meet the other.

There is, anyway, a simpler argument for the non-exemplification of the property of moral goodness, as this seems ordinarily to be understood. The property is both non-relational and such that necessarily, if you believe that something has it, then you want this something to exist. But it is hard to believe that there can ever be such a necessary connection. Whatever non-relational property F we take, believing that x is F will not make you want x to exist, unless you want there to be as much F-ness as possible, and believe that since x is F its existence contributes to this end. But it is possible that someone who believes that x is F, and wants there to be as much F-ness as possible, also believes, not that x's existence contributes to this end, but rather that it is possible for x not to exist and that there would be more F-ness if x did not exist. Such a person will believe that x is F but not want x. Since such a person is possible, there is no non-relational property, either of goodness or of anything else, such that necessarily, if you believe that something has it, then you want this something to exist.

5

Freedom and Natural Order

No incoherence has emerged in the desire for extra possibility freedom. When decisions free in that sense are wanted for the sake of moral responsibility, then the desire has a doubtful internal proposition. But even if someone, finally unable to accept the objectivist metaphysic which ordinary conceptions of morality seem to presuppose, were to stop wanting there to be free decisions for the sake of what is ordinarily called moral responsibility, his desire for their existence would probably still survive in one of the forms that I discussed in Chapter 3. Let me turn then to the third question about want and belief conflicts proposed at the end of Chapter 2.

With p as the proposition which the victim of a first-order want and belief conflict wants to be true but believes to be false, the third question was: Is there good evidence for not-p which is better evidence than any evidence for p? If the victim's belief that not-p was originally based on his conviction that there was good evidence for not-p, and he afterwards abandons that conviction, then his belief that not-p is liable to collapse. So the information that there is no good evidence for not-p is useful in the resolution of conflicts in which not-p is believed. As I explained in Chapter 2, this is not to say that continuing to believe not-p without good evidence for p is on every value theory about belief bad. Nor is it even to say that a victim, wondering whether to go on believing that not-p, and applying his own value theory, need always ask himself whether he has good evidence for what he believes. If p is the proposition which the victim of a first-order conflict believes to be false, then the answer to our question about evidence will also be of interest to the victim of a related second-order conflict, who wants but believes he lacks a true belief in that same proposition p. The second-order victim may not be willing to resolve matters by acquiring a belief that p unless he thinks that it is not the case that there is good evidence for not-p which is better than any evidence for p.

What does *p* represent in the conflicts we are now considering? If we leave out conflicts in which the victim wants free decisions for the sake of moral responsibility, *p* represents either 'There are S-free decisions', 'There are C-free decisions', or 'There are *-free decisions'. Roughly put, the aim of this chapter is to see whether there is good evidence, in the shape of a deterministic or other general thesis about regularity in the world, for the non-existence of *-free decisions. I take it as obvious that if there is no such evidence against the existence of *-free decisions, then there is also no evidence of this kind for the non-existence of S-free and C-free decisions which are not *-free.

Let us say that a thesis of natural order is any proposition which implies that natural laws or regularities are prevalent. Not all theses of natural order are deterministic. That every event falls under a universal law of nature is a thesis of natural order. But the label applies also to such doctrines as that every event falls under a statistical law, or that every mental event falls under a psycho-physical law, or that every rational decision falls under a psychological law, and likewise to various doctrines about the prevalence of true spatio-temporally unrestricted generalizations. In these terms, my aim in this chapter is to see whether the existence of *-free decisions is excluded by any evidentially well supported thesis of natural order. In the first section I consider the relation between *-freedom and theses of natural order under what in Chapter 3 I called a demystified interpretation of counterfactuals. In Section 2 I consider the same question on the basis of what I there called a Lewis-style interpretation. I hope that, as described, the two interpretations are general enough to stand between them for all possible interpretations.

1. *-FREEDOM AND DEMYSTIFIED COUNTERFACTUALS

Consider this thesis of natural order:

D For any true propositions *p* and *q* which respectively describe the state of the world at an instant and at an earlier instant, there is a set of true spatio-temporally unrestricted generalizations whose conjunction with *q* entails *p*.

Given the demystified interpretation of counterfactuals in general which I described earlier on, the following argument shows D to be incompatible with the existence of *-free-decisions:

(a) D.

(b) N *-freely decided at t to A.

(c) There is a true proposition describing the state of the world just before t whose conjunction with a set of true spatio-temporally unrestricted generalizations entails that N decided at t to A.   (from (a) and (b))

(d) If N had decided at t not to A, the state of the world just before t would have been exactly as it actually was.
       (from (b))

(e) Whenever something like N's deciding at t not to A occurs, it is immediately preceded by a state of the world like the actual state of the world just before t.   (from (d))

(f) Sometimes an actual state of the world like the actual state of the world just before t is immediately followed by something like N's deciding at t not to A.   (from (e))

(g) There is no true proposition describing the state of the world just before t whose conjunction with a set of true spatio-temporally unrestricted generalizations entails that N decided at t to A.   (from (f))

Since (c) and (g) cannot both be true, and since each follows from the conjunction of the two premisses (a) and (b), these two premisses cannot both be true. So given that each premiss is consistent, the two premisses are incompatible. On a demystified interpretation of counterfactuals (d) entails (e) because on that interpretation the putting forward of a counterfactual is nothing more that a convenient way of asserting or conversationally implying various propositions about the actual world, and in the case of (d) the generalization (e) will be at least one of the propositions actually asserted (see above, p. 28). On a Lewis-style interpretation of counterfactuals (d) does not entail (e). On a Lewis-style interpretation, (d) is true if and only if either (i) it is impossible that

(A) N decides at t not to A

or (ii) some possible world in which it is true both that (A) and that

(B) the state of the world just before *t* is exactly like the state of
     the actual world just before *t*

is more similar to the actual world than any world in which (A)
and not-(B) hold. But even if (e) were false, a possible world in
which both (A) and (B) hold might still be more similar to the
actual world than any world in which (A) and not-(B) hold.
This is why I have to consider the implications of a Lewis-style
interpretation separately.

Is there good evidence for D's truth, and better evidence for its
truth than there is for its falsity? If so, and given the validity of
(a)–(g), there is good evidence for the non-existence of *-free
decisions, and better evidence than any for their existence.

What has, on the contrary, very often been claimed is that there
is good evidence for D's falsity and better evidence than for its
truth. According to D, for any true propositions *p* and *q* which
respectively describe the world at an instant and at an earlier
instant, there is a set of true spatio-temporally unrestricted generalizations whose conjunction with *q* entails *p*. Quantum mechanics
is supposed to provide good evidence that if *q* and *p* describe
physical states of the world there are no spatio-temporally unrestricted generalizations whose conjunction with *q* entails more
that that *p* has a certain probability. Swinburne has a simple
argument to this effect. If his argument is sound, there is good
evidence for D's falsity, at least if we are allowed to ignore the
unlikely possibility that any true proposition describing the physical state of the world at some instant is nevertheless entailed by
the conjunction of a set of true spatio-temporally unrestricted
generalizations and a proposition describing both its physical and
its mental state at some earlier instant.

If a certain theory in some field is supported by observations better than
any other theory, we are only justified in supposing that its laws are not
the most fundamental laws, governing phenomena in the field, if we are
justified in suspecting that one day some more fundamental theory will
be confirmed better . . . But if we have evidence that in some respect no
more fundamental theory will ever be established, we must surely take
the laws of the theory which we have in that respect as the fundamental
laws governing phenomena.[1]

---

[1] Swinburne (1986), 240.

T_2 will be a more fundamental theory than T_1 if it predicts whatever T_1 predicts but more than T_1 predicts. Thus, if we have a theory whose laws are universal and which is better confirmed than all rival theories in its field, we should assume that some events fall under these laws unless we suspect that a more fundamental theory, whose laws are statistical, can be both constructed and confirmed. And if we have a statistical theory which is better confirmed than all rival theories in its field, we should assume that some events are merely statistically related, unless we suspect that a more fundamental theory whose laws are universal can be both constructed and confirmed. Now quantum theory is a statistical theory, and is better confirmed than all rival theories in the field. We could perhaps construct 'a more fundamental theory consisting of universal law-like statements which explained the subsequent destination of photons by properties which they possessed on leaving the source, their possession of which made inevitable their destination'.[2] But we could not confirm this more fundamental theory, if quantum theory is true, because we can never simultaneously measure the position and momentum of sub-atomic particles. Hence whatever evidence there is for quantum theory is also evidence that no more fundamental non-statistical theory will be confirmed. But there is good evidence for quantum theory. So there is good evidence that no more fundamental non-statistical theory will be constructed and confirmed. Hence we should conclude that some events are merely statistically related.

Let us suppose for the moment that this or some other appeal to quantum mechanics shows that there is better evidence for the falsity of D than any evidence for its truth. There may still even on this assumption be some more modest relative of D for which there is good evidence, and better evidence than any for its falsity. And if D is incompatible with the existence of *-free decisions, the same may be true for similar reasons of this more modest relative. Here are two candidates for the role:

D* For any true proposition p describing somebody's decision and any true proposition q describing that person's neurophysiological state just beforehand there is a set of true spatio-temporally unrestricted generalizations whose conjunction with q entails p.

----

[2] Swinburne (1986), 242.

and

S For any true propositions p and q which respectively describe
the state of the world at an instant and at an earlier instant,
there is a set of true spatio-temporally unrestricted statistical
generalizations whose conjunction with q entails that there is a
probability R $(0<R<1)$ that the state of the world described
by p will occur.

Let us consider D* and S in turn.

If we replace D, in (a)–(g), by D*, then obviously the argument goes through as before. And if we can assume that decisions
are non-identical to physical events, and also that no true spatio-
temporally unrestricted generalization correlates mental and
physical events, then we can conclude that no quantum mechanical argument tells against D*. Is there then good evidence for
D*, and better evidence than there is for its falsity?

It is true that for some kinds of decisions we will probably
never gain knowledge of particular spatio-temporally unrestricted
generalizations which would enable them to be predicted from
what we know about antecedent neurophysiological states. But
we cannot conclude from this that D* is false. Suppose a scientist
tells you, perhaps using a code, that on receipt of his very message
you will be in a neurophysiological state such that, according to a
true spatio-temporally unrestricted generalization linking neurophysiological states and decisions (a true N → D generalization),
you will then immediately decide to A. If you are interested in
discovering the truth-value of what you are told, you will naturally
try to falsify it. And one easy method is to decide not to A. But
people are often interested in discovering the truth-value of scientific claims, especially when these are used to predict their own
decisions. And so there is good reason to suppose that any N → D
generalization will in fact be falsified, if it is used in conjunction
with a true proposition about a neurophysiological state to make
a prediction of the form 'You will decide to A immediately after
receiving this prediction'. But it does not follow that there is no
true N → D generalization whose conjunction with a description
of your neurophysiological state on receipt of the prediction that
you will decide to A entails that you will decide *not* to A. And so,
even if you do decide not to A, on receipt of the prediction that
you will decide to A, it does not follow that there are any actual

decisions which are not entailed by conjunctions of true N → D generalizations and true descriptions of antecedent neurophysiological states, and hence it does not follow that D* is false. Whatever actual decision you take, on being told that according to a true N → D generalization you will on receipt of this message be in a state such that you will immediately decide to A, it is always possible that there is some N → D generalization, unfalsified by your decision, whose conjunction with a description of your neurophysiological state entails that you do indeed take that decision.

Swinburne thinks that a good argument for the actual falsity of determinism about human behaviour can be based on the existence of what he calls 'counter-suggestible agents', i.e. scientifically minded people interested in testing as easily as possible claims about the springs of their own behaviour.[3] He argues that for any true deterministic theory T linking brain states and bodily movements it would probably be possible to give a counter-suggestible agent a signal that he has just been found in a brain state such that on receipt of the signal and given the truth of T a particular movement will occur in his body. Since the agent is counter-suggestible he will take the opportunity to falsify T by bringing about a result which excludes the predicted movement. So probably there is no true deterministic theory linking brain states and bodily movements. If this argument were sound it could, I think, be adapted to show that D* is probably false: for 'true deterministic theory linking brain states and bodily movements' read 'true spatio-temporally unrestricted generalization of the type referred to in D*'. But, so far as I can see, it is always possible that there is some other unknown true deterministic theory whose conjunction with a description of your brain state on reception of the signal about the implications of the current and doomed theory entails that you will do whatever you in fact do on receipt of that signal. Swinburne may be right that, once a particular deterministic theory has been formulated, it will probably always be possible to signal to a counter-suggestible person enough of its implications to allow that person to falsify it. What he does not seem to show is that if there is a true deterministic theory, then probably it will at some time be formulated.

[3] Swinburne (1986), 252–61.

But even if there is no good evidence for the falsity of D*, there may still be no good evidence for its truth. And I do not in fact know of any convincing evidence for that. One might try to support D* by extrapolation from the past successes of neuro-science. Honderich does indeed argue on that basis for a thesis of natural order which seems to entail D*. This thesis, which he calls a determinism, is the conjunction of three propositions, the Correlation Hypothesis, the Hypothesis on the Causation of Neural Pairs, and the Hypothesis on the Causation of Actions. But D* seems to be entailed just by the conjunction of the first two of these, viz.,

CH For each mental event of a given type there exists some simultaneous neural event of one of a certain set of types. The existence of the neural event necessitates the existence of the mental event, the mental event thus being necessary to the neural event. Any other neural event of any of the mentioned set of types will stand in the same relation to another mental event of the given type,

and

HP Each psychoneural pair, which is to say a mental event and a neural event which are a single effect and in a lesser sense a single cause—each such pair is in fact the effect of the initial elements of a certain causal sequence. The initial elements are (i) neural and other bodily elements just prior to the first mental element in the existence of the person in question, and (ii) direct environmental elements then and thereafter.[4]

Neuroscience, according to Honderich, 'confirms psychoneural intimacy', for '(i) In very many cases, a set n of neural facts is often, or very often, or in all experiment and observation, accom-panied by a certain mental phenomenon m . . . (ii) In very many cases, a set n of neural facts is taken as guaranteeing a mental phenomenon m'.[5] And since all psychophysical identity theories are false, only CH allows for psychoneural intimacy. What of HP?

With respect to pain and pleasure, there is the fact that the causal history of certain peptides gives detail to the proposition of the neural and bodily causation of the neural events associated with lesser pain or the absence

    [4] Honderich (1988), 247–8.
    [5] Ibid. 284.

of pain. So with the emotions. Various known facts give content to the causal propostion in this connection. As for consciousness, all that was said suggests . . . that there is a very considerable knowledge of neural and bodily causal antecedents of associated neural events. One can mention the development and functioning of the hippocampus and of the corpus callosum. Finally, with respect to the higher functions, the development and functioning of the speech areas of the cortex are of obvious relevance, as are facts of chemical function and of such disorders as schizophrenia.[6]

The difficulty with this argument lies, I think, in the general principle of inference which it employs. This seems to be something like 'Many Xs are known to be Ys; no Xs are known not to be Ys, so probably all Xs are Ys'. Surely this is vitiated by the inability of the generalization to explain its instances, to unify otherwise conspicuously diverse phenomena? That all emeralds are green hardly explains the fact that all the numerous past observed emeralds have been green. Nor, to take just one element in Honderich's determinism, would CH explain the fact that 'for many mental events of a given type there exists some simultaneous neural event of one of a certain set of types, etc.' CH and HP are non-explanatory metaphysical generalizations which do not stand in an evidential relation to their instances which is like the relation in which scientific theories stand to the explananda by which they are confirmed.

Now let us consider

S For any true propositions p and q which respectively describe the state of the world at an instant and at an earlier instant, there is a set of true spatio-temporally unrestricted statistical generalizations whose conjunction with q entails that there is a probability R $(0<R<1)$ that the state of the world described by p will occur.

Is it true that both (i) S is incompatible with the existence of *-free decisions, and (ii) there is good evidence for the truth of S which is better than any evidence for its falsity? S does look a more likely thesis than either D or D*, but we need not go into that because so far as I can see there is no way to show, within the constraints of a demystified conception of counterfactuals, that S excludes the existence of *-free decisions. Certainly it will not do just to modify (a)–(g) in the most obvious way. That would give us the following argument:

(a1) S.

(b) N *-freely decided at t to A.

(c1) There is a true proposition describing the state of the world just before t whose conjunction with a set of true spatio-temporally unrestricted statistical generalizations entails that there is a probability R ($0<R<1$) that N decided at t not to A. (from (a1) and (b))

(d) If N had decided at t not to A, the state of the world just before t would have been exactly as it actually was.

(from (b))

(e) Whenever something like N's deciding at t not to A occurs, it is immediately preceded by a state of the world like the actual state of the world just before t. (from (d))

(f) Sometimes an actual state of the world like the actual state of the world before t is immediately followed by something like N's deciding at t not to A. (from (e))

(g1) There is no true proposition describing the state of the world just before t whose conjunction with a set of true spatio-temporally unrestricted generalizations entails that there is a probability R ($0<R<1$) that N decided at t to A.

And this argument breaks down because (g1) does not follow from (f). In the original argument (a)–(g), (f) is incompatible with the conjunction of D and 'N decided at t to A', and hence entails (g), because this conjunction entails that every actual state of the world exactly like the state of the world just before t is immediately followed by a decision on the part of somebody like N to A, and nobody can simultaneously decide to A and decide not to A. But (f) is compatible with the conjunction of S and 'N decided at t to A', and hence does not entail (g1), because all that this conjunction entails is that for any actual state of the world exactly like the state of the world just before t there is a probability R that it will be immediately followed by a decision on the part of someone like N to A. And since $R<1$, what the conjunction entails is consistent with there being *some* occasions on which there is a state of the world exactly like the state of the world just before t, and this state is not immediately followed by a decision to A.

And if this minimally modified version of (a)–(g) does not show that the existence of *-free decisions is incompatible with S, neither will a correspondingly modified version of (a)–(g) show that the existence of *-free decisions is incompatible with the hybrid of D and S which we get if we drop the 'statistical' from S and allow the probability R to have any value up to and including 1. This is fortunate, because the hybrid of D and S looks more likely to be true even than S.

  We are looking for a thesis of natural order which satisfies these two conditions: (i) it is incompatible with the existence of *-free decisions, and (ii) there is good evidence for its truth which is better than any evidence for its falsity. We have been assuming that Swinburne's or some other appeal to quantum mechanics shows that D fails (ii). Quite independently of any quantum mechanical argument D* also seems to fail (ii). S or the hybrid of D and S may pass (ii), but both seem to fail (i). What if neither Swinburne's nor any other appeal to quantum mechanics does show that D fails (ii)? It seems unlikely that D will pass (ii) if D* fails it. For although D does not entail D*, it is hard to see how we could construct any positive argument for D which did not use the principle of inference which I criticized in arguments for D*. So I am inclined to conclude that on a demystified conception of counterfactuals, and regardless of the soundness or otherwise of anti-deterministic appeals to quantum mechanics, no thesis of natural order satisfies both (i) and (ii).

2. *-FREEDOM AND LEWIS-STYLE COUNTERFACTUALS

What conclusions would we reach on whether the existence of *-free decisions is incompatible with some well-supported thesis of natural order, if we assumed a Lewis-style rather than a demystified interpretation of counterfactuals? The argument I gave for D's incompatibility with the existence of *-free decisions does not work on a Lewis-style interpretation, and neither will parallel incompatibility arguments for any of our relatives of D.

  To formulate a thesis of natural order which will exclude the existence of *-free decisions on a Lewis-style interpretation we need the notion of an iron law of nature. I will say that a proposition fits that description only if it is a true spatio-temporally unrestricted generalization such that nobody is ever free to make a decision such that if he had made it the generalization would be false. Now consider

D1　For any true propositions *p* and *q* which respectively describe the state of the world at an instant and at an earlier instant, there is a set of iron laws of nature whose conjunction with *q* entails *p*.

The following argument shows that on a Lewis-style interpretation of counterfactuals, D1 is incompatible with the existence of *-free decisions:

(a)　D1.

(b)　*N* *-freely decided at *t* to *A*.

(c)　There is a true proposition describing the state of the world just before *t* whose conjunction with a set of iron laws of nature entails that *N* decided at *t* to *A*.　　(from (a) and (b))

(d)　*N* could have decided at *t* not to *A*.　　　　　　(from (b))

(e)　If *N* had decided at *t* not to *A* the state of the world just before *t* would have been exactly as it actually was.

　　　　　　　　　　　　　　　　　　　　　　(from (b))

(f)　*N* could have made a decision at *t* such that if he had made it a proposition which is an iron law of nature would have been false.　　　　　　　　　　(from (c), (d) and (e))

(f) is self-contradictory, on our definition of iron laws of nature. But (f) follows from (c), (d), and (e), and hence from (a) and (b). So (a) and (b) cannot both be true. Why does (f) follow from (c), (d), and (e)? (e) entails that if *N* had decided not to *A*, it would have been false that whenever there are states exactly like the state of the world just before *N*'s decision to *A*, these are always immediately followed by decisions to *A*. But according to (c) this last generalization not merely is true but would have been true even if *N* had decided at *t* not to *A*. The idea is not that (e) entails a proposition about the actual world which is incompatible with the set of true generalizations about decisions to *A* referred to in (c). That would be true on a demystified interpretation of counterfactuals. The idea is rather that (e) entails something about possible worlds which is incompatible with what must be true of possible worlds if the generalizations referred to in (c) are iron laws of nature.

Obviously a similar argument will establish that the existence of free decisions is incompatible with

D1* For any true proposition *p* describing somebody's decision and any true proposition *q* describing that person's neurophysiological state just beforehand there is a set of iron laws of nature whose conjunction with *q* entails *p*.

Now consider

S1 For any true propositions *p* and *q* which respectively describe the state of the world at an instant and at an earlier instant, there is a set of iron statistical laws of nature whose conjunction with *q* entails that there is a probability R $(0>R>1)$ that the state of the world described by *p* will occur,

where a true spatio-temporally unrestricted statistical generalization is an iron statistical law only if nobody would have made a decision such that had he made it the generalization would have been false. Can the argument (a)–(f) be modified so as to show that *-free decisions would be excluded by S1? Here is the obvious revision:

(a1) S1.

(b) N *-freely decided at *t* to A.

(c1) There is a true proposition describing the state of the world just before *t* whose conjunction with a set of iron statistical laws of nature entails that there is a probability R $(0<R<1)$ that N decided at *t* to A.   (from (a1) and (b))

(d) N could have decided at *t* not to A.   (from b))

(e) If N had decided at *t* not to A the state of the world just before *t* would have been exactly as it actually was.

(from (b))

(f1) N could have made a decision at *t* such that if he had made it a proposition which is an iron statistical law of nature would have been false.   (from (c1), (d), and (e))

The idea is that, given (e), if N had decided at *t* not to A, there would have been one more decision not to A which is preceded by a state of the world just like the actual state of the world at *t*. The probability that states like that are followed by decisions to A would therefore have been different from R. But since, according to (c1) it is an iron statistical law that this probability is R, it follows from (c1), (d), and (e), and hence also from (a1) and (b), that N could have made a decision such that if he had made it an iron statistical law would have been false. But this is impossible, so (a1) and (b) cannot both be true. S is compatible with *-freedom of decision, on a demystified conception of counterfactuals, because it is compatible with all those propositions about the actual world to which on this conception (e) is equivalent. S1 is supposed to be incompatible with *-freedom of decision, on a Lewis-style conception of counterfactuals, because (e) entails something about possible worlds which cannot be true if the generalizations referred to in (c1) are iron statistical laws of nature.

But the argument is invalid. It does not in fact follow from (e) that if N had decided not to A, there would have been one more decision not to A which is preceded by a state of the world just like the actual state of the world at t. For (e) is compatible with the proposition that if N had decided at t not to A, then somebody else would have made a decision to A, preceded by a state of the world exactly like the actual state of the world at t, which he would not otherwise have made, and so R would have remained the same even if N had decided at t not to A.

To meet this objection, we could revise the definition of an iron statistical law. On our revised definition, a true spatio-temporally unrestricted statistical generalization will be an iron statistical law only if nobody would have made a decision such that had he made it, and if, had he made it, nobody else would have made a contrary decision, preceded by the same sort of state of the world, then the generalization would have been false. Maybe the argument will work if 'iron statistical law' is taken throughout in this revised sense, and if (f1) is replaced by

(f2) N would have made a decision at t such that if he had made it, and if, had he made it, nobody else would have made a contrary decision, preceded by a state of the world exactly like the actual state of the world at t, which he would not otherwise have made, a proposition which is an iron statistical law of nature would have been false.

There is however a further difficulty. Maybe the argument will work if statistical laws are of the form 'x% of As are Bs'. But it may seem that a statistical law, as distinct from a statistical fact, must apply to As severally, or distributively, and not merely collectively. For example, even if it were true that '50 per cent of all radium atoms, if left alone, not subjected to nuclear bombardment and so on, disintegrate within a period of 1590 years from the time at which they became radium atoms', this would not be a statistical law, because it might be that in the whole history of the universe, only 2^n million radium atoms ever have come or ever will come into existence, that the first half of these, the first 2^{n-1} million, all disintegrate within 1590 years of their becoming radium atoms, while none of the other half ever have disintegrated or ever will. For there to be a statistical law, 'the proportionality of the outcome must be exhibited repeatedly, it must in some way crop up wherever the antecedent conditions occur'.[7]

Suppose that, in order to allow for this distributiveness or severality, we take a statistical law to say that in long actual runs of A's the frequency of B's usually approaches a common limit.[8] Then, if some individual A which is a B had not been a B, this by itself would be consistent with the law. And so, in our revised argument, (f2) will not follow from (c1), (d), and (e). Possibly this objection would be met be redefining an iron statistical law yet again, so as to require that nobody would have made a decision such that had he made it, and if, had he made it, nobody else would have made a contrary decision, the statistical fact underlying the law would have been false.

But it is futile for our purposes to prolong this process of re-definition unless there is good evidence for the iron statistical thesis with which we eventually end up. And so far from that being the case, there does not in fact seem to be good evidence for any iron theses of natural order, statistical or non-statistical. I suggest moreover that there would still be no good evidence for any iron thesis of natural order even if there were good evidence for some thesis of natural order, such as D or D* or S, which refers only to true generalizations and not to iron laws.

The objection will be made that it must at least be possible to have good evidence that some propositions are iron laws of nature as distinct from mere spatio-temporally unrestricted generaliza-tions because otherwise we would never have good evidence that any proposition was a law of nature, as distinct from a true accidental generalization. If they are to be distinguishable from

[7] Mackie (1974), 235.
[8] Ibid. 241.

accidental generalizations at all, laws must hold of natural necessity, or, more fundamentally perhaps, they must support counterfactual conditionals, which would be impossible if they did not
have a modal content. But then, how can we possibly make sense
of the necessity here, unless we explain it precisely in terms of
human powers, and more particularly by saying that the necessity
which distinguishes a law from an accidental generalization consists precisely in the fact that if p is a law of nature, nobody is
able to make p false? Might not freedom to make a decision, such
that if one did make it p would be false, be a special case of that
ability to make p false in terms of whose absence natural necessity
must be explained?

Sympathetic though I am to the idea of explaining modal concepts in this way, I do not find this objection very plausible. There
is a difference between having good evidence that some particular
propositions are laws of nature, and having overriding evidence
that every event falls under a law of nature. And why, anyway,
should we assume that there are any laws of nature, as distinct
from true accidental generalizations? What, after all, is 'drawing
a distinction between laws and accidental generalizations'? Is
it finding a property which people who call regularities laws of
nature actually or potentially believe that these regularities must
possess if they are to be called laws of nature rather than accidental generalizations? Or is it finding a property, not of the
form 'being believed to be F', which really is possessed by all
those generalizations which people call laws of nature, and is not
possessed by those generalizations which they call accidental?

Take the second interpretation. I may agree for the sake of
argument that the regularities which people call laws of nature
would possess a property of this kind not possessed by the regularities which they call accidental generalizations only if they
were iron laws of nature. But this will not commit me to the belief
that all or even any of the regularities which people call laws of
nature really are iron laws of nature. Since the existence of iron
laws, or the existence of good evidence for a hypothesis about
their prevalence, is one of the questions at issue, it cannot be
taken for granted that any distinction must be preserved whose
preservation would require that all the regularities called laws of
nature are iron laws. If on the other hand 'drawing a distinction
between laws and accidental generalizations' is taken in the first

way, then the truth of my thesis that there is no good evidence for iron theses of natural order will not prevent us from drawing the distinction. Even if there are no iron laws of nature at all, it may still be true that people are unwilling to call a regularity a law of nature rather than a true accidental generalization unless they believe that it is an iron law. The mere fact that the ordinary concept of a law of nature is such and such is no evidence that the concept actually applies to anything.[9]

At this point someone who accepted a Lewis-style interpretation of counterfactuals might abandon iron theses of natural order as potential evidence for the non-existence of *-free decisions and turn his attention back to theses like

D For any true propositions p and q which respectively describe the state of the world at an instant and at an earlier instant, there is a set of true spatio-temporally unrestricted generalizations whose conjunction with q entails p.

Although a demystified interpretation of counterfactuals is necessary to sustain an actual incompatibility between D and the existence of *-free decisions, one might easily still think that even on a Lewis-style interpretation D's truth would make it very unlikely that there are *-free decisions. I did indeed suggest earlier on that any positive argument for D would probably be vitiated by its reliance on some form of induction by simple enumeration. But let us at least see what exactly this new move amounts to.

The argument would be as follows. Suppose there are *-free decisions. Then probably there are enormous numbers of cases in which this or that person who could have taken a decision did not do so. And more particularly it is probable that some of the generalizations referred to in D are such that they have very many instances in which this or that person could have made the generalization false by taking a decision which he did not in fact take. But in that case it is very unlikely that D is true. For if, on each of very many independent occasions, an outcome of a certain type is

---

[9] For a denial that there is any further property possessed by all the true spatio-temporally unrestricted generalizations which people call laws of nature, see Van Fraassen (1989), pts. i and ii. For a defence of the Mill–Ramsey–Lewis hypothesis that the only further property of such generalizations is that they fit in neatly with other such generalizations to form a strong and simple deductive system, see Earman (1986), ch. 5.

possible, then there is a good chance that on at least one of these occasions it is actual.

One can be sceptical about this argument without being sceptical about the general principle about actuality and possibility on which it relies.[10] Suppose that most of the generalizations in D have many instances, and that there are many occasions on which someone or other has the unexercised power to take a decision which would have made false one or other of the generalizations in D. It may still be true that each generalization in D, which someone or other has the unexercised power to make false, has relatively few instances.

Given the general principle about actuality and possibility one might indeed try to argue against the existence of *-free decisions without appealing to the likely truth of any thesis about natural order. Suppose I *-freely decide to A. Then, it may be said, there is a finite though possibly very brief period of time up to the time of my decision during which I am able to decide to A but do not. But then, given the general principle about actuality and possibility, it is highly improbable that I make or begin to make my decision to A at the precise instant when I do make it or begin to make it, and at none of the infinitely many instants in the preceding period during which I am able to make it or begin to make it but do not. So it is highly improbable that my actual decision to A is in fact *-free at all.[11] But the most that this argument can show is that it is highly improbable that there are any decisions which are both *-free and S-free. If the ability to decide to A is part of what I possess when I have a veridical experience as of being able to decide to A and able to decide not to A, then doubtless I possess the ability for a finite period of time. But it does not seem to make sense to say that there is a finite period of time during which the conditional is true by virtue of whose truth my decision to A would be C-free.

---

[10] For an interesting discussion of some similar general principles and their relations with various forms of the principle of sufficient reason, see Kane (1986). The Aristotelian doctrine that whatever is always possible is at some time actual has, he says, surfaced again among theoretical physicists in the form of 'Gell-Mann's totalitarian principle': anything not prohibited is compulsory.

[11] Cf. Brentano (1925), 265–7.

6

Palliatives

THE third question to be asked about want and belief conflicts, on the programme of Chapter 2, was about the evidential status of the proposition which in first-order conflicts is believed to be false. And in the last chapter I made some progress with this question, so far as it concerns conflicts about free decisions. It did at any rate seem that, whatever interpretation of counterfactuals we take, no thesis of natural order is both well supported by evidence and incompatible even with the probable existence of *-free decisions. There may yet be evidence of quite a different kind for the non-existence of *-free and indeed S- and C-free decisions. A new kind of doubt will in fact emerge in Chapter 8. But this must wait. And, allowing for the worst, I now turn to the last of the four questions about want and belief conflicts proposed at the end of Chapter 2. This is the one about palliatives.

With p as the proposition which the victim of a first-order conflict wants to be true but believes to be false, we were to ask: Is there is a proposition q such that (i) if p then probably at least not-q, (ii) the victim wants q to be true, (iii) the victim does not already believe that not-q? Suppose it has somehow been decided that the first-order conflict should not be resolved by abolition of one or other of the two conflicting attitudes. Then the victim's recognition that there is a proposition q which meets these conditions will at least diminish the strength of his desire for p to be true. And the palliative will apply also to those related second-order conflicts in which the victim wants but believes he lacks a true belief in that same proposition p, but does not positively believe that p is false. For this victim, as we are assuming, also wants p to be true. I now ask then whether there is a value of q which meets the three conditions when p stands for the various desiderata in the central want and belief conflicts about free decisions. If it turns out that despite what I have said about theses of natural order there is still good evidence for the non-existence of the kinds of free decisions which we want to exist, then our first-order conflicts may need a palliative. But even if there is no evidence of this kind, a palliative may still be needed. Mere absence of evidence for the non-existence of free decisions does not help the second-order victim: what he wants is positive evidence that free decisions do exist.

In the first section of the chapter I consider palliatives for conflicts in which the existence of *-free decisions is the object of desire, and in the second section palliatives for those in which what is wanted is the existence of S- and C-free decisions which are not *-free. In the third section I relate the argument of this and the previous chapter to some current discussions of 'Incompatibilism'.

I. ORDER-BASED PALLIATIVES

As we saw in the last chapter, various theses of natural order are, on one or other of our two interpretations of counterfactuals, incompatible with the existence of *-free decisions. If then there are theses of natural order which we want to be true and do not believe to be false, there is a chance that these very same theses will figure in palliatives for conflicts about *-free decisions. I will start by seeing how this idea works out on a demystified interpretation of counterfactuals, and then I will do the same with a Lewis-style interpretation.

On a demystified interpretation of counterfactuals 'There are *-free decisions' entails the negation of

D For any true propositions p and q which respectively describe the state of the world at an instant and at an earlier instant, there is a set of true spatio-temporally unrestricted generalizations whose conjunction with q entails p.

So if D is a proposition which the victim of a want and belief conflict about *-free decisions wants to be true, and if he does not already believe that D is false, then on a demystified interpretation there is a palliative for his conflict. If it is a first-order conflict that we are considering, a belief in D may be one of the very things that helped to generate the conflict, and in this case the victim will certainly not already believe that D is false. There is a palliative for this particular victim if he wants D to be true. And it is easy to imagine how he might want D to be true, even though he also thinks that it is incompatible with the freedom he wants. For D's truth is a necessary condition for complete predictive knowledge. The difficulty, though, is that for this particular victim a D-based palliative may turn out to be unnecessary. As we saw in the last chapter, there are quantum mechanical arguments for D's falsity. Fortunately, I did not have to decide on their merits. But if any of them really is sound, then the partly D-generated conflict could perhaps be resolved by abolishing the belief element. Furthermore, the existence of these arguments threatens the efficacy of a D-based palliative for want and belief conflicts about *-freedom which are not even partly generated by a belief in D. Among such conflicts would be second-order conflicts partly generated by a failure to believe in the falsity of

D* For any true proposition p describing somebody's decision and any true proposition q describing that person's neuro-physiological state just beforehand there is a set of true spatio-temporally unrestricted generalizations whose conjunction with q entails p.

For if D is to figure in a palliative it is necessary not only that we want it to be true, but that no argument convinces us of its falsity.

What is needed then is a proposition which we want to be true, which probably at least would be false if there were free decisions, and for whose falsity there would be no good evidence even if some quantum mechanical argument for D's falsity were sound. The obvious candidate is D*. The truth of D* is desirable as a necessary condition for predictive knowledge of human behaviour. As I said in the last chapter, demystified assumptions about counterfactuals make D* incompatible with the existence of *-free decisions if D is. And as I also said, there does not seem to be any good evidence for D*'s falsity.

There is this objection. In the last chapter I defended D* against an argument of Swinburne's about counter-suggestibility. But I was only able to do this by assuming that some of the generalizations to which D* refers will never be formulated. But is this assumption compatible with our reason for wanting D* to be true? The truth of D*, like the truth of D, is desirable as a necessary condition for predictive knowledge, and predictions cannot be made with the aid of unformulated generalizations.

I reply that, even if we exclude from D*'s scope decisions taken by counter-suggestible people in response to scientific predictions about how they will decide, we will still want the correspondingly weakened version of D* to be true. And although the weakened version of D* is compatible with the existence of *-free decisions, it will still be incompatible with something that, in wanting there to be *-free decisions, we want to be true, viz. that there are *-free decisions *not* taken by counter-suggestible people in response to scientific predictions about how they will decide.

There is another seeming palliative. Consider

(R) Most decisions are taken for a reason.

It could be argued that probably if there are *-free decisions then (R) is false. It is unlikely that *-free decisions, if they exist, make up only a minority of decisions in general, so probably, if there are *-free decisions, some of them are taken for a reason. But necessarily, if a decision is taken for a reason then it is caused by a belief on the decider's part about its conduciveness to what he wants. And necessarily, it might be thought, no *-free decisions are caused. So if we want (R) to be true and do not already believe it false, we have another palliative for want and belief conflicts about *-free decisions.

Difficulties could be made about the claim that necessarily no *-free decisions are caused. Maybe one can accept that the existence of *-free decisions is incompatible with such theses of natural order as D and D* without having to accept this further thesis about causality. But the palliative is in any case dubious because it is far from clear that we want (R) to be true. Given that I now believe that my decision to A would satisfy my wants, I can hardly mind if this belief now causes me to decide to A. But I may well be much less happy about the causation of my future decisions by my future beliefs about how they satisfy my wants, or about the causation of other people's decisions by their beliefs about how their decisions satisfy their wants. For I may have no confidence in the truth either of other people's beliefs or of my own future beliefs about such matters, and no confidence either that I will not, or that others do not, have wants which I now want not to exist. If in these ways I have no confidence in the rule of subjective reason, then it can hardly console me for the absence of *-freedom.

Now let me consider the question of palliatives on Lewis-style interpretations of counterfactuals. Do conflicts about *-free decisions also have order-based palliatives on those interpretations? The argument of the last chapter for D's incompatibility with the existence of *-free decisions does not, as we saw, work on Lewis-style assumptions. Nor therefore does the essentially similar argument for the conclusion that the existence of these decisions is excluded by D*. There was, however, an argument, valid on Lewis-style assumptions, for the exclusion of *-free decisions by an analogue of D which employed the notion of iron laws of nature. A proposition is an iron law of nature, I said, only if it is a true spatio-temporally unrestricted generalization such that nobody is ever free to make a decision such that if he had made it the generalization would be false. The analogue of D was

D1 For any true propositions p and q which respectively describe the state of the world at an instant and at an earlier instant, there is a set of iron laws of nature whose conjunction with q entails p.

And the argument for D1's incompatibility with the existence of *-free decisions was as follows:

(a) D1.

(b) N *-freely decided at t to A.

(c) There is a true proposition describing the state of the world just before t whose conjunction with a set of iron laws of nature entails that N decided at t to A.   from (a) and (b))

(d) N could have decided at t not to A.   (from (b))

(e) If N had decided at t not to A the state of the world just before t would have been exactly as it actually was.
                                                                  (from (b))

(f) N could have made a decision at t such that if he had made it a proposition which is an iron law of nature would have been false.   (from (c), (d) and (e)

(f) is self-contradictory, on our definition of iron laws of nature. But (f) follows from (c), (d), and (e), and hence from (a) and (b).

So (a) and (b) cannot both be true. Why does (f) follow from (c), (d), and (e)? (e) entails that if N had decided not to A, it would have been false that whenever there are states exactly like the state of the world just before N's decision to A, these are always immediately followed by decisions to A. But according to (c) this last generalization not merely is true but would have been true even if N had decided at t not to A. The idea is not that (e) entails a proposition about the actual world which is incompatible with the set of a true generalizations about decisions to A referred to in (c). That would be true on a demystified interpretation of counterfactuals. The idea is rather that (e) entails something about possible worlds which is incompatible with what must be true of possible worlds if the generalizations referred to in (c) are iron laws of nature.

Now since D1 entails

D   For any true propositions p and q which respectively describe the state of the world at an instant and at an earlier instant, there is a set of true spatio-temporally unrestricted generalizations whose conjunction with q entails p,

quantum mechanical arguments against D, if there is anything in them, tell equally against D1. But just as, when we were considering palliatives on the demystified interpretation of counterfactuals we replaced D by

D* For any true proposition p describing somebody's decision and any true proposition q describing that person's neurophysiological state just beforehand there is a set of true spatio-temporally unrestricted generalizations whose conjunction with q entails p,

so, now that we are working on Lewis-style assumptions, we can replace D1 by

D1* For any true proposition p describing somebody's decision and any true proposition q describing that person's neurophysiological state just beforehand there is a set of iron laws of nature whose conjunction with q entails p.

And if (a)–(f) shows that D1 is incompatible with the existence of *-free decisions, then essentially the same argument will show that the same is true of D1*. So we will have a D1*-based palliative for conflicts about *-free decisions if (i) we want D1* to be true, and (ii) there is no convincing argument for its falsity. I fear, though, that even if (ii) is true (i) is false. You might want D* to be true for the sake of predictive knowledge. Or at least you might for this reason want the truth of some version of D* qualified to exclude the falsifying decisions of the counter-suggestible. But once you have distinguished between D* and D1* and realized that the latter entails but is not entailed by the former, you would not want the truth of the latter, as distinct from the former, for the sake of predictive knowledge, unless you believed that what differentiates the latter from the former is also necessary for predictive knowledge. And if you did believe that then you would, I think, be wrong.

Someone may say that although D* does not entail D1* it is nevertheless highly unlikely that the former is true and the latter false. Suppose that people are always free to make decisions such that if any of those decisions are made at least one of the generalizations referred to in D* is false. Then surely it is highly unlikely that D* is true. D* would only be immune to this charge of probable falsehood if, instead of referring to spatio-temporally unrestricted generalizations, it referred to iron laws of nature. But then it would be identical to D1*. So probably, if the truth of D* is necessary for predictive knowledge, so also is the truth of D1*. This objection was, however, met at the end of the previous chapter. It looks, then, as if on Lewis-style assumptions about counterfactuals no order-based palliative is available for conflicts about *-free decisions.

2. S- AND C-FREE DECISIONS

Is there a palliative for want and belief conflicts about decisions which are S- or C-free but not *-free? Our arguments about the relations between theses of natural order and the existence of *-free decisions cannot, I think, be adapted to support any parallel conclusions about the existence of S- or C-free decisions which are not *-free. It follows from the conjunction of D and

(1) At t N made a non-*-free but S- or C-free decision to A

that

(2) There is a true proposition describing the state of the world just before t whose conjunction with a set of true spatio-

temporally unrestricted generalizations entails that N decided at t to A.

And it follows from the conjunction of D1 and (1) that

(3) There is a true proposition describing the state of the world just before t whose conjunction with a set of iron laws of nature entails that N decided at t to A.

But it does not follow from (1) that if N had decided at t not to A then the state of the world just before t would have been exactly as it actually was. So on neither of our two interpretations of counterfactuals does it follow from (1) either that (2) is false or that (3) is false.

Someone might object that it is in any case necessarily true that if N had decided at t to A he could not have made a decision at t such that if he had made it then the state of the world would have been different from what it actually was at any time before t. The necessity here stems from the fact that the past is fixed, and is quite independent of whether or not N *-freely decided at t to A. If this is right, and if we grant a demystified interpretation of counterfactuals, the existence of non-*-free decisions will be incompatible with D. And, on a Lewis-style interpretation of counterfactuals, their existence will be incompatible with D1. It is true that the past is fixed in a sense which requires that if an event e has occurred before t nobody could have made a decision at t such that if he had made that decision it would have been true both that e occurred before t and that e did not occur before t. But it is not true that the past is fixed in a sense which requires that if e occurred before t nobody could have made a decision at t such that if he had made it then it would have been true that e did not occur before t. And neither 'N S-freely decided at t to A' nor 'N C-freely decided at t to A' entails 'N could have decided at t not to A' in a sense which is incompatible with 'If N had decided at t not to A then things just before t would have been different'.

There might, however, be a theological or depth-psychological palliative for want and belief conflicts about decisions which are S- or C-free but not *-free. There might be some hypothesis about God or the unconscious which we want to be true, which we do not disbelieve, and which also entails that there are no S- or C-free decisions even of the non-*-kind, or at least no S- or C-free human decisions even of the non-*-kind.

Arguments for the incompatibility of free decisions and the foreknowledge of a timebound God work, I suspect, only when 'free' is taken in a ∗-sense. 'God knows at all times before t that N will decide at t to A' entails that N did not freely decide at t to A if 'N freely decided at t to A' is interpreted so as to entail 'if N had decided at t not to A then the state of the world just before t would have been just as it actually was'. For if N had decided at t not to A, and the state of the world just before t had been just as it actually was, then just before t God would have believed that N would decide at t to A, and this belief would have been false, which is impossible if God is necessarily omniscient. But this argument will not work if 'N freely decided to t to A' is interpreted so as to be compatible with 'if N had decided at t not to A then the state of the world just before t would not have been just as it actually was'.

Free decisions of at any rate one non-∗ kind do, however, seem to be excluded by the hypothesis of an omnipotent God. 'N C-freely decided at t to A' entails a conditional of the form 'If X had been the case N would have decided at t not to A'. Let us distinguish between two kinds of C-freedom, according to whether or not 'N C-freely decided at t to A' also entails 'It is not the case that N would have decided at t not to A only if someone else had decided that N would so decide'. Suppose that there is a God who is omnipotent 'in the sense that God's effective willing, or not willing, is *logically equivalent* to the obtaining, or not, of every contingent state of affairs that is not a state of God's own willing'.[1] Then, at least on a demystified interpretation of counterfactuals, N would have decided at t not to A only if God had decided that he would so decide, and N will therefore have lacked one kind of C-freedom to decide at t to A.

We can also identify a non-∗-freedom of decision which is excluded by a familiar 'Freudian' hypothesis. Suppose that all decisions to A are caused in the following way. There is something the decider wants and to which he believes that Aing is conducive; these wants and beliefs together cause his decision; and these wants and beliefs are unconscious in the sense that he does not know or even believe that he has them. If all decisions to A are caused in this way, then N will not have the kind of C-freedom to

---

[1] Ross (1980), 614.

decide to *A* which requires it to be true both that he could have reflected on and disapproved of the wants and beliefs which caused him to decide at *t* to *A*, and that only if he had thus disapproved of these wants and beliefs would he have decided at *t* not to *A*.

3. PRE-NATAL INCOMPATIBILISM

In this and the last chapter I have been considering whether, in our central want and belief conflicts about free decisions, the existence of the free decisions which we want to exist is excluded by certain theses of natural order. The last chapter was about the possible abolition of the belief element in such conflicts. With that in mind I asked whether the existence of the free decisions in question is excluded by any thesis of natural order for which we have good evidence. The present chapter has been about palliatives, and I have asked whether the existence of the free decisions in question is excluded by any thesis of natural order which we want to be true and for whose falsity there is no good evidence. Various determinisms were among the theses of natural order that I have been discussing in these two chapters, and the reader will have been reminded of current disputes about 'Incompatibilism'. It is I think worth making some explicit comparisons.

Attention has been focused recently on what we can call the pre-natal argument for the incompatibility of determinism and free physical action. The basic idea, as described by van Inwagen, is this: 'If determinism is true, then our acts are the consequences of the laws of nature and events in the remote past. But it is not up to us what went on before we were born, and neither is it up to us what the laws of nature are. Therefore, the consequences of these things (including our present acts) are not up to us'.[2] Van Inwagen goes on to defend three more developed versions of this line of thought.[3] I will look at just one of these. 'Determinism', in the version I look at, is defined as the conjunction of the following two theses: (a) for every instant of time, there is a proposition that expresses the state of the world at that instant; (b) if *p* and *q* are any propositions that express the state of the world at some

---

[2] Van Inwagen (1983), 16.
[3] There is a similar argument, descending from Ginet (1966), in Ginet (1990), ch. 5.

instant, then the conjunction of p with the laws of nature entails q. To show that determinism, so defined, is incompatible with the thesis that we are able to act otherwise than we do, van Inwagen asks us to imagine a man, 'J', who refrains from raising his hand at a certain time, 'T'. Let 'P_0' denote a proposition which describes the state of the world at some time prior to J's birth, let 'P' denote a proposition which describes the state of the world at the time T when J failed to raise his hand, and let L denote the conjunction into a single proposition of all the laws of nature. We then have the following simple argument, consisting of six premises and a conclusion which follows from their conjunction:

(vI 1) If determinism is true, then the conjunction of P_0 and L entails P.

(vI 2) It is not possible that J has raised his hand at T and P be true.

(vI 3) If (vI 2) is true, then if J could have raised his hand at T, J could have rendered P false.

(vI 4) If J could have rendered P false, and if the conjunction of P_0 and L entails P, then J could have rendered the conjunction of P_0 and L false.

(vI 5) If J could have rendered the conjunction of P_0 and L false, then J could have rendered L false.

(vI 6) J could not have rendered L false.

(vI 7) If determinism is true, J could not have raised his hand at T.

It is easy to construct an analogous argument which refers to decisions rather than physical actions. Imagine a man, J, who refrains from deciding at t to A; let P_0 denote a proposition which describes the state of the world at some time prior to J's birth, P a proposition which describes the state of the world at T, and L the conjunction into a single proposition of all the laws of nature. We then have:

(1) If determinism is true, then the conjunction of P_0 and L entails P.

(2) If J had decided at T to A, then P would be false.

(3) If (2) is true, then if J was free to decide at T to A, then J was free to render P false.

(4) If J was free to render P false, and if the conjunction of P_0 and

L entails P, then J was free to render the conjunction of P_0 and L false.

(5) If J was free to render the conjunction of P_0 and L false, then J was free to render L false.

(6) J was not free to render L false.

(7) If determinism is true, J was not free to decide at T to *A*.

Laws of nature, in van Inwagen's own argument, are so defined that although they apply to hand movements they do not apply to decisions: they are restricted by fiat to propositions which apply non-vacuously to things which are not rational agents. This is because he wants to use 'law of nature' in such a way that 'It is necessary that, for every person *x* and every proposition *y*, if *y* is a law of nature then *x* cannot render *y* false', but thinks that there are psychological generalizations to which this principle may not apply, and which it is nevertheless 'tempting' to call laws.[4] But we would still have a close analogue of van Inwagen's argument if we dropped the fiat and upheld the weaker principle that necessarily no-one is free to render a law of nature false by making a decision. And if the laws of nature which it refers to are understood in that way, then van Inwagen's determinism entails, though it is not entailed by,

D1 For any true propositions *p* and *q* which respectively describe the state of the world at an instant and at an earlier instant, there is a set of iron laws of nature whose conjunction with *q* entails *p*.

Current disputes about the cogency of van Inwagen's and similar arguments illustrate a point which I made at the beginning of Chapter 3, namely that without want and belief conflict resolution as a conscious objective it is hard to see what principle there can be for choosing among the various senses of 'freedom' and 'determinism' on which the validity of any incompatibilist argument is bound to turn. Fischer, in a useful survey of some recent writing, notes two different responses to arguments like van Inwagen's. There is 'multiple-pasts compatibilism', which initially challenges (VI 5), and there is 'local-miracle compatibilism', which initially challenges (VI 6). According to the multiple-pasts compatibilist, we must distinguish between

---

[4] Van Inwagen (1983), 63–4.

two ways in which we might be thought to be powerless over the past. Suppose proposition b says that some event e_1 occurred at time t_1. The compatibilist wishes to distinguish between two ways in which an agent might be said to be powerless to affect b:

(FP 1) If e_1 occurred at t, then no agent can at any time later than t_1 initiate a causal sequence issuing in e_1's *not* occurring at t_1.

(FP 2) If e_1 occurred at t_1, then no agent can at any time later than t_1 perform an action such that if he were to perform it, e_1 would not have occurred at t_1.

The multiple-pasts compatibilist claims that, whereas (FP 1) is valid, it is not equally clear that (FP 2) is valid. The multiple-pasts compatibilist takes the (FP 2) sense to be the pertinent sense, and in this sense, he points out that the fixity-of-the-past premise , . . is false.[5]

The local-miracle compatibilist, who rejects (vI 6),

distinguishes two senses in which we might lack power over the laws of nature:

(FL 1) No agent can ever perform an act that itself would be or would cause a law-breaking event.

(FL 2) No agent can ever so act that a law-breaking event would (at some point) have occurred.

The local-miracle compatibilist points out that whereas (FL 1) is valid, (FL 2) is not obviously valid, and although compatibilism (of this sort) must deny (FL 2), it needn't deny (FL 1). The local-miracle compatibilist takes (FL 2) to be the pertinent sense, and he points out that, in this sense, the fixity-of-the-laws premise . . . is false.[6]

One way of answering the multiple-pasts compatibilist would be to concede that, interpreted so as to deny (FP 2), (vI 5) is not self-evidently true, but to build it into the very definition of 'free action' that J freely refrained from raising his hand only if he could have raised it by doing something such that if he had done it things up to then would have been the same. With free action defined in that way, it would still follow from the conjunction of determinism and 'J freely refrained from raising his hand' that J could have rendered (P_0 and L) false. But it would also follow from that conjunction that he could have rendered (P_0 and L) false without rendering P_0 false, and so we would still get the

---

[5] Fischer (1986), 35.
[6] Ibid. 36.

alleged absurdity that he could have rendered L false. Would this
be a legitimate answer? It depends on the actual purpose of the
argument thus defended. Suppose the purpose is to illuminate
the relations between determinism as van Inwagen defines it and
the kind of freedom we want. And suppose there is some independent reason to think that we want a freedom such that if
N freely Aed, (i) he was able not to A, and (ii) if he had not Aed
things up to then would have been the same. The move would
be legitimate, relative to that purpose. But there is no way to
decide whether the move is legitimate without reference to some
purpose, and since neither van Inwagen nor his multiple-pasts
compatibilist opponents consider possible purposes, it is not
surprising that the match seems to be drawn. In fact, I am not sure
that we do want a freedom such that if N freely Aed then (i) he
was able not to A, and (ii) if he had not Aed things up to then
would have been the same. What we may well want, as I argued in
Chapter 3, is *-freedom of decision, which belongs to N's decision
to A only if (i) he was able to decide not to A, and if he had
decided not to A then things just beforehand would have been the
same. Nor would the purpose which I imagined be a very good
one: determinism as van Inwagen defines it does not seem either to
be well supported by evidence or something that we want to be
true. But the present point is only that some purpose or other has
to be specified before we can even begin to assess the multiple-
pasts compatibilist's objection.

Van Inwagen's own method with the multiple-pasts objection is
to define 's can render p false' in such a way that it is impossible
to render a proposition about the past false, impossible not only
to initiate backwards causation, but even to do something such
that if one had done it things beforehand would have gone differently. His definition is as follows: 'It is within s's power to
arrange or modify the concrete objects that constitute his environment in some way such that it is not possible in the broadly
logical sense that he arrange or modify those objects in that way
and the past have been exactly as it in fact was and p be true'.[7]
And this does certainly leave him open to an *ad hominem* objection. He claims that his defences of the various premises in his
argument 'do not in any clear sense presuppose that statements of

---

[7] Van Inwagen (1983), 68.

ability are not disguised conditionals'.[8] But suppose 'It was in *s*'s power to *A* at *t*' does mean something of the form 'If *X* had been the case before *t* then *s* would have *A*ed at *t*'. Then, by van Inwagen's definition, '*s* could have rendered *p* false at *t*' will mean 'If *X* had been the case before *t*, then *s* would have done something such that necessarily, in the broadly logical sense, if he had done it, and the past had been exactly as it in fact was, then *p* would have been false'. But this in turn will mean 'If *X* had been the case before *t*, and the past had been exactly as it was, then *s* would have done something such that necessarily, in the broadly logical sense, if he had done it then *p* would have been false'. Now 'the past', in this conditional, means 'what took place before *t*'. But then it follows that the antecedent of the conditional is necessarily false and hence that the whole conditional necessarily true. So on a conditional interpretation of 'It was in *s*'s power to *A* at *t*' *s* could have rendered any proposition false at *t*, and that of course will destroy van Inwagen's argument, one essential premiss of which is

(vI 6) J could not have rendered L false.

But the objection could be met by redefining 'free action' in such a way that if you act freely you could have done otherwise but not in any conditionally analysable sense. And the legitimacy of *that* move could again not be attacked or defended without some reference to the overall purpose of the argument.

The same moral emerges when we consider 'local-miracle compatibilism'. This is elaborated in a paper by David Lewis.[9] For reasons of his own, Lewis maintains that if J had raised his hand P_0 would still have been true, and he focuses accordingly on

(vI 6) J could not have rendered L false.

He looks for a principle which would allow him to reject (vI 6) without making him say that people are able to break laws. The principle he comes up with is that, although I do not have the ability to do something such that if I did it my act itself would be a law-breaking event, and although I do not have the ability to do something such that if I did it my act would cause a law-breaking event, I do have the ability to do something such that if I

---

[8] Ibid. 121.
[9] Lewis (1981).

did it some law would be broken. If J had raised his hand, then the course of events would have diverged from the actual course of events a little while beforehand, and at the point of divergence there would have been a law-breaking event. 'That is not to say that anything would have been a law and broken—that is a contradiction in terms if, as I suppose, any genuine law is at least an unbroken regularity. Rather, if L had not been true, something that is in fact a law, and unbroken, would have been broken, and no law'.[10] But what if we reject (vI 6) simply on the grounds that it is logically possible that J could have raised his hand even if this very act itself would have been a law-breaking event? If the reply is that the laws of nature referred to in the determinism we are discussing are so defined as to make that a logical impossibility, then we want to know why it is that particular determinism that we are discussing. According to Lewis, that I am able to break a law is 'incredible'; all we can believe is that I am able to do something such that if I did it a law would be broken. Maybe on our ordinary concept of a law, the first thesis is incredible because self-contradictory. But that does not make it any less likely that the only regularities in the world are ones that if they are to be called laws at all can be called laws only in a sense on which it is coherent to say that I am able to break a law. And until we know what evidence there is that these are not the only regularities that prevail, or at least why we should want stronger regularities than these to prevail, we do not seem to have any good reason to select for discussion a determinism which refers to laws so defined that it is incredible that I am able to break them.

---

[10] Lewis (1986), 292.

7

Free Will and Free Action

I HAVE now made some progress with all the questions of Chapter 2, so far as they concern our central want and belief conflicts about free decisions. In the first-order conflicts which are, as I argued or assumed, likely to afflict us, S-free, C-free and *-free decisions are what we want there to be. In none of these conflicts could I find any incoherence in the content of the desire. Only those desires based on objectivist beliefs about moral responsibility seemed to be based on doubtful internal propositions. On neither demystified nor Lewis-style assumptions about counterfactuals did there appear to be any thesis of natural order which was both incompatible with the existence of *-free decisions and supported by good evidence. It was not clear that if a palliative was still needed for first- or second-order conflicts about *-freedom then Lewis-style assumptions about counterfactuals would allow it to be found. Nor was it clear that on any assumptions about counterfactuals a palliative could be found for conflicts about S- and C-free decisions which are not *-free. But on demystified assumptions about counterfactuals, conflicts about *-free decisions would have a palliative in the shape of D*, or a weakened version of the same.

As we will see in the next chapter, more radical doubts are liable to arise about free decisions than any I have so far considered. But decisions, I am assuming, are but one kind of actions, and before taking up these further doubts, I will say something in this present chapter about how, whatever their origins, conflicts about free decisions are related to conflicts about those free actions which are not decisions. In the first section I describe an actual or potential sense of 'action', and an actual or potential sense of 'decision', such that decisions are a species of actions. In Section 2 I consider whether, on these senses of 'action' and 'decision', and with 'freedom' taken in the various senses displayed in Chapter 3, more would need to be said on conflicts about free decisions which are not actions than could be inferred pretty well mechanically from an ideally complete study of conflicts just about free decisions. Section 3 contains some of the few extra things which would in fact need to be said. The conditions which in Section 1 I take to be necessary and sufficient for events to be actions or decisions are I think ones which most people would on reflection believe to be satisfied by all and only the events they ordinarily call by these names.

1. ACTION

An action, in the sense with which I will work from now onwards, is an event which is either (i) a volition, or (ii) generated by a volition, or (iii) of a type some instances of which are so related to a volition that the volition generates another event.

'Volition' I define in terms of a certain particular kind of introspectible quality. Any mental event which exhibits a quality of this kind I call a volition. Decisions exhibit a particular introspectible quality. The same or in some cases a similar quality is exhibited in making an effort, attending, judging or mentally assenting, forming an intention, and willing something to be the case. All these events I call volitions. By 'willing' I shall not mean what occurs when there is volition of any kind: I keep the word for that particular kind of volition which is willing something to be the case. 'Voliting' suggests itself if a term is needed for what occurs when there is volition of any kind.

Decisions are then in my usage a sub-class of volitions, which are in turn a sub-class of actions. By decisions I mean decisions to act rather than decisions that something is the case: the latter I call judgements or mental assentings. Decisions are distinguished from some other volitions by the fact that they require previous deliberation or at least an awareness of alternatives, from others both by this fact and by the fact that we employ the concept of action in describing the contents of decisions. When one forms an intention or makes an effort one always forms an intention or makes an effort to act, just as when one decides one always decides to act. But neither forming an intention nor making an effort requires previous deliberation or awareness of alternatives. Neither do attending, mentally assenting, or willing something to be the case. And volitions of these last three kinds also differ from decisions in that use of the concept of action does not always need to be made in describing their contents. I may for instance will that I shall act or will you to act, but I may also will that the orange stops rolling before it reaches the edge of the table.[1]

Some writers join wanting to deciding and willing in a single category or continuum. But I think that there is a clear phenomenological division between wanting and all the kinds of events which I have called volitions. Wanting, when it is more than a mere disposition to behave, feels not like actual willing or deciding but like a pressure towards willing or deciding to act, or towards willing that something is the case. It may be that one cannot will or decide without occurrently wanting, but one can want without willing and without at the time experiencing anything like willing or deciding.

What is it for an event to be generated by a volition? N's Aing is generated by his Bing if and only if he As by Bing. Examples of Aing by Bing are: giving a signal by raising one's arm, raising one's arm by deciding to raise it, pleasing one's instructor by paying attention, going back on one's previous decision to X by deciding to Y. Generation is never the same as causation. If, when I raise my arm by deciding to raise it, raising it and deciding to raise it are two different events, still the deciding to raise it will be a part of raising it. Since nothing can cause itself, nothing can cause a whole of which it is itself a part, and my deciding to raise it cannot cause my raising it. What my deciding to raise my arm does cause, when it generates my raising my arm, is my arm's going up. But in other cases in which I A by Bing, such as that in

---

[1] Mulligan and Smith ((1986), 117; cf. Smith (1987), 206) distinguish between states, whose temporal parts are homogeneous, processes, whose temporal parts are not homogeneous, and events, which are temporally extensionless boundaries of processes or states. Decisions they assign to the category of events: they are boundaries to processes of deliberation. As I conceive them, decisions, and volitions more generally, would on the contrary be in these terms processes or states. When by deciding to act we bring a process of deliberation to an end, we can, I think, be aware of something which exhibits a quality, and is distinct from what has occurred during the process of deliberation. I do not see how such a thing could not have temporal parts. For a more detailed description of the something which in my view has to be temporally extended see Pfänder's 'Motive und Motivation' (1911), in Pfänder (1963).

which by deciding to Y I go back on my previous decision to X, no part of the Aing is caused by the Bing.

Why is it sufficient for an event to be an action that it is of a type some instances of which are so related to a volition that the volition generates another event? Because I do not want my working sense of 'action' to be too eccentric. Ordinary usage allows there to be action without any actual volition on the agent's part, and so does the sufficiency of this condition. We ordinarily allow that when a sleeping man raised his arm he acted, and likewise count it as action when someone unthinkingly fidgets, taps his foot, or scratches his hand, or automatically walks across the room. This, I think, is because events which otherwise resemble these events often are caused by volitions which thereby generate events which we accordingly call actions. Swinburne says that what makes things like mindless tappings actions is that we 'allow them to happen and could at any instant if [we] so chose, stop them. The volition is, in these cases, no decision: it is a giving of permission; but not the active permission of signing a permission form, but the passive permission of doing nothing to stop something. So much action is a matter of the agent not stopping his body from doing what it does naturally under its own steam.'[2] If this is right then we could instead take it as sufficient for an event to be an action that it is of a type which the agent is able, by willing, to prevent. Or we might prefer Aune's version: when we say things like 'S moves his arm when asleep', the 'import of what we are saying . . . is that the man's body moved in the way it would move if he voluntarily moved it.'[3]

Action as I have defined it can be compared with action as described by Prichard. He thought it necessary and sufficient for an event to be an action that it is a volition and more particularly that it is a willing:

When, e.g., we think of ourselves as having moved our hand, we are thinking of ourselves as having performed an activity of a certain kind, and, it almost goes without saying, a *mental* activity of a certain kind. . . . If we ask 'What is the word used for this special kind of activity?' the answer, it seems, has to be 'willing' . . . while we know the general character of that to which we refer when we use the word 'willing', this

[2] Swinburne (1986), 94.
[3] Aune (1973), 22.

character is *sui generis* and so incapable of being defined, i.e. of having its nature expressed in terms of the nature of other things.... Thus obviously, as Locke insisted, willing is different from desiring, and again, willing is not, as some psychologists would have it, a species of something called conation of which desiring is another species... in addition, plainly, willing is not resolving, nor attending to a difficult object, as James holds, nor for that matter attending to anything, nor, again, consenting to the reality of what is attended to, nor, indeed, consenting to anything.[4]

There are three respects in which my definition is more liberal. Firstly, I count as actions volitions which are not willings. Secondly, Prichard rejects the idea that an event is an action if generated by a willing because he thinks that when we talk for example of moving a finger we are simply describing a willing in terms of its effect.[5] And thirdly Prichard does not require anything like my third condition: he thinks that always, in what we would call action, willing is something of which we are 'dimly aware'.[6]

Every action is either basic or non-basic, and an action is basic if and only if not generated by any other action. Plainly, all volitions are basic actions: you do not decide to do something, or pay attention to something, by doing anything else, even if having done something else causes you to decide or attend. Are all basic actions volitions? Not quite, because events like the sleeping man's

---

[4] Prichard (1949), 190.

[5] Loc. cit.

[6] Several writers have recently advanced what they call volitional theories of action, whether as conceptual analyses of some kind or as speculations about what happens to be the case. But in most of them the willings, tryings, or volitions are not introspectible events with a distinctive phenomenal character. In Davis (1979) volitions are functionally defined (p. 18). Donagan (1987) offers a non-functionalist theory, in which volitions are not S-volitions but 'rational appetites', and Zimmerman (1984) a brilliantly organized Chisholm-style treatment of eighteen problems about action, with 'volition' used as an undefined term. O'Shaughnessy believes that in every case of bodily action there occurs a striving or trying with distinctive phenomenal properties. But this striving is not volition, because according to O'Shaughnessy we know a priori that some physical non-psychological action is part of it: he dissociates himself from 'the suffocatingly interiorist and indeed obscurantist world of quasi-magical volitionism' ((1980, ii, p. xx). The doctrine is supported by an argument for the conclusion that successful strivings or tryings to take bodily actions are identical with those actions. Hornsby likewise identifies successful trying with action, but manages to resist the conclusion that e.g. trying to raise one's arm has, when successful, an arm rising as a part: her tryings, unlike O'Shaughnessy's, are 'inner' events. They are, however, certainly not volitions, for they have no 'phenomenal

raising his arm, which are on my definition actions even though
neither volitions nor generated by volitions, are presumably not
generated by any other actions either. But if we postulate, as we
may care to, a primary sense of action on which it is necessary and
sufficient for an event to be an action that it is either a volition or
generated by a volition then an action is basic if and only if it is a
volition.

It will be objected that non-flukiness needs to be written into
any non-eccentric definition of action, perhaps by way of the
definition of generation. I decide to raise my arm but, unknown to
me, it will go up only if somebody else makes it go up. Knowing
that I have decided to raise it, you make it go up. Do I raise it by
deciding to raise it? Do I even act at all? Or is it that, although
my raising it is an action, it is an unintentional action? I shall
assume the latter, and say something about intentional action a
little later on.

Would it be better to say with Prichard that one and the same
action can have different descriptions than that one action may
generate another, that one thing can be done by doing something
else? Would it be better to talk of different action-descriptions
than of different actions? When we say naïvely that somebody did
something by doing something else, is it not strictly speaking a
matter of doing one thing under two different descriptions? If we
say naïvely that he raised his arm by deciding to raise it, is it not
really the case that he decided to raise his arm and that his arm's
going up is an effect of that decision, in terms of which the
decision itself can be described? I think that once we see that 'he
raised his arm by deciding to raise it' is logically equivalent to 'he
decided to raise his arm and this caused it to go up', we need not
insist that 'really' there was only one thing that he did, the rest

character' ((1980), 58). Of recent writers, I come closest to Ginet. He holds that it
is sufficient for an event to be (correctly called?) an action that it is a mental
occurrence with what he describes as an 'actish phenomenal quality', and that it is
also suffcient that it is generated by such a simple mental act. But he does not
mention anything like my third condition. He believes that, at least in the case of
bodily action, an actish quality is always experienced, though not always noticed.
'Even when I walk "automatically", without thinking about it, there is a way in
which I experience my exerting my legs... [which] is *actish* in its phenomenal
quality' ((1990), 25). I can attend to this aspect of my experience, and when I do
so, 'it is like paying attention to the pain I have been feeling in order to be sure
whether or not it has moved slightly' (p. 27).

being 'up to nature', and we need not feel obliged to show the inadequacy of all theoretical criteria for individuating actions, on which there are two things that he did. To insist that there was only one thing that he did is indeed to dramatize the fact that there was only one volition, but in a way which misleadingly suggests that there is something wrong both with our ordinary talk of there being two things that he did, and that we are not free to accept general principles of individuation, like Goldman's, on which there are two things he did.[7]

As already noted, some volitions have a content which cannot be described without using the notion of action. When you decide, you decide to act; when you form an intention, the intention is to act. It could seem that this vitiates my definition. We do not want to say that a volition is an action only if, like attending, or willing an orange to stop rolling, it is not a volition to act. If, however, some volitions are essentially volitions to act, how can we have a complete grasp of the general notion of volition unless we have already grasped the notion of action? The solution, I suggest, is to see that volitions to act are closely related to willings whose contents can be described without using the concept of action, and this relation is such that no unanalysably special kind of volition would be missing from the array of volitions if these willings were substituted for volitions to act. In attention to something and in willing that something is the case different relations can be discerned between the content of the volition and the introspectible quality of the volition. And this makes for a difference in kind between the two volitions. There is no parallel difference between those willings, such as decisions, whose contents are described by using the concept of action, and those whose contents are not so described. Suppose I will my arm to go up, expect it to go up as a result, and know that if it does then I shall have raised my arm, and hence acted, by my willing it to go up. I might then subsequently say for short that I willed that I should raise my arm, and indeed from then onwards always when it comes to the point make use of this loose abbreviation, recognizing that only an abbreviated description of my mental state would be lost if I reverted to willing that my arm goes up when knowing that if it does I will have acted. No special kind of volition, no special

---

[7] Goldman (1970), 10–11.

relation between introspectible quality and variable content would be lost if there were no volitions to act, but only volitions whose contents could be described without using the concept of action and which were accompanied by beliefs on the part of the agents that their volitions would generate actions. And no special type of volition, no special relation between quality and content would be lost if there were only volitions whose contents could be described without using the concept of action, and which did in fact generate actions, but whose agents did not possess the concept of action and therefore did not have the accompanying belief that their volitions would generate actions. There are indeed advantages, from the self-conscious agent's point of view, in restricting volitions to those whose contents are not described in terms of action. Suppose I decide to A, recognizing that my Aing would be generated by a volition. Either (i) the generating volition would be identical to my decision to A, or (ii) this is not the case. If (i), I decide to take an action part of which I will have already taken. And it seems impossible to decide to act, recognizing this about the action decided on. But surely the self-conscious decider does often expect the action on which he decides to be generated by that selfsame decision.

Action as I define it can be contrasted with action defined merely as bodily behaviour caused or non-deviantly caused by the owner's wants or wants and beliefs, or as bodily behaviour caused or non-deviantly caused by those mental states of the owner which make his behaviour under some description rational. Such definitions do strike me as eccentric. One might think that this is because in ordinary usage there is an obvious difference between acting and being passively propelled by one's own attitudes. But this raises the difficult question of why it is not ordinarily supposed that one is passively propelled by one's own volitions. One thing that clearly does make these definitions eccentric is that ordinary usage allows for mental acts which do not essentially involve any bodily behaviour. There is also a problem about rationality. Ordinary usage allows there to be such a thing as action which is non-rational under any description. Someone may perfectly well A rather than B even though he judges that Bing is better than Aing, given the evidence that he has. Davidson, defending a rationality definition, recognizes this, but maintains that in such cases the agent will still make an unconditional 'all-out' judgement to the effect that he is to *A*. The all-out judgement, which he calls a 'pure intention', rationalizes the *A*ing.[8] At this point, as it seems to me, 'rationality' has been emptied of meaning.

It will be useful also to have working senses of 'voluntary action' and 'intentional action'. Here too the conditions I take to be necessary and sufficient seem to be ones which most people would on reflection believe to be satisfied by all and only the events which they call by these names.

A voluntary action I take to be either a volition, or a willing action, taken without coercion or even reluctance, or just an action generated by a volition.

N's *A*ing is intentional, on a first approximation, if and only if either (i) it is a volition, or (ii) (a) it is generated by one of his volitions, (b) the process of generation is non-fluky, and (c) at some time at or after the time of the volition which generated his *A*ing, but not after his *A*ing, he believes that he is *A*ing or that he is doing something by which he will *A*.[9] If *N*'s *A*ing is generated by a volition then (b) is necessary for it to be intentional because otherwise we would have to say such things as that he killed her intentionally if he decided to kill her, by this decision pulled the trigger, believed at this point that by pulling the trigger he would kill her, and although did indeed kill her by pulling the trigger, did so only because when the shot missed it set off a totally unexpected avalanche which killed them both. Condition (c) is necessary because otherwise we would have to say such things as

---

[8] Davidson (1980), Essay 5.

[9] Cf. Ginet (1990), 87: 'Given that "*S*'s *V*ing at *t*" is a canonical designator of an action, "*S*'s *V*ing at *t* was *intentional*" is true if and only if either

(1) "*S*'s *V*ing at *t*" designates a simple action,

(2) It designates a complex action of which the following is true: "*S*'s *V*ing at *t* consists of some action, *S*'s *A*ing at *t*, plus that action's causing certain results or its occurring in certain circumstances, where

    (a) *S*'s *A*ing at *t* was intentional and

    (b) (i) At *t*, *S* believed of her *A*ing that she would or might thereby *V* and

        (ii) At *t*, in what *S* knew that had not then slipped her mind, *S* had justification for this belief that was not, at the same time, justification for believing a proposition too far from the truth as to how she was actually going thereby to *V*", or

(3) It designates an aggregate of actions each of which was intentional and of each of which the following is true: "When *S* performed it, *S* believed of it and of the other component actions already performed or being performed that they would or might be parts of her *V*ing".'

that he killed her intentionally if he decided to set fire to her house, by this decision set fire to it, by setting fire to it killed her, and there was nothing abnormal about the causal chain linking his decision to her death, but all the same there was no time during the process at which he believed that he was killing her or doing anything by which he would kill her.

I doubt, however, whether we would stay close enough to ordinary usage if (b) and (c) were taken to be jointly sufficient for *N*'s volition-generated *A*ing to be intentional, and doubt that we would get the right kind of a jointly sufficient condition if we also required that *N* wanted to *A*. You can *A* non-flukily, and believe that you are *A*ing, and want to *A*, but still never have decided to *A* or have willed the precise state of affairs whose causation by your volition constitutes your *A*ing. Suppose *N* decided to set fire to her house, by this decision set fire to it, and by setting fire to it killed her; there was, moreover, nothing abnormal about the causal chain linking his decision to her death, he believed when he set fire to it that he would thereby kill her, and he wanted to kill her. He may still conceivably have regarded her death as an unavoidable by-product of his only volition, of the only thing that he actually decided to do, which was to set fire to her house. And in this case I think we would say that he did not kill her intentionally.

English law seems now almost to have agreed that some condition over and above (b) and (c) needs to be satisfied. In *Hancock and Shankland* (1986) H and S were miners on strike.

They objected to miner (X) going to work. X was going to work in a taxi driven by the deceased, Wilkie (W). H and S pushed a concrete block weighing 46 lbs. from a bridge over the road along which X was being driven by W . . . The block struck the taxi's windscreen and killed W . . . the Crown decided to pursue the charge of murder. The defence was that H and S intended to block the road but not to kill or do serious bodily harm to anyone . . . H and S were convicted of murder, the Court of Appeal quashed their conviction.[10]

The Crown appealed to the House of Lords and the Crown's appeal was dismissed. The ground for the dismissal seems to have been not that there was insufficient evidence that H and S believed that by dropping the block they would cause X's death, but that even if they had foreseen this consequence they might still, as they

---

[10] Smith and Hogan (1986), 592.

claimed, not have intended to kill X. As Lord Scarman put it, in *Maloney* (1985) '... the House made it absolutely clear that fore-sight of consequences is no more than evidence of the existence of the intent; it must be considered, and its weight assessed, together with all other evidence in the case. Foresight does not necessarily imply the existence of intention.'[11] There is, however, still a residual unclarity about the relevance of the distinction between foresight of highly probable consequences, and foresight of certain consequences. In *Maloney* a good deal of reliance was placed on Lord Hailsham's speech in *Hyam* (1985).[12] Lord Hailsham had insisted that the surgeon in a heart-transplant operation will not intend his patient to die even if he recognizes that there is at least a high degree of probability that his action will kill the patient. But he also insisted that if a man blows up an aircraft in order to get insurance money, and some passengers are killed, then the saboteur would have intended to kill them, and it is a case of murder. His reason seems to be that the saboteur would have been certain that some passengers would die in the explosion. It is not clear why the condition, which H and S could have failed to satisfy even if they had thought that the death of W was a highly probable consequence of their action, is not also a condition which even the aircraft saboteur could fail to satisfy.

What condition over and above (b) and (c) must N's volition-generated Aing in fact satisfy if it is to be intentional in a non-eccentric sense? A natural suggestion is that he must have willed that he would A. But suppose that N raises his arm by willing his arm to go up, and the generation is non-fluky, and he believes that by willing his arm to go up he raises his arm. No extra volition in the shape of a willing that he would raise his arm seems necessary for his raising his arm to be intentional. Let us distinguish between what, using the word in a technical sense, we can call the result of an action generated by a volition, and the volition which generates the action. The result of my raising my arm is that my arm goes up, of his killing her that she dies.[13] We might then say that N's volition-generated Aing is intentional only if he willed the result of his Aing. A difficulty is that as I have defined 'action' some actions do not consist of volitions and results caused by those volitions. If,

[11] Ibid. 593.
[12] Ibid. 307–10.
[13] I take over the 'result' terminology from McCann (1974), 452.

by deciding to Y, I go back on my previous decision to X, my going back on my previous decision has no part which stands to the whole of my action as my arm's going up stands to my raising my arm. I will call N's volition-generated Aing intentional only if either it has what is in the technical sense a result and this result is willed by N, or it has no result, in which case (b) and (c) are jointly sufficient. Thus N intentionally raised his arm only if, in addition to its being true that his raising his arm was non-flukily generated by one of his volitions, and that at some point on or after the time of this volition but not after his Aing he believed that he was Aing or that he was doing something by which he would A, he willed that his arm should go up. This willing may or may not be identical to the volition which generated his action. It is on the other hand sufficient for N to have intentionally gone back on his previous decision to X, that his decision to Y generates this backsliding as it could hardly not do in a non-fluky way, and that at the time of his decision to Y he did indeed believe that he was thereby going back on his previous decision to X. In *Hyam*, Lord Hailsham not only repudiated the idea that in law you necessarily intend what you foresee to be the highly probable consequences of your voluntary actions, but also endorsed Asquith LJ's interpretation of intention in *Cunliffe* v. *Goodman* (1950):

An 'intention' ... connotes a state of affairs which the party 'intending' ... does more than merely contemplate. It connotes a state of affairs which, on the contrary, he decides, so far as in him lies, to bring about, and which, in point of possibility, he has a reasonable prospect of being able to bring about, by his own act of volition.[14]

Not too far, I think, from the definition suggested: the 'party "intending"' acts intentionally, and if his action had a result, then for 'state of affairs which he decides to bring about' we can perhaps read ' result which he wills'.[15]

---

[14] Smith and Hogan (1986), 309.

[15] I do not deny that other senses of 'intentional action' are also current. Suppose that today I decide that tomorrow I will write to Mary. When tomorrow I do write, my action may be generated by a volition of tomorrow, but non-flukily caused by today's decision. If tomorrow's action would have been intentional by the definition I have been labouring with even if it had not been so caused by today's decision, then it looks as if there is another sense of 'intentional action' which this definition does not capture. Or suppose that I decide to walk home, and this generates my action of walking home. Would we not say that each particular step I take is intentional, even though I do not will the result of any particular

2. FREE ACTION

With 'action' and 'decision' taken as I have just defined them, and 'freedom taken in the senses displayed in Chapter 3, want and belief conflicts may arise about free actions which are not free decisions. What if anything would have to be said about the resolution of such conflicts which could not be very rapidly inferred from a proper treatment of conflicts about free decisions?

An action is free, I shall assume, only if it is intentional. On the definition of 'intentional' proposed in the last section, it follows that an action is free only if it is either a volition or generated by a volition. I do not think that once conflicts about free decisions had been properly treated anything substantially new would need to be said on conflicts about the freedom of volitions which like non-deliberative willings and acts of attending are not decisions. Let us turn then to conflicts about those free actions which are generated by volitions.

As I noted at the beginning of Chapter 3, 'N freely Aed' can mean simply that one of the components of N's Aing was a willing which did indeed cause an event of just the type willed.[16] Freedom of this kind I will call freedom of play. I borrow the name from Gerard Manley Hopkins who in his fragment *On Personality, Grace and Free Will* contrasted it or a case of it with freedom of pitch and freedom of field:

> it is freedom of pitch to be able to choose for yourself which of several doors you will go in by; it is freedom of play to go unhindered to it and through the one you choose; but suppose all were false doors or locked but the very one you happened to choose and you do not know it, there is here wanting freedom of field.[17]

Now it is sufficient for an action to exhibit freedom of play that one of its components is a decision which causes a physical event of just the type willed. People want there to be decisions which

---

step? If so, then we must postulate yet another sense of 'intentional action', on which N's volition-generated Aing is intentional if and only if he is caused to A by his deciding to B and by his unconscious belief that his Aing is a means to B's result. (Cf. Swinburne (1986), 94–5.)

[16] Cf. Schopenhauer, *Essay on the Freedom of the Will*, 6: according to 'the original, purely empirical and hence popular concept of freedom ... "free" means "in accordance with one's own will".'

[17] Hopkins (ed. Devlin 1959), 149.

are effective in this way, but are liable to be impressed by old philosophical doubts about the possibility of psycho-physical interaction. So there are want and belief conflicts about freedom of play. And no help can be got in their resolution from any treatment purely of conflicts about free decisions.

Since decisions do not have volitions as parts they cannot exhibit freedom of play. The same goes for volitions which are not decisions. But there are other senses of 'free', listed in Chapter 3, in which intentional actions can be called free whether or not they are volitions or generated by volitions. They may be free in either a negative or a positive extra possibility sense. They may be hierarchically coherent, or autonomous, or free in the sole authorship sense. And they may be unconstrained. Does more need to be said on conflicts about volition-generated actions free in these further senses?

I suggested in Chapter 3 that, short of suspecting that there are no decisions at all, we are not liable to suspect either that there are no hierarchically coherent decisions or that there are no unconstrained decisions. It is, I think, equally plain that, short of suspecting that there are no volition-generated actions at all, we are not liable to suspect either that there are no hierarchically coherent actions of that kind or that there are no unconstrained actions of that kind. And reasons, if there were any, for suspecting that there are no volition-generated actions would either be reasons for suspecting that there are no volitions, and would therefore have been dealt with in a complete treatment of conflicts about free decisions, or they would be reasons for doubting that volitions can generate actions, and would therefore be dealt with in a treatment of freedom of play. So the only substantially new things which would need to be said on conflicts about volition-generated actions free in the hierarchical coherence and lack of constraint senses are things which would be said in a proper treatment of conflicts about freedom of play.

Conflicts about volition-generated actions free in the autonomy and sole authorship senses are a different case because, as we saw in Chapter 3, there may be conflicts about the existence of decisions free in these senses which are not based merely on doubts about the very existence of decisions. But I do not think that anything more would need to be said about 'true responsibility' and sole authorship as applied to volition-generated actions than I said when discussing free decisions.

This leaves us with conflicts about volition-generated actions free in extra possibility senses. Either the victim of such conflicts suspects that there are no volition-generated actions at all, or he does not suspect this. We have already seen that in the first case nothing substantially more would need to be said than would already have been said in a proper treatment of conflicts about free decisions and about freedom of play. So let us assume the second case, and take positive and negative extra possibility in turn.

N's *A*ing was free in a negative extra possibility sense, it will be remembered, only if he was able not to *A*, and in a positive extra possibility sense, only if he was able to do something other than *A*ing. If (a) N's action of *A*ing is intentional and volition-generated, and the extra possibility is negative, then his ability not to *A* will presumably be either (a i) an ability not to will in the way or ways necessary for his action to be intentional, or (a ii) an ability to prevent the effectiveness of the volition or volitions necessary for his action to be intentional. If (b) his action of *A*ing is intentional and volition-generated, and the extra possibility is positive, then his ability to do something other than *A*ing is presumably either (b i) an ability just to will to do something else, or (b ii) an ability to take a different volition-generated action.

Suppose someone wants there to be intentional and volition-generated actions which are free in a negative extra possibility sense but believes that there are none. I do not see why he should believe that ability (a ii) is always lacking. And although he may well believe that ability (a i) is always lacking, he will probably not believe this unless he thinks that it is excluded by determinism or some other thesis of natural order. But the questions which the philosopher will raise at this point are substantially the same as the ones which he will already have raised about the relations between theses of natural order and negative extra possibility freedom of decision. Decisions are only a species of volitions. But, so far as these issues go, the differences between decisions and other volitions are irrelevant.

Now suppose that someone wants there to be intentional and volition-generated actions which are free in a positive extra possibility but believes that there are none. If the victim believes that ability (b i) is lacking it will again probably be because he thinks that it is excluded by some thesis of natural order. If he thinks that ability (b ii) is lacking it will be either (1) because he thinks that people cannot manage the volition necessary for the alternative action, or (2) because he thinks that, though possible for people to manage, the volition would not be effective. If (1), it will once again probably be because he thinks that the volition is excluded by a thesis of natural order. If (2), then what he thinks is hard to reconcile with the existence of any effective volitions. And if he does doubt the existence of effective volitions in general then his doubts will have been dealt with in a proper treatment of freedom of play.

The general conclusion is that, given a complete treatment of conflicts about free decisions, the only conflicts about free actions other than free decisions on which anything substantially new would need to be said are conflicts about freedom of play. To these I now finally turn.

3. FREEDOM OF PLAY

People want there to be physically effective decisions, but they are, as I said, liable to be impressed by old doubts about the possibility of psycho-physical interaction.

Consider this triad

(1) Some decisions cause bodily movements.

(2) There are sufficient physical causes of all bodily movements.

(3) No decisions are physical events.

Victims of want and belief conflicts about freedom of play may think that the triad is inconsistent and that it is more reasonable to drop (1) than either (2) or (3).[18]

Is there in fact good evidence on these lines for the non-existence of physically effective decisions? Even if we grant (2) and (3), it is difficult to find a reasonable interpretation of (1) on which the triad is inconsistent. If we take (1) to mean that some decisions are INUS conditions of bodily movements, then there is no inconsistency. If a is an INUS condition of b then there is a set of events s which is a sufficient but non-necessary condition for b, and a is an insufficient but necessary member of s. Since a

---

[18] For similar triads and different remedies see e.g. Armstrong (1968), 32–3; Carruthers (1986), 63–6; and the more elaborate but, to me at least, impenetrably obscure treatment in Peacocke (1979), 134–143.

can be an INUS condition of *b*, even though there is some other set of events besides *s* which is sufficient for *b*, *b* can have some sufficient purely physical cause, even if *a* is non-physical. To get an inconsistency we would have to turn (1) into the fantastic hypothesis that decisions are necessary causal conditions of bodily movements. And even then there would be no inconsistency on a pure regularity interpretation of 'necessary causal condition' and 'sufficient physical cause'. 'Whenever B-type events occur they are immediately preceded by A-type events' is perfectly compatible with 'Whenever C-type events occur they are immediately followed by A-type events', even if B-type events are not a species of C-type events. To get inconsistency in the triad, even on our fantastic version of (1), we would have to take '*a* is a necessary causal condition for *b*' to mean '*a* precedes *b* and if *a* had not occurred then even if everything else had remained unchanged *b* would not have occurred', and '*a* is a sufficient causal condition for *b*' to mean '*a* precedes *b*, and even if everything other than *a*'s occurrence had changed *b* would still have occurred', the two counterfactuals being interpreted Lewis-style. But then (2) would become

(2a) For any bit of bodily behaviour *b*, there is an antecedent set of physical events *s* such that even if everything other than *s*'s occurrence had changed, *b* would still have occurred.

And (2a) is much less plausible than (2).

Suppose we keep to the INUS condition version of (1). Is there in this case any revised version of (2) which will make the triad inconsistent? So far as I can see, (2) would need to be replaced by

(2b) For every bodily event there is at least one set of events which is a sufficient causal condition of that event, and no bodily event has, as a sufficient causal condition, a set of events any of whose members is a non-physical event.

But (2b) is surely less plausible than (2), and we might well prefer to restore consistency by dropping (2b) rather than by dropping (1). And even if we were unwilling to drop (2b) we might still prefer to keep (1) by dropping (3), which loses its aura of self-evidence once we begin to enquire more closely into what exactly is meant by a physical event. In one sense of 'physical event', (3), so far from being necessarily true, is in fact trivially false. This is the sense used by Davidson when he says that for an event to be physical is for it to be 'picked out by descriptions or open sentences that contain only the physical vocabulary essentially'.[19] In this sense, all events are physical, just as all events are mental. Given any event, we can always find another event, picked out by a purely physical description, with which it is simultaneous, just as we can always find another event, picked out by a purely mental description, with which it is simultaneous. There would also be no reason to accept (3), if a physical event were defined simply as one of those changes in things in themselves which explain our experience, but which are known, in Russell's words, 'only as regards their space-time structure', events composed of qualities 'so completely unknown that we cannot say either that they are, or that they are not, different from the qualities that we know as belonging to mental events'.[20] If, however, we take a physical event to be a change in the non-dispositional, non-relational, and commonsensically physical properties of an object, such as its colour qualities, then it is reasonable to doubt, not only that there is any good evidence for (2b), but also that there is any good evidence for the existence of physical events at all.

[19] Davidson (1980), 211.
[20] Russell (1948), 427.

8

Volition

WANT and belief conflicts about free decisions are still liable to afflict a person who is not in the least impressed by the old and new difficulties earlier discussed about how extra possibility freedom can be reconciled with order in nature, and has no desire either for sole authorship or an unattainable 'true responsibility'. Initially, let us suppose, you at least believe that there are decisions. But the concept of a decision, like the more general concept of a volition, is the concept of an object with a quality. And for anyone who naïvely believes that any such object exists a distinction lies in wait between experiences as of there being objects with the quality in question, and objects with that quality whose existence is independent of experiences as of their existence. We distinguish for example between experiences as of qualitatively coloured external objects, and real qualitatively coloured objects which exist independently of any experiences as of their existence. Once we have drawn this distinction we may lose our initial naïve belief in the existence of qualitatively coloured external objects, or even come positively to disbelieve in the existence of such things, and move over to the belief that real objects existing independently of experiences as of their existence are coloured only in a dispositional sense. Initially believing that there are decisions, you are in the same way liable to distinguish between experiences as of qualitative volitions, and real volitions occurring independently of any experiences as of their occurrence. And then, having drawn the distinction, you may lose your naïve belief in the existence of volitions, or even come positively to disbelieve in the existence of real volitions, and come to believe that no event which occurs independently of experience is a volition in anything but a dispositional sense. If even after these changes you want there to be free decisions the belief element in the want and belief conflict which then afflicts you will be sustained not by doubts about how decisions can be free but rather by doubts about whether there are real decisions at all.

Am I ignoring the difference between experiences in which a property is represented as being possessed by something, and those in which this is not the case? Experiences as of coloured things belong to the first kind, experiences of pain belong to the second. If volitional experiences also belong to the second kind, then no question is likely to arise about whether volitions exist independently of experiences as of their existence. I think, however, that experiences as of volitions are analogous not to experiences of pain, but to experiences as of being in pain. In an experience of pain, a mental event of being in pain, no property is represented as possessed by something. But in an experience as of being in pain the property of being in pain is represented to the subject as possessed by himself. Equally, in a volition no property is represented as possessed by something. But in an experience as of a volition, the volition is represented to the subject as his own. Like experiences as of qualitatively coloured things, experiences as of willing represent properties as possessed. Unlike experiences as of coloured things, they represent properties as possessed by events which somehow belong to or are part of the subjects of those very experiences.

It would be a mistake to think that the only want and belief conflicts which doubts about the existence of real qualitative volitions can help to produce are conflicts about freedom. Such doubts can also help to produce conflicts in which the object of desire is, not that there are free decisions or free volitions or any of the other events that I am calling free actions, but just that there are real volitions. Nor is it the case that, whenever you want real volitions to exist, and believe that they do not, or fail to believe that they do, you want them to exist for the sake of there being free decisions or volitions or free volition-generated actions. Some writers do admittedly present it as a conceptual truth that there cannot be such a thing as a non-free volition, or at least a non-free willing. 'When, deliberating how to gratify a wish, you arrive at a practical conclusion, you only appear to choose to act on it if it is not in your power to choose not to . . .'[1] Or, as Duns Scotus puts it somewhere, 'Experitur enim qui vult se posse non velle.' English law seems to be on the other side:

---

[1] Donagan (1987), 170.

No act is punishable if it is done involuntarily: and an involuntary act in this context . . . means an act which is done by the muscles without any control of the mind . . . ⟨But⟩ when a man is charged with murder, and it appears that he knew what he was doing, but that he could not resist it, then his assertion 'I couldn't help myself' is no defence in itself . . . though it may go towards a defence of diminished responsibility . . . it does not render his act involuntary so as to entitle him to an unqualified acquittal. (Lord Denning in *Bratty* v. *Attorney-General for Northern Ireland* (1963)[2]

But whoever is right, it may still be possible to want there to be volitions without wanting there to be free volitions. It is possible not to want the logical consequences of what one wants.

For what, other than for the sake of freedom, do we want there to be real volitions?

'It is better that a man wills nothing than that he does not will.' Nietzsche's remark echoes throughout the rhetoric of fascism. 'The core of national socialism is a revolutionary creative will that needs no ideological crutches . . . It has no fixed aim' (Hitler).[3] But is what even the fascist values for its own sake really willing, as distinct from effective willing, or willing which causes the physical change willed? Results seem necessary, as when Mussolini, by an act of will, halted the lava flowing down Mount Etna. Mightn't a mere experience as of willing have been just as effective?

There are other ways in which the existence of real volitions is liable to be an object of desire. It is easy to think that if we did not really will we would not even exist as subjects of experiences. Volition, in the shape of an act of attention, can easily seem necessary for any experience, perhaps even for any kind of thought. But someone who wants there to be real volitions for the sake of his own existence will not be afflicted by much of a conflict in consequence of doubts about whether his volitional experiences are non-veridical. Simply by believing that he is thus afflicted he would be committed to the belief that real volitions exist, which is just what, in a first-order conflict, he would also believe to be false, and in a second-order conflict believe that he does not believe. Neither conflict would survive the victim's

[2] Smith and Hogan (1986), 196.
[3] Quoted in O'Sullivan (1983), 138.

recognition of these elementary facts. But less ephemeral conflicts are liable to arise in those who doubt the veridicality of volitional experiences. If we think we have experiences as of willing then we want there to be real volitions if only for the sake of not being under a repeated illusion. We want there to be real volitions for the same reason that, if we think we have experiences as of S-freely deciding, we want there to be S-free decisions (see Chapter 3, Section 3). It may be that the ultimate resolution of conflicts generated by this kind of desire will come from an argument to the effect that the victim must really will if he is to exist at all. But one can want there to be real volitions, and doubt whether they exist, without at the same time self-defeatingly wanting them to exist for the sake of one's own existence.

In this chapter and the next I discuss conflicts based on doubts about the existence of real volitions. I confine the discussion to conflicts in which the object of desire is simply that there are real volitions, and do not apply the conclusions I reach to conflicts about freedom until my general summary at the end of Chapter 9.

Of the four questions which by the conflict-resolving programme of Chapter 2 I should be asking of conflicts about real volitions, I shall in fact consider just two. They are: Does the desire for there to be real volitions have a coherent content?, and Is there is good evidence for the non-existence of real volitions which is better evidence than any for their existence? In order for there to be conflicts about real volitions, it is not necessary that anyone actually has experiences as of there being real volitions. It is enough that people should want there to be veridical experiences of these kinds and believe that there are no veridical experiences of these kinds. But I assume that in order for the wants in these conflicts to have a coherent content it is necessary though not sufficient that there actually are experiences as of real volitions. I think that there are, and try to provide some evidence for this in the first section of the chapter. Readers who already agree with me on this point should turn directly to Section 2, in which I try by the exploration of colour analogies to see whether, even if there are experiences as of real volitions, conflicts about real volitions have an incoherent content. The question about evidence for the non-existence of real volitions is considered in the next chapter.

I. MORE ON THE PHENOMENA

There are, I suggested, two senses of 'volition' which someone might try to apply to real events, to events whose occurrence is not dependent on any experience which anyone has as of their occurrence. A real event might be called a volition in the sense of an event which actually has a quality of the distinctive kind with which experiences as of volitions are supposed to acquaint us. Or it might be called a volition only in the sense that it has the power to give an introspective observer an experience as of a real volition. The first sense of 'volition', which we could call the S-sense, is analogous to the S-sense of 'freedom' which I postulated in the first section of Chapter 3, on the doubtful assumption that there are experiences as of having the power to decide. And the distinction between the two senses of 'volition' is, as I suggested, also analogous to the distinction we need between two senses of, say, 'red', on the assumption, not in the least doubtful, that there are *sui generis* colour experiences.

I should say of a pillar-box that it is 'red'. If I came to distinguish between the pillar-box and the visual sensibile which I sense when I look at a pillar-box, I should say that the sensibile is 'red' too. As applied to the pillar-box the word 'red' is a dispositional adjective; as applied to the visual sensibile it is non-dispositional. By saying that the pillar-box is red I mean *at least* that, if any normal observer were to look at it in daylight, it would look red to him. And I *might* mean no more than this. By saying that the visual sensibile is red I mean something which could not possibly be expressed by a conditional sentence. A man *may* believe that the pillar-box is red in the non-dispositional sense also.[4]

The S-sense of volition is analogous to the non-dispositional or as we can also call it S-sense of red. And in the conflicts to be considered in this and the next chapter it is S-volitions whose existence is the object of desire. Unless I say otherwise volition will in fact always be used in the S-sense from now onwards.[5]

---

[4] Broad (1933), 148.
[5] The prevalence of functionalist theories means in fact that the S-sense of volition needs to be distinguished from two different dispositional senses. 'According to functionalism, the essential or defining feature of any type of mental state is the set of causal relations it bears to (1) environmental effects on the body, (2) other types of mental states, and (3) bodily behaviour. Pain, for example,

Among modern analytical philosophers even experiences as of
S-volitions are objects of almost universal disbelief. Sometimes this
attitude is part of a more general functionalist or materialist
opposition to the existence of any mental states whose contents
have phenomenal properties. But disbelief in the special phenomenal content of experiences as of volitions is also almost universal
even among those philosophers who are prepared, in the usual
somewhat dowager-like terminology, to 'countenance' a special
phenomenal content in experiences of colour, sound, or pain. And
there is at least one writer, namely Searle, who, though he thinks
that there are distinctive 'experiences of acting', usually generated
by causally efficacious and episodic intentions which are components of all actions and not analysable in terms of wants and
beliefs, still refuses to believe in introspectible acts of will.[6] I begin
with a few hostile words on the materialists' opposition to the
existence of volitional experiences.

characteristically results from some bodily damage or trauma; it causes distress,
annoyance, and practical reasoning aimed at relief; any state that plays exactly that
functional role is a pain, according to functionalism. Similarly, other types of
mental states (sensations, fears, beliefs and so on) are also defined by their unique
causal roles in a complex economy of internal states mediating sensory outputs and
behavioural inputs.' (Churchland (1984), 36) So (a) there is a dispositional sense of
'volition' which is defined in terms of the S-sense, and is analogous to the
dispositional sense of 'red'. Just as to call an object red can be to say that it has the
power in standard circumstances to produce in normal observers experiences as of
an S-red object, so to say that a volition occurs can be to say that an event occurs
which has the power to produce in normal introspection an experience as of an
S-volition. And (b) there is the dispositional sense of volition which functionalists
pursue. Volitions in this sense will not be events which have the power to produce
experiences as of S-volitions. They will be mental events defined by their causal
relations with bodily and environmental as well as with other mental events, and
these other mental events will not necessarily even be the functionalist surrogates
of experiences as of S-volitions.
   A dispositional property, I suggest, is one whose ascription to an individual
entails a subjunctive conditional which does not itself entail that the individual has
that property. Thus 'x is fragile' entails 'if x were suitably dropped it would break',
but that conditional does not itself entail 'x is fragile'. For if x is fragile it has other
properties, including perhaps dispositional ones, which explain why that
conditional is true. If we take 'red' in its S-sense, take it as the name of a quality
with which we are acquainted through visual experience, then 'x is red' entails
various subjunctive conditionals. For instance, it entails the conditional that if N
were to believe that x is red, he would believe something true. But that conditional
itself entails that x is red, and so I think does every other subjunctive conditional
which is entailed by 'x is red' with red taken in the S-sense. So S-redness comes out
as non-dispositional. Cf. Mellor (1982–3), 96–7; (1974), 157–81.
   [6] See Searle (1983), 87–91.

Someone might sketch out a model on which introspection does not acquaint us with any quality but consists merely in the acquisition of information which enables us to engage in discriminatory behaviour. Just as, in a behavioural theory of external perception, our pre-scientific concept of red is, in Armstrong's words, 'all blank or gap', apart from being the concept of something falling under a determinable, so, in a behavioural theory of introspection, our pre-scientific concept of a volition might be 'all blank'. In each case, it is liable to be thought, a gap theory is easier than its rivals to reconcile with an antecedently plausible materialist world view. But, as Armstrong notes,

if we 'reduce' the secondary qualities of objects to purely physical properties of objects, then ... we will not be able to form a coherent conception of a physical object ... if we look at the properties of objects that physicists are prepared to allow them, such as mass, electric charge, or momentum, these show a distressing tendency to dissolve into *relations* that one object has to another. What, then, are the things that have these relations to each other? Must they not have a non-relational nature if they are to sustain relations? But what is this nature? Physics does not tell us. It is here that the secondary qualities, conceived of as irreducible properties, are thrown into the breach to provide the stuffing for matter.[7]

Armstrong's reply to the difficulty is as follows

we must admit that such things as electrons are *individual objects* ... Yet it seems madness to say that the electron has any of the secondary qualities ... So the problem of non-relational nature *must* be solved for electrons without bringing in the secondary qualities. And if the problem can be solved for electrons without appealing to the secondary qualities, surely it can be solved for physical objects generally without appealing to the secondary qualities?[8]

But I should have thought that until the problem is actually solved and we know what in its non-relational nature matter might be we have no reason to think that a materialist world-view even requires a gap theory of volitions. If it is mad to suppose that external objects are S-coloured, there might indeed be no non-relational properties left for them to have other than the S-volitional properties which our experiences reveal.

[7] Armstrong (1968), 282.
[8] Ibid. 282–3.

One might, however, doubt the existence of such experiences, not on the grounds that this would be difficult to reconcile with some antecedently plausible world-view, but simply on the grounds that one never oneself actually has experiences as of S-volitions. At this point it is worth looking back to some findings of early twentieth-century introspectionist psychology.

In the experiments of Michotte and Prüm, the subjects were instructed as follows: 'A card will appear on which two numbers will be found. Various mathematical operations can be carried out with these numbers. Choose between, for example, addition and subtraction. Decide for some definite reason, and then react.'[9] Anxious not to distract attention from any volitional phenomena to the actual realization of the operation decided on, the experimenters required, as 'reaction', not that the chosen operation should be carried out, but merely that a button should be pressed once a choice had in fact been made. Cards were displayed many times to a group of six subjects, who reported what they then experienced. Some protocols speak of a 'consciousness of action', distinct from any muscular sensation, emotion, or sense of strain, and more than a mere judgement about the relative difficulty of the operations being considered:

At the point of decision, the consciousness of determining something was very clear. I take particular note of that, when I compare this phenomenon with the way in which a content of consciousness arises through association. In the latter case 'I say it' was not appropriate in the same sense as in the former, in which indeed it as it were pronounced itself. It is precisely here that I find something willed, voluntary. It is something absolutely different from a feeling of muscular activity.[10]

In the protocols, this consciousness of action—

can only be expressed in the infinitive; c'est la conscience de 'faire', d''agir', de 'désigner', de 'se tourner vers', de 'dire', de 'laisser aller', etc. No particular consciousness of self emerged in the course of these experiences, and the subjects are struck by this. It seems puzzling to them. They say: 'I am not able not to say that it is myself who did it, and yet I find no phenomenon at all which in the course of the experience manifests the self.'[11]

---

[9] Michotte and Prüm (1910), 128.
[10] Ibid. 192.
[11] Ibid. 194.

At around the same time, Ach performed experiments designed to measure the strength of resolutions to carry out instructions which conflicted with artificially induced habits.[12] He was indeed later on critical of Michotte's procedures, and his assistant Luderitz, repeating Michotte's experiment, got no reports of 'consciousness of action'.[13] But the acts of will reported in Ach's own experiments, and in further experiments by Luderitz, in which choices were actually to be implemented, were still much the same as those reported by Michotte. Ach summarizes the phenomena reported as follows. The 'energetic act of will (intention)' has two main features (Momente), and two subsidiary features:

1. The objective feature of the intention with the content of the task.... 2. The immediate feature, which finds its expression in the experience-fragment 'I really will' and which is especially characterised by the appearance of the self-aspect of the mental events.... 3. With the energetic act of will more or less strongly marked expressions of sensations of tension also supervene (perceptual feature). 4. A further phenomenon accompanying the whole process of energetic willing is the consciousness of effort (accompanying feature).[14]

Or, as a final example, there are the experiments of Honoria Wells in which subjects who had learned to associate nonsense words with various pleasant and unpleasant tastes, were instructed to choose between pairs of liquids identified by those words, and to drink the chosen liquid. In many cases the subjects found it difficult to make a choice. And in these cases they again reported 'consciousness of action', involving the self, and different from muscular and kinaesthetic sensations. For example:

Vab–Laip. Realised I did not want to drink either. Hesitation, and a vague mental content containing thoughts about negative motivation. Still more hesitation. Then with a distinct reference to 'Self', I designated *Laip* with a strong consciousness of action.

Vab–Laip repeated; unpleasure strongly marked... Then an intentional direction to *Vab* with the knowledge, 'They are both bad, that's the worst'. 'I will', strongly auditorily and kinaesthetically. Tension from eyes, neck and forehead which almost masked my consciousness of action. The consciousness of action seemed to be similar to my intentional

---

[12] Ach (1910).
[13] Ach (1935), 372.
[14] Ibid. 201. For a fuller description see Ach (1910), 237–49.

direction. This is how I can discriminate it out of the naked sensations of muscular effort . . .[15]

Surely in these reports we have the kind of naïve conviction that there are indeed S-volitions which reflection would resolve into the more cautious belief that there are experiences as of S-volitions. Although expecting or wanting one's experience to have a certain content is not, in normally honest people, a sufficient condition for having experience with that content, it may, as the introspectionist psychologists were well aware, be a necessary condition. So it would hardly be surprising if contemporary analytical philosophers, brought up on Ryle's witticisms about ghostly thrusts, were ill-prepared for the introspection of experiences as of volitions. Ach, Michotte, and their followers had less inhibited subjects.

Ryle's polemics are indeed still influential enough for it to be worth making a detailed comparison between the volitions which are the object of his attack and the volitions as of whose existence I claim that we have experiences, and whose existence is desired in want and belief conflicts.[16]

Volitions, in Ryle's usage, and in what he claims to be a traditional usage of philosophers since the days of late antiquity, are entities which satisfy at least the following conditions. (i) They are mental but not bodily or physical, (ii) they are qualitatively distinctive objects of introspective awareness, (iii) they can cause bodily behaviour, (iv) they cannot occur without causing actions, (v) they are actions, (vi) actions are voluntary only if caused by them, and (vii) they are themselves voluntary.[17] A final condition, on which Ryle says that only some writers insist, is that entities are volitions only if (viii) they are 'identical' to 'settlements of indecisions,' or 'processes of resolving or making our minds up to do something', or processes of 'nerving or bracing ourselves to do something'.[18] About these conditions, Ryle makes the following claims. (A) It is a fundamental mistake to suppose that any entities satisfy (i). (B) Even if some entities could satisfy (i), the causal relation referred to in (iii) and (iv) is too mysterious to obtain. (C)

---

[15] Wells (1927), 85.
[16] For recent endorsements of Ryle on volitions, see Smith and Jones (1986), 126–7; Kenny (1989), 32–3.
[17] Ryle (1963), 62–6.
[18] Ibid. 66–7.

It is logically impossible for the three conditions (v), (vi), and (vii) to be simultaneously satisfied unless, absurdly, actions are caused by prior actions *ad infinitum*. (D) Entities can satisfy (ii) only if 'ordinary men' or at least those trained in the dictions appropriate to the description of their inner, as distinct from 'their overt, behaviour' can easily answer some simple questions about them which in fact they find it difficult or impossible to answer. (E) No entity can satisfy both (vi) and (viii).

Which of Ryle's eight conditions must be satisfied by volitions as I defined them in the last chapter and as they figure in the want and belief conflicts which I am analysing in this book? (iv) and (vi) are, I think, the only conditions not thus required. (iv) drops out because, although volitions as I defined them can be effective, they certainly do not have to be: one can easily decide to do something and then not do it. (vi) drops out because volitions, according to the last chapter, are themselves a subclass of voluntary actions. But if these two conditions are not necessary for volitions as I defined them, then neither of the perfectly justified claims (C) and (E) that Ryle makes about these two conditions can impugn the existence of volitions as I define them or the existence of experiences as of such volitions. And of his remaining claims, (A), (B), and (D), none seems to have much force.

With (A), I revert to Armstrong's difficulty: it is hard even to understand the doctrine of psycho-physical identity that Ryle is here asserting, until the nature of distinctively physical non-relational properties has been specified. (B), that psycho-physical causal interaction is too mysterious to obtain, is relevant to conflicts about actions causally generated by volitions. But it is not relevant to conflicts actually about volitions, unless in these conflicts the existence of volitions is wanted for the sake of the actions which they causally generate. It is in any case, as I showed in the last chapter, difficult to find a true interpretation of (B). That leaves us with (D).

The questions which according to (D) it is difficult or impossible to answer about volitions conceived of as entities which satisfy condition (ii) are about how volitions are to be described:

Can they be sudden or gradual, strong or weak, difficult or easy, enjoyable or disagreeable? Can they be accelerated, decelerated, interrupted, or suspended? Can people be efficient or inefficient at them? Can we take lessons in executing them? Are they fatiguing or distracting? Can I do two or seven of them synchronously? Can I remember executing them? Can I execute them, while thinking of other things, or while dreaming? Can they become habitual? Can I forget how to do them? Can I mistakenly believe that I have executed one, when I have not, or that I have not executed one, when I have? At which moment was the boy going through a volition to take the high dive? When he set his foot on the ladder? When he took his first deep breath? When he counted off 'One, two, three—Go', but did not go? Very, very shortly before he sprang? What would his own answer be to these questions?[19]

Doubtless much work needs to be done in the pure phenomenology of volition. But in order to meet Ryle's point, that there are no definite data here at all, it is enough to sketch the answers that do in fact quite easily suggest themselves to his rhetorical questions when 'volitions' are taken as real decisions and doubts suspended about the veridicality of our experience.

Real decisions, then, if they existed, could be sudden; they could also be expected. They could not, however, be gradual, in the sense that they were completed by a series of stages which imperceptibly shaded off into each other and in which the initial stage was nevertheless perceptibly different from the final stage. Since real decisions would be temporally extended entities (see Chapter 7, Section 1) they could in principle be accelerated, decelerated, interrupted, or suspended, even though we would not know how to do any of these things either to our own or to other people's decisions. Since we would not make real decisions by doing anything else, we could not be efficient or inefficient at them, or take lessons which would make us more efficient at them. We could, however, if we wanted to, have lessons in which we practised deciding. Real decisions could indeed be tiring, and I could easily be distracted from my contemplation of some scene by my sudden decision to go and get myself a drink. We could not simultaneously make more than one decision. We could remember past decisions. I could decide while thinking of other things or dreaming only if thinkings and dreamings were not themselves volitions or non-causally generated by volitions. Certain types of decisions could become habitual, and I could forget how to decide by becoming totally indecisive. I can mistakenly believe that I

[19] Ryle (1963), 63.

have decided when I have not, because it is conceivable that my experience as of deciding is not veridical. If there are real decisions then I can mistakenly believe that I have not decided when I have because it is conceivable that real decision should occur without there being any experience as of deciding. The boy may have decided to dive at any time before he dived and he may or may not give a correct answer if I ask him whether he decided at such and such a time.

2. QUALITIES AND COHERENCE

It is easy to think that the desire for there to be real volitions has an incoherent content, even after one has distinguished volitions from the entities attacked by Ryle, and even if one is prepared to assume that there are at least experiences as of real volitions. For it is easy to think that no qualities grasped only through experience can be instantiated by any real object or event, any object or event whose existence or occurrence is not dependent on experiences as of its existence or occurrence. The general principle about qualities grasped only through experience has often been defended by reference to the case of colour qualities, and I will look at that case in some detail. 'The noumenal inconsistency thesis about S-colours' will be my name for the thesis that, although there are experiences as of things with non-dispositional colour qualities, it is incoherent to suppose that something whose existence is not dependent on experience has a non-dispositional colour quality as distinct from a power to produce experiences as of a qualitatively coloured external thing. Suppose experience acquaints us with S-colours. And suppose that there are no good arguments for the noumenal inconsistency thesis about S-colours. Then, I assume, there are no good arguments for the parallel thesis that, although there are experiences as of real volitions, it is incoherent to suppose that there are real volitions.

The noumenal inconsistency thesis about colours is not an immediately obvious truth. According to McDowell, believing that it is coherent to suppose that there are colour properties which are not secondary but primary ('that is, which characterize things independently of their perceivers'), and yet resemble colours as they figure in our experience, is no better than believing in the coherence of 'a conception of amusingness which was fully intelligible otherwise than in terms of the characteristic human responses to what is amusing, but which nevertheless contrived somehow to retain the "phenomenal" aspect of amusingness as we experience it in those responses.' He would 'sympathize with anyone who found this idea incoherent'.[20] But does denial of the noumenal inconsistency thesis oblige us to believe that objects can be coloured 'independently of their perceivers', coloured in a sense 'fully intelligible otherwise than in terms of characteristic human responses to what is coloured'? Yes and no. It obliges us to believe that real objects can be coloured in a sense other than that they have the power to produce experiences as of coloured objects. But it does not oblige us to hold the absurd view that non-dispositional senses of colour terms are intelligible to people who have not had colour experiences of the sort produced by objects which have the corresponding dispositional colours. The first view can easily seem incoherent if, as in McDowell's polemic, it is not clearly distinguished from the second.

The difficulty of establishing the noumenal inconsistency thesis is also underestimated in McGinn's recent study, *The Subjective View*. While stressing that colour experiences are fully intelligible only to those who have enjoyed them, and insisting, against 'adverbial' theories of perception, that '"looks red" is semantically complex, having "red" as a semantically significant constituent',[21] McGinn also claims that we know a priori that external things are red only in the sense (roughly) that they look red to some perceivers.[22] We have this a priori knowledge because this is how 'the' concept of red is to be 'analysed', and this even though on his own admission the semantic complexity of 'looks red' makes this analysis of 'external things are red' an analysis only in something of the sense that 'Jumbo is taller than most elephants' is an analysis of 'Jumbo is a tall elephant'.[23] But if 'red' is a semantically significant constituent of 'looks red' does it or does it not there designate a non-dispositional property? And if it does there

---

[20] McDowell (1983), 4. His target is Mackie, according to whom 'the contents of our experience are not undetectably labelled as such: mind-independence is not a part of what we perceive, and certainly not a part from which it would be impossible to abstract, for constructive use elsewhere, other parts of that experiential content' ((1976), 68–9).

[21] McGinn (1983), 6.

[22] Ibid. 114.

[23] Ibid. 7.

designate a non-dispositional property, how exactly do we know a priori that this property is not possessed by things in themselves? After a series of experiments with such claims as that 'it is possible for a concept *C* to be analysable in terms of condition *A* without it following that if it looks as if *C* is satisfied it must look as if *A* holds',[24] and that it may not really be 'right to say of someone looking at a red object that it looks *non*-relationally red to him, as distinct from its not looking relationally red',[25] McGinn reluctantly grants that there seems to be '*something* right in the idea, exploited by the argument for the representational theory of perception, that objects look *intrinsically* red'.[26] But if there is enough right in this idea for 'red' to be the name of a non-dispositional property, we must once again ask how exactly we know a priori that this non-dispositional property is not possessed by external objects. McGinn's reluctance to admit that external objects look intrinsically red seems to derive from the conviction that if they did we would be committed either to the view that 'secondary quality experience contains an error' or to a representational theory of perception on which 'the immediate objects of perception are mental items ("sense data")'.[27] But he does not explain why exactly this is such an uncomfortable consequence.[28]

The noumenal inconsistency thesis calls, then, for a proper argument. And any such argument, we should note, will have the pitfall to circumvent which Moore identified in his 'Refutation of Idealism'. If we learn what 'blue' means, in its S-sense, only through experience as of something blue, then presumably we

---

[24] Ibid. 134.
[25] Ibid. 136 n. 8.
[26] Loc. cit.
[27] Ibid. 129.
[28] It is very difficult to find anywhere in recent philosophy of perception a straightforward recognition that adjectives like red are simply ambiguous. In his *Sense and Content* Peacocke distinguishes between red' and red. '*x* is red' he takes to mean '*x* is disposed in normal circumstances to cause the region of the visual field in which it is presented to be red' in normal humans', where red' stands for a 'sensational property' of the visual field ((1983), 39). Sensational properties are those which an experience has in virtue of some aspect—other than its representational content—of what it is like to have that experience (ibid. 5). Peacocke's 'red'', like my 'S-red', stands for a non-dispositional property with which we are acquainted in experience. But he builds it into the definition of red' that this experience does not represent external objects to be red', whereas I have allowed, following Broad (see n. 4 above), that experience can represent objects to be S-red.

also learn only through experience the meaning of the phrase 'experience as of something S-blue'. Suppose that there is some argument from the premiss about how we learn the S-sense of 'blue' to the conclusion that there are not real S-blue things, but only experiences as of S-blue things. Then there will also be an argument from the parallel premiss about how we learn the meaning of 'experience as of something S-blue' to the conclusion that there are no experiences as of S-blue things but only experiences as of experiences as of S-blue things. And further parallel reasoning would lead us to the quite obviously false conclusion that no matter how often we iterate 'experience as of' in front of 'experience as of something blue', we do not really have experiences of the kind we thereby attempt to describe.

In the search for an argument for the noumenal inconsistency thesis about S-colours one turns naturally to Berkeley:

But, say you, surely there is nothing easier than to imagine trees, for instance, in a park, or books existing in a closet, and nobody by to perceive them. I answer, you may so, there is no difficulty in it: but what is all this, I beseech you, more than framing in your mind certain ideas which you call *books* and *trees*, and at the same time omitting to frame the idea of anyone that may perceive them? This therefore is nothing to the purpose: it only shows you have the power of imagining or framing ideas in your mind; but it doth not show that you can conceive it possible, the objects of your thought may exist without the mind: to make this out, it is necessary that you conceive them existing unconceived or unthought of, which is a manifest repugnancy.[29]

A standard criticism is that Berkeley conflates two different propositions, viz. 'It is not the case that there is a person and a thing such that the person truly supposes that that thing is not thought of' and 'No one truly supposes that there is something which is not thought of'. The first proposition is necessarily true, but the second, which is the one whose truth Berkeley needs in order to establish his general conclusion about material substance, is not necessarily true, and Berkeley has not in fact shown it to be true at all.[30] Let us however take him, as Foster and Robinson suggest, to be claiming—

[29] *Principles of Human Knowledge*, part I, sect. 23 (Luce and Jessop edn., ii. 50).
[30] See Mackie (1976), 52–4.

first that it is impossible to conceive of a sensible object (at least in a way which reveals its sensible character) without imagining it; second, that it is impossible to imagine an object without imagining that one perceives it. Berkeley's point would then be that we cannot make sense of the supposition that there are unperceived sensible objects, since any attempt to form a concrete conception of something's being sensible but unperceived is self-defeating. To form a conception of the object we would have to imagine ourselves perceiving it and thus its being perceived becomes part of the content of the perception.[31]

Both claims need some supporting argument, and with the second, at least, I do not see what this could be. To imagine something, according to Peacocke, 'is always at least to imagine, from the inside, being in some conscious state'.[32] This in turn involves 'S-imagining' that certain conditions are fulfilled by the imagined conscious state, where S-imagining, though it is not supposing, 'shares with supposition the property that what is S-imagined is not determined by the subject's images'.[33] Thus if you imagine being at the helm of a yacht, you imagine from the inside having an experience and also S-imagine that your imagined experience is perceptual. And if you imagine from the inside an experience as of being at the helm of a yacht, you S-imagine that your imagined experience may or may not be perceptual. Equally, if you imagine a tree, you imagine from the inside an experience, and S-imagine that your experience is perceptual. I do not, however, see any plausibility in Peacocke's initial principle that to imagine something is always to imagine from the inside being in some conscious state. Imagining from the inside being in some conscious state has to be more than imagining something which might also have figured merely in the content of a real conscious state, otherwise there would be no imagined whole conscious state which one could S-imagine to fulfil any conditions. But surely there are cases in which you are simply too interested in what you imagine also to imagine being in any conscious state. You imagine her eyes, and are so caught up by the image itself that you have no attention left for any such extra content of imagination as your whole conscious state. And besides, if to imagine a tree is, at least, to imagine from the inside an experience as of a tree, why is it not the case that

[31] Foster and Robinson (1985), 4.
[32] Peacocke (1985), 21.
[33] Ibid. 25.

imagining an experience as of a tree is at least imagining from the inside an experience as of having an experience as of a tree, and so on *ad infinitum*? Peacocke denies that to imagine being in the state of having an experience as of Waterloo Bridge is at least to imagine from the inside an experience as of being in the state of having an experience as of Waterloo Bridge. 'Imagining having an experience of a given kind', he insists, 'is *just* imagining having an experience of that kind.'[34] But no reason is given for this restriction.

There is a tenacious attempt to improve on Berkeley in Sprigge's *The Vindication of Absolute Idealism*. He claims that we cannot imagine an S-coloured thing as existing outside a mind's perceptual experience. This is not because to imagine anything is to imagine being in a conscious state, but rather because when one has an experience as of an S-coloured thing the latter presents itself as having 'subject-implying qualities'. It presents itself as having positive or negative aesthetic value, and as part of a Gestalt, as for example part of a foreground or background. It also presents itself as having a 'perspectival character': what is coloured has a shape presented as determined by a point of view.[35] The thought seems to be that when you imagine an S-coloured thing, you must also imagine the subject implied by subject-implying qualities of the type which an S-coloured thing would be presented as having if you were to have an experience as of an S-coloured thing. But I do not see why I could not have an aesthetic attitude to my imagined S-coloured object, or organize my imagined S-coloured object in a Gestalt, without its being true that my attitude and my organization are themselves part of my imagined world, themselves imagined. Nor, as regards perspectival character, does it follow that because, in experience, what is presented is presented as having a shape, and because this shape is determined by the point of view of the subject, the active imagination of an S-coloured thing will have a content in which the shape of the thing is presented as inseparable from an imagined position of the agent.

The only other seeming route I can think of to the noumenal inconsistency thesis about S-colours would be from an adverbial

---

[34] Ibid. 12 n. 5.
[35] Sprigge (1983), 116–17.

theory of perception, a theory dispensing with isolatable and detachable S-colour qualities altogether.

According to Chisholm 'there exists a y such that y appears Fly to X' can be taken to mean the same as 'y appears F to x', and 'the adjectives which follow the verb "appear" are *not* predicates qualifying an appearance or way of appearing'. Thus the adjective 'rectangular' as it is used in 'The window appears rectangular' is not a predicate attributing a characteristic to the way in which the window appears. Rather the two words 'appears rectangular' constitute a predicate which attributes a certain characteristic to the window.[36] Complex expressions like 'appears rectangular', or 'looks centaurian', might, he suggests, be replaced by single words, for example by 'lookscentaurian'.[37] Similarly the subject who was traditionally said to experience a red sensation, without there being any implication that an external red object exists, 'does not stand in a sentient relation to an *object* which is a red sensation; rather, he is sentient *in a certain way*—a way that we could describe as "redly" . . . For philosophical purposes it is convenient to use "is appeared to" in place of "senses".'[38] Chisholm stresses that the expression 'being appeared to redly' can be given a sense which is not equivalent to the sense of any of the following expressions: 'being appeared to by something that is red'; 'being appeared to in the way in which one is normally appeared to by things that are red'; 'being appeared to in the way in which one believes that red things normally appear'.[39]

It is not entirely clear just how optional Chisholm himself thinks that these ways of talking are. He does say that if we agree with Locke that some predicates, like 'rectangular', which designate the primary qualities of things, may also be used, without ambiguity or change of meaning, to designate the ways in which some things appear, then 'no one . . . can show that we are mistaken'.[40] But someone might argue not merely that it is preferable to talk in Chisholm's way, rather than to talk for instance of red sensations or red sense-data, but also somehow compulsory, and that what makes it compulsory compels us also

[36] Chisholm (1957), 132.
[37] Ibid. 116.
[38] Chisholm (1981), 93.
[39] Loc. cit.
[40] Chisholm (1957), 133.

to recognize that there are no isolatable or detachable pre-scientifically graspable S-qualities of redness, blueness, etc., which could be possessed by mind-independent objects. Blue, bitter, sweet, etc., might, as Ducasse puts it, be 'names not of objects of experience nor of species of objects of experience, but of *species of experience itself* . . . the noun "blue" is the word we use to mention merely a certain *kind* of activity (just as are the nouns "waltz", "leap", etc.).'[41]

Efforts have been made to show that adverbial descriptions of experience, so far from being compulsory, cannot even allow, as they obviously should, that 'I sense red-square-ly' entails 'I sense redly'. To explain why the entailment holds, it would be necessary either to grant that the meaning of 'red-square-ly' is after all built out of independently semantically significant components like 'red' and 'square', or to interpret 'I sense redly' as 'I sense red-some-shape-ly' and take the latter as a genus to which 'I sense red-square-ly' belongs. Jackson claims that if we try to preserve the adverbial description by offering the second explanation then we shall have no reason to believe that 'red-square-ly', rather than say 'red-square-fuzzy-ly' is a 'basic mode of sensing', and he complains more generally that for any n in 'I sense $F_1 - \ldots - F_n$-ly' we can be forced to abandon $F_1 - \ldots - F_n$-ly in favour of $F_1 - \ldots - F_n - F_{n+1}$-ly as a basic mode of sensing.[42] But I cannot see the force of this point. On an act-object account, a sense datum would have just as many properties as a perceiver in fact discriminates in any one perceptual episode. We would not have to believe in basic sense data with a number of properties n such that nobody ever has sense data with more than n properties. Why then must there be basic modes of sensing? Jackson also thinks that it is difficult to give a satisfactory adverbial rendering of what would be described in act-object language as my simultaneously having two different after-images, one red and one green. One would have to say either that, at one and the same given time, I am sensing both redly and non-redly, or that I am sensing redly with respect to one thing and non-redly with respect to another. The first alternative makes one out to be doing something impossible. As to the second, we are to ask 'What are these things

---

[41] Ducasse (1942), 232–3.
[42] Jackson (1977), 68.

with respect to which I am sensing?' If there are no physical things in the offing, 'It is hard to see what they could be other than the mental objects of the act-object theory'.[43] But my present interest in the adverbial description of sensation is that it may help us to deny that there are S-colours and by analogy volitional qualities, and in this way resolve want and belief conflicts about volition. So long as the mental objects to whose existence the adverbial description commits us did not have S-colours, the adverbial description might still serve this purpose, even if it turned out not to be quite so different from the act-object description as one might initially have supposed.

Is there anything which positively constrains us to adopt adverbial descriptions? One might say this. The evident unintelligibility of the suggestion that some things in themselves are noisy or sweet in some pre-scientifically graspable non-dispositional sense compels us to deny that there is any such non-dispositional property of noisiness or sweetness at all, and hence to accept an adverbial account of sound and taste experiences. But if there are no non-dispositional properties of noisiness or sweetness, how is it that there are non-dispositional colour properties? This is a challenge to the believer in S-colours, rather than a positive argument for the adverbial description of colour-sensations. And in any case, it is a challenge that can be met. The phenomenologist, trying to give a full description of what experiencing blue or red is like without importing the subject's beliefs about external causes, has to say that there is an experience as of *something's* being blue or red. But in the case of taste or sound experiences, he cannot improve on phrases of the form 'experience of such and such a sound (taste)'. We can understand how things in themselves can be red because our experiences of red are already as of *something* red. The 'as of something red' description leaves room for us to understand how something which really does exist when not experienced could be red in the same sense. No room is left for this kind of understanding in the case of experiences of sound or taste, because they are not experiences as of *something* having a sound or a taste but at most experiences of e.g. noisiness or sweetness, accompanied by beliefs about material objects which cause the experience.

[43] Ibid. 69.

The only positive argument for adverbialism that I know of appears in John Foster's *The Case for Idealism*. Colours, according to Foster, are somehow *realized*, not merely conceived of. We have to grant this, he thinks, in order to account for the fact that, even when they have exactly the same content, episodes of sensing and episodes of imagining differ in their intrinsic character. But it is impossible to explain how colours are realized, as distinct from merely conceived, unless we say, following Ducasse, that colours are the sensation-types of which particular episodes of sensing colours are the self-revealing tokens or instances. We do not *explain* the difference if we say that in sensing a colour we are aware of a content, for we are also aware of a content when we conceive a colour. But if we do say that colours are sensation-types, instanced in particular episodes of sensing, then according to Foster we can deduce that colours, or as he calls them, colour-qualia, cannot have an ultimate non-sensory realization. A complete visual quale, i.e. a visual colour-expanse or colour-pattern, cannot have an ultimate non-sensory realization because 'for the existence of a sensation, nothing more is required than an ultimate realization of the quale.'[44] Nor is it possible to detach colours from visual extension, and say that they can have an ultimate non-sensory realization by themselves.

I find this unconvincing for two reasons. Firstly, what has to be but so far as I can see not shown by Foster is that colours are *only* sensation-types and not also types whose tokens include, say, the particular non-dispositional rednesses of things in themselves. My second objection is to Foster's claim that particular episodes of sensing colours are self-revealing, or objects of consciousness. Clearly this is something he must claim if there is to be any chance that his description will fit the phenomena. There is some object of consciousness in every episode of sensing, and if we agree with Foster that the particular episode of sensing does not itself consist of awareness of an object, then the object of consciousness can only be that episode itself. But surely one can sense a colour without being aware that one is sensing it, without being aware of the whole episode of sensing it.

The noumenal inconsistency thesis about S-colours seems, then, to be unsupported. And so, I conclude, is the parallel thesis about volitions.

[44] Foster (1982), 106.

9

Evidence

THE two questions which on the Chapter 2 programme I was to ask of want and belief conflicts about volitions as such were: Does the desire for there to be real volitions have a coherent content?, and Is there good evidence for the non-existence of real volitions which is better evidence than any for their existence? Having failed in the previous chapter to find any incoherence in the content of the desire, I now turn to the evidential status of the opposing belief. Arguments against the existence of volitions are considered in the first section. And in the second, more speculative section I consider some arguments for supposing that they do exist.

1. ANOTHER COLOUR ANALOGY

Some writers who reject the noumenal inconsistency thesis about S-colours nevertheless think it reasonable to deny that S-colours are possessed by things whose existence is independent of experience. Have they an argument, an analogue of which will reveal good evidence for the falsity of 'There are real volitions'? I should stress that what these writers deny is not just that (i) when an external thing appears to have a particular S-colour, that is the S-colour it has, nor just that (ii) external things have those of their seeming S-colours which we especially want them to have. They also deny that (iii) external things have any S-colours whatsoever. (i) is certainly to be rejected, on the grounds that if it were true, the S-colour of the thing itself would change as often as its seeming S-colour, or its parts would be as different in their S-colours as the seeming S-colours of its different parts. ('If you look at port wine in a slim conical glass held against the light, its colours range from pale yellow at the bottom, through orange to ruby-red, and, as the reader can verify for himself, a bathful would look almost black.'[1]) As for (ii), one can hardly expect her eyes really to be just that shade of blue one so admires. But (iii) does not entail either (i) or (ii). As Hardin puts it, '... the practitioner of commonsense metaphysics might be globally right about the ontological status of colours, but almost always wrong in judging what colours things have.'[2]

In Chapter 8 of his *Perception* Frank Jackson defines a scientific property as 'a property appealed to by current science in explaining the causal effect of one material thing on another material thing, or a logical consequence of such a property or properties', and he argues that 'only if colour were a scientific property would we have reason to believe that material things were coloured'. And from here he moves rapidly to the conclusion that it is 'reasonable to assert that ... colour ... is not a property of material things'. For 'although the precise status of Occam's razor is a matter of dispute, it seems clear that properties we have no reason to believe are possessed by material things are properties we ought not to ascribe to them.'[3] Mackie makes what seems to be a similar move in his *Problems from Locke*:

the literal ascription of colours, as we see colours, and the like, to material things, to light, and so on, forms no part of the explanation of what goes on in the physical world in the processes which lead on to our having the sensations and perceptions that we have.[4]

Admittedly physics does not itself tell us that no such properties are there. This denial is a further, philosophical step; but it is one which is at least prima facie reasonable in the light of the successes of physical theory.[5]

The philosophical principle of economy of postulation ... supplies a reason for not introducing supposedly objective qualities of kinds for which physics has no need.[6]

But Mackie and Jackson are not really claiming that there is good evidence for the thesis that material objects lack colour qualities. The idea is rather that since we lack good evidence that material

[1] Mundle (1971), 134.
[2] Hardin (1988), 61. For more on want and belief conflicts about S-colours themselves, see my (1986).
[3] Jackson (1977), 123.
[4] Mackie (1976), 18.
[5] Ibid. 19.
[6] Ibid. 20.

objects *do* have colour qualities, we *ought* to believe that they do not. This is an ethical claim. Compare the famous passage of Russell's on favouritism and secondary qualities:

There is no colour which pre-eminently appears to be *the* colour of the table, or even of any one particular part of the table—it appears to be of different colours from different points of view . . . And . . . even from a given point of view the colour will seem different by artificial light, or to a colour-blind man, or to a man wearing blue spectacles, while in the dark there will be no colour at all, though to touch and hearing the table will be unchanged. Thus colour is not something inherent in the table, but something depending upon the table and the spectator and the way the light falls on the table. When, in ordinary life, we speak of *the* colour of the table, we only mean the sort of colour which it will seem to have to a normal spectator from an ordinary point of view under usual conditions of light. But the other colours which appear under other conditions have just as good a right to be considered real; and therefore, to avoid favouritism, we are compelled to deny that, in itself, the table has any one particular colour.[7]

Jackson and Mackie think that, lacking good evidence that a material object has some colour quality or other, we ought to believe that it has none. Russell thinks that if, for each particular colour quality which a material object appears to have, we lack good evidence that it has that quality, we ought to believe that it has no colour quality. Since these writers think that we ought to believe that material objects lack colour qualities, rather than claim that there is good evidence that material objects lack colour qualities, there is no analogue here to support the thesis that there is good evidence for non-existence of real volitions.

It has to be admitted that scientific explanations of volitional experience are unlikely when they eventually appear to postulate the independent occurrence of real volitions. For no accepted scientific explanations of other types of experience postulate the independent exemplification of the qualities we refer to in describing the content of the experience explained. For example, the orthodox theory of radiation, accepted as the simplest explanation of colour experiences, does not suppose that external things have S-colours. It refers rather to the wave-length composition of the light which is reflected by the external thing and

---

[7] Russell (1912), 13–14.

which strikes the retina of the observer, and to the relation between this wave-length composition, the molecular structure of
the external thing, and the wave-length composition of the in-
cident light. But I do not think there is anything very damaging
in this admission. Maybe it is true that

(A) If q is a set of experiential data then q is good evidence for
p if p is entailed by the simplest explanation of q.

But it does not follow from (A) that the explanatory redun-
dancy of a proposition not entailed by experiential data is evidence for the falsity of that proposition. Someone may say that
the latter, stronger doctrine is merely a self-evident principle of
parsimony. But if it commits us to taking on the extra belief that
these explanatorily redundant propositions are false, then from
one point of view it is distinctly less parsimonious than (A), which
at most commits us not to believe that they are true. I conclude
then that colour-analogies reveal no good evidence for the contingent non-existence of real volitions. Nor, for that matter, is
there a sound volitional analogue of the argument against supposing that when an external thing appears to have a particular
S-colour, that is the S-colour it really has. A real volition would
not be a persisting thing which could be observed at different
times under different observational conditions, like a pair of eyes
or a glass of port. Nor would it be simultaneously observable by
more than one observer. It would not present different appearances to the same observer at different times or different appearances to different observers at the same time.

2. MATTER AND SELF

If there is no good evidence for the non-existence of real volitions,
is there perhaps good evidence that they do exist? And if evidence
for their existence will not come from any special role which
they are likely to play in the eventual scientific explanation of
volitional experience, can it perhaps come from a general vol-
untaristic metaphysics? According to Russell, things outside us
must have intrinsic, non-dispositional, non-relational, not purely
spatio-temporal properties, but science gives us no knowledge
of what these are. It tells us only about the relational and dis-

positional properties *of* these unknown properties, yields only a structural or topic-neutral theory of matter. Suppose we accept this. The hypothesis then suggests itself, as it did to Russell, that the intrinsic nature of the physical world is mental. If we could first vindicate this general mentalist hypothesis then perhaps by some supplementary argument we could subsequently attribute to physical things not just unspecified mental properties but precisely the real volitions whose existence we want.

That physical things are mental is not the only coherent hypothesis about their intrinsic properties. There is, as we earlier saw, no inconsistency in the supposition that colour qualities are intrinsic properties of external objects. We can also coherently suppose that the intrinsic properties are of an unknown kind with which our experience leaves us entirely unacquainted. According to Mackie—

it is reasonable to postulate that there is a relatively permanent quantitative something-or-other intrinsic to objects and additive in all their normal combinations. In saying that an object has such and such a mass we may reasonably opt for the interpretation that this is to say that it is such that a certain set of conditionals holds, and that though this style of introduction is dispositional, what is introduced is an intrinsic, quantitative, but otherwise mainly unknown feature.[8]

Why then should the mentalist hypothesis be preferred?

One possible answer is that, since non-relational mental properties are known to be instantiated by things other than mere contents of experience, and no other non-relational properties are known to be thus instantiated, probably mental properties are the only non-relational properties which are thus instantiated. 'Surely it is good sense to take the one example of a thing which we know concretely as thing in itself as our paradigm for conceiving the nature of the other concrete things in themselves which we know are there as noumenal backing or basis of our phenomenal physical world.'[9] Inferences of this general type are popular among metaphysicians. Honderich makes one in his extrapolation of a mind–brain determinism from the findings of neuro-science (see Chapter 5, Section 1). Those who believe that mental states are essentially inner states apt to cause overt be-

[8] Mackie (1973), 151.
[9] Sprigge (1983), 105.

haviour sometimes argue that, although it is consistent to suppose that the owner of these inner states is a spiritual substance, it is equally consistent to suppose that they are owned by the brain, and that since we already know that some physical substances exist, we should prefer the hypothesis which allows us to suppose that all substances are physical. But as earlier noted, such inferences are dubious. It is simpler, no doubt, for one kind rather than two kinds of non-relational properties to be instantiated. But it is not necessary for a causal explanation of experience that we say anything at all about what the particular intrinsic properties are, changes in which constitute the causes. Certain specifications of those intrinsic properties may indeed give us a unity in what would otherwise have seemed diverse. But we do not gain much unity from the postulation of a simple resemblance between noumenal and known. Consider by contrast the theistic hypothesis that both those features of the world which we admire and also our admiration of them are produced by a transcendent being which itself has those very same features. Causal explanations of these features of the world and of our attitudes to them could be given without postulating such a being, but the postulate does nevertheless markedly unify. It is not just that the unknown is supposed to resemble the known. Rather, two otherwise diverse parts of the known are supposed both to resemble the same unknown.[10]

It may admittedly be possible to establish a more limited mentalism without relying on the inferential principle which I have criticized. Suppose that for any non-physical qualitative change in N's mental state, there would be some simultaneous change

[10] The unity gained by a causally redundant postulation of specific intrinsic qualities in the unobserved should not be confused with that gained from the mere description of unsuspected analogies between superficially diverse observable phenomena. The latter is what for example Schopenhauer provides. After all the explanations of 'etiology', our representations 'still stand quite strange before us'. 'The philosophical investigator must always feel in regard to the complete etiology of the whole of nature like a man who, without knowing how, is brought into a company quite unknown to him, each member of which in turn presents to him another as his friend and cousin, and thus makes them sufficiently acquainted. The man himself, however, while assuring each person introduced of his pleasure at meeting him, always has on his lips the question: "But how the devil do I stand to the whole company?"' (*The World as Will and Representation*, i. 98). The strangeness is to be abolished by tracing the omnipresent expression or objectification of Will in nature. Given, however, that there are no causal relations between phenomena and Schopenhauer's thing in itself, it is hard to see how tracing Will's

in the experiences as of N's brain which would be enjoyed by an ideally well-equipped and receptive observer. May not the qualitative changes which would directly cause those experiences of the observer, and which dualists would take to be physical qualitative changes distinct from, though correlated with, the non-physical qualitative mental changes in N, be precisely identical with those non-physical qualitative mental changes in N? Several writers, such as Schlick and, with qualifications, Russell himself, have accepted some such a theory of the relations between brain and mind, whilst balking at any general mentalism or panpsychism.[11] The theory could be defended not on the grounds that it minimizes the number of distinct kinds of non-relational properties, but on the grounds that it enables us to simplify some at least of our causal explanations of the ideal observer's experiences. Consider this dualistic model. N's time t experience,

objectification can be more than a metaphor for the detection of analogies between human volition and other natural phenomena. Everything turns out to resemble one and the same thing. The stone's flight, for example, resembles my deliberate action. 'Spinoza (Ep. 62) says that if a stone projected through the air had consciousness, it would imagine it was flying of its own will. I add merely that the stone would be right... what in the case of the stone appears as cohesion, gravitation, rigidity in the assumed condition is by its inner nature the same as what I recognize in myself as will, and which the stone would recognize as will, if knowledge were added in its case also' (ibid. i. 126). Cf. Max Scheler on the German bombardment of Rheims cathedral in the First World War: 'if the cathedral had been capable of thinking and feeling it would have realized that the force firing the cannons was part of the same force that had once created this heaven-storming Gothic masterpiece' (quoted in Grunberger (1974), 386–7). 'Hermeneutic' interpretations of Freudian theory make that into a similar enterprise.

[11] If A is looking at a red flower and B is an ideally well equipped and receptive observer simultaneously looking at A's brain then according to Schlick there is no distinct process in A's brain with which A's experience would run parallel or interact. And we must not suppose that through the intuitive images in B's consciousness the properties of A's brain have been directly grasped. A's experience is the qualitative reality that causes B's consciousness, a reality which is at the same time physical because it can be designated by means of the spatio-temporal quantitative concepts of science (Schlick (1925), 311–13). Schlick does nevertheless completely reject the hypothesis, entailed by pan-psychism, that 'all being designated by means of natural scientific concepts is mental' (328). Cf. Russell, in a passage from which I have already quoted: '... while mental events and their qualities can be known without inference, physical events are known only as regards their space-time structure.' This allows us to say that where events in brains are concerned, some at least of them are thoughts. But 'when we come to events in physical space-time where there are no brains..., the qualities that compose such events are unknown—so completely unknown that we cannot say either that they are, or that they are not, different from the qualities that we know as belonging to mental events' (Russell (1948), 246–7). Russell's theory is, however, easy to misinterpret. On his usual understanding of perception, the brain

which is accompanied by a time t qualitative change in N's brain, causes a time t_1 change in N's brain, which in turn causes a time t_2 change in the ideal observer's experience as of N's time t_1 brain. Since the t_1 change in N's brain is presumably also caused by the time t change in N's brain, the time t causal antecedents of the observer's time t_2 experiences include both mental and non-mental changes in N. On our monistic alternative, however, the observer's time t_2 experience has only a single time t causal antecedent. The time t_1 event which directly causes the observer's time t_2 experience is in fact a time t_1 experience of N's, and not, as the dualist says, a distinct brain event. And there is no time t brain event, distinct from N's time t experience, by which N's time t_1 experience is caused.

But how do we move even from this limited mentalism to the existence of real volitions? When others wonder whether the direct cause of the observer's experiences as of N's brain has for its non-relational properties colour qualities or unknown features, the limited mentalist postulates mental properties. But why should these properties include real volitions, rather than just experiences as of volitions? Someone might at this point appeal to a new principle of simplicity: when it comes to explanations of experience as of something's having a non-relational property F, there is a special and truth-indicating simplicity in those which make F itself a non-relational property of the substance whose causal powers explain the experience. But on that principle, the

events which are perceivings are not only mental in a sense which could not be captured by any topic-neutral analysis of mentality, but also possessed of phenomenal properties like non-dispositional colour qualities. This is because he eliminates from perceiving, and indeed from thought in general, everything but the content of the act: 'The distinction between "seeing the sun"' as a mental event, and the immediate object of my seeing, is now generally rejected as invalid, and in this view I concur ((1948), 220); 'The occurrence of the content of a thought constitutes the occurrence of the thought' ((1921), 2) So far at least as some brain events are concerned, Russell's conclusions therefore entail those that we would have reached on the basis of the general speculation that the intrinsic properties which all physical objects must possess are in fact S-colour qualities. If we start with this general speculation, we seem to have no means of knowing which particular colour quality any physical object has. On Russell's theory we at least know that the brain events with which visual perceivings are identified have the colour of the perceptual content. For an attempt to combine these conclusions of Russell's with the admission that as well as perceptual content there is awareness of this content, see Lockwood (1989), ch. 10, and for a good defence of a mentalistic mind–brain identity theory shorn of Russellian idiosyncrasies see Maxwell (1978).

existence of real volitions on the part of N could be derived from N's own experiences as of volitions, regardless of whether these real volitions are among the mental features which could be postulated as direct causes of the observer's experiences as of N's brain. And anyway, the principle itself seems unduly permisssive. Even if, in a non-causal unification, we may postulate what has to exist for otherwise diverse things to resemble a single common thing, we do not have here an instance of that inference. The postulated F-substance only resembles experiences which already resemble each other in their as-of-F content.

But let us, in a final speculation, assume the more demanding principle of non-causal unification, which requires the same unknown to resemble otherwise diverse parts of the known. There are real experiences. Suppose we know that experiencing is an act of attention to a content. Then there are at least real acts of attention. Now there are experiences as of volitions other than acts of attention. And if experiencing is an act of attention we can move by the principle of non-causal unification to the further conclusion that there are real volitions other than acts of attention. An explanation of experiences as of volitions other than acts of attention need not postulate that these experiences are caused by real volitions of the types that they are experiences as of. But that postulate would nevertheless unify. The real volitions would resemble the contents of the experiences. And they would also resemble the whole experiences themselves. For the latter, as we are supposing, are themselves volitions. Two diverse parts of the known would resemble the same unknown.

How, though, can we know that experiencing is an act of attention to a content? By supposing this we can at least explain away those seeming deliverances of introspection which would otherwise oblige us to accept either a paradoxical or a merely negative doctrine of subject and agent. It is often claimed as a datum of introspection that in experience there is a something to which a content is presented and in volition a something by which an event is willed and that neither something is identical to any experience or volition or bundle of experiences or volitions. Only one positive thesis has ever been advanced as to what actually constitutes this subject or agent, namely that it is a brain or body. To say that the subject or agent is a spiritual substance is only to say what it is not. And there is, as I shall argue, a paradox in the solitary positive suggestion. But perhaps, when you are aware of experiencing something scarlet, what you are aware of is not precisely a something to which the content 'something scarlet' is presented, but only a something seemingly distinct from and yet somehow intimately linked to the content 'something scarlet'. And perhaps, when you are aware of willing, you are aware, not precisely of a something by which an event is willed, but only of a something which is distinct both from what is willed and from the quality of the volition. I think that, if it is granted that experience just is attention to a content, then we can say what in each case the distinct something is without postulating either an agent or a subject whose nature could only be further and positively specified as a brain or body.

What, other than a subject which might be a brain or body or spiritual substance, could the dimly introspectible something be, which, in an experience as of something scarlet, is intimately linked to the content 'something scarlet'? The answer is that if experiencing is attending, and if attending is a kind of volition, then the something could be the introspectible conative quality of the attending itself, that quality, distinct from what is attended to, which makes it an act of attention. What, other than an agent which might be a brain or body, could the dimly introspectible something be, which, in an experience as of willing something or as of attending to something, is distinct both from what is ostensibly willed or attended to and from the conative quality of the ostensible willing or attending, and yet intimately linked to both of these things? The answer is that it could be the conative quality of a further volition, which is itself an act of attending. The position could be this. We have experience X as of willing that p. A something is revealed in this which is distinct both from the content and from the quality of the ostensible willing that p. 'Attention to ...' replaces 'experience as of ...'. So experience X as of willing that p is attention X to ostensible willing that p. Attention X has, however, its own introspectible conative quality. And the something, distinct both from the content and from the quality of willing that p, and dimly revealed when there is attention X to ostensible willing that p, is, not a real or ostensible agent, but the distinctive conative quality of attention X. When there is attention X to an ostensible willing that p, there is also attention W to attention X, and the quality of attention X which is part of the content of attention W is the something, distinct both from the content and from the quality of the ostensible willing that *p*, that there is awareness as of when there is attention X to the ostensible willing that *p*. What goes for experience as of willing that *p*, goes also for experience as of attending to something, such as a scarlet content. The something dimly revealed, which is distinct both from the scarlet content and the quality of the ostensible attention to that content, is the quality of a further act of attention, whose content is the ostensible act of attention to the scarlet content. By regarding experiencing as an act of attention to a content, we have then an alternative to the theory that in experience and volition there is an indeterminately presented subject or agent further to be specified as a brain or body or spiritual substance.

Objection One. It cannot be the case that all supposed presentations of content are really only acts of attention, for to attend is itself to focus or concentrate on part of an already presented content. If all presentations of content were acts of attention, every such act of attention would be preceded by an infinite series of acts of attention, each member of which would have a broader content than its successor. And that is absurd.

Reply. Attending to a content is not the same as focusing or concentrating on a content. By attending to a content I mean sustaining or keeping hold of a content, and this need not involve any selection from a wider content previously attended to.

Objection Two. There can be no volition without a previous or simultaneous idea or image. If for example I will my arm to go up I must have, or have had, an idea or image of its going up. The idea or image must, however, be simply presented to a subject rather than actively attended to, otherwise every volition would have to be preceded or accompanied by an infinite series of volitions. So it cannot be the case that all supposed presentations to subjects are really just acts of attention.

Reply. Suppose that the necessary image is presented to the subject at the very time of the volition, and that the volition has an agent who is identical to this subject. How could the agent act at all, if at precisely the time of his action he was occupied with the reception of a presentation? It seems then that if the idea or image were presented to the subject at the very time of the volition, then this act would either have no agent, or, absurdly, would have an agent who was not identical to the subject. Suppose then that the idea or image is presented to the subject before the volition. Its presentation would then presumably stand in a causal relation to the subsequent volition. But the volition has its own content, and cause and effect are distinct existences. So we can conceive of the volition as occurring with its own content and without the previous presentation.

Objection Three. If there were no presentations of content but only acts of attention, then there would be no veridical perception. The content of an act of attention would be produced by the act rather than by those parts of the mind-independent world which the content seemingly represented.

Reply. We are concerned only with what it is possible to conceive, and maybe it is possible to conceive that there is no veridical perception. And anyway, a whole act of attention could still be caused by those parts of the mind-independent world which were represented by the content of that act.

It seems, then, that by regarding experiencing as an act of attention we can elaborate a coherent and reductively voluntarist alternative to both bodily or cerebral and spiritual conceptions of subject and agent. What now are the disadvantages in the latter conceptions? What grounds do we have for preferring the voluntarist alternative, and hence for accepting that experiencing is an act of attention, and hence for accepting that, given the principle of non-causal unification, there are real volitions of all the kinds as of which we have experiences? In the spiritual conception there is an obvious negativity. And, in what for convenience I will call the materialist conception, there is a less obvious difficulty about causation.[12]

---

[12] In fact, the bodily or cerebral conception of subject or agent does often appeal to those who are anxious to preserve some vestige of the strong materialist doctrine that people have only material properties, and yet at the same time are convinced that some mental properties are irreducibly non-material. They can say

The difficulty about causation is this. Let us say that an event E_1 is causally related to an event E_n if either E_1 causes E_n, or E_1 causes an event which causes E_n, or E_1 causes an event which causes an event which causes E_n, or . . . , and so on. Then we surely know that if there are real volitions then sometimes at least the event which is the beginning of the brain or body which a materialist would regard as the agent of some volition is causally related to that volition. But it is hard to see how, on the materialist's theory of the agent, we could know that this causal relation holds.

How does the materialist think that volitions are related to the brains or bodies which are their agents? Presumably he thinks that it is not a mere contingent truth that there are no volitions without agents. Suppose then that, even though, as I have argued, experiences as of volitions do not reveal real or ostensible agents, it is impossible for a real volition to occur without an agent. From the propositions that there cannot be volitions without agents and that those agents are in fact brains or bodies, it does not follow that it is impossible for there to be volitions without brains or bodies. That conclusion would follow only if it were necessarily true that the agents are brains or bodies. But if it were impossible for there to be volitions without brains or bodies, and impossible also for these brains or bodies not to have beginnings, then it would also be impossible for volitions to occur without these beginnings. And on any reasonably demystified conception of causation, E_1 is causally related to E_n only if it is possible for E_1 to occur without E_n. Now I do not see how the materialist can be confident that it is not necessarily true that agents are

that at least the owner of mental properties is material. There is a seeming endorsement of this weak materialism in Mackie's (1976) '. . . we seem to be left with a distinctive set of mental properties which, even if we *say* that they too are physical, are unlike other physical properties' (p. 168). But the concept of personal identity . . . is the concept of something that turns out to be the continuity of the structure of a certain part of the body' (201). 'A materialist view of the thinker is less controversial than a materialist view of thoughts' (202). Other sympathizers succumb in the end to ill-explained scruples. McGinn notes that 'we could hold mental properties to be irreducible and *sui generis* without holding that their substance is a subject or object distinct from any physical object, specifically, distinct from the body' ((1982), 26). But there is a mystery in 'how a physical organ of the body . . . could be the basis of consciousness' (36). According to Nagel, the mental cannot be reduced to or analysed in terms of the physical ((1986), 48), and 'the persisting locus of mental states and activities . . . is as a matter of fact the intact brain' (40). But there is something 'strange' about the conjunction of these two propositions: it 'has the faintly sickening odour of something put together in the metaphysical laboratory' (51, 49).

brains or bodies, and hence that it possible for there to be volitions without brains or bodies, unless he knows that it is inconsistent to suppose that agents are spiritual substances. The notion of a spiritual substance is, however, too ill-specified for him to have this knowledge. Nor do I see how the materialist can be confident that it is possible for brains or bodies to be beginningless.[13] So the materialist is, I think, forced into the paradoxical admission that he does not know that the beginning of the brain or body which he takes to be the agent is sometimes causally related to a volition of that agent.

Why does a reasonably demystified conception of causation require that if E_1 is causally related to E_n, then E_n can occur without E_1? Suppose we accept the two Humean principles that any true causal statement could have been false and that any event could have caused any other event. We must then accept as a third principle that if one event causes another then there is nothing which makes it impossible for the second event to occur without the first. For if we deny this then we are also obliged to deny not only that if one event causes another then this could not have been the case but also that it could have been the case that the second event was instead caused by an event which would have caused the actual first event not to have occurred.[14] It does,

[13] 'There is a ... curious asymmetry in our intuitions. Something infinitely old makes the mind boggle in a way in which something with an infinite future does not. Wittgenstein in a lecture once asked his audience to imagine coming across a man who is saying, "... 5, 1, 4, 1, 3—finished!", and, when asked what he had been doing, replies that he has just finished reciting the complete decimal expansion of π backwards—something he has been doing at a steady rate for all of past eternity. There is a special way in which this story strikes us as absurd, a way in which the corresponding story about a man beginning to recite the complete decimal expansion of π and carrying on forever does not strike us as absurd.' (Moore (1990), 44.)

[14] Kevin Mulligan has proposed this counterexample to the third principle: my judging causes my sadness, even though it is impossible for that sadness to occur without my judgement. But suppose more particularly that this is the case: I am sad that Mary is in London. Maybe what this amounts to is that I am sad, while at the same time judging that Mary is in London and believing that my sadness is caused by this judgement. On that analysis it would of course be impossible for me to be sad that Mary is in London without my judging that she is. But if my judgement does cause my sadness, it is only my feeling that it causes, and not the whole complex of states and events which is my sadness that Mary is in London. Since my judgement is part of the whole complex, it cannot cause the whole complex without causing itself. What is caused, in the example, is not the same as what cannot occur without that cause; the third principle seems therefore to survive.

however, follow from our third principle that if E_1 is causally related to E_n then it is possible that E_n should occur without E_1.[15]

To summarize. If experiencing is an act of attention to a content then the relatively demanding principle of non-causal unification allows us to infer real volitions of all the types as of which we have experiences. We have a coherent positive alternative to the materialist theory of subject and agent if, and, so far as I can see, only if, experiencing is an act of attention to a content. And we need a positive alternative to that theory, given what we know about how the beginnings of brains or bodies are causally related to volitions.[16]

3. GENERAL SUMMARY

I will now try to incorporate the speculations of the last section in a general summary of the last seven chapters.

Even if we believe that there are real decisions and other real volitions, we may still believe that no real decisions are *-free, and even believe that none are effective. But we want decisions to be effective, and it is as well from a conflict-resolving standpoint also to assume that we want them to be *-free. Taking it for the sake of argument that real volitions are conceivable, I was unable to discover an incoherence in the content of these desires. Nor did they seem to depend on dubious internal propositions. Nor could I find good evidence, in the shape of a thesis of natural order, for the negations of the desiderata. Order-based palliatives

---

[15] Consider the series $E_1, \ldots E_{n-1}, E_n$. If it is possible that both E_1's immediate successor occurs and E_1 does not, and possible that both E_1's immediate successor occurs and all the events after E_1 up to and including E_n occur, then it is possible that both E_n occurs and E_1 does not. But if E_1 is causally related to E_n then all the events after E_1 up to and including E_n actually do occur and it is therefore possible for them to occur. So if the third principle is correct, and if E_1 is causally related to E_n, it is possible that E_n should occur without E_1.

[16] There is a rather different criticism of the bodily or cerebral theory of subject or agent in my (1992), from which I have borrowed some parts of this section. I argue there that if, as some people want, the theory is to be genuinely materialistic, a genuine vestige of the strong but untenable doctrine that people have only material properties, then the material must have ontological primacy. That primacy, however, is difficult to secure except on a theory of universals which we should in any case reject in favour of a pure particularism or tropism of the kind defended by Husserl, D. C. Williams, and K. Campbell.

would in any case be available for some of these conflicts, at least on a demystified interpretation of counterfactuals. So much for the freedom part of the 'free-will problem'.

But then it appeared that even the very existence of real volitions could be doubted. With no real volitions there would be no real decisions, free or unfree, effective or ineffective, and indeed no free actions. Even if there were no good evidence for unfreedom or inefficacy, want and belief conflicts about free and effective decisions and about other free actions could still persist. There would anyway be want and belief conflicts simply about real volitions. But what finally emerges, if there is anything in my speculations about non-causal unification, is that without real volitions, no want and belief conflict would even have a victim. For if experiencing is attending, and other kinds of volitions are real, then non-dispositional mental life is itself a succession of real volitions. A person either just is a succession of real volitions, or at any rate could not exist without some such succession. Neither the body nor any part of it is the indeterminately introspected agent and subject, the something by which events are willed and to which contents are presented and without which volition and experience are inconceivable. There is no agent or subject of this kind.

It is to be remarked that *choice* in the sense of the taking of one and leaving of another real alternative is not what freedom of pitch really and strictly lies in. It is choice as when in English we say 'because I choose', which means no more than (and with precision does mean) I instress my will to so-and-so. ... So also *pitch* is ultimately simple positiveness, that by which being differs from and is more than nothing and not-being, and it is with precision expressed by the English *do* (the simple auxiliary). ... And such 'doing-be', and the thread or chain of such pitches or 'doing-be's, prior to nature's being overlaid, is self, personality; but it is not truly self: self or personality then truly comes into being when the self or person comes into being with the accession of nature.[17]

---

[17] Gerard Manley Hopkins, 'On Personality, Grace and Free Will', in Devlin (1959), 150–1.

10

A Programme Subsumed

As well as supporting the theses just summarized, the last seven chapters have, I hope, also illustrated a method. As I stressed in the Introduction, adoption of this method does not leave the utility of metaphysics simply to take care of itself. Or to put it in another way, randomness is reduced. Take any doctrine of metaphysics. Is it true? If the answer is to be Yes or No, and the doctrine is ambiguous, then a meaning must be selected. But by what principle of selection? Take 'Freedom is compatible with determinism'. Is it true? I wondered in Chapter 3 and again at the end of Chapter 6 whether in some current Yes answers to this question a perfectly random selection had not been made from the large array of different Incompatibilisms allowed for by the combined ambiguity of 'determinism' and 'freedom'. On the method proposed, we ignore all questions but those to which answers are necessary for the identification or resolution of want and belief conflicts. Instead of asking whether freedom is compatible with determinism, we ask whether there is any evidentially well-supported determinism which is incompatible with a freedom we want to possess. Or, looking at it for once in a different way, whether there is any evidentially well-supported thesis of freedom which is incompatible with a determinism we want to be true. How could the original stock question have any non-random answer if we do not reveal and try to resolve the want and belief conflicts which explain its now customary centrality?

Exactly the same treatment can be applied to many other prominent enigmas. Is moral objectivism true? Is the foundationalist theory of epistemic justification true? The physical theory of personal identity over time? The materialist theory of the mind? The regularity theory of causation? Heavily ambiguous questions, without exception. Which meanings do we choose? Those in which the truth of the 'theory', or of its negation, is liable to be an object of desire, and yet also seems to be desired in vain. Then we can try systematically to resolve or mitigate the conflict.

To pursue just two of these further examples. There will be a want and belief conflict about moral objectivism if we take that to entail that some actions have properties such that necessarily if you know that an action has that property then you want or even decide to take it if you believe you can. Why want moral objectivism to be true? For the sake of its being true, or for the sake of something else? But what else? A degree of practical agreement otherwise unattainable? Would the desire in that case have a doubtful internal proposition? Has the desire in any case a coherent content? If so, is there after all good evidence that the desideratum is false? Metaphysicians of morals do not systematically address these questions. Sometimes indeed they are happy enough just to find something true to which the labels of 'moral objectivism' or 'moral realism' can without too much eccentricity be applied. Or again, there will be a want and belief conflict about foundationalism in the theory of epistemic justification if by that we mean the doctrine that a person could have a fairly extensive belief-system in which what he believed was exhaustively divided between privileged propositions which it would not be bad for him to believe without evidence, and nonprivileged propositions which it would be bad for him to believe without evidence but which could nevertheless all be evidentially supported by the privileged. The various disjointed efforts of epistemologists with the 'regress of justification' could be transmuted into questions about the internal propositions of the desire to possess such a belief-system and the coherence of the content of that desire.

As we moved from one old question to another, connections could of course be established, not only with those scattered studies which do already focus on what we want to be true about some aspect of the nature of things,[1] but also with some of the more topic-neutral programmes of current analytical metaphysics. Mackie proposed that the philosopher should aim to provide both conceptual and 'factual' analyses of our most general concepts, and has himself provided such analyses for the concepts of causation and of moral judgement.[2] If conceptual analyses often incidentally describe what we uncritically want to be the case, and

[1] Parfit's (1971) and (1984) studies of personal identity are a conspicuous example.
[2] See Mackie (1974), 59–60; (1977), ch. 1; and for his general theory of philosophical analysis (1973), ch. 1.

factual analyses often describe those residues of our uncritical desiderata for which there is good evidence, then Mackie-style findings could be used in a piecemeal conflict-resolving programme. So also could the results of another neo-Humean enterprise: Blackburn's quasi-realism. For part of the aim here is to show that in cases where we want it to be true but ought not to believe that things in themselves have certain properties, there are sufficiently strong analogies between what we naïvely want and the residual reality for it not to be misleading to go on talking as we ordinarily do.[3]

But however extensive the application of a conflict-resolving method, the accumulated results are liable to lack unity. And the final question I want to consider is whether a piecemeal programme of want and belief conflict resolution cannot be subsumed under and integrated by some further and more ambitious project. In the first section of this chapter I discuss a formalistic suggestion, in the second section something better.

1. DIALECTICS

If you want p to be true but believe it to be false, then although you might not in the least mind having either attitude if you did not have the other, their simultaneous possession is irksome by virtue of your awareness of the logical relation between their contents. Described in that way, want and belief conflicts take on the appearance of a special case. In addition to irksome pairs of separately acceptable attitudes, one a want and the other a belief, there could furthermore be pairs of wants, and pairs of beliefs, or at any rate of inclinations to believe: want and belief conflicts could be subsumed under the same genus as Buridan's Ass predicaments, and the conflicts generated by antinomies, in which we are inclined to believe each of some pair of propositions while not seeing how to avoid the inconsistency to which this seems to commit us. In addition to pairs of separately acceptable attitudes, irksome to their owner because of his beliefs about the logical relations between their contents, there will also be sets irksome for that reason with any number of members.

---

[3] See Blackburn (1984), 170–223.

If we can fix the whole genus, we can see the project of meta-physical want and belief conflict resolution as just part of a pro-gramme in which all species of such collectively irksome and metaphysical sets are dissolved or neutralized.

Let us define an A-set as a set of attitudes, all simultaneously owned by the same person and all either wants or beliefs. Con-tents of wants and beliefs, as we can suppose, are given by sen-tences. These may or may not be ambiguous or meaningless. Each sentence giving the content of a member of an A-set may express more than one definite proposition; each such sentence may or may not express any definite proposition at all. Next let us define a B-set as a A-set in which each content of each component want or belief determines just one definite and self-consistent proposition, but in which the whole set of these pro-positions is inconsistent. Could we now say, at least as a first approximation, that the broader programme to which the re-solution of metaphysical want and belief conflicts belongs is the programme of helping people to be rid at an acceptable cost of the unwelcome conviction or suspicion that some of their meta-physical A-sets are B-sets? We may try to show that at least one sentence giving the content of an attitude in the A-set is ambigu-ous, and can be taken to express a proposition such that the whole set of propositions expressed by the sentences giving the contents of the attitudes is not inconsistent after all. We may try to show that some want in the set rests on a doubtful internal proposition. And so on.

This description would need some refinement. For one thing, one might not always mind owning what one takes to be a B-set, as originally defined. There would be nothing particularly dis-turbing about believing that p and q are incompatible while be-lieving that one wants p to be true and wants q to be true if one wanted p's truth very much more than one wanted q's truth. And if we operate with degrees of belief, instead of belief *simpliciter*, there is in the same way nothing disturbing about thinking one has an A-set in which one has different degrees of belief in each of a pair of incompatible propositions, so long as the subjective probabilities obey the axioms of the probability calculus and add up to 1. So perhaps, in the definition of 'A-set', we should sub-stitute 'degree of belief' for 'belief' and stipulate that no two wants in an A-set are to be of equal strength, and that all degrees of belief in an A-set obey the probability axioms.

We should also consider cases in which one or more of the attitudes in a A-set is an attitude towards an attitude, as for example wanting or believing that one wants something, or that one believes something to a certain degree. One can want to be rid of certain A-sets containing attitudes towards attitudes, even though one does not think that these are A-sets on the original or modified definition. Suppose for example that I want to believe p and want to believe q, but believe that p and q are inconsistent. I will want to be rid of one of these two attitudes even if the two wants are of unequal strength. But even if p and q are inconsistent, my A-set will not be a B-set, even on our modified definition. To cover cases of this kind, we can distinguish between direct, indirect and ultimate contents of wants and beliefs. Let us say that if I want or believe that p, then p stands for the direct content of my want or belief, and that if p is a proposition which entails either that I want that p_1 or that I believe that p_1, then p_1 stands for the first indirect content of my belief that p, and so on. Let us also say that a direct or indirect content of my want or belief is the ultimate content of that want or belief if it does not express a proposition which either entails that I want something to be the case or that I believe that I want something to be the case. Thus if I want a drink, 'I have a drink' is the direct and ultimate content of my want. If I want to know that I am safe, 'I know that I am safe' is the first indirect content of my want. Since 'I know that I am safe' entails both 'I believe that I am safe' and 'I am safe' these stand for second indirect contents of my want. We can then redefine a A-set as a B-set in which each component want or degree of belief determines just one definite and self-consistent proposition, and the whole set of propositions expressing the ultimate contents of these attitudes is inconsistent.

The programme of helping people to get rid of the unwelcome suspicion that some of their metaphysical A-sets are B-sets would, I think, be especially congenial to philosophers of the dialectical tradition. Progress is to be made through the resolution of a conflict. As a kind of dialectical philosophy, this random anti-B-set programme could be contrasted with enterprises of two other kinds. There is the Hegelian programme of ordering all conflicts in some single finite series, through which one progresses, as a ship 'tacking against the wind blowing head on from its ultimate destination',[4] to a saving grasp of the Absolute Idea. And then there is dialectical thought of an entirely non-therapeutic kind in which the aim is just to assemble tragic or bourgeois-confounding or merely curious instances of inner and interpersonal strife.

One objection to a general anti-B-set programme is the difficulty of seeing what one would have to do in order to complete it. Unless one can somehow group B-sets by what their propositions are about, it seems impossible to anticipate which kinds of B-sets are liable to afflict one. One would be fighting forever against a guerrilla army perpetually replenished by the fertility of one's own confusion.

Also, the ostensibly unifying formal concept of a B-set masks differences of urgency among the various conflicts it covers. Compare want and belief conflicts with antinomies, or rather the conflicts of attitudes which antinomies generate. These are also covered by the same B-set description. An antinomy is a seeming contradiction supported by an argument which we do not know how precisely to fault. There are actually two cases. (1) An unambiguous sentence expresses a proposition of the form 'p and not-p', and there is an argument for this proposition the details of whose deficiency escape us. (2) An ambiguous sentence which seems to express nothing but a contradiction can also express a non-contradictory conjunction, and what seemed like a good argument for p and not-p, can be disambiguated into a pair of arguments, one of which may really be a good argument for the non-contradictory conjunction. Russell's Class Paradox would on some views illustrate the first case. We have the unambiguous sentence 'the class of all classes that are not members of themselves both is, and is not, a member of itself', and to reject the argument for the contradiction which this expresses we must reject the principle that for any condition you can formulate there is a class whose members are the things meeting this condition.[5] The so-called Dynamical Antinomies of Kant's first Critique illustrate the second case. In each antinomy thesis and antithesis can

[4] McTaggart (1896), 146–7.
[5] Quine (1966), 3–30.

be joined together in a single sentence which expresses a self-contradictory proposition, and the arguments for the thesis and the antithesis can be joined together in a single argument whose conclusion is that sentence. In effect, Kant's resolution is to show that the single sentence we then get is ambiguous and also expresses a non-contradictory conjunction both conjuncts of which may really be supported by propositions expressed by the ambiguous premisses of the single argument. Thus in the third antinomy, the thesis affirms that there must be a 'causality through freedom' as well as a 'causality according to the laws of nature', and the antithesis affirms that all causality is according to the laws of nature. Kant's scrutiny is, however, supposed to reveal that the thesis contradicts the antithesis only if both are taken to be about the phenomenal world, and that there may be a transcendentally free first cause of the whole series of appearances even though there is no 'causality through freedom' within the series. Being baffled by an antinomy is one way of believing one owns a B-set. The plausible body of argument makes one want to believe that p and also makes one want to believe that not-p, and one appears to have two wants whose indirect and ultimate contents determine an inconsistent pair of propositions. One finds it irksome to own both wants because one believes it impossible to believe both that p and that not-p, and the arguments do not give one a preference for believing either. But the B-set description disguises the fact that bafflement by antinomies is less irksome than affliction by want and belief conflicts. Even if there really is a pair of incompatible propositions each of which one is inclined to believe, one does know in advance that at least one of the two propositions is false, so that one or other of the attitudes can be abandoned with impunity. But there is no such prior assurance in the case of wanting p to be true while believing it false. Each attitude can be perfectly reasonable, and their joint possession a permanent affliction.

I think, then, that no extra unity is gained just by locating want and belief conflicts in a wider collection of oppositions. There is, however, a genuine way in which the piecemeal programme of metaphysical conflict resolution can be unified. For, as I will now try to show, there is a single overriding goal, the construction of a set of evaluative world-views, to which help with each conflict can be seen as a contribution.

2. WORLD-VIEWS

Suppose you ask yourself these questions. Of which kind or kinds of things do I want there to be at least one instance? How many instances of that kind or kinds do I want there to be? The questions, it is understood, are about what you want to be the case for its own sake, about your ultimate desiderata. If you now ask, of each kind, whether it really is instantiated to the extent you want, and there is some kind of which you are forced to answer that it is not, then there are questions of how if at all that can be altered by human action; can we multiply instances, or even produce an instance where no instance has ever existed before? Answers to these questions either suggest courses of action which you will want for the sake of what you want to exist for its own sake, or, if it appears that nothing can be done, questions suggest themselves about whether it would really have been better if something could have been done, or if some particular kind had already been instantiated to the extent that you want. Maybe, if it had been, that would have stopped there being instances of some other kind; maybe instances of one of your favoured kinds cannot be produced without destroying instances of another.

A unified and reasoned set of answers to this series of questions constitutes a world-view. Many familiar ideologies can be reformulated in these terms. In secular humanism, for example, nothing is wanted for its own sake but the existence of people, or at any rate the satisfaction of human wants. Action to satisfy these wants has no supernatural reinforcement and can only exploit the regularity of nature. On a secular aestheticism the only things wanted for their own sakes are sensuous qualities, unified structures of such qualities, mathematical structures, unified plans of action successfully carried out. People are valued only as bearers or makers of these qualities, structures and sequences of action. On a Schopenhauerian world-view nothing is wanted for its own sake but the avoidance of frustrated desire, and because the world is essentially blind will the only effective way to that is the total abolition of individual desire: art is valuable only as distraction from the treadmill, morality only as the first stage of self-annihilation. On a traditional theistic world-view nothing is wanted for its own sake but God's existence and the effectiveness of his will; what he wills includes things which on some secular world-views are wanted for their own sakes, and he offers grace to reinforce the free human action by which he wills that some of the things he wills can be achieved. (Or, better perhaps, for anything other than God's existence which is wanted for its own sake, wanting that other thing for its own sake is an attitude wanted only for the sake of wanting what God wants for its own sake.[6])

World-views have both critical and casuistical applications. They can be combined with detailed empirical beliefs to yield more detailed plans of action, both private projects and public policies. And existing plans of action, patterns of activity or aspiration, even particular actions and desires, can be criticized in the light of a world-view and a set of detailed empirical beliefs. Is this or that plan or pattern of action or desire itself an instance of a kind whose instantiation is, in the world-view, consciously wanted for its own sake? Does it, alternatively, make some causal contribution to the instantiation of such a kind? Such casuistry and criticism can be autobiographical, as when the author, with an eye to actual or potential allies, applies his own world-view, using his own detailed empirical beliefs. It can also be *ad hominem*, as when the author, with an interest in the prediction of behaviour or the diffusion of consistency, applies an alien world-view, using the detailed empirical beliefs of those who accept it. And there are also neutral brands of casuistry and criticism, in which the author aims to apply universally shared elements of different world-views with the aid of universally shared empirical beliefs.

World-views may or may not be self-critical. A world-view describes what somebody wants for its own sake and contains statements about how far these wants are or can be jointly satisfied. A self-critical world-view will try to show that belief in some at least of these statements is itself an instance of a kind of thing wanted for its own sake or itself a causal condition for the instantiation of such a kind. It will in other words contain an epistemology or ethics of belief to which it will show that at least some part of itself conforms. Every task traditionally called philosophical finds its place somewhere in the construction or application of a self-critical world-view. But some studies traditionally called

---

[6] See Adams (1986).

philosophical—normative social theory or applied ethics—are at the same time indistinguishable from more or less ill-informed applied psychology or social science. And others—conceptual analysis or logical criticism—are or should be part of the daily work of every special scientist. But if philosophy is defined as the construction, not application, of self-critical world-views, then its task is distinct from anything which is or could be attempted by any special science.

How does the study of metaphysical want and belief conflicts fit into this conception of philosophy? Consider, if you like, a conflict between wanting there to be special properties of good-ness and believing that there are none. The effort to resolve or mitigate the conflict necessarily produces a preliminary sketch of one fragment of a world-view. In deliberating on the conflict, one naturally asks whether the existence of the properties is some-thing the victim wants for its own sake or for the sake of some-thing else that he wants for its own sake, and if the latter, whether his desire for their existence depends on a false belief. One would also ask whether the victim really ought to believe that there are no such properties. And one might in the end have to ask whether, if there were such properties, something else would be false which the victim wants to be true. But these are just the questions which the world-view constructor poses about every kind of thing whose instantiation he might want for its own sake. And since his task is too huge for him to dispense with partial and preliminary sketches he can be glad of piecemeal efforts to resolve or mitigate particular metaphysical want and belief conflicts, even though improved solutions may well be deducible from his ultimate construction.

List of Works Cited

ACH, N., *Über den Willensakt und das Temperament* (Leipzig, 1910).
—— *Analyse des Willens* (Berlin, 1935).
ADAMS, R., 'The Problem of Total Devotion', in R. Audi and W. Wainwright (eds.), *Rationality, Religious Belief and Moral Commitment* (Ithaca, N.Y., 1986), 169–94.
ARMSTRONG, D. M., *A Materialist Theory of the Mind* (London, 1968).
AUNE, B., *Reason and Action* (Dordrecht, 1973).
AYER, A. J., 'Freedom and Necessity', in *Philosophical Essays* (London, 1954), 271–84.
BALDWIN, T., 'Ethical Non-Naturalism', in I. Hacking (ed.), *Exercises in Analysis* (Cambridge, 1985), 23–45.
BERKELEY, *Philosophical Commentaries* and *Principles of Human Knowledge*, in A. A. Luce and T. E. Jessop (eds.), *The Works of George Berkeley* (Edinburgh, 1948–57).
BLACKBURN, S., 'Moral Realism', in J. Casey (ed.), *Morality and Moral Reasoning* (London, 1971), 101–24.
—— *Spreading the Word* (Oxford, 1984).
—— 'Supervenience Revisited' in I. Hacking (ed.), *Exercises in Analysis* (Cambridge, 1985), 47–67.
BRENTANO, F., *The Foundation and Construction of Ethics* (1925; tr. E. Schneewind, London, 1973).
BROAD, C. D., *Examination of McTaggart's Philosophy*, i (Cambridge, 1933).
—— 'Determinism, Indeterminism and Libertarianism', in *Ethics and the History of Philosophy* (London, 1952), 195–217.
CARRUTHERS, P., *Introducing Persons* (London, 1986).
CHISHOLM, R. M., *Perceiving* (New York, 1957).
—— *The First Person* (Minneapolis, 1981).
CHURCHLAND, P. M., *Matter and Consciousness* (Cambridge, Mass., 1984).
DAVIDSON, D., *Essays on Actions and Events* (Oxford, 1980).
DAVIS, L., *Theory of Action* (Englewood Cliffs, N.J., 1979).
DENNETT, D. C., *Elbow Room* (Cambridge, Mass., 1984).
DONAGAN, A., *Choice* (London, 1987).

DUCASSE, C. J., 'Moore's "The Refutation of Idealism"', in P. Schilpp (ed.), *The Philosophy of G. E. Moore* (Evanston, Ill., 1942), 223–51.

EARMAN, J., *A Primer on Determinism* (Dordrecht, 1986).

FISCHER, J. M., 'Introduction: Responsibility and Freedom', in J. M. Fischer (ed.), *Moral Responsibility* (Ithaca, N.Y., 1986), 9–61.

FOSTER, J., *The Case for Idealism* (London, 1982).

—— and ROBINSON, H. (eds.), *Essays on Berkeley* (Oxford, 1985).

FRAASSEN, B. VAN, *Laws and Symmetry* (Oxford, 1989).

FRANKFURT, H., 'Alternate Possibilities and Moral Responsibility', *Journal of Philosophy*, 66 (1969), 828–39; repr. in J. M. Fischer (ed.), *Moral Responsibility*, 143–52.

—— 'Freedom of the Will and the Concept of a Person', *Journal of Philosophy*, 68 (1971), 5–20; repr. in G. Watson (ed.), *Free Will* (Oxford, 1982), 81–95.

FRANKL, V., *Man's Search for Meaning* (tr. I. Lasch, London, 1964).

GINET, C., 'Might we have no choice?', in K. Lehrer (ed.), *Freedom and Determinism* (New York, 1966), 87–104.

—— *On Action* (Cambridge, 1990).

GOLDMAN, A., *A Theory of Human Action* (Englewood Cliffs, N.J., 1970).

GRUNBERGER, R., *A Social History of the Third Reich* (Harmondsworth, 1974).

HARDIN, C. L., *Colour for Philosophers* (Indianapolis, 1988).

HONDERICH, T., *A Theory of Determinism* (Oxford, 1988).

HOPKINS, G. M., 'On Personality, Grace and Free Will', in C. Devlin (ed.), *Sermons and Devotional Writings* (Oxford, 1959), 146–59.

HORNSBY, J., *Actions* (London, 1980).

INWAGEN, P. VAN, *An Essay on Free Will* (Oxford, 1983).

JACKSON, F., *Perception* (Cambridge, 1977).

JAMES, W., *Principles of Psychology* (1890; Dover edn., New York, 1950).

JEFFREY, R., *The Logic of Decision* (2nd edn., Chicago, 1983).

KANE, R., *Free Will and Values* (Albany, N.Y., 1985).

—— 'Principles of Reason', *Erkenntnis*, 24 (1986), 115–36.

KENNY, A., *The Metaphysics of Mind* (Oxford, 1989).

LEHRER, K., 'An empirical disproof of determinism?', in K. Lehrer (ed.), *Freedom and Determinism* (New York, 1966), 175–202.

—— 'Cans without ifs', *Analysis*, 29 (1968–9), 29–32.

LEWIS, D., 'Are we free to break the laws?', *Theoria*, 47 (1981), 113–21; repr. in *Philosophical Papers*, ii (Oxford, 1986), 291–8.

LLOYD, A. C., 'The Self in Berkeley's Philosophy', in J. Foster and H. Robinson (eds.), *Essays on Berkeley* (Oxford, 1985), 187–209.

LOCKE, D., 'Three Concepts of Free Action', *Proceedings of the Aristotelian Society*, supp. vol. 49 (1975), 95–112.

LOCKWOOD, M., *Mind, Brain and the Quantum* (Oxford, 1989).

McCANN, H., 'Volition and Basic Action', *Philosophical Review*, 83 (1974), 451–73.

McDOWELL, J., 'Aesthetic Value, Objectivity and the Fabric of the World', in E. Schaper (ed.), *Pleasure, Preference and Value* (Cambridge, 1983), 1–16.

McGINN, C., *The Character of Mind* (Oxford, 1982).

—— *The Subjective View* (Oxford, 1983).

MACKIE, J. L., *Truth, Probability and Paradox* (Oxford, 1973).

—— *The Cement of the Universe* (Oxford, 1974).

—— *Problems from Locke* (Oxford, 1976).

—— *Ethics* (Harmondsworth, 1977).

McTAGGART, J. M. E., *Studies in the Hegelian Dialectic* (Cambridge, 1896).

MAXWELL, G., 'Rigid Designators and Mind-Brain Identity', in C. Wade Savage (ed.), *Perception and Cognition* (Minneapolis, 1978), 365–403.

MELLOR, D. H., 'In Defense of Dispositions', *Philosophical Review*, 83 (1974), 157–81.

—— 'Counting Corners Correctly', *Analysis*, 42 (1982–3), 96–7.

MICHOTTE, A. and PRÜM, E., 'Étude expérimentale sur le choix voluntaire', *Archives de Psychologie*, 10 (1910), 113–320.

MOORE, A., *The Infinite* (London, 1990).

MULLIGAN, K., and SMITH, B., 'A Relational Theory of the Act', *Topoi*, 5 (1986), 115–30.

MUNDLE, C. W. K., *Perception: Facts and Theories* (Oxford, 1971).

NAGEL, T., *The View from Nowhere* (Oxford, 1986).

NATHAN, N. M. L., 'Simple Colours', *Philosophy*, 61 (1986), 345–53.

—— 'Weak Materialism', in H. Robinson (ed.), *Objections to Physicalism* (Oxford, 1992).

NOZICK, R., *Philosophical Explanations* (Cambridge, Mass., 1981).

O'SHAUGHNESSY, B., *The Will* (Cambridge, 1980).

O'SULLIVAN, L., *Fascism* (London, 1983).

PARFIT, D., 'Personal Identity', *Philosophical Review*, 80 (1971), 3–27.

—— *Reasons and Persons* (Oxford, 1984).

PEACOCKE, C., *Holistic Explanation* (Oxford, 1979).

—— *Sense and Content* (Oxford, 1983).

—— 'Imagination, Experience and Possibility', in J. Foster and H. Robinson (eds.), Essays on Berkeley (Oxford, 1985), 19–35.

PFÄNDER, A., *Phänomenologie des Wollens* (2nd edn., Tübingen, 1963).

POLLOCK, J., *Contemporary Theories of Knowledge* (London, 1987).

PRICHARD, H. A., 'Acting, Willing and Desiring', in *Moral Obligation* (Oxford, 1949), 187–98.

QUINE, W. V., 'The Ways of Paradox', in *The Ways of Paradox and Other Essays* (New York, 1966), 3–20.

ROSS, J. F., 'Creation', *Journal of Philosophy*, 77 (1980), 614–29.

RUSSELL, B., *The Problems of Philosophy* (London, 1912).

—— *The Analysis of Mind* (London, 1921).

—— *Human Knowledge: Its Scope and Limits* (London, 1948).

RYLE, G., *The Concept of Mind* (1949; Penguin edn., Harmondsworth, 1963).

SCHLICK, M., *General Theory of Knowledge* (1925; tr. A. Blumberg, Vienna and New York, 1974).

SCHOPENHAUER, *The World as Will and Representation* (tr. E. J. F. Payne, New York, 1966).

—— *Essay on the Freedom of the Will* (tr. K. Kolenda, Indianapolis, 1960).

SEARLE, J., *Intentionality* (Cambridge, 1983).

SMITH, B., 'On the Cognition of States of Affairs', in K. Mulligan (ed.), *Speech Act and Sachverhalt* (Dordrecht, 1987), 189–225.

SMITH, J. C., and HOGAN, B., *Criminal Law: Cases and Materials* (3rd edn., London, 1986).

SMITH, P., and JONES, O. R., *The Philosophy of Mind* (Cambridge, 1986).

SPRIGGE, T., *The Vindication of Absolute Idealism* (Edinburgh, 1983).

STRAWSON, G., *Freedom and Belief* (Oxford, 1986).

SWINBURNE, R. G., *The Coherence of Theism* (Oxford, 1977).

—— *The Evolution of the Soul* (Oxford, 1986).

WELLS, H. M., 'The Phenomenology of Acts of Choice', *British Journal of Psychology*, monograph supplement 4 (1927), 1–155.

ZIMMERMAN, M. J., *An Essay on Human Action* (New York, 1984).

Index

D0142791

Victorian Urban Settings

LITERATURE AND SOCIETY IN VICTORIAN BRITAIN
VOLUME I
GARLAND REFERENCE LIBRARY OF THE HUMANITIES
VOLUME 1889

Literature and Society in Victorian Britain

Sally Mitchell, *Series Editor*

Victorian Urban Settings
Essays on the Nineteenth-Century
City and Its Contexts
edited by Debra N. Mancoff
and D.J. Trela

Victorian Urban Settings

Essays on the Nineteenth-Century City and Its Contexts

Edited by
Debra N. Mancoff and D.J. Trela

Garland Publishing, Inc.
New York and London
1996

Library of Congress Cataloging-in-Publication Data

Victorian urban settings : essays on the nineteenth-century city and its contexts / [edited by] Debra N. Mancoff and D.J. Trela.
       p.   cm. — (Garland reference library of the humanities ; v. 1889.
Literature and society in Victorian Britain ; v. 1)
    "Originally presented as conference papers at the 1993 annual meeting of
the Midwest Victorian Studies Association"—Pref.
    Includes index.
    ISBN 0-8153-1949-5 (alk. paper)
    1. Great Britain—History—Victoria, 1837–1901—Congresses. 2. City
and town life—Great Britain—History—19th century—Congresses. 3. Cities and towns—Great Britain—History—19th century—Congresses. 4. English fiction—19th century—History and criticism—Congresses. 5. London
(England)—History—1800–1950—Congresses. 6. City and town life in
literature—Congresses. 7. London (England)—In literature—Congresses.
8. Cities and towns in literature—Congresses. 9. City and town life in art—
Congresses. 10. London (England)—In art—Congresses. 11. Cities and
towns in art—Congresses. I. Mancoff, Debra N., 1950–   . II. Trela,
D. J. (Dale J.) III. Midwest Victorian Studies Association. Meeting (1993)
IV. Series: Garland reference library of the humanities ; vol. 1889. V. Series: Garland reference library of the humanities. Literature and society in
Victorian Britain ; v. 1.
DA550.V544 1996
941.081—dc20   96-12754
                                                                  CIP

Printed on acid-free, 250-year-life paper
Manufactured in the United States of America

Contents

List of Plates

1. Building elevations on Cannon Street, London, detail nos. 52-76. (James Bunstone Bunning, artist.) Pen, ink, and watercolor on paper. Original 143½ x 21¾ inches, 1856. Corporation of London Records Office.
2. Building elevations on Cannon Street, London, detail, Unity Association Buildings to no. 94. (James Bunstone Bunning, artist.) Pen, ink, and watercolor on paper. Original 143½ x 21¾ inches, 1856. Corporation of London Records Office.
3. Building elevations on Cannon Street, London, detail nos. 110-126. (James Bunstone Bunning, artist.) Pen, ink, and watercolor on paper. Original 143½ x 21¾ inches, 1856. Corporation of London Records Office.
4. Perspective view of Berens, Blumberg and Company, nos. 2-6 Cannon St. (William Hoskings, architect.) Engraving. *Illustrated London News* (1856) 17.
5. Map of Scotland showing the homes of the poets.
6. George Cruikshank. "London Going out of Town," in George Cruikshank, *Scraps and Sketches*, Part II. London: George Cruikshank, 1829. Collection of the Grunwald Center for the Graphic Arts, UCLA, Richard Vogler Cruikshank Collection.
7. George Cruikshank. "Seven Dials," in Charles Dickens, *Sketches by Boz*. London: John Macrone, 1837. From the *Graphic Works of George Cruikshank*, New York, Dover Publications, 1979.
8. George Cruikshank. "Oliver Claimed by his Affectionate Friends," in Charles Dickens, "Oliver Twist," *Bentley's Miscellany*, 1837-1839. From the *Graphic Works of George Cruikshank*, New York, Dover Publications, 1979.

Preface

*I*n nineteenth-century Britain, the city was the stage for life. From avenues to alleys, from the concert stage to the music hall, from the meanest market to the grandest gallery, Victorian culture displayed a distinctive urban orientation. Every mode of expression – literary, musical, theatrical, architectural, visual – flourished in metropolitan communities. A striking reciprocity resulted; as the city shaped the cultural identity for Victorian England, cultural and artistic activity shaped the city.

This reciprocal development is the unifying subject for *Victorian Urban Settings: Essays on the Nineteenth-Century City and Its Contexts.* The eleven interdisciplinary essays were originally presented as conference papers at the 1993 annual meeting of the Midwest Victorian Studies Association. Approaching the topic of the city as a cultural agent from the points of view of diverse fields, including art history, literary criticism, history, biography, and urban planning, proved a productive path of inquiry and a provocative stimulus for discussion. The present collection retains the multifaceted, interdisciplinary approach of the conference, as well as its central thematic question: How did the selection (or rejection) of an urban setting provide the context for a representative product of Victorian art or culture?

In his introduction "An Age of Great Cities," Harold Perkin paints a vivid portrait of Victorian Britain as the premier industrialized nation. Perkin's themes lay the groundwork for the essays that follow: the impact of changing population on established social structures, the transformation of the townscape, the quest for identity in the course of relocation, the physical restructuring of the inner city and suburbs, and the increased disparity between the enclaves of the rich and the poor. Although Perkin exposes the harsh realities of evolving industrial society, he also considers the new cultural advantages that pioneered programs of mutual aid and self-improvement on an unprecedented scale. Both the problems and the solutions resonate with our contemporary urban circumstance, suggesting that the current state of the city is the rich and burdensome legacy of its Victorian predecessor.

The first group of essays, "Mapping the Victorian City," investigates the character of the city through creative definitions of topography. In "Commercial Sites: The Early Victorian Development of Cannon Street," Linda R. Krause charts the expansion of Cannon Street in central London, detailing builders' and architects' responses to both changing architectural aesthetics and shifting commercial demands dating from the Regency to the mid-Victorian era. The early Victorian mixture of warehouses, large and small company offices and ground-floor shops maintained a balance between competing commercial demands, Krause argues, that late-Victorian monumentality lost as development grew more impersonal. Mary Burgan examines a very different mode of civic topography in "Mapping Contagion in Victorian London: Disease in the East End" by documenting the marginalizing and typing according to class and income that occurred throughout London. Her essay surveys primarily middle-class responses to poverty and its attendant filth and contagion. While responses to the mapping of contagion could lead to reforms like the creation of Victoria Park, which provided fresh air and open spaces for the working classes, it also not surprisingly generated fears about proximity to poverty. Moving the focus from the city to the suburbs, Joseph F. Lamb's essay "Symbols of Success in Suburbia: The Establishment of Artists' Communities in Late Victorian London," follows London's art elite as they leave the confines of the city. The new and distinctive building type – "the studio home" – proved to be more than a measure of an artist's financial success; it became a public statement of the role of the artist as social celebrity.

The second section, "Constructing Identity in an Urban Setting," considers how the city as social entity intersected with the defining actions of specific communities. Two essays address cultural invention as a response to the grim reality of urban poverty. In "London, Dickens, and the Theatre of Homelessness," Murray Baumgarten identifies a "social economy of theatrical representation" in the novels of Charles Dickens. No Victorian writer was more intimately connected with or attached to the city than Dickens, and Baumgarten sees in his work the potential of the urban world as a moral site, a glimmer of hope that bridges divisions of class and society. In contrast to other essays in this collection (especially Burgan, Prasch and Jacobs) Baumgarten sees Dickens's emphasis on the interactions between classes in London more positively as a classroom for "city-knowing" and "city-thinking." With all its problems, the urban world is also the site of moral self-making. By contrast, Edward Jacobs examines an active – and textual – response to economic oppression in "Disvaluing the Popular: London Street Culture, 'Industrial Literacy,' and the Emergence of Mass Culture in Victorian England." "Penny gaff" theatricals and penny fiction "bloods" emerged in the context of a distinctive street culture that was largely eradicated by police action and legislative campaigns by the early 1850s. Essentially the street culture of the time resisted regularization by refusing to conform to rote, assembly line techniques in industry or education. Primarily for this reason, Jacobs argues, this street culture was destroyed rather than absorbed or altered by the industrial juggernaut. Much as rural life-styles were changed by industrialization, so also was city life.

The remaining two essays in this section consider women's responses to the disruption of relocation. In "The City, the Country, and Communities of Singing Women: Music in the Novels of Elizabeth Gaskell," Alisa M. Clapp defines the importance of community music-making for uprooted women. For many women in Gaskell's novels childhood songs and musical memories mark the single, unsevered link to home and an oasis of community that the rural immigrant can find in her new urban home. So long as community, which Clapp connects with Gaskell's rural aesthetic, was fostered, women were in some sense safe. However, as a form of personal display or aggrandizement, Gaskell associated music with urban individualism and danger and therefore viewed it far less favorably. Florence S. Boos considers the power of poetry as a force of self-identification in "'Oor Location': Scotswomen Poets and the Transition from Rural to Urban Culture." Subjected to land clearances, industrialization, and economic decline, a small but distinctive group of women writers – nearly forgotten today – preserved their culture and their language in their poems and songs even as their physical ties to the land were destroyed. These poets did not produce a unified message but rather documented and bitterly deplored changes that – like Gaskell's women – they had no real opportunity to resist.

In the final section "Imaging the Victorian City," the authors assess how the visual record of the urban experience influenced public opinions about the city and its circumstances. Anne L. Helmreich explores Cruikshank's satirical and didactic art in its London context in "Reforming London: George Cruikshank and the Victorian Age." Although best known as a master of Regency caricature, his shift in the early Victorian era to social reform, family values and the crusade for temperance paralleled and even helped to shape corresponding changes in British urban culture. His art also begins to view the poor as "other," a perspective increasingly common in the Victorian period and particularly graphically reinforced by later photographers. Two articles address this use of the new medium. In "Photography and the Image of the London Poor," Thomas Prasch charts the manipulative practices of posed pictures, passed off as documentary evidence, in segregating the disadvantaged and defining them as a separate race. This view could have the added effect of limiting society's responsibility to the worse off since racial differences could not be overcome through charity, education, slum clearance or other reforms. Prasch shows how photographic images by John Thomson were based on earlier conventions drawn from paintings that were now used to perpetuate Victorian values. Similarly, in "Midnight Scenes and Social Photographs: Thomas Annan's Glasgow," Ian Spring demonstrates that the aesthetics of a photograph – in terms of light, angle, and shot – shape the perceptions of a city and its population. Spring's analysis of Annan's photography as an "ethnographic practice" imprinted on its subjects carries on the racial typing themes of both Thomas Prasch and Mary Burgan. Spring further suggests that far from Annan's work generating reform of slum conditions, as is often thought, his photographs resulted from Victorian fascination with an "other" that was about to disappear due to planned slum clearances.

The role of self-definition is the subject for Sarah V. Barnes's "Lessons in Stone: Architecture and Academic Ethos in an Urban Setting." Barnes explores the multiple reasons for the collegiate-Gothic design for what became the University of Manchester. Alfred Waterhouse's designs were functional, buildable and adaptable. They were particularly appropriate for a modern, urban university oriented to the sciences but still teaching the humanities. In short, "Gothic Revival" was also pre-eminently Victorian and as such well-suited to an industrial urban setting. Through her inquiry into the use of an historicist style for a new and innovative building site, Barnes presents the quadrangle of the University of Manchester as a metaphor for civic pride, social mobility, and middle-class identity.

Each of these sections explores different cultural issues, but as an ensemble they present a detailed and vital portrait of the Victorian urban experience. Our objective in this portrayal was neither comprehensive nor definitive, but to demonstrate that the diversity of the Victorian city as a background for cultural expression demanded from scholars a diversity in methodology. This collection celebrates both the richness of Victorian urban contexts and the riches of interdisciplinary scholarship. From a single point of departure we hope to suggest varied routes to explore this complex and paradoxical society.

A collection of essays is in every way a collaborative effort. First and foremost, the editors of *Victorian Urban*

Settings would like to thank the authors for their hard work throughout the challenging process of transforming a collection of conference papers into an integrated ensemble of essays. On the authors' behalf we thank the following institutions – the Annan Gallery; the City Art Center, Edinburgh; Corporation of the London Records Office; Dover Publications; Grunwald Center for the Graphic Arts, UCLA at the Armand Hammer Museum of Art; the Lilly Library at Indiana University; and the University of Manchester Communications Office – for allowing us to reproduce works from their collections. We also extend our thanks to those who made the original conference possible, the officers and the executive board of the Midwest Victorian Studies Association, in particular MVSA President Patrick Brantlinger. Special appreciation goes to Linda K. Hughes and John R. Reed for their advice at the start of the project. We would like to acknowledge the generous support of our home institutions, Beloit College and Roosevelt University, with a special note of gratitude to Provost Stuart Fagan and Arts and Sciences Dean Ronald Tallman for their continuing support. David Heesen of Beloit College prepared the manuscript with diligence and care. And finally, we thank the two people without whom this project would not have been possible. Sally Mitchell, editor of the Garland Publishing's Literature and Society in Victorian Britain series, gave us encouragement by selecting our work as the lead entry in her new series and Gary Kuris, with his expertise and good humor, gave the support we needed along the way.

Debra N. Mancoff, Beloit College
D.J. Trela, Roosevelt University

Victorian Urban Settings

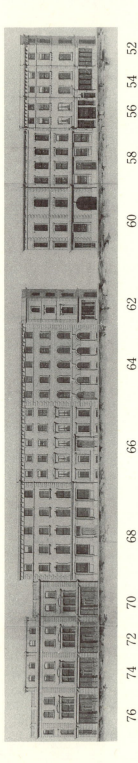

76   74   72   70   68   66   64   62   60   58   56   54   52

1. *Building elevations on Cannon Street, London, detail nos. 52–76. (James Bunstone Bunning, artist.) Pen, ink, and watercolor on paper. Original 143½ x 21¾ inches, 1856. Corporation of London Records Office.*

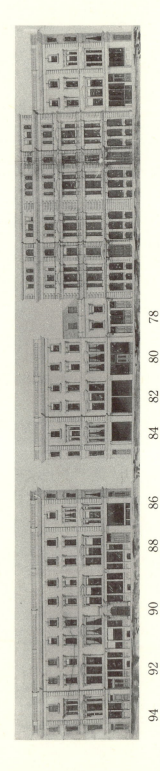

94   92   90   88   86   84   82   80   78

2. *Building elevations on Cannon Street, London, detail, Unity Association Buildings to no. 94. (James Bunstone Bunning, artist.) Pen, ink, and watercolor on paper. Original 143½ x 21¾ inches, 1856. Corporation of London Records Office.*

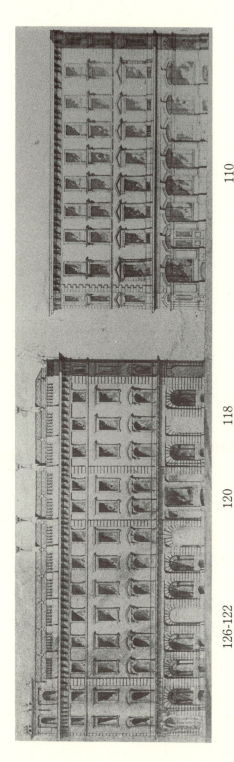

3. Building elevations on Cannon Street, London, detail nos. 110-126. (James Bunstone Bunning, artist.) Pen, ink, and watercolor on paper. Original 143½ x 21¾ inches, 1856. Corporation of London Records Office.

110

118

120

126-122

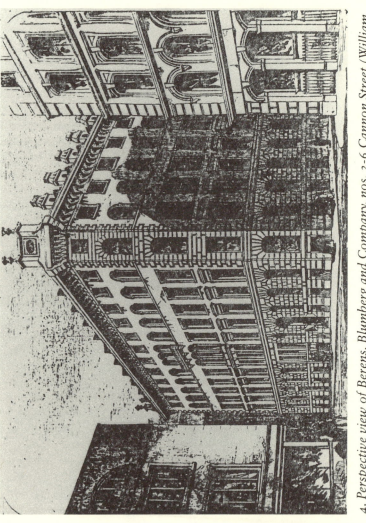

4. *Perspective view of Berens, Blumberg and Company, nos. 2-6 Cannon Street (William Hoskings, architect.) Engraving.* Illustrated London News (*1856*) 17.

Inverness

Aberdeen ⑤

⑤

Glasgow
•②

Edinburgh

5. Map of Scotland showing the homes of the poets.

6. George Cruikshank. "London Going out of Town," in George Cruikshank, Scraps and Sketches, Part II. London: George Cruikshank, 1829. Collection of the Grunwald Center for the Graphic Arts, UCLA, Richard Vogler Cruikshank Collection.

141

7. *George Cruikshank.* "Seven Dials," *in Charles Dickens,* Sketches by Boz. *London: John Macrone, 1837. From the* Graphic Works of George Cruikshank, *New York, Dover Publications, 1979.*

8. George Cruikshank. *"Oliver Claimed by his Affectionate Friends,"* in *Charles Dickens, "Oliver Twist,"* Bentley's Miscellany, *1837-1839. From the* Graphic Works of George Cruikshank, *New York, Dover Publications, 1979.*

9. George Cruikshank. "Battle of A-gin-Court," in George Cruikshank, The Comic Almanack. London: Tilt and Bogue, October 1838. From the Graphic Works of George Cruikshank, New York, Dover Publications, 1979.

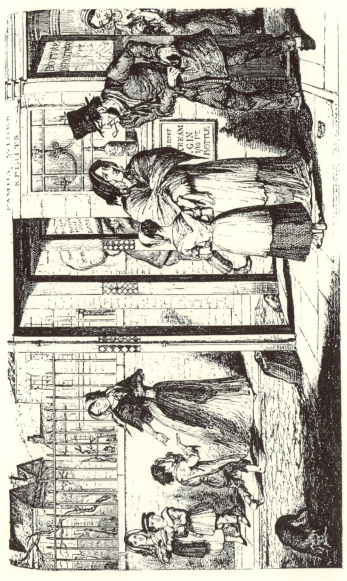

10. George Cruikshank. "Unable to find Employment, . . ." in George Cruikshank, The Bottle. London: D. Bogue, 1847. From the Graphic Works of George Cruikshank, New York, Dover Publications, 1979.

11. George Cruikshank. "The Maniac Father . . ." in George Cruikshank, The Drunkard's Children. London: D. Bogue, 1848. Collection of the Grunwald Center for the Graphic Arts, UCLA, Richard Vogler Cruikshank Collection.

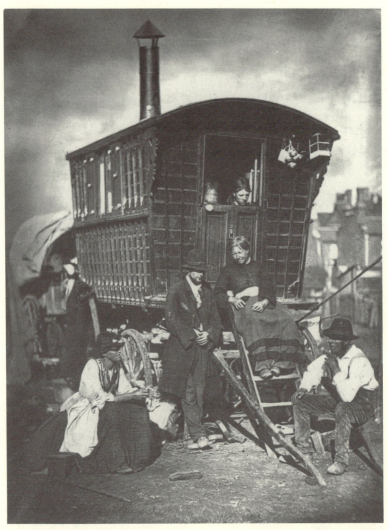

12. *John Thomson.* "London Nomades," *in John Thomson and Adolphe Smith*, Street Life in London. *London: Sampson Low, Marston, Searle and Rivington, 1877, facing 10. Photograph. Courtesy of Lilly Library, Indiana University, Bloomington.*

THE LONDON COSTERMONGER.

" Here Pertaters ! Kearots and Turnups ! fine Brockello-o-o ! "

[*From a Daguerreotype by* BEARD.]

13. Richard Beard. "The London Costermonger," in Henry Mayhew,
London Labour and the Labouring Poor (4 volumes). London: Griffin,
Bohn and Company, 1861-62, 1:13. Engraving after daguerreotype.
Courtesy of Lilly Library, Indiana University, Bloomington.

THE RAT-CATCHERS OF THE SEWERS.

*14. Richard Beard. "The Rat-Catcher of the Sewers," in Henry Mayhew,
London Labour and the Labouring Poor (4 volumes). London: Griffin,
Bohn and Company, 1861-62, 3: facing 425. Engraving after daguerreo-
type. Courtesy of Lilly Library, Indiana University, Bloomington.*

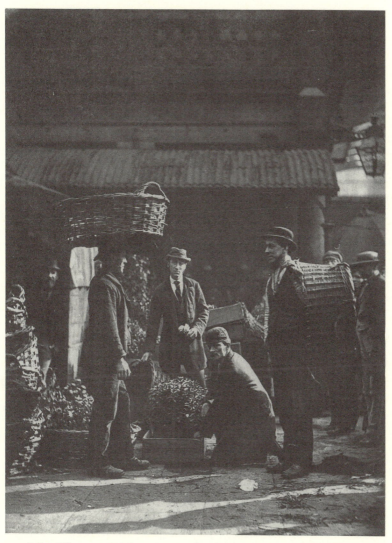

15. *John Thomson. "Covent Garden Labourers," in John Thomson and Adolphe Smith,* Street Life in London. *London: Sampson Low, Marston, Searle and Rivington, 1877, 74. Photograph. Courtesy of Lilly Library, Indiana University, Bloomington.*

16. *John Thomson. "The 'Crawlers,'" in John Thomson and Adolphe Smith,* Street Life in London. *London: Sampson Low, Marston, Searle and Rivington, 1877, 117. Photograph. Courtesy of Lilly Library, Indiana University, Bloomington.*

17. David Octavius Hill. In Memoriam: The Calton, *1862. Oil on panel, 6³/₄ x 8⁵/₈ inches. City Art Centre, Edinburgh.*

18. *George Cruikshank. Frontispiece for* Midnight Scenes and Social Photographs, *by Shadow (Alexander Brown), published Glasgow, 1858.*

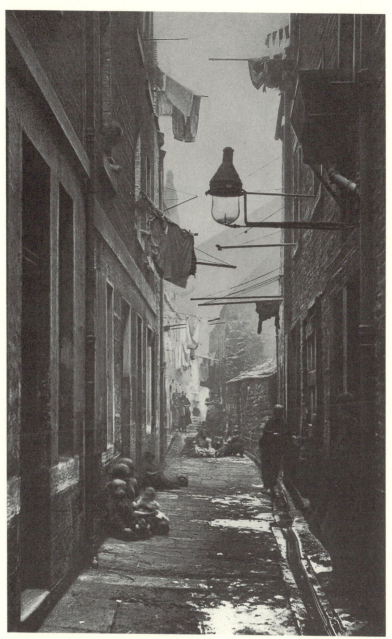

19. Thomas Annan. 80 High Street, Glasgow, 1868. Calotype. T&R Annan & Sons, Ltd.

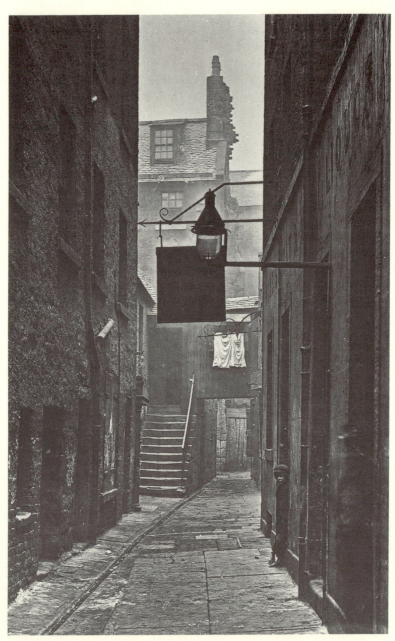

20. Thomas Annan. 18 Saltmarket, Glasgow, 1868. Calotype. T&R Annan & Sons, Ltd.

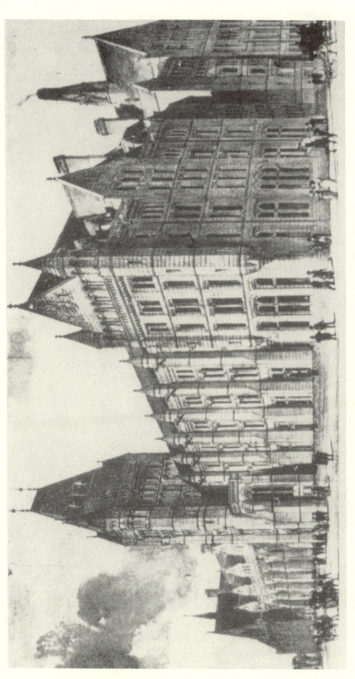

21. Alfred Waterhouse. "Manchester Architecture: Owens College," in The Builder November 7, 1896: 380. University of Manchester, School of Architecture Collection.

22. *David Wrightson. "Manchester Town Hall in 1977," in J.H.G. Archer, "A Civic Achievement: the Building of Manchester Town Hall. Part I. The Commissioning,"* Transactions of the Lancaster and Cheshire Antiquarian Society *81 (1982): 2.*

23. A. Brothers. "The Owens College," in H.B. Charlton, Portrait of a University, 1851- 1951. Manchester: Manchester University Press, 1951, (facing page 5).

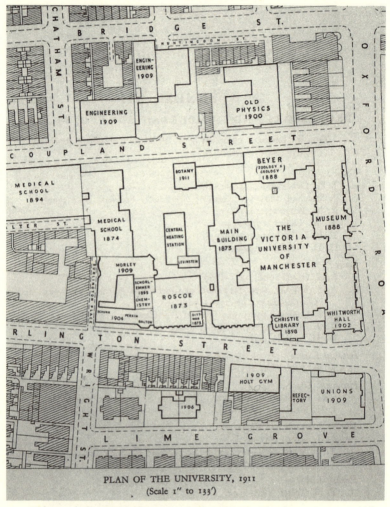

PLAN OF THE UNIVERSITY, 1911
(Scale 1" to 133')

24. *"Plan of the University, 1911," in H.B. Charlton*, Portrait of a University, 1851- 1951. *Manchester: Manchester University Press*, 1951, 171.

25. "The Oxford Road Frontage with the Whitworth Hall, 1902," H.B. Charlton, Portrait of a University, 1851-1951. Manchester: Manchester University Press, 1951, (facing page 75).

Introduction:
An Age of Great Cities

Harold Perkin

*I*n 1843 Robert Vaughan published a prescient book entitled *The Age of Great Cities*. A Dissenting minister who believed that the Victorian urban middle classes were the moral leaders of society and would purge the corruption and selfishness of the feudal aristocracy and tame the fecklessness and violence of the working masses, he affirmed that "If any nation is to be lost or saved by the character of its great cities, our own is that nation." Modern industry and the new railways

> will necessarily tend to swell the larger towns into still greater magnitude and to diminish the weight of many smaller places, as well as of the rural population generally in social affairs. Everywhere we trace this disposition to converge upon great points. It avails nothing to complain of this tendency as novel, inconsiderate, hazardous. The pressure towards such an issue is irresistible, nor do we see the slightest prospect of it ceasing to do so. (91)

He was right. Eight years later the Census reported that for the first time in any country the urban population had outgrown the rural. In 1801 four out of five Britons lived in the countryside; by 1901 four out of five lived in towns, most of them larger than all but a dozen or so towns in the eighteenth century. For the master narrative of the Victorians was not simply that they lived in an age of great cities but that they lived in urban settings that were increasing in size and population at accelerating speed.

Both the urgent social problems and the dynamic progress can be traced to this explosive urban growth. George Cruikshank's famous cartoon of "London Going out of Town" reproduced in Anne Helmreich's chapter in this volume, showing "the march of bricks and mortar" across the green surrounding fields, epitomized the experience of most Victorians. As the *Manchester Guardian* observed on 17 November 1832, "The manufacturing system as it exists in Great Britain, and the inconceivably rapid increase of large towns under it, are without previous parallel in the history of the world." But London and many pre-industrial cities grew as fast as the new factory towns and, surprisingly, the fastest growing towns were the new seaside resorts which catered for the growing leisure of an urbanized and affluent society (Perkin, *Crowd*, Ch. 5). The population of Britain more than trebled during the nineteenth century, from 10.5 to 37 million, and most of the natural increase went to the towns and suburbs. The social problems of poverty, overcrowding, public health, crime, law and order, drunkenness, and mental illness – none of them new but all of a novel scale and intensity – stemmed from the crowding together of vast numbers of newcomers in locations totally unprepared for their coming. But so too did the solutions to those problems, forced on reluctant, often makeshift local and national government departments by "the pressure of facts" against the prevailing philosophy of *laissez-faire.* And, contrary to much contemporary nostalgia which yearned for the supposed social harmony and benevolent paternalism of the rural past, the growing towns contrived to create the institutions of a civilized social life, from new churches and chapels to gentlemen's clubs and workers' friendly societies, from pubs and temperance meetings to music halls and brass bands, from theaters and libraries to hospitals and colleges, on a scale unknown in the "Merrie England" of the mythical past. The "insensate industrial town" was pullulating with life, far more so than Oliver Goldsmith's lost "sweet Auburns" of the eighteenth century or the somnolent television suburbs of the late twentieth.

The difficulty for the Victorians was that the problems came first, the solutions only later. Partly because of this, there were really three Victorian ages not one, whose urban experiences were almost as different as if they had been in three different lands. The first age, from the accession of the Queen in 1837 to the Great Exhibiton of 1851, was the age of Thackeray and the early Dickens, of the aristocratic Pitt Crawley and the adventuress Becky Sharp, of Oliver Twist, Bill Sykes and the criminal under-world of pre-industrial London, and of the violent strikes and Chartist riots in the new industrial towns. The second, from 1851 to the early seventies, was the so-called mid-Victorian boom, the age of Anthony Trollope and George Eliot, of the condescending Pallisers and the benevolent Dorothea Casaubon, of Gladstone and John Bright and their reconciliation between the classes in the capacious Liberal Party, of what I have called elsewhere a viable class society in which the classes learned to live with each other without violence and tried to find solutions to their prob-lems (Perkin, *Origins*, Ch. 9).[1] The third, from the mid-seventies to the Queen's death, was the age of Oscar Wilde and Bernard Shaw, of skepticism and questioning, of frivolous plutocrats and solemn socialists, of Lord Ran-dolph Churchill and Joseph Chamberlain, Tory Demo-crats and Social Imperialists, and the first fears of Brit-ain's economic and imperial decline.

This is of course a vast oversimplification of a three-generation period which is still thought of as a unified whole, the source of "Victorian values" for ignorant and meretricious politicians, but which we now know to have been diverse, pluralistic, full of contradictory trends and countercurrents that swirled around each other in waves and eddies too fast and numerous to photograph. Yet the main stream flowed strongly enough in each age, carrying boats large and small along with it, to discern the general directions, which still influence Britons' lives today. For the Victorians, in all three generations, created our mod-ern world, and they created it in the cities.

1. *Fear and Loathing in the Early Victorian City*

The first impact of the growing towns on the Victorian imagination was one of fear and loathing. Foreign observers were struck by the foulness and stench, the violence and disorder of British cities. A French visitor, Leon Faucher in 1844 bracketed the new industrial towns with the old commercial cities for equal condemnation:

> The centres of industrialism are seats of corruption, in which the population enjoy an atmosphere neither more salubrious nor moral, than in those large towns, which are formed by the demands of commerce. From this point of view, *Manchester appears almost on a level with London or Liverpool.* (Faucher 90-91)

Frederick Engels in the same year thought no city could be worse than Manchester. Behind the main thoroughfares with their shops of dazzling splendour and the affluent houses of the bourgeoisie lay the miserable and squalid slums of the working classes. Right in the middle by the cathedral, from Ducie Bridge over the River Irk,

> One looks into piles of rubbish, the refuse, filth, and decaying matter of the courts on the steep left bank of the river. Here one house is packed very closely upon another, and because of the steep pitch of the bank a part of every house is visible. All of them are blackened with smoke, crumbling, old, with broken window panes and window frames. The background is formed by old factory buildings, which resemble barracks. On the right, low-lying bank stands a long row of houses and factories. . . .The background here is formed by the paupers' cemetery and the stations of the railways to Liverpool and Leeds. Behind there is the workhouse, Manchester's 'Poor Law Bastille.' It is built on a hill, like a citadel, and from behind its high walls and battlements looks down threateningly upon the working-class quarter that lies below. (Engels 60)

Manchester was the "shock city of the age," in Asa Briggs's phrase, which foreigners and English southerners visited to see the future and fear it (Briggs, Ch. 3), but in fact this was its pre-industrial core, much like the older commercial cities, and it was the Victorians' task to replace these warrens with neat gridirons of solidly built row houses, some of which still survive in gentrified condition. Edwin

Chadwick's famous *Sanitary Report* of 1842 found that the wynds and courts of the pre-industrial cities like London, Edinburgh and Bristol were far more offensive and disease-ridden with cholera, typhoid and "low fever" (typhus). Industrial Birmingham, by contrast, was "distinguished apparently by an immunity to fever, and the general health of the population is high, although the occupations are such as are elsewhere deemed prejudicial to health" (357).

Contemporary moralists like Joseph Fletcher, school inspector and moral statistician, blamed all the social problems of the age on the concentration of "the masses employed in mining and manufacturing pursuits":

> Here, brought into close neighbourhood, and estranged from the influence of superior example, they are subject to temptations, hazards, and incitements far beyond those which approach the rural cottage; ignorant and largely depraved, they are likewise capable of combination [in trade unions and political movements]; and exigencies of a reeling alternation of prosperity and adversity; to say nothing of all the evils which improvidence and heathenism pour out upon themselves. (193-94)

Despite the middle- and upper-class fears of mass violence, however, political crimes arising out of strikes and Chartist riots formed only a tiny fraction of the total, averaging only 170 per annum in 1834-56 and only 425 per annum in 1857-92, when police activity and records were much fuller and the population larger. More specifically, "riot and sedition," an offence introduced in 1839 to deal with Chartist violence, increased from 231 arrests in that year to 962 in 1842, but then shrank to 2 in 1844 and 1 in 1855 before disappearing out of view (Gatrell and Hadden 371-72). Fear of revolt and revolution was far more vivid than the actuality.

Civil crime, on the other hand, was booming in the early nineteenth century. All the towns, industrial, pre-industrial and leisure resorts, suffered from a rising wave of crime, as newcomers flooded into crowded spaces and overwhelmed the old social controls and mainly amateur defenses of law and order before the new professional police and community values could establish themselves. Between 1805 and 1848, the numbers committed to trial for indictable offences in England and Wales multplied more than six-fold, from 4,605 to 30,369, and the numbers convicted more than eight-fold, from 2,783 to 22,900 (Porter 365). This was no statistical artefact of increased police activity, since the new "preventive police," in London from 1829, the boroughs from 1839, and the counties only from 1856, left prosecution entirely to the victims. Most crimes were against property (theft, burglary and larceny), and rose and fell before 1857 with unemployment and depression – only later did the cycle reverse, with "opportunity crime" rising and falling with prosperity (MacNab; Gatrell and Hadden 367-69, 377, 385). The later nineteenth century saw a remarkable decline in reported crime, down to levels scarcely seen before or since, a testimony to the success of the Victorians in solving their most pressing social problems.

Much the same trajectory was taken by the female escape from urban poverty, prostitution. Here again, the older commercial centers and leisure towns offered better pickings than the new factory towns, whose more affluent male inhabitants resorted to the nearest city for their clandestine pleasures. Faucher in 1844 estimated known prostitutes in London at 15,000 and in Liverpool at 2,000, compared with only 750 in Manchester and 300 in Paisley. Other estimates for London in the 1840s ranged from 7,000 to 80,000; Mayhew reported 41,954 "disorderly prostitutes" arrested between 1850 and 1860 (Faucher 42n; Vaughan 227; Mayhew 215, 262-63). Yet, like crime in general, prostitution seems to have declined, or at least was more discreet, in the later nineteenth century, again to levels not seen before or since: an international survey on prostitution described London in 1914 as a gigantic "open-air cathedral" (Gatrell and Hadden 377; Harris 211)!

Drunkenness was rampant in early Victorian cities, as the gin palaces of the cartoons and the rantings of the temperance lecturers bear witness. Again, this was not new, as Hogarth's squalid "Gin Lane" and prosperous "Beer Street" of a hundred years earlier show, but it was on a new plane in the burgeoning towns of the industrial age. The temperance movement, as its name implies, set out to wean the poor from hard liquor on to more wholesome beer with some success, but beer itself increased to record levels of consumption in the 1870s, and became the target for "teetotallers" who eschewed alcohol of any kind. Temperance cafes and hotels, music halls and concerts offered alternatives to the universal pub but never replaced it. Later in the century the movement nearly captured the Liberal Party and closed down many pubs, with probably more loss to the Liberal vote than Irish Home Rule, but once again demonstrating how the Victorians tried to solve their problems by overkill (Harrison *passim*).

Given the fear and loathing of the new urban masses, it was not surprising that the affluent began to flee the cities. Faucher noted "the absence of the higher classes" in Manchester:

> The town, strictly speaking, . . . is only inhabited by shopkeepers and operatives; the merchants and manufacturers have detached villas situated in the country. This mode of existence excludes social intercourse, and leads to total absenteeism. And thus, at the very moment when the engines are stopped, and the counting houses closed, everything which was the thought – the authority – the impulsive force – the moral order of this immense industrial combination, flies from the town, and disappears in an instant. The rich man spreads his couch amid the beauties of the surrounding country and abandons the town to the operatives, publicans, mendicants, thieves, and prostitutes, merely taking the precaution to leave behind a police force [under the local Police Act of 1815], whose duty it is to preserve some little of material order in this pellmell of society. (Faucher 26-27)

London and some of the old country towns like Bath and York continued to have rich and poor living cheek by jowl, with courts and tenements hidden just behind the elegant squares and terraces, since the servant-keeping classes needed the services of the poor, the street traders, food and coal deliverers, crossing sweepers, and garbage collectors to maintain their labor-intensive life style. Even there the social distance between East End and West End was almost oriental. As Francis Place explained to Richard Cobden in 1840 in an attempt to explain why the Anti-Corn Law League could not unite the metropolis as it did the northern towns,

> London differs very widely from Manchester, and, indeed, from every other place on the face of the earth. It has no

> local or particular interest as a town, not even as to politics.
> Its several boroughs in this respect are like so many very
> populous places at a distance from one another, and the
> inhabitants of any one of them know nothing, or next to
> nothing, of the proceedings in any other, and not much
> indeed of their own.

Segregation and mutual ignorance led to hostility between
the workers and the rest, since fear and loathing worked
in both directions:

> The leaders – those among them who pay attention to public
> matters – are one and all at enmity with every other class
> of society. . . .They call the middle classes 'shopocrats,'
> 'usurers' (all profit being usury), 'moneymongers,' 'tyrants
> and oppressors of the working people,' and they link the
> middle classes with the aristocracy under the dignified
> appellation of 'murderers of society,' 'murderers of the
> people.' (Wallas 393-94)

In the face of such eye-witness evidence it is difficult
to agree with some "post-modern" historians who reject
the very existence of class in the nineteenth century or
dismiss it as only one factor among many, notably populism, gender, and patriotism. Reacting against "vulgar
Marxism," they seem to think that class conflict can only
exist between labor and capital, that it must be violent and
destructive to the brink of civil war, and that transparent
attempts by Liberal politicians like Cobden and Bright to
unite the middle and working classes against the landed
aristocracy, or by Tory paternalists like Shaftesbury and
Disraeli to unite workers and aristocrats against the industrial bourgeoisie, do not count because they cut across
Marx's binomial analysis. Sometimes the approach verges
on obscurantism, as when "The consciousness of *a class*
need not, and has not been, the consciousness of *class*,"
or working-class self-expression is transmogrified into
"labourist populism" (Joyce, *Visions* 332, 339-40, and
Joyce, *Class*).

The Victorians themselves were never so coy about
using class language to differentiate the many layers of
society, and they expressed their differences in solid,
material, non-textual ways: in different churches and
chapels for the different social groups and different pew
rents within them, different hotels and pubs and different

lounges and bars in them, different theaters ("legitimate," music halls and "penny gaffs") and different accommodations inside (pit, stalls, dress circle, balcony, and "the gods"), different sports and leisure pursuits ("soccer" versus "rugger," field sports and lawn tennis versus the inner city "monkey run" of ogling, strolling teenage "mashers"), different holiday resorts (Blackpool versus Southport, Southend versus Bournemouth), even three classes of railway travel to get there. Above all, they voted for class segregation with their feet and their pockets. The cities grew physically by the flight of the higher classes as far from their inferiors as their capacity to pay rents or house prices and travel costs would carry them. Geographical segregation had begun even before the railways came, with separate areas of the towns for different classes, the wealthier gravitating towards the prevailing winds of the west and up the surrounding hills where the air and water were purer, leaving the inner core around the business district to the slums of the casual workers and the underclass. The railways, and the horse buses from the 1840s, enabled them to live further away, and created inner rings of skilled working- and lower middle-class suburbs around all the towns, and outer rings of middle and upper middle-class suburbs around the villages along the railway lines, like beads on radiating strings. Even the skilled workers with regular wages and hours were able later in the century to live some way out with the aid of the workmen's trains at penny fares, which developed the whole north-east quarter of London as a working-class district. If putting one's money where one's mouth is is an earnest of one's belief, the Victorians proved their awareness of class in the most visible and material way.

Suburbanization also enabled the middle and better-off working classes to separate work from home and to enjoy the benefits of a comfortable domestic life. This gave to women, as Leonore Davidoff and Catherine Hall have shown, a leading role in the formation of class and of bourgeois values, constructing a network of familial and female support based on the sexual division of labor in capitalist society. Men and women of the bourgeoisie adopted different class identities and a different class language, and women claimed for themselves moral and religious leadership in the domestic sphere (Davidoff and Hall).

Nevertheless, gender alone did not determine female roles: women took their power and influence from their wealth and status. The *grandes dames* of high society like Lady Londonderry or Lady Holland brooked no disrespect from doctors or lawyers, and made or broke the careers of rising politicians like Disraeli or Gladstone, while middle-class ladies dealt with shopkeepers and workmen as mere servants. Even the "respectable" wives of skilled workers treated the "roughs," the drunks and the wifebeaters as beneath contempt. Class was not made up of individuals but of generational chains of families, and women and marriage were the key links in the chain (J. Perkin, *Women*; J. Perkin, *Victorian*).

The salience of class does not mean that class conflict remained violent, a sort of covert civil war, or that people were not drawn to other interests cutting across class. They could be patriotic, nationalistic, imperialist, proud of their local community, religious sect or sports team, loyal to employers or landlords, male chauvinist or proto-feminist, without losing their sense of place in the social hierarchy, which is the essence of class-consciousness.

One master rival for their attachment and support was occupational hierarchy. However much the wage-earner might resent exploitation by the boss, or the farmer or field laborer by the landlord, he was well aware of their inter-dependence, and a crisis in the textile industry or agriculture, like the Cotton Famine or the Great Depression, could be disastrous for them both. At times it was impossible to tell whether a protest movement owed more to class or to vertical interest: the Anti-Corn Law League, for example, was as much an attack by the exporting manufacturers, both workers and capitalists, on the landed interest, both farmers and landlords, as of the middle class against the aristocracy. At such times, typically in the transitional early Victorian age, society was like shot silk, with the warp of occupational hierarchy and the weft of class cutting across each other and shining on the surface according to the play of the light and the angle of view.

That depended on how men – and women, since they were the main bearers of social attitudes for their families – saw their interest, as linking them with those above them in the social pyramid or with those on the same level. As David Hume said in the previous century, "Though men be much governed by interest; yet even interest itself, and all human affairs, are governed by *opinion*" (Hume 1:125). To that extent the post-modernists are right, but to less effect than they imagine, since the opinion once formed becomes as much a material fact as a farm, a factory, or a city. The lay-out of Victorian cities was a geographical expression of contemporary social attitudes, which turned class-aversion into physical patterns on the ground. The suburbs were the material witness of the class-consciousness of the Victorians, which survived the fear and loathing of the first generation and lived on into the less conflict-ridden second.

2. Mid-Victorian Prosperity: A Viable Class Society

Somewhere between the last Chartist petition of 1848 and the Great Exhibition of 1851 opinion on class relations changed abruptly. Chartist violence and the threat of revolution died down, the great crime wave began to subside, and industrial conflicts began to issue in bargaining rather than violent strikes. A period of calm, "an age of equipoise," and a "mid-Victorian boom" ensued which lasted down to the eve of the Great Depression of 1874-96. This interlude of apparent prosperity and social harmony is something of a puzzle to economic historians, since economic growth was no faster than before, and real wages may have stagnated somewhat because of slowly rising prices. But there is no mistaking the change in "feel"; social protest died away, fear of the poor changed to curiosity, politics became a competition between Liberals and Tories for the adherence of the skilled working class, crises were limited to marginal concerns like "Papal aggression" or anti-Irish riots, or to mild pressure for parliamentary reform which both Parties were willing to concede. The change from the "over my dead body" response to the Chartists in the 1840s to the Dutch auction by Gladstone and Disraeli in 1866-67 over how far down the scale the franchise should go shows how dramatically the socio-political atmosphere had been transformed.

The reasons for this change are somewhat elusive. Mild inflation lubricated the struggle for income and made it easier for employers to concede wage increases, tenants to pay rents, and governments to cut taxes. The political reforms of "the age of improvement" began to pay off: the local initiatives in public health in Manchester, Liverpool, Birmingham and other pioneering cities culminated in the Public Health Acts of 1848 and 1866; industrial legislation, especially the Mines Act of 1842 and the Ten Hours Act of 1847, helped to improve hours and conditions for women and child workers; the Food and Drugs Act of 1860 helped clean up the food supply to the towns; the Police Acts of 1839 and 1856 helped to reverse the tide of crime; and the modifications of the poor law in 1847 and the 1860s for the unemployed and for children and old people in the workhouse helped reduce the harshness of the regime. All these affected life in the towns for the better, but perhaps the most important thing was the effect of time and the settling down of the first generation of town-dwellers into what became mature communities with their own values and social controls. This was the urban aspect of the viable class society of mid-Victorian Britain.

The mid-Victorian cities benefited from a whole range of institutions which the previous generation had begun to build up in the hard times. The urban bourgeoisie consolidated its hegemony, by contrast with the informal networks of the pre-industrial aristocracy based on a federation of country houses, by building great civic institutions: commodity and stock exchanges, chambers of commerce, Liberal and Conservative clubs, literary and philosophical societies, masonic and other lodges, university colleges, local charities and hospitals, and above all a whole range of governmental institutions from poor law guardians and improvement commissions to gas and water supply bodies and the municipal corporations themselves. They came to express bourgeois pride and power in great civic buildings, above all in the splendid town halls through which the cities vied with each other in displays of wealth and magnificence. Manchester's immense town hall, Gothic without and Pre-Raphaelite within, Birmingham's enormous "Parthenon," Leeds' gigantic neo-classical temple, all spoke to the pride of their urban elites and their surprising preference for beauty and grandeur over utility and thrift (Briggs 134-35; 156-83; 196). Victorian values were far more collectivist and less materialist than their modern free market admirers suppose.

Nonetheless, the civic fathers who prided themselves on the wealth, importance and even the dirt and smoke of their cities – "Where's there's muck there's brass," as northern industrialists boasted – continued their nightly retreat to residences in the suburbs and countryside. As G. M. Young observed of the mid-century, "The best society in Manchester is trying to get out of it" (Briggs 70). Their flight was facilitated by the new horse buses and railways, the latter intended to be "iron bridges" connecting the city centers, but soon used by the middle class as escape chutes to the outer suburbs and country villages. Thus the late Victorian age was to see the most segregated society, by class, income, culture, and location of any generation before or since.

3. The Late Victorian City: Plutocracy and Poverty

In the late nineteenth century the economic and social climate changed once again, bringing in a new age far more diverse and paradoxical than its two predecessors. Social harmony and confidence in progress were both given a blow by the "Great Depression" of 1874-96, the first downturn in the pace of economic growth since industrialism began. The rate of increase in industrial production was halved, from 3.6 per cent per annum in the 1850s and 1860s to 1.8 per cent p.a. in the late 1870s to the 1890s (Saul 37). National income per head, including expanding services like education, the professions and government, held up until the late 1890s, but there is no doubt that in the last quarter of the century British capitalism reached a climacteric.

The result, as in all such recessions, was a questioning of the system. Did British industrialists and merchants, asked Alfred Marshall, work as hard as their fathers and grandfathers? Why were foreigners, notably the Germans and the Americans, asked books like *Made in Germany* (1878), able to make better and cheaper products and steal our markets? Why didn't we protect our home market as they did, asked the Fair Trade League (1881), with industrial tariffs? Shouldn't capitalism be scrapped, asked the new socialist societies, the Social Democratic Federation (1881), the Socialist League (1884), and the Fabian Society (1884), and replaced by a collectivist utopia? Shouldn't it at least pay a living wage to the unskilled, asked the match-girls, gas workers and dockers of the New Unionism (1889 onwards), and give them bargaining rights over pay and conditions? Weren't the urban poor too numerous and undernourished to be physically capable of work, asked the social surveyors Charles Booth and Seebohm Rowntree, and shouldn't they be removed from competition with the fit workers? Shouldn't at least the elderly poor be given old age pensions, asked Booth and Joseph Chamberlain, to keep them out of the workhouse? Weren't most urban workers too unfit for service in the army, asked General Sir Frederick Maurice of the Boer War volunteers; and wasn't the struggle for existence now between nations, asked Karl Pearson and Benjamin Kidd, so that mass poverty was a threat to the survival of the British Empire? Such questions highlighted the change from a mainly rural to a mainly urban population, and posed Britain against the still mainly rural countries of the continent with endless supplies of mass peasant conscripts raised in fresh air with wholesome country food.

Despite the gloom, the Great Depression, paradoxically, saw a faster rise in living standards than ever before. This was because falling prices, especially of imported food and raw materials, raised purchasing power for everyone, and left more disposable income for other consumer goods. Retail prices fell by 40 per cent between the early 1870s and the late 1890s, raising purchasing power by an astonishing 67 per cent, not allowing for any increase in money incomes.[2] For some economic historians like Berwick Saul, this was "the pay-off of the Industrial Revolution." Not everybody gained so much. Landlords in the corn-growing south and east saw their rents fall dramatically, but their counterparts in the pastoral north and west supplying milk and meat to the towns saw their real rentals rise enormously, while the urban landowners in the expanding cities made a killing, since town rents and house prices rose against the trend, and the great urban landlords became the backbone of a new plutocracy.

The new prosperity, cutting against the grain of the psychological depression, could be seen on the ground, especially in the cities. The new department stores like Harrods and Selfridges, and chain stores like Liptons tea shops and the Maypole dairies, the new consumer goods and services like gas stoves, electric light, telephones, bicycles, horse trams and the electric "tube," and latterly a few motor cars for the very rich, new sports grounds like football stadiums, greyhound tracks, and "pedestrian" running grounds, more holidays and growing resorts like Blackpool with its famous Tower and Southend with its mile-long pier, all spoke to the enhanced purchasing power of all classes except the very poor.

The paradox of discontent in the midst of prosperity was exacerbated by a widening of the distribution of income. The rich, despite their protests, were getting richer, and the poor, if not poorer, more numerous. The gap between rich and poor was probably greater in the late Victorian age than at any time before or since (Perkin, *Rise* 28-36). According to Dudley Baxter in 1867, the upper and upper-middle classes, 2 per cent of all families, received 37 per cent of the national income while the working classes, 74 per cent, received 39 per cent. Sir Leo Chiozza Money, a rich Fabian banker for whom seven eighths of the population lived in "poverty," found in 1904 that 3 per cent of families received 34 per cent while 88 per cent received only 51 per cent: "the United Kingdom is seen to contain a great multitude of poor people, veneered over with a thin layer of the comfortable and rich" (Baxter 15; Money 41-3).

At the top there emerged a new plutocracy, a merger of the richest urban landowners, like the Dukes of Portland, Bedford and Westminster, with new corporate business men like the railway magnate Richard Potter, the diamond millionaire Sir Julius Wernher, the ironmaster Sir John Guest (Lord Wimborne), or the soap and fats king W. H. Lever. These national and international capitalists were on a new plane above the old industrialists and merchants of the provincial cities, and enjoyed an affluent life style in the great houses of the West End and the grand hotels of cosmopolitan capitals and spas. As an elderly member of the old aristocracy, Lady Dorothy Nevill, a descendant of Sir Robert Walpole, reminisced,

> In the old days Society was an assemblage of people who, either by birth, intellect or aptitude, were ladies and gentlemen in the true sense of the word....Now all this is changed, in fact, Society (a word obsolete in its old sense) is, to use a vulgar expression, 'on the make.' (Nevill 100)

Beatrice Webb, daughter and hostess of the Chairman of the Midland Railway, largest company in the world, and President of the Canadian Pacific Railroad, saw the only qualification for membership of "this remarkable amalgam, London Society and country house life" as "great wealth and the possession of some form of power over other people." Of a dinner party at Sir Julius Wernher's Bath House (bought from the poorer Marquess of Bath) she remarked:

> There might have been a Goddess of Gold erected for overt worship – the impression of worship, in thought, feeling, and action, could hardly have been stronger. (Webb, *Apprenticeship* 48-49; *Partnership* 347)

The solid provincial merchants and manufacturers of the industrial towns, like her grandfather Sir Richard Potter, cotton merchant and first Mayor of Manchester, had been left behind and relegated, like the smaller landed gentry, to the second rank, and their cities had been sidelined by the larger metropolitan economy and culture. The City of London became the center of world banking and finance, turning its back on domestic industry and drawing its rentier income from its global investments.

At the other end of society, fear of the poor returned in a new form. No longer the fear and loathing of the riotous and criminal urban poor of the first Victorian age, or the anthropological curiosity of the second, it was a fear that an isolated, undernourished, diseased yet hedonistic and feckless working mass was dragging down the country and threatening the decline of Britain and the Empire in the now intensified competition for world trade and imperial power. As the "New Liberal" politician Charles Masterman put it in the new century, "the crowded quarters of the working classes" had produced "a characteristic *physical* type of towndweller: stunted, narrow chested, easily wearied, yet voluble, excitable, with little ballast, stamina or endurance – seeking stimulus in drink, in betting, in any accustomed conflicts at home or abroad" (8).

This analysis reflected the social surveys of Charles Booth and Seebohm Rowntree, who found 31 per cent of the people of London – 35 per cent of East Enders and 28 per cent of the people of York (43 per cent of the working class there) living in poverty. In fact, their definitions of poverty were somewhat elastic, and the real underclass were the 8.4 per cent of Londoners (12.4 per cent of East Enders) Booth found "in want and distress" and the 10 per cent in York (25.5 per cent of the working class) Rowntree placed in "primary poverty," the state of having insufficient resources to keep them healthy and fit for work (Booth, vols. 1-2; Rowntree 111, 117-18). It also reflected the army recruitment figures in the Boer War, which General Maurice claimed showed that three out of five volunteers were unfit to serve, though the army's own estimate was 35 per cent (see "Miles," "Where," and Maurice, "National"). Such fears of the declining health, physique and mental capacity of the working classes led to the Committee on Physical Deterioration whose Report in 1904 demonstrated the appalling condition of the poor, but sensibly affirmed that the decline, if any, was not irreversible but could be cured by better feeding, medical treatment, fresh air and exercise. The Report was to lead to the first tentative measures of what we now call the welfare state: school meals and medical inspection, old age pensions, town planning and slum clearance, national insurance

against sickness and unemployment. Meanwhile, however, the fear that the poor physical and mental condition
of the lower working class of the towns would undermine
Britain's world leadership in trade and empire evoked the
"National Efficiency" movement of Lord Rosebery and Sidney Webb and converted many Social Darwinists from the
struggle for survival between individuals to the collectivist
struggle between nations, thus paving the way for social
reform (Perkin, *Professional* 155-59).

The problem was aggravated by the physical segregation of the classes, increased by the development of cheap
public transport: the suburban railways, beginning with
the London underground in the 1860s and spread still
further by the electric tube in the 1890s, the cheap work-
man's trains that turned the whole north-east quarter of
London into working-class suburbs, and the new feeder
lines and stations that carried the middle classes further
north-west and south, and surrounded all the major cities
with octupus-like arms of railway suburbs. From the
salubrious heights of Hampstead and Highgate the middle
classes looked down, wrote Masterman, "upon the huge
and smoky area of tumbled tenements which stretches at
their feet," anticipating "the boiling over of the cauldron"
(9).

Leaving aside the West End with its elegant squares
and terraces for the rich and a few similar areas in Edinburgh, Newcastle and Bristol, the middle classes lived as
far from the madding crowd as they could afford, and
sorted themselves out according to the rents or house
prices and travel costs they could pay. Each railway suburb had its own status and social tone. Kathleen Chorley,
daughter of the engineer who designed the first underground electric locomotive in 1890, wrote of the Manchester railway suburbs to the south-west, "Snobbery was also
geographical." Alderley Edge, where she lived alongside
the wealthier business and higher professional commut-
ers, could not speak to Wilmslow, where the lesser man-
agers and office workers lived, or to Peover further out,
where the manager of the Bank of England's Manchester
branch lived in state, and her mother was positively em-
barrassed to receive an invitation to lunch from Lady

Stanley of Alderley Park and the county gentry. On the north side Stella Davies, daughter of a traveling salesman living in a substantial "end terrace" in Crumpsall, was not allowed to play with the working-class children who lived in the cottages alongside their large garden, nor with the business employer's children who lived next door (Chorley 155-57; Davies 63-64).

There were pull as well as push factors. Nostalgia for a lost rural idyll when all ranks lived together in paternalistic harmony – a mythical past which never existed – drew people outwards to create miniature landed estates, one-acre gardens around detached villas or tiny aprons of lawn and flower beds in front and back of semi-detached houses, built close together before the car arrived to open up the driveway to the garage. Late Victorian suburban houses had to be within walking distance of the railway station and can still be recognized on the ground by their density, unlike the looser texture of the twentieth-century infilling of the motorized suburbs (Perkin, *Railway*, Ch. 9; Perkin, *Automobile*, Ch. 9).

In the smoke and dirt, swarming tenements and grid-iron row houses of the inner cities the late Victorian working classes lived "a life apart" and developed a separate culture of their own. Some historians have discovered "a remaking of the working class" in this period, when locational segregation and the sense of abandonment by the rest of society expressed itself in new institutions such as the new mass unions and the Independent Labour Party and in a retreat into a sullen, despairing outlook in the isolated ghettos of the inner city (see Meacham; Jones, "Working" and *Languages*). This has to be set against the sympathy shown by the press and the middle classes for the match-girls and the striking dockers, the new university settlements in the slums manned by Oxbridge graduates, the psychological impact of the poverty surveys, the committees on old age pensions, the workmen's compensation act, the "jingoism" of many workers in colonial conflicts like the Boer War, and their support for the Liberal and Tory Parties far in excess of new Labour.

Class politics are only one aspect of class awareness, and no one in late Victorian England could be unaware of the precise differences in appearance, dress, physique, manners, and above all accent between persons of different social standing in the streets. Working men, for example, were on average two inches shorter than the middle class, and four inches shorter than the upper class. They might dress somewhat like their "betters" on Sundays, but their every-day attire was unmistakably plebeian. As that "squashed cabbage leaf," the flower seller Eliza Doolittle exclaimed in Bernard Shaw's *Pygmalion*, "He's a gentleman – look at his boots." Above all, they betrayed themselves by their accents. As her creator said, "One Englishman cannot open his mouth without being despised by another Englishman." Frank Harris, that epitome of the Victorian upper-class rake and pornographer – Victorian avocations in all three periods – summed it up: "Snobbery is the religion of England" (Harris 730). For snobbery was the driving force behind the explosion of the cities into the suburbs and beyond, leaving the inner core, except for a few islands of plutocratic affluence like Mayfair and Belgravia, to the unskilled and the underclass. The cities were the theater in which the Victorians played out their drama, or pantomime, of class relations, first in fearfulness and conflict, then in harmony and peaceful bargaining, and finally in a segregated dance of distrust and apprehension. It would take two world wars, a real great depression, and the affluent, motorized society of the late twentieth century to begin to break down, to some extent only, the social and physical barriers they created.

*   *   *   *   *

The British still live, to a larger extent than they recognize, in the material framework created by the Victorians. The road patterns and suburban railways, the chief public buildings and landmarks, the town halls and commercial exchanges, the art galleries and museums, the libraries and theaters, the hospitals and universities, the public parks and most of the churches, were Victorian creations. The office buildings and tower blocks of the twentieth century are so anonymous and boring that the eye filters them out and sees only the Victorian core of the city. It is only outside the city centers that the twentieth century imposes, in the housing estates and shopping malls, the motorways and airports, the theme parks and motels, and all the clamor of advertising signs, fast food restaurants, and gas stations on the way in. Of course, the twentieth-century love affair with the motor car has over-loaded the cities and is in process of choking them to death, forcing them to ease the stranglehold with pedestrian shopping streets, speed bumps, and one-way traffic schemes.

Just as Robert Vaughan insisted in 1843, the cities are still, despite television, portable telephones, and all the paraphernalia of information technology, the bearers of civilization, the centers of culture, the scenes of politics and commerce, and the springs of ideas and creativity. Even the nostalgia for the rural past is an artefact of city dwellers seeking an escape from overcrowding and pollution. The "wilderness" was a Victorian urban creation, by the Commons Preservation Society, the Ramblers Association, the Cyclists Touring Association, and the National Trust, all of whom were opposed by most landowners and farmers.

As Joseph Cowen, proprietor of the *Newcastle Chronicle* wrote in 1877,

> The gathering of men into crowds has some drawbacks, yet the concentration of citizens, like the concentration of soldiers, is a source of strength. The ancient boroughs were the arks and shrines of freedom. Today, behind the dull roar of our machinery, the bellowing of our blast furnaces, the panting of the locomotives and the gentle ticking of the electric telegraph . . . we can hear the songs of children who are fed and clad, and the acclaim of a world made free by these agencies. When people declaim against the noise and dirt of the busy centres of population, they should remember the liberty we enjoy as a consequence of the mental activity and enterprise which have been generated by the contact of mind with mind brought together in great towns. (Briggs 64-65)

Such self-confidence helps to explain the phenomenal success of the Victorian bourgeoisie.

The urban problems of congestion and crime, pollution and stress, are the price city dwellers and suburbanites pay, and willingly, for the amenities they share, of access to work, entertainment, leisure facilities, art and culture, the media, advanced medicine, higher education, and government itself, all of which are centered in the cities. Even the remotest country dwellers are now latched on to the city, via the telephone, radio and television, e-mail and the internet, and the emergency services. What we have lost are the civic pride and sense of community that the Victorians created out of the raw settlements of early industrialism, and their appetite for moral progress and civic improvement. They pioneered the age of great cities, and we have to reform and revive our faith in them.

Notes

1. The novelists thought they were writing of earlier generations but their social values were of their own age.
2. Mitchell & Deane, 472-72: Rousseaux Index of Retail Prices: average 1870-74 = 122.3; 1895-99 = 74.2 (average of 1865 and 1885 = 100).

Works Cited

Baxter, Dudley. *The National Income*. London: Macmillan, 1968.

Booth, Charles. *Life and Labour of the People of London*, vols. 1 & 2. London: Macmillan, 1889-1903.

Briggs, Asa. *Victorian Cities*. London: Odhams, 1963.

Chadwick, Edwin. *Report on the Sanitary Condition of the Labouring Population of Great Britain*. 1842; rpt. ed. M. W. Flinn, Edinburgh University Press, 1965.

Chorley, Lady Kathleen. *Manchester Made Them*. London: Faber, 1950.

Davidoff, Leonore and Catherine Hall. *Family Fortunes: Men and Women of the English Middle Class, 1780-1850*. London: Hutchinson; Chicago: University of Chicago Press, 1987.

Davies, C. Stella. *North Country Bred*. London: Routledge, 1963.

Engels, Frederick. *The Condition of the Working Class in England*. Oxford University Press, 1958.

Faucher, Leon. *Manchester in 1844*. Manchester, 1845.

Fletcher, Joseph. "Moral and Educational Statistics of England and Wales," *Statistical Journal* 10 (1847): 193-94.

Gatrell, V. A. C. and T. B. Hadden, "Criminal Statistics and Their Interpretation," in E. A. Wrigley, ed., *Nineteenth-Century Society* (Cambridge University Press, 1972): 371-72.

Harris, Frank. *My Life and Loves*; 1925; rpt. ed. John F. Gallagher. New York: Grove, 1963.

Harris, Jose. *Private Lives, Public Spirit: A Social History of Britain, 1879-1914*. Oxford University Press, 1993.

Harrison, Brian. *Drink and the Victorians: The Temperance Question in England, 1815-1872*. London: Faber, 1971.

Hume, David. *Essays, Moral, Political, and Literary*, vol. 1. London, 1875.

Jones, Gareth Stedman. *Languages of Class: Studies in English Working-Class History, 1832-1982*. Cambridge University Press, 1983.

_____. "Working-class Culture and Working-class Politics in London, 1870-1900; Notes on the Remaking of a Working Class," *Journal of Social History* 7 (Summer 1974): 460-508.

Joyce, Patrick. *Visions of the People: Industrial England and the Question of Class, 1848-1914*. Cambridge University Press, 1991.

_____, ed. *Class*. Oxford University Press, 1995

MacNab, K. K. "Aspects of the History of Crime in England and Wales, 1805-60," D.Phil. diss., University of Sussex, 1965.

Manchester Guardian.

Masterman, C. F. G. *The Condition of England*. London: Methuen, 1909.

_____. *The Heart of the Empire*. London: T. Fisher Unwin, 1902.

Mayhew, Henry. *London Labour and the London Poor*. 4 vols. London, 1861-62.

Meacham, Standish. *A Life Apart: The English Working Class, 1890-1914*. Cambridge: Harvard University Press, 1977.

Maurice, Sir John Frederick. "National Health: A Soldier's Study," *Contemporary Review* 83 (Jan. 1903): 41-56

"Miles" [Sir John Frederick Maurice]. "Where to Get Men," *Contemporary Review* 81 (Jan. 1902): 78-86.

Mitchell, B. R. and Phyllis Deane. *Abstract of British Historical Statistics*. Cambridge University Press, 1962.

Money, Leo Chiozza. *Riches and Poverty*. London: Methuen, 1905.

Nevill, Ralph, ed. *The Reminiscences of Lady Dorothy Nevill*. London: E. Arnold, 1906.

Perkin, Harold. *The Age of the Automobile*. London: Quartet Books, 1976.

_____. *The Age of the Railway*. Newton Abbot: David and Charles, 1971.

_____. *The Origins of Modern English Society*. London: Routledge, 1969.

_____. *The Rise of Professional Society: England Since 1880*. London: Routledge, 1989.

_____. *The Structured Crowd*. Totowa: Barnes and Noble; Brighton: Harvester Press, 1981.

Perkin, Joan. *Victorian Women*. New York University Press, 1995.

_____. *Women and Marriage in 19th Century England*. London: Routledge, 1986.

Porter, G. R. *The Progress of the Nation*. 1851; London: Methuen, 1912.

Rowntree, B. S. *Poverty: A Study of Town Life*. London: Longmans, 1901.

Saul, S. B. *The Myth of the Great Depression, 1873-1896*. London: Macmillan; New York: St. Martin's, 1969.

Vaughan, Robert. *The Age of Great Cities*. London: Jackson and Walford, 1843.

Wallas, Graham. *Life of Francis Place, 1771-1834*. London and New York: Longmans, 1898.

Webb, Beatrice. *My Apprenticeship*. London: Longman's, 1926.

_____. *Our Partnership*. Cambridge University Press, 1948.

1

Commercial Sites: The Early Victorian Development of Cannon Street

Linda R. Krause

> New Cannon Street [is] our present *beau idéal par excel-*
> *lence*. In this street very great things have been done . . .
> [we have] wholesale warehouses, insurance offices, and
> other businesses which may fairly vie with some of the
> palaces of Venice, Paris, and Verona, and . . . outdo many
> of them. (*CEAJ* 20: 87)

*I*n 1847 and again in 1850 the British Parliament passed
acts authorizing the widening and extension of Cannon Street
in the City of London. An improvement of this medieval
thoroughfare, which cut northwesterly through the heart of
London, had been proposed since the seventeenth century.
The need was genuine: traffic between London Bridge and St.
Paul's Cathedral proceeded glacially along a torturous, narrow, disjointed route. But more than facilitating east-west
access, the Cannon Street improvement promised to revolu-
tionize the City's streetscape. For beyond correcting the roadway and architecture in that locale, commentators hoped

Cannon Street would set the tone for elevating the quality of architecture throughout commercial London.

Concerted efforts at improving the city's streetscapes were rare in mid-nineteenth-century London because neither Parliament nor the monarch were empowered to initiate the kind of comprehensive urban development one might see, for example, in Paris. In the first three decades of the century London did boast two extensive street improvements: Regent Street (built largely between 1817-23) and King William Street (developed from 1829-35). But by mid-century both of these were receiving mixed to poor reviews from Early Victorian critics. Their criticism of late Georgian street design, and their faith in Cannon Street as the new *beau idéal* of urban streetscapes will be addressed shortly.

For historians Cannon Street provides an unusual chance to investigate several significant issues: urban aesthetics, commercial real estate development, and the architect's role in commercial building. Urban aesthetics were being redefined immediately prior to and during the street's development. Although this new aesthetic appears in various London streets, Cannon Street is the first comprehensive scheme to consistently exhibit these changes. At mid-century the City was changing from domestically-scaled buildings, which often served as residences as well as business premises, to monumental commercial chambers entirely dedicated to business purposes. This change of scale and function is realized in Cannon Street. Owing in part to such changes, and in part to a perceived threat from builders, London's architects increasingly undertook commercial commissions. As Cannon Street contains both builder-designed and architect-designed works, it permits comparison of the designers' respective roles and contributions. Finally, the Cannon Street improvement, precisely because it is relatively well documented, allows us to compare Early Victorian expectations and achievements.

Among the earliest and most persistent expectations about Cannon Street was that it would be a positive alternative to Regency and other late Georgian street improvements. By the mid-1830s such improvements as seen in Regent Street and King William Street were so roundly condemned that it is worth revisiting these sites to gain some perspective on Georgian and Regency practices.

Regent Street, located in London's fashionable West End, was planned as a *via triumphalis* linking the newly developed Regent's Park with a proposed new royal residence, Carlton House. Architect John Nash designed the park buildings, Carlton House (which was modified into terrace housing), and the basic plan of the thoroughfare. Although he designed only a small section of the buildings that lined Regent Street, his aesthetic was accepted by other builders involved in this extensive development. Typically, Nash's neo-Classical vocabulary includes colonnades, pediments, and a consistent cream-colored wall treatment. The brick buildings are faced with stucco that is scored to mimic smoothly laid stone (ashlar masonry). Manufactured ornamental fittings include cast iron (railings, columns) and Portland cement (small sculptural elements).

King William Street was begun in conjunction with the rebuilding of London Bridge in 1824. Developed between 1829 and 1835, this broad thoroughfare is the northern approach road to the bridge. The route extends northwesterly from Wren's Monument to the 1666 fire of London to the important intersection of Cornhill, Lombard Street, Princes Street, and Threadneedle Street. At this intersection are some of London's most prestigious government and financial institutions: the Royal Exchange, Bank of England, and Mansion House. One might have expected the buildings of King William Street to echo the architectural monumentality of these institutions. But, with few exceptions – Henry Roberts's substantial Fishmonger's Hall (1831-4) comes to mind – the street's architecture was similar to that in Regent Street: domestically-scaled, stucco-covered, neo-Classical buildings containing commercial and residential premises.

Both Regent Street and King William Street were initially praised.[1] But negative comments about these Late Georgian commercial developments appeared as early as the 1830s and were common during the 1840s. One critic noted that Regent Street offered "a lesson that shall instruct more by teaching what is to be avoided, than by showing what is to be followed" (*BA* 1845: 224). The lesson that Early Victorian critics learned covered many areas: building materials, building design, and the role of the architect in improving street architecture.

Few topics elicited more negative commentary than late Georgian building materials. The attack occurred on several fronts. Pre-cast materials (cast iron, Portland cement ornament, plate glass) and stucco were thought to degrade architecture. They were considered sham (stucco parades as stone), they concealed poor workmanship (stucco covers bad brick masonry), and they were pre-fabricated (inexpensive cast work is inherently inferior to hand-carved ornament). Henry Bowman, a contemporary critic, noted how pervasive these materials had become when he declared that, "[in] ninety-nine buildings out of a hundred, where there is any quantity of ornament, it is sure to consist of casts either metal, plaster, cement, artificial stone, compo, [or] papier maché" (318). Another critic claimed that stucco encouraged poor workmanship, because

> [The] builder [thinks nothing of] how badly he may do his work without the defects being found out before he has been paid; a wraprascal of stucco covers the multitude of his sins; the worse the brickwork is, the more readily the stucco adheres to it; and if there is a sinking in the foundation or a crack in the walls, the first is "of no consequence" and the last is "easily filled up." Such is the process of London building. (*CEAJ* 5:245)

While it is certainly true that stucco might conceal slipshod construction, there is nothing inherently inferior in the material. This cementious substance had been used successfully as a surface embellishment for centuries. In tracking the complaints against stucco and cast ornaments, it is increasingly apparent that the arguments are not driven by a simple desire for good construction. Rather, they comprise a complex mixture of ethical, aesthetic, and professional concerns.

Early Victorian critics held that the builder who used stucco and cast ornamentation defrauded his client and the client who used them defrauded the public. Bowman, pointing to this duplicity, claims that

> [We] see . . . hundreds of houses which every body knows to be built of brick, but which from some fancy or other, are made to appear as though they were built of stone, betraying at once, the pride of the proprietor in desiring an expensive material, and his poverty in being unable to obtain it. (318)

Augustus Welby Pugin and John Ruskin, widely read architectural critics, echoed these sentiments. In *True Principles* (1841), Pugin describes a typical Regency dry goods shop that "apes to be something after the palace of the Caesars . . . [where] the mock stone columns are fixed over a front of plate glass to exhibit the astonishing bargains; while low-ticketed goods are hung out over the trophies of war" (48). Ruskin, in *The Seven Lamps of Architecture* (1849), considers pre-fabricated ornament "an imposition, a vulgarity, an impertinence, and a sin" (8:83).

Early Victorian critics also opposed the use, or as they saw it overuse, of classical columns and pilasters. Such decorative elements were "ridiculous affectations . . . mean and insignificant" (*CEAJ* 5:245). Fancy neo-Classical ornamentation was considered a lure for unwary shoppers; shopfronts became mere billboards. Both Pugin and Ruskin recognized and abhorred the fact that shopkeepers used their facades as a form of advertising. Pugin disliked the shopfronts because he saw them as sham, aiming to appear more expensive than they were. Ruskin hated these boldly decorated shops because they lured citizens to the shops like "moths to a candle" (8:158).

In decrying Georgian architecture, Early Victorian criticism went beyond individual buildings to attack the effect of the entire street ensemble. Regency and late Georgian street architecture did have a rather uniform, two-dimensional appearance. All surfaces were covered in stucco, the style was consistently neo-Classical, and the low-relief cast ornamentation was often banal. Additionally, it was common Georgian practice to line the street with terrace houses that appeared as a series of narrow,

vertical strips.   Early Victorian commentators preferred
the high relief that resulted from hand carved, stone
ornaments and the massiveness that came from treating
each property as an independently articulated block. For
them, the Georgian street ensemble seemed thin, boring,
and cheap.[2]

Many Early Victorian critics held both builders and
architects responsible for what they deemed inferior street
architecture. Builders (contractors) were accused of ac-
ceding to client demands. To Victorians, such collusion
amounted to a marriage of the base and tasteless (Leeds,
"London Shops": 44; *BA* 1850: 227). If a client wanted to
open the entire ground floor to huge plate glass windows,
showy gilt ornament, and gaudy signage, the builder was
happy to accommodate. Architects were faulted for thinking that street architecture was beneath their consideration. Early Victorian commentators believed that architects were better educated than builders but that their
education placed too much emphasis on grandiose
schemes that had little or no practical application (Leeds,
"Shop Fronts": 437).   They reasoned that if architects
applied their talents to ordinary buildings, street architecture would improve.   To make the case that architects
were capable of designing handsome street ensembles,
some critics pointed to the buildings rising in Pall Mall.

Pall Mall, a West End street of luxurious, private clubhouses designed primarily in the 1830s, became the very
model of a good architectural street ensemble. The clubhouses, especially those built after 1835, were inspired by
Italian Renaissance palazzi. They were austerely orna-
mented stone edifices. Presented as a series of block-like,
independently articulated buildings, they offered a cubic
or three-dimensional character markedly different from
the two-dimensional effect of Regency work.   The clubhouses eschewed stucco; cast ornament and columns
were rare. As a whole the street projects stylistic conform-
ity without absolute uniformity. It is a prestigious street,
announcing wealth, security, and privilege.

That Pall Mall was seen as a possible standard for a
commercial thoroughfare such as Cannon Street was not
surprising for the palazzo style had already been appropri-

ated for commercial buildings. By the late 1840s it was the preferred style for housing prominent insurance companies, banks, and large wholesale warehouses (Hitchcock 1:345-407). Perhaps more important, in an age of associationism, Early Victorian entrepreneurs found the palazzo an apt metaphor. Likening themselves to latter-day Renaissance merchant princes, these businessmen readily adopted the style of Renaissance palaces for their own commercial premises. With Pall Mall as an example of what to emulate, and Regency streets lessons in what to avoid, the designers of Cannon Street could, it was hoped, create a new, monumental, commercial thoroughfare.

The history of Cannon Street is long and complicated but as that history bears directly on the cohesion of its street architecture, we might briefly consider it. The new thoroughfare had its origins in old Cannon Street, a narrow, medieval stretch of road that went from Clements Lane to Walbrook. At its eastern end, Cannon Street connected with East Cheap which in turn linked it to Fish Street, an important access road to London Bridge. At its western end, old Cannon Street led to Budge Row, then to Watling Street, the ancient Roman road that terminated at St. Paul's. Together, these congested streets and lanes constituted the principal east to west route across the City.

Proposals to create a broad new thoroughfare between London Bridge and St. Paul's appeared shortly after the Great Fire of 1666. Among the most famous proposals were those submitted by Christopher Wren and John Evelyn. Neither of these Baroque plans was adopted, and a good opportunity to rebuild the destroyed area was lost. For some, like Joshua Reynolds writing in the eighteenth century, the jumble of City streets was desirable (213). But the London Common Council found little to recommend these congested lanes. In the early nineteenth century they considered a proposal for a new east-west thoroughfare, similar to Wren's, offered by architect George Dance, Jr., the Clerk of City Works. This new street would be part of a large scheme to rebuild London Bridge and create King William Street. The bridge was completed in 1824 and King William Street was created between 1829 and 1835, but the east-west route was abandoned. Finally in 1847 Parliament passed an act authorizing the widening of old Cannon Street from King William Street to Dowgate Hill and continuing the line of Cannon Street from Dowgate to Queen Street (*Local Acts,* 1847: 4093). What is important to remember is that in this initial section of the street, the northern side of old Cannon Street was not altered and the street was widened by razing buildings only on the southern side. New construction, therefore, was restricted to one side of the street. Thus, the kind of comprehensive and unified environment envisioned by Early Victorian commentators was impossible. Under the direction of City Architect James Bunstone Bunning demolition proceeded but, due to notification laws and complex negotiations with landowners, construction did not proceed until 1851. Meanwhile, in 1850 Parliament passed an act authorizing the creation of a new street that would extend the line of Cannon Street from Queen Street to St. Paul's Churchyard (*Local Acts,* 1850: 781). With the passage of this second act there would be a single great thoroughfare linking two of Wren's most famous works: the Monument to the Fire at London Bridge and St. Paul's Cathedral.

A set of drawings, signed, stamped, and possibly executed by Bunning, provides a comprehensive view of the street improvement in the mid-1850s. Several of the buildings on Cannon Street are stylistically similar to Bunning's own work of this period yet his name is not associated with any building here. And although, as City Architect, he was nominally in charge of the Cannon Street improvement, he did not control the design of individual buildings. Indeed, such control would have been unusual because City Architects had no such power. Further, the Cannon Street improvement was not completed until the 1870s, long after Bunning's involvement. In the course of its construction, commercial architecture underwent dramatic changes in style and size. Buildings erected in Cannon Street in the 1870s respond to High Victorian, rather than Early Victorian, aesthetics. Despite the lack of governmental control, initially the new architecture of

Cannon Street was surprisingly coherent. It is not possible here to analyze all of the new buildings in Cannon
Street; instead, representative works that illustrate new
conditions and responses will be discussed.

Clearly the most significant change in Cannon Street
was that the new construction was entirely given over to
commercial premises. These consisted primarily of office
buildings (commercial chambers), insurance companies,
and wholesale warehouses. In many of the smaller office
buildings the ground story was let to retailers. Designers,
now free to work at a non-residential scale, eliminated the
Georgian terrace housing pattern. Other noteworthy
changes in Cannon Street revealed a general rejection of
Regency building practices. There was relatively little
stucco, ornamentation was restrained, and there were few
decorative columns. Most of the building designs incorporated buff colored brick with buff colored cement or stone
trim. Two frequent motifs – relatively new to London's
commercial street architecture – were splayed (chamfered)
corners and Palladian windows.

Given the opportunity that a street improvement afforded, and the expectations this improvement raised, the
very first buildings in Cannon Street might seem disap-
pointing. Nos. 64-68 and 52-56 (Plate 1) are modest
structures not radically different from Georgian residential stock. They are designed by the builder James Browne
and were considered undistinguished in their day. Yet
Browne's use of the monochromatic brick and Portland
cement trim departs from standard Georgian practice as
does his use of a chamfered corner. These signal features
indicate, I believe, a different attitude toward street architecture.

Browne's splayed corner at 52 Cannon Street is reminiscent of a similar corner treatment introduced by Charles Robert Cockerell at his palazzo-inspired Sun Fire Insurance Offices in Threadneedle Street in 1840. Cockerell, departing from standard Renaissance practice,
splayed the corner of the Insurance company offices in
order to accommodate certain site conditions. But he
turned this expedient into an asset by using the now
highly visible corner (clearly seen from all streets ap-

proaching the intersection) to accommodate the company's main entrance and logo. Browne's building, occupied by The Emperor Insurance Company, uses the splayed corner in precisely the same way. The corner houses the main entrance which is surmounted by the company logo. (The "Emperor" symbol is now obscured by signage of later tenants). I maintain that the consistently splayed corner treatments in Cannon Street acknowledge the new role of street architecture as commercial advertising. Not every corner property takes advantage of this advertising opportunity but many do and the implications for architecture are worth considering.

By the 1840s it was increasingly common for large banks and insurance companies to use their corporate headquarters to suggest the probity, wealth, and prestige of the company. Huge sums of money were expended on these palatial premises and an image of the building frequently appeared in company advertisements and on company stationery. One might say that Early Victorian London introduces the public to the notion of the identifiable corporate building, a notion still seen in such famous buildings as Sears Tower in Chicago, Citicorp in New York, and the Transamerica Tower in San Francisco. Browne's tenants could hardly claim to compete with large insurance companies and banks, but they could take advantage of the splayed corner in much the way Cockerell's Sun Insurance does: to create a business entrance visible from several directions, and to use the corner to mount identifiable company emblems. The splayed corner, so common in Cannon Street, actually anticipates contemporary practices. In speaking of the Las Vegas commercial strip, Robert Venturi notes that the huge casino signs and billboards are inflected toward the highway to maximize notice by passersby in automobiles (Venturi 51-52). The splayed corner works similarly in Cannon Street for pedestrians.

Other Cannon Street builders, while continuing Browne's novel corner treatment, were less timid about departing from his essentially Georgian elevations. An important parliamentary act passed in 1851 hastened the demise of simple Georgian fenestration: the repeal of the window tax. Builders quickly seized upon this relaxation of an onerous duty that had made extensive windows prohibitively expensive in all but the most extravagant public and private structures. Now ordinary street architecture could include more varied and elaborate window treatments. Although simple sash windows would still be used in Cannon Street, increasingly architects and builders used more and larger windows as well as windows arranged in groups. This change suited the commercial tenants who needed additional light to illuminate offices and display areas. Many Cannon Street buildings were designed by the contracting firm of William Lawrence and Sons, and it is Lawrence who introduced Palladian window motifs (Plate 1, nos. 70-6; Plate 2, nos. 80-94).[3] Here, tri-partite Palladian windows effectively triple the glazed area of the facade. The benefits of such extensive fenestration were immediately apparent, and each successive generation of entrepreneurs expanded the use of glass until ultimately, in the twentieth century, the modern curtain wall presents buildings that appear entirely glazed.

What is significant about Lawrence's work is not simply the window treatment but that the firm used a motif routinely associated with architect-designed buildings. We may recall that Early Victorian critics hoped Cannon Street would be the locus of professional architects rather than builders. But the records reveal that overwhelmingly builders designed the street's architecture. Interestingly, and unexpectedly, it was the architects who learned from the builders and not the reverse. Nowhere is this more apparent than in Unity Association Buildings designed by the prominent architect John Belcher and completed in 1854 (Plate 2). Though much larger than Lawrence's buildings, Unity Association employs the same Palladian window motif and materials. Here, I believe, is a case where builder and architect collaborated; or at least the architect took his cue from the builder.

The denigration of builders' work by professional architects of the period is clearly self-serving, and the truth as presented in Cannon Street proves otherwise. Not only did architects borrow design concepts from builders but builders successfully competed with architects for large scale commissions. George Myers, a highly respected builder who worked for many leading architects, introduced the palazzo style to Cannon Street. Erected during 1852-3, and situated between Martin's Lane and Laurence Pountney Lane, no. 110 has the monumental scale of a palazzo (Plate 3). It was larger and taller than earlier office buildings in the street. It was also the first new building in the street to be faced in stone, and the first to use Cockerell's motif of haunched (segmental) arches over the ground story windows. In 1854 the *British Almanac* described it as having an "Italian character, with varied window dressings . . . [and a] carefully treated design" (*BA* 1854: 257). This brief notice was the only positive comment afforded the work of a builder in Cannon Street. However, there can be no question that Myers' work compares favorably with contemporary commercial architecture designed by architects. We are left, then, to assume that its lack of notice by architectural journals is an intentional slight meant to perpetuate the myth of professional superiority.

Architects working in Cannon Street also produced some handsome buildings. Indeed the thoroughfare is bracketed by two very grand palazzo style warehouses: Henry Dawson's wholesale warehouse constructed between 1852-4 at 126-120 Cannon Street for Henry and Eneas Dawson's Stationers[4] (Plate 3), and William Hosking's large wholesale warehouse for the importing firm of Berens, Blumberg and Company built in 1854 and located at nos. 2,4,6 Cannon Street (Plate 4). Both of these buildings were impressive stone structures. Their strongly articulated ashlar masonry cornices, bases, and quoined corners fostered a sense of massiveness. These were austere, serious buildings with all the "gravitas" of High Renaissance palazzi. They would not look out of place among West End clubhouses, and they seem to fulfill the Early Victorian hope that Cannon Street would be a commercial Pall Mall. That such grand premises were, in fact, rare in Cannon Street may have more to do with economics than aesthetics.

Early Victorian architectural commentators held that better street architecture would result from hiring architects who would use substantial building materials and have the good sense to copy such time-honored urban precedents as Italian Renaissance palazzi. Occasionally, as in the work of Dawson and Hosking, this happens. In both cases a single tenant hired an architect and assumed the cost of erecting a palatial building. Most buildings in Cannon Street, however, were built on speculation. Speculative buildings were not commissioned by a client; rather, the builder assumed construction costs with the expectation of realizing a return on his investment through leasing space in the completed building. Owing to the inherent uncertainty of market conditions, this is a riskier venture than commissioned buildings and one that encourages builders to keep construction costs low. Unsurprisingly, speculative builders in Cannon Street typically produced functional, unpretentious buildings.

The speculative nature of most Cannon Street architecture foreclosed other early Victorian expectations. Both in Cannon Street and elsewhere in mid-nineteenth-century London, architects worked primarily on large scale, commissioned projects. Their salary, typically 5% of construction costs, could only be guaranteed if there was a client. Yet most commercial work in London was small scale and speculative. Individual purveyors of goods and services, lacking the capital to commission their own business premises, leased space in the new commercial chambers. Cannon Street is a good example of this trend toward speculative commercial chambers. The first buildings were quite modest but as the street improvement developed, the office buildings became larger. Larger buildings housed more tenants which, in turn, diminished the risk of lost income. Builders, who traditionally assumed the risks of speculative commercial work, established a foothold in the office building market. As demand for rental space increased, builders constructed ever larger and more profitable commercial chambers.

As we have seen, the belief that good design was restricted to architects was not borne out in Cannon Street. Builders produced well-designed commissioned and speculative works. Further, the notion that Cannon Street should be a commercial Pall Mall was an aesthetic judgment that lacked an understanding of how well-functioning commercial streets work. A commercial Pall Mall could only be possible if it consisted entirely of buildings housing large, private concerns: banks, insurance companies, prominent wholesalers. Yet such streets are rare and actually undesirable. Streets filled with palatial premises, though visually impressive, would have reduced pedestrian activity because banks, insurance companies, and wholesalers did not attract casual customers. Consequently, only those working or transacting business in such premises would be drawn to the area. Street activity primarily would consist of businessmen and employees entering and leaving the buildings.

Precisely because it was not a commercial version of Pall Mall, Cannon Street offered a more lively environment. Among the banks, insurers, and wholesalers were commercial chambers whose upper stories were filled with small business concerns and professional offices, and whose ground stories were filled with shops. Shops and offices attract a more diverse clientele. Shops also create more pedestrian activity. This mixture of single-tenant "foreground" buildings, often designed by architects, and multiple-tenant "background" buildings often designed by builders, assured a variety of rentable spaces and a crucial diversity of tenants. Without such diversity, Cannon Street would not have been commercially viable, and without ground floor rental space, street activity would have been drastically reduced.

The lessons we learn from Cannon Street are many. When Early Victorian commentators sought an aesthetically uniform street of palatial business premises they were short-sighted. Commercial thoroughfares succeed when there are diverse users, goods, and services that result from buildings of different scale and function. Cannon Street offered this. Contemporary critics wrongly assumed that architect-designed buildings were necessarily better than builder-designed work. Cannon Street further revealed that architects and builders could collaborate effectively. Architects were perhaps more sensitive to contemporary aesthetic preferences, while builders better understood market conditions. But these distinctions are frequently blurred.

For many Early Victorian writers on architecture the use of advertising – whether in large, plate glass shop windows, gaudy signs, or Carlyle's famous seven-foot lath-and-plaster hat – was distasteful. Yet Victorian entrepreneurs increasingly used architecture to advertise their businesses. In Cannon Street the splayed corners afforded a new opportunity to attract customers and to promote businesses. Early Victorians railed against stucco and manufactured ornament. Their aversion, based both on aesthetic and moral grounds, may well have inspired Cannon Street architects and builders to reduce the amount of ornamentation and virtually eliminate stucco. But one could also find sound economic reasons for the change. Stucco and lavish ornament increased the building's cost. Builders, always mindful to keep costs low, simply returned to an earlier Georgian mode of leaving their brick buildings unstuccoed.

Judged according to the criteria set down by early Victorian architectural critics, Cannon Street was a failure. Yet I would argue that those criteria were too narrowly construed. As recent studies have shown, successful streets offer a variety of building types, functions, and scales. They attract a diverse group of users and encourage varied activities. (Anderson *passim*) In the 1850s the designers of Cannon Street created a humanely scaled and varied commercial thoroughfare. In the 1870s, by the time the Cannon Street improvement was completed, the transformation of commercial London was well underway. The latest buildings in the street dramatically departed from the works just discussed. Cannon Street commercial buildings became larger, taller, and costlier. Huge warehouses filled the western end of the street. There were few shops. Cannon Street became, what too many commercial thoroughfares would become: monumental, anonymous, and underpopulated.

Notes

1. On Regency London, see James Elmes and Thomas Shepherd, *Metropolitan Improvements*, (London: n.p., 1827): 1: 2. On King William Street, see William Gaspey, *Tallis's Illustrated London*, (London: John Tallis, 1851-2): 1: 310.
2. William Henry Leeds, a prominent and prolific critic, wrote scathing reviews of late Georgian architecture. His comments on street ensembles appear in "Architecture" and "Candidus's Notebook . . .," *CEAJ* 7 (1844): 294.
3. The Palladian window is named for the Italian High Renaissance architect, Andrea Palladio, who used the motif in many of his buildings. It consists of a large, arched, central window or door opening abutted on either side by lower, flat-headed openings. The motif was modified in Cannon Street to consist of a flat headed central window topped by an unglazed, segmental arch.
4. This was likely a family commission offered to Dawson, who was a young architect at the time, by his relatives.

Abbreviations

BA: *Companion to the British Almanac*
CEAJ: *The Civil Engineer and Architect's Journal*

Works Cited

Anderson, Stanford, ed. *On Streets*. Cambridge and London: MIT Press, 1986.
"Architectural Improvements of London." *CEAJ* 20 (1857): 87.
BA, 1845, 224.
BA, 1850, 22.
BA, 1854, 257.
Bowman, Henry. "Remarks on the Present State of Architectural Taste and Practice in Our Large Towns." *CEAJ* 6 (1843): 318.
Great Britain, *Local Acts*, 10 and 11 Vict., c. 280 (1847): 4093.
Great Britain, *Local Acts*, 13 and 14 Vict., c. 56 (1850): 781.
Hitchcock, Henry-Russell. *Early Victorian Architecture in Great Britain*. 1954. New York: Da Capo Press, 1972.
Leeds, William Henry. "Architecture of Shop Fronts." *Westminster Review* 36 (1841): 436-55.
[Leeds, William Henry] Candidus. "London Shops." *CEAJ* 3 (1840): 44.
Pugin, A[ugustus] Welby. *The True Principles of Pointed or Christian Architecture . . .* 1853; rpt. Oxford: St. Barnabas Press, 1969.
Reynolds, Sir Joshua. *Discourses on Art*. Intro. Robert R. Wark. New York: Collier Books, 1966.
Ruskin, John. *The Seven Lamps of Architecture*, in *The Works of John Ruskin*. Ed. E.T. Cook and Alexander Wedderburn. London: George Allen, 1903: 8.
"The Threadneedle Street Structure," *CEAJ* 5 (1842): 245.

Venturi, Robert, Denise Scott Brown, and Steven Izenour. *Learning from Las Vegas: The Forgotten Symbolism of Architectural Form.* Cambridge and London: MIT Press, 1977.

2

Mapping Contagion in Victorian London: Disease in the East End

Mary Burgan

*P*eter Keating has noted a Victorian tendency to represent the unknown dangers of the East End of London in analogy with "darkest Africa" (13-15). He suggests that the discoveries that lurked in the unexplored neighborhoods of poverty east and north of the Tower Bridge were as mysterious and threatening to middle-class Londoners as the savagery imagined in the last unexplored continent of British Imperialism. Indeed, the mysterious world of the East End was imagined as more hazardous because of its nearness to home, to the heart of London itself. The imagery of Empire featured the condition of urban poverty in a topographical nexus, but geography was not the only metaphorical matrix that located the sites of the London poor in a rhetorical borderland between danger and safety. Almost inevitably, topography was conjoined with anatomy in a figure of the city as a body. Anatomy was an activating trope in this variation on the cartography of London because it fastened upon the fear of infection, of disease as threatening the entire body when in fact it affected only one part. Geography as anatomy thus became a feature of many Victorian representations of London. Such a combination suggested the relation of the poor to the rich of London not only in terms of distance but in terms of a connection summoned to instruct and warn the middle-class city-dweller.

As Victorian London was constructed both as a place and a body, writers on London were drawn to anatomical metaphors for the city: its river as the blood stream, St Paul's as the soul, and its outlying suburbs as appendages or organs. Wordsworth's sonnet "Composed upon Westminster Bridge, September 3, 1802" invoked such a trope by imagining London as a great, living organism. In exclaiming that "all that mighty heart is lying still" in the last line of his sonnet, Wordsworth articulated a physiological image that suggests the strength of a giant, but also the possibility of a paroxysmal dissolution.

In *Past and Present* (1843), Carlyle used the story of the Irish Widow who proved her sisterhood by spreading "typhus fever" to seventeen citizens of Edinburgh to contrast the failure of kinship in industrial society with the more humane ministrations of the black woman and her daughter who helped Mungo Park recuperate from illness in Africa. His famous exemplum combined the motif of exploration with that of a contagion that might stop the mighty hearts of cities in catastrophic infection; thus he helped to set up a master Victorian narrative of the poor, wandering out of their ordinary neighborhoods to infest the whole of society. But it was Dickens who transcribed this narrative of contagion onto the map of Victorian London, naming neighborhoods and streets in such a way as to provide future cartographers with landmarks that represented pathology as well as pathos in Victorian urban experience. Dickens's mapping in *Bleak House* (1853) likewise figured the city as an organism, robust in the variety of its places, but also threatened by disease from within. Jo the crossing-sweeper (who actually resides in the slums within the neighborhoods around the Inns of Court), carries the fever that he contracts in the dark purlieus in central London westward, to respectable and healthy areas. Jo's wandering to the pastoral environs of St. Albans figures the threat of contagion from the London of mid-century industrial migration to midland farms and country houses, even though he is not, strictly, a representative of that east of London that came to signify darkest Africa to late Victorian social explorers. The segregation of squalor in the East End was amalgamated in the popular imagination in the last quarter of the century. Dickens's 1853 geography of the westward movement of disease was thus premonitory. The cholera epidemic of the late fifties and the death of the Prince Consort from typhus in 1861 were landmark events that enforced the realization that disease was likely to move from east to west. Perhaps it was the widening circumference for these social infections that caused Dickens to extend the geography of disease in *Our Mutual Friend* (1864). There he locates the movement of contagion between the East End docks and the rest of the city, imaging the Thames as a river of corruption that washes up its dead among the already debilitated poor. Thus while the literary representation of the East End as an exotic heart of darkness may have served as a travelogue of wonders for Victorians who sat safely at home, there was little comfort in imagining the East End as a festering locus of fatality that could bring cholera, consumption, typhus, and venereal infection to the wards of Highgate, Hampstead, Westminster, and even Buckingham Palace.

In routing such avenues of infection, Dickens appropriated a geographical discourse that was apocalyptic and melodramatic, but that discourse was also functional as a spur to reform. It was, indeed, instrumental in practical Victorian efforts to change the actual map of London. For as the century progressed, the reformation of London's streets and neighborhoods was governed by the awareness of place itself as salubrious or polluted; the grammar of disease inflected the rhetoric of reform which led to the creation of public spaces, the programs of early sociology, and measures of public health. This essay will survey these public responses to the geography of contagion, noting several significant instances: the creation of Victoria Park in the East End, the depiction of slum life as an incurable disease by naturalist writers, the elaboration of Charles Booth's "poverty maps" of London, and the segregation of the poor of the city for the treatment of chest diseases. While the geographical plotting of disease could become a powerful impetus in efforts to alleviate the illnesses of the poor, however, it could also motivate the kind of fear that led to efforts to coerce sufferers into quarantine. Thus it should become clear that efforts to define and provide space for the poor also involved segregation. Critics of *Bleak House*, most significantly D.A. Miller, have noted Dickens's own ambivalence between cure and control, freedom in the country and the metropolitan prison. This ambivalence is perhaps most active in his division of the sources of restoration of health and reconciliation between Alan Woodcourt, the doctor, and Inspector Bucket, the policeman. The following analysis will show that such ambivalence also marks civic texts that targeted the East End as a locus of Victorian contagion through the nineteenth century.

* * * * *

Among the earliest elaborations of the East End as a site of disease were the debates that led to the establishment of Victoria Park. The effort to have a park in the East End led to the formulation in 1840 of a petition to the young Queen to set the project in motion. The petition was notable for its description of the neighborhoods that made up the Tower Hamlets, enumerating their multifarious commercial benefits and calling attention to the phenomenal growth and crowding of their population of "400,000 souls, nearly double that of any City or Town within the British Dominions" (Poulsen 18). Respectful in its emphasis on the inequity implicit in the absence of a royal park in this part of London – only gently alluding to the unfairness of the West Enders' enjoyment of St. James, Green, Hyde and Regent's Parks – the petition made the threat of disease an argument that might prove more effective than the demands of justice. It spoke of the lack of "air, exercise or healthful recreation" for East End workers, and it referred to the far-reaching effects of such deprivation: "Fever is constantly prevailing in these places, which are indeed declared on competent authority to be 'the main sources and seats of the Fevers of the Metropolis'"(18). These fevers were, of course, moralized:

"Unable to breathe the pure air of Heaven with their families, multitudes are driven into habits of intemperance, bringing in their train demoralization, disease and death" (18).

Victoria Park was approved and opened in 1845. Compared with the great royal parks in the West End, Victoria Park was modest in the extreme: it was small, and it had few amenities. Eventually, it acquired ponds for boating and bathing, playing grounds, and the plantation of a relatively small variety of trees for shade as well as horticultural instruction. This elaboration of the impulse to make the park a site for acquiring useful knowledge led to the stocking of some exotic birds to accommodate the East End fascination with ornithology, the provision of an array of flowers for East End carpet gardeners, and even the installation of a flock of sheep (which helped by grazing as well as providing a pastoral aura). One of the most popular attractions was a pagoda on an island in one of the ponds. This structure served as a reminder to East Enders that there were places more exotic than their own.

Despite its popularity among East Enders, Victoria Park and its few amenities had to be defended against encroachments throughout the century. Most particularly, the citizens of the park had to fight for its share of the "pure air of Heaven." A major crisis in its history was successfully negotiated through public petition in 1864 when the Imperial Gas, Light and Coke Company attempted to build a huge gas works just east of the park. The call for a public meeting to resist this encroachment warned that "Hundreds of thousands who have been able to enjoy pure air and healthful recreation . . . will be obliged to inhale a poisoned atmosphere, and the only park the East End Population have to recruit their health will be utterly destroyed" (Poulsen 80).

Since Victoria Park was instigated as a measure of public health, it is not surprising that it was also imagined anatomically, as an organ in the body of London. The acceptance of this standard view of London as a huge body was embedded in many views of London's parks. For example in a 1907 survey of *London Parks and Gardens*,

Mrs. Cecil ("Citizen and Gardener of London"), apostro-
phized the parks of London as the source of health:

> He who loves not only London itself with a patriotic venera-
> tion, but also his fellow-men, will not rest with the inspec-
> tion of the beautiful. He will journey eastward into the
> heart of the mighty city, and see its seething millions at
> work, its dismal poverty, its relentless hardness. . . . but
> apart from all ideas of social reform, from legislative action
> or philanthropic theories, there is one thin line of colour
> running through the gloomy picture. The parks and gar-
> dens of London form bright spots in the landscape. . . .
> From the utilitarian point of view they are essential. They
> bring new supplies of oxygen, and allow the freer circulation
> of health-giving fresh air. They are not less useful as places
> of exercise and recreation. They waft a breath of nature
> where it is most needed. (2)

Of course, in mid-century, the notion of the transmission of disease was as yet uninformed by bacteriology; the
metaphor of contagion involved only rudimentary notions
of transmission through the environment. Contaminated
water had long been seen as the main avenue of disease,
and so increasing the provision of safe water for bathing
and for drinking was a continuing factor in the evolution
of Victoria Park. The park was granted its only unbe-
grudged bequest in 1862 when an ornate drinking foun-
tain was dedicated as the gift of Angela Burdett-Coutts.
Miss Coutts took the first drink, toasting the health of the
10,000 East Enders who attended the ceremony (Poulsen
59).

If fresh water was considered critical to public health
through the earliest sanitary reforms of the Victorian
Period, fresh air became a more pressing consideration as
urban London became dark with pollution. The imagery
of air infiltrates descriptions of the unhealthy atmosphere
of the East End, both in the petition for Victoria Park and
the subsequent defenses of its salutary role in protecting
against working-class disease. Indeed, the quality of the
air was often noted as a feature of other, better neighborhoods in guidebooks to London. When E.V. Lucas apos-
trophizes Hampstead Heath as London's "lung" in his
1906 guidebook (197), he is carrying on a tourist tradition
of looking for the freshest air in the city.

If Hampstead was mapped as the lung of London, the East End was mapped as the seat of typhus and consumption, the most virulent and wasting social diseases of the nineteenth-century. Even syphilis, the other nineteenth-century scourge, held fewer terrors for the poor. It did not "gallop," it did not affect the young (especially young women), and its cause was relatively well understood. Kelley's *Post Office Guide to London in 1862* laid out this pattern of mortality from East End diseases in its charts and numbers. Of all the deaths for the past year reported in this compendium, miasmatic (typhus) diseases counted for 14,459 among the environmentally caused afflictions, while tuberculosis took 10,824 from the "constitutional" category. Only 206 deaths were assigned to the category of "generative organs," although the writer lamented the extent of growth ("threefold what they were in 1849") of deaths "due to a profligate indulgence of the passions" (35). This survey rejoices in the reduction of deaths as effected by "more complete drainage and the consequent improved habits of cleanliness" (35), but the assignment of tuberculosis to "constitutional diseases" denotes the continuing lack of knowledge of its etiology. Florence Nightingale was an ardent proponent of the "foul air" theory of consumption, and her theory was endorsed by an international gathering of public health experts in London in 1862 (Smith 31). And early medical statistics proved that consumption killed many more working-class citizens in the East End than it did in the northern and western regions of London. Thus it was especially appropriate that a committee of Quaker benefactors should have set up the London Hospital for Diseases of the Chest on the southwest border of Victoria Park in 1848. This hospital catered to consumptives among the poor in the East End; more affluent urban consumptives were likely to take refuge in private nursing homes, many of which were located in Hampstead.

London guidebooks, and surveys of London's parks, tended to neglect Victoria Park as an attraction for visitors.[1] On occasion, writers like Mrs. Evelyn Cecil would embrace the only park in the East End in a patriotic gesture, but for all intents and purposes, it was "off the map." Even today, it is difficult to find, and in the Victorian era, it could be reached only by way of trams and omnibuses. Its inaccessibility segregated it from the general London public. Like the rest of the topography of the East End, then, Victoria Park tended to be erased in mid- and late-Victorian geographical renditions of London. Meanwhile, the rare literary representations of the East End picked up on the notion of geography as pathology. Fictional descriptions of the East End as a pathological node in London set up a convention that embedded evolutionary determinism in evocations of the mean streets of east central and east end neighborhoods. When George Gissing describes in *The Nether World* (1889) an outing into Essex, he stages a view from the train passing from Clerkenwell through Bethnal Green that employs lurid medical detail. The description emphasizes the crowding and the air:

> Over the pest-stricken regions of East London, sweltering in sunshine which served only to reveal the intimacies of abomination; across miles of a city of the damned, such as thought never conceived before this age of ours; above streets swarming with a nameless populace, cruelly exposed by the unwonted light of heaven; stopping at stations which it crushes the heart to think should be the destination of any mortal; the train made its way at length beyond the outmost limits of dread. (164)

It is no surprise that as the novel unfolds in a dreary chronicle of last-minute failure, this environment has crushed every character. And Arthur Morrison begins his *A Child of the Jago* in 1896 with a description of the air of becalmed Shoreditch, stagnating under a lurid, coppery sky: "Below, the hot, heavy air lay a rank oppression on the contorted forms of those who made for sleep on the pavement: and in it, and through it all, there rose from the foul earth and the grimed walls a close, mingled stink – the odour from the Jago" (45). Morrison's fictions, like Gissing's, record the moral inertia and mental stupefaction wrought by these surroundings. The East End is a place of social diseases as well as pallid complexions, bad teeth, and stunted growth.

Both of these writers of the East End represented London as hiding its sites of disease in segregation from the rest of the city. They reveal unknown neighborhoods where weary inhabitants endure the desperation either of being stranded or of fighting against wasted bodies and minds to find a way out. It is significant that their diagnoses enlarge the afflictions linked to place, for they participate in the modern medicalization of alcoholism, domestic violence, and mental impairment, adding them to the spectrum of illnesses caused by environment. While Gissing and Morrison imply the risk of contagion for their readers, they eventually emphasize the self-fulfilling prophecy of life in the East End. Their characters will never move out far enough to do more to the middle classes than burglarize an occasional home in a fringe neighborhood like Islington. Their address to daily life in the atmosphere of the slums blocks the occasional romanticism of Dickens's depictions of slum communities like Mrs. Plornish's in *Little Dorritt*, communities in which the irrepressible forces of imaginative health find occasions to celebrate and "take the air." They also seem less inclined than a heroic Carlyle to preach the possibility of cure. Beset by the Darwinian premonition that their condition is the result rather than the cause of the devolution of slum dwellers, Gissing and Morrison grimly confront the hereditary nature of East End disease. They see illness as so deeply permeating their characters that it can hardly be treated by external reform. In this emphasis on the internalization of the disease geography, the sober rhetoric of Gissing and Morrison echoes that of the sociological reformers who examined the East End with a newly scientific gaze at the end of the nineteenth century. It is significant that such gazes recorded a variety of findings on actual maps of the city, for several mid-century maps of London were coded for particular attractions (Hyde 27). For example, in 1892, Sidney Webb exhibited a map of London on which all public houses had been marked with red dots, which he characterized as "London's scarlet fever." Drink had indeed become a disease in the minds of social reformers.

This shifting emphasis in the imaging of London as a system of health or disease is implicit in the mapping of London done over the last decade of the nineteenth century by Charles Booth. Booth's study – which set out originally simply to describe in detail the wealth or poverty of neighborhoods in London – eventually made visible the threat of contagion while studiously avoiding the sentimental appeal (or determinism) of the individual case history that might be featured in literary representations of London's poor. Booth devised a color coding, derived from a door-to-door assessment of London neighborhoods. The results of this canvass were then plotted on "Stanford's Library Map of London and Its Suburbs," a highly detailed (six inches to the mile) charting of London, first published in 1862 and then updated on a regular basis until the end of the century. Booth's seven-point color scheme assigned yellow to wealthy streets, red to well-to-do, pink to comfortable middle class, purple to comfort mixed with poverty, light blue to standard poverty, dark blue to deep poverty, and black to areas of deepest poverty mixed with crime. It seems not too fanciful to suggest that Booth's economic project mimics the methods of the medical anatomist, dissecting the body of the city in order to arrive at a surgical remedy. Indeed, a glance at the streets surrounding Victoria Park, with its designation of red and pink for the life-blood of the middle-class dwellings built along the approach roads, visually represents London as a circulatory system. Within that arterial system of middle-class well-being on main streets, there lurks the infection of various shades of blue poverty in back streets. The pockets of disease in the city are encapsulated behind the fronts erected in the main thoroughfares by the affluent. It is significant that the development of Victoria Park included a real estate development for upper-middle-class houses that were to face the park itself; lower-class housing was to be placed behind these stately buildings, cut off from the park's green lawns. When the streets turn to dark blue and black on Booth's maps, in places like the Jago near Petticoat Lane, they denote sites which require curative removal through the razing of infested housing and the forced resocialization of the redeemable poor.

Although the texts that Booth's maps accompany provide details of the crowding and lack of healthy open spaces in the East End, the attention of his analysis was focused primarily upon the economics of the inhabitants of its various streets. His textual discourse runs upon an arithmetical rather than a medical base; he is more interested in the competition for wages than in contagion, remarking that "The disease from which society suffers is the unrestricted competition in industry of the needy and the helpless" (*Life and Labour*, 162).

Booth's final solution rejects philanthropy and its curative efforts to help the poor help themselves. Like Gissing and Morrison, he had close contact with the streets of the East End, and that intimacy suggested that without drastic measures the poor were destined to be trapped in their city of dreadful night. Thus his text asks for the forced take-over of the blue and black bands in a kind of national hospital: "To effectually deal with the whole class . . . – for the State to nurse the helpless and incompetent as we in our own families nurse the old, the young, and the sick, and provide for those who are not competent to provide for themselves – may seem an impossible undertaking, but nothing less than this will enable self-respecting labour to obtain its full remuneration and the nation its raised standard of life" (165). Booth's prescription of "limited Socialism" would affect only the lowest class, and thus protect the healthy individualism of the other classes. Further, his system would seek to liberate the children of this coerced class from their hereditary ills. Sanitized by their isolation from the rest of society, they might be able to move up in the world at a later time. Booth's methods and achievement in surveying the poverty of London are well known, while the maps which he attached to each of the volumes of his study are endlessly fascinating in their detail.[2] The text itself has been less analyzed for its prescriptions. Their application of the idea of quarantine for irremediable poverty brings to full circle a half century of the mapping of London as a diseased body, giving up on early notions of systemic cure to be effected through sanitary reform and provision of open public spaces.

Eventually, such a therapeutic construction of the poor as diseased conjoined with a bacteriological imperative in the medical policing of the East End and other London working-class areas. The surveyors in Booth's project (who included early socialists like Graham Balfour and Beatrice Webb) were prototypes of the environmental hygienists of the turn of the century. They did not have coercive authority, but their model of house-to-house survey was repeated by health workers, especially those who were charged with identifying consumptives so as to force them into sanatoriums. The discovery of the tuberculin bacillus by Robert Koch in 1883 would eventually initiate extensive public health measures designed to eradicate infection. Given scientific evidence that diseases could be spread not so much by general atmospheric conditions as by human interchanges, the state was empowered to take measures against human agents of infection. This hygienic imperative may have accounted for the change in housing styles – the substitution of "laboratory" developments for ramshackle buildings and the preference for washable and sterilizable surroundings, especially for the poor (Smith 121-22). The work of René and Jean Dubos revealed that wholesale declines of tuberculosis within large populations had derived as much from higher standards of nutrition and sanitation as from the miracle drugs developed in the 1940s. F.B. Smith has told the story of this new motive for the disease surveillance of the industrial cities of Great Britain. In it the Inspector of Police becomes the Inspector of Health who finds a scientific reason to take the alien East Ender in hand and move him or her into new urban and suburban landmarks: the Poor House Infirmaries and sanatoriums with their spartan regimes of fresh air, supervised food, and utter isolation from whatever human life and culture the streets of the East End offered its masses.

This life and culture has not been fully charted: it belonged to people who had no written texts beyond their single park and the names of their streets. As Murray Baumgarten suggests in his essay in this volume, they are imagined in Dickens's "theatre of homelessness," but their stages and props have disappeared. There are, to be sure, some landmarks remaining: Angela Burdett-Coutts's Peabody Buildings, a children's centre at Bethnal Green, and the almost derelict grounds of Victoria Park. Even today, however, the most famous map of London – the brightly colored underground map that promises visitors access to the most important places – skirts the East End. It goes as far as the Angel station, but it leaves names like Victoria Park, Stamford Hill, Stepney, Hackney, and Bethnal Green off the grid that defines London for those who do not know the history of neighborhoods where communities of the working poor survived illness, quarantine, and hopeless diagnoses by the experts. They emerged from such predictions, however, as the heroic resisters of the twentieth century's most determined effort to exterminate them. It was the East End that Hitler targeted most viciously in his bombing of London in the Second World War. Had he read the novels of Dickens, he might have realized that despite the conditions of life there, the people possessed a sense of their own place as a location that could not be eradicated from the map of London.

Notes

1. For example, my informal survey of a selection of London guidebooks in the Library of Congress has failed to uncover any directions to Victoria Park. See Cooper, Lucas, and Tranter.
2. These have been preserved by the London Topographical Society in an atlas which reproduces the maps without Booth's text.

Works Cited

Barker, Felix and Peter Jackson. *The History of London in Maps.* London: Barrie & Jenkins, 1990.

Booth, Charles. *Charles Booth's Descriptive Map of London Poverty, 1889.* London: London Topographical Society, 1984.

_____. *Life and Labour of the People in London.* New York: Macmillan, 1902.

Carlyle, Thomas. *Past and Present.* 1843; rpt. Boston: Houghton Mifflin, 1965.

Cooper, Charles S. *The Outdoor Monuments of London: Statues, Memorial Buildings, Tablets and War Memorials.* London: The Homeland Assoc., 1928.

Church, Richard. *The Royal Parks of London.* London: H.M.S.O., 1956.

Dubos, René, and Jean. *The White Plague: Tuberculosis, Man, and Society.* 1952. New Brunswick, NJ: Rutgers University Press, 1987.

Gissing, George. *The Nether World.* 1889; rpt. London: Dent, 1973.

Hyde, Ralph. *Printed Maps of Victorian London, 1851-1900.* Fokkstone: Dawson's, 1975.

Hyde, Ralph, ed. *Stanford's Library Map of London and Its Suburbs.* 1860; rpt. London: Harry Margary with Guildhall Library, 1980.

Keating, P.J., ed. *Into Unknown England, 1866-1913: Selections from the Social Explorers.* Manchester: Manchester University Press, 1976.

Kelley, Edward Robert. *Kelley's Post Office Guide to London in 1862: Visitor's Handbook to the Metropolis and Companion to the Directory with Map.* London: Simpkin, Marshall, 1862.

Lucas, E.V. *A Wanderer in London.* London: Macmillan, 1906.

Miller, D.A. *The Novel and the Police.* Berkeley: University of California Press, 1988.

Morrison, Arthur. *A Child of the Jago.* 1896; rpt. Woodbridge: Boydell Press, 1982.

Poulsen, Charles. *Victoria Park: A Study in the History of East London.* London: Stepney Books, 1976.

Rockley, Alicia Margaret (Tyssen-Amherst) Cecil. *London Parks and Gardens.* London: Constable, 1907.

Rosen, George. "Disease, Debility, and Death," in H.J. Dyos and Michael Wolff, eds., *The Victorian City: Images and Realities.* London: Routledge, 1973, 625-68.

Smith, F.B. *The Retreat of Tuberculosis: 1850-1950.* London: Croom Helm, 1988.

Stanford, Edward. *Stanford's Library Map of London and Its Suburbs.* London, 1862.

Tranter, George. *Visitor's Guide – Showing How to Spend a Week in London.* [London, ca. 1891]

Wordsworth, William. "Composed upon Westminster Bridge, September 3, 1802" in *Norton Anthology of British Literature,* 6th ed. New York: Norton, 1993, 2: 198.

3

Symbols of Success in Suburbia: The Establishment of Artists' Communities in Late Victorian London

Joseph F. Lamb

Few moments in the history of British art have proven more favorable to contemporary artists than the period of the 1860s through the late 1880s. During this brief era British artists enjoyed unprecedented popularity among a broad and admiring public, their fame surpassing the adulation exhibited for such other popular artistic professions as novelist, playwright, and poet. Rare was the social event or high society dinner without a well-known or promising visual artist at hand. Of course, new found fame had its price, and frequent comments are found in artists' memoirs and journals concerning the constant demands upon their time. Thomas Sidney Cooper's statement is typical: "The late hours of London society, with the excitement consequent upon the numerous social gatherings that I was called upon to attend, combined with my continued hard work and close attention to my professional duties, began at last to make such really serious inroads upon my health" (Cooper 2:79).

This elevated social status of the visual artist was a reflection of British society's rapidly changing attitudes towards the arts. In a time of enormous prosperity, investment in contemporary art signified social status, and collectors spent with wild abandon. Scores of artists – primarily but not exclusively male painters who were members of the Royal Academy – received unprecedented prices for works of art or for reproductive engravings after their more popular paintings. The social status of artists rose significantly with the support of these many collectors who, in turn, enhanced their own image by socializing with artists.

The day's popular press responded to and helped to perpetuate this profession's social and worldly success by devoting unprecedented attention to contemporary art and artists.[1] Similar to the attention reserved for cinema and popular music celebrities today, illustrated articles featuring not only the art but the life styles of contemporary artists became regular features in such widely read journals as *Harper's New Monthly Magazine, The Illustrated London News, Strand Magazine,* and *Punch.* Sections devoted to art topics touted everything from upcoming works from the brushes of painters to their favorite vacation locales or their new houses. Popular artists soon discovered that while substantial media coverage helped advance one's career, it was a decidedly mixed blessing. Readers inundated their heroes with requests for advice, art lessons, and even money. Hamo Thornycroft noted in 1893, "I have been pestered lately more than usual with enquiries for my autograph and permissions to see my studio, owing no doubt to the illustrated article in the *Strand* for September."[2] Nevertheless, by the late nineteenth century, constant press coverage had been fully established as a necessary ingredient of a successful career.

As Thornycroft's comment indicates, references to where and how their favorite artists lived were of special interest to the art-loving public. Anyone even vaguely interested in British contemporary art knew that later

Victorian artists were most likely to be found happily ensconced in London within one of the four most popular artists' communities of Chelsea, Hampstead, Kensington, or St. John's Wood. Joseph Hatton's 1883 *Harper's New Monthly Magazine* article, "Some Glimpses of Artistic London," is a typical example of the type of journalism which made these London colonies renowned throughout the western world. The author takes us on what is essentially a walking tour of Kensington, St. John's Wood, and Hampstead, all the while waxing rapturously over the variety of residences and lifestyles to be found flourishing in these newly fashionable neighborhoods (Hatton 828-50). Such was the fame of "artistic London" that these four communities became part of any well-bred foreigner's itinerary whenever she or he visited that great capital. One writer effectively captured a sense of the popularity of these artists' colonies when he noted that an invitation to visit the painter Alma-Tadema's St. John's Wood residence, one of London's most spectacular, was "sufficient in itself to bring a Yankee across the Herring Pond" (Smith 210).

Although Chelsea, Hampstead, Kensington, and St. John's Wood did not collectively emerge as the four major artistic centers until the 1870s, all these regions had previously attracted artists. J.M.W. Turner, John Martin, and others had discovered the joys of Chelsea; George Romney, Clarkson Stanfield, and John Constable the rural wonders of Hampstead; Augustus Wall Callcott, John Linnell, Paul Sandby, and David Wilkie the quiet beauties of Kensington; while Edwin Landseer, C.R. Leslie, and John Rossi were among the first artists to settle in lush St. John's Wood. However, despite artistic associations before the 1870s, these areas attracted only the small minority of artists who were content to live some distance from most of their peers and patrons.

Georgian artists preferred inner London, with those who could afford it residing at smart addresses just south of Regent's Park, at Belgravia, Bloomsbury, Fitzroy Square, Marleybone, Mayfair, and especially, North Soho.[3] By the early Victorian decades this sense of a single true artistic center briefly faded, as many artists abandoned these established locales while settling elsewhere in a seemingly haphazard fashion. The most obvious new trend to emerge at this time was a slow westwards movement into South Kensington, Kensington, Campden Hill, and – by the 1860s – Holland Park.[4] It was not until the 1870s that the migratory habits of British artists once again clearly stabilized, with Chelsea, Hampstead, Kensington, and St. John's Wood emerging as London's most popular artists' communities.[5] These areas would remain synonymous with contemporary art until the late 1890s, when younger artists established Camden Town and elsewhere as viable and preferable options.

It is the purpose of this essay to consider the significance of the establishment of artists' colonies in London's new suburbs rather than the long favored inner city locales. It is my belief that this wholesale change of address is an important factor which must be considered when attempting to understand the unprecedented popularity British contemporary art enjoyed during the 1860s-80s; without the benefits derived from these new addresses, the later Victorian "golden age of British art" would have proven less fecund. In considering the importance of this shift of London's artist population, I will address two main issues: Why did Victorian artists reject the central London favored by past generations of artists in favor of regions outwards, and how did artists benefit from this establishment of new artists' communities?

While several reasons can be given as to why the once beloved artists' haunts of the West End fell from grace, chief among them was that attribute we now associate with many a modern American metropolis, the demise of the once grand areas of the inner city. By the 1870s artists dreaming of worldly success would never have contemplated establishing themselves at formerly chic Georgian and early Victorian addresses. The likes of Bloomsbury or Fitzroy Square and Newman Street, once renowned as the addresses of such illustrious Royal Academicians as Sir Charles Eastlake or Benjamin West, were now dilapitated areas, attracting only poor and struggling artists searching for cheap rents with large north windows perfect for painting, artists willing by necessity rather than by inclination to live London's version of a Bohemian life style.   Thus young artists such as Edward Burne-Jones, Luke Fildes, and J.A.M. Whistler, at the beginning rather than the height of their careers, resided in these depressing flats only until their finances allowed them to escape to more comfortable, and more fashionable addresses.   The painter-illustrator Harry Furniss recalled, "If the haunts and trysting-places of the Bohemian verged on squalor, the homes and studios of the artists presented in most cases an aspect of faded grandeur . . . houses which at one time were the homes of the elite of London" (Furniss 46).

Why didn't later Victorian artists simply continue to live in those areas of inner London which remained well-kempt?   Conscious decisions of this nature became particularly relevant in the 1860s and 1870s, when excess cash derived from the newly flourishing market of contemporary art meant that dozens of artists suddenly possessed the financial freedom to choose precisely where they might most favorably reside.   From a broad perspective, one can argue that this profession's collective decision to vacate traditional artists' quarters reflects the fact that artists wishing to flourish in the increasingly competitive field of the visual arts were *forced* to seek newly fashionable addresses.   In an age of unprecedented wealth and consumption among the middle classes, materialistic display of personal status, riches, and success meant all. Many of those very patrons most willing to pay the highest prices for modern art needed to be reassured that the art they were buying was created by the finest artists and, in addition, was a safe investment.   Many collectors naively believed was that a fine address and impressive residence was a certain gauge of these two factors.   After all, how could these artists live so well but for the fact that many patrons before them had already made similar, satisfactory aesthetic and financial decisions?   Thus artists well understood that to continue to reside in unfashionable quarters of London would be to the ambitious professional artist of the 1860s-80s a social and thus professional kiss of death.   Playing by the rules came to mean that to maintain a suitable residence at a proper address greatly increased one's odds of worldly success. Such thinking helps to explain why many artists abandoned inner city homes even when they were clearly content with them. For instance, the newly popular portraitist Frank Holl, already in possession of a secluded and picturesque Camden Square residence complete with "one of the finest studios in London," decided in 1881 to have Richard Norman Shaw build him a home on newly smart Fitzjohn's Avenue, Hampstead, despite the fact that his entire family was quite content where they were (Reynolds 136).

Where then were artists with sufficiently deep resources to find socially acceptable and professionally attractive new addresses in the ever changing and expanding London landscape? Seen in its simplest terms, many artists were among that first wave of urban Londoners who decided to move into areas previously virtually untouched by London's inevitable sprawl outwards. London's population growth and resulting building boom was so swift that within a few short decades hamlets which had in some cases managed to retain a village-like atmosphere into the 1870s were suddenly engulfed by the metropolitan city. Kensington, for example, grew from 27,000 in 1841 to 163,000 just forty years later (Gaunt 208). Similarly St. John's Wood – which when many young artists discovered its attractions in the 1860s was "with its trees and gardens a thing apart from the noisy bustling city of which it was but an outskirt – one could hardly call it a 'suburb'" – likewise found its population rapidly burgeoning (Smith 123-24). If many artists were savvy enough to move into areas which fast became London's most favored new addresses, it is frankly fruitless to credit them with possessing a special foresight or wisdom. With the city's population growing at an unprecedented rate, artists were, for the most part, among the first wave of innumerable middle-class professionals who chose to purchase or usually build homes in the only spaces readily available to them, the surrounding suburbs. Thus by chance, fashion, and momentum – more often than by design – many a late Victorian artist moved to suburbia, living in the midst of the very middle classes who would support and admire their careers. It is, however, worth noting that due to the peculiar nature of their profession, artists could become a part of the first urban generation to move to these locales with few complications. After all, the products they created were painted or sculpted within their very residences. This meant they initially had less need than most professionals within their income bracket (doctors, lawyers) for fine high street commercial areas, or avenues lined almost exclusively with wealthy individuals or well paved streets. As long as they continued to have ready access to the Royal Academy and their favorite dealers or patrons, many were content to live in areas just beginning to undergo great transformations.

If the above statements help us to understand how artists came to move into the still wide open spaces immediately surrounding London, it does not tell us why they specifically preferred Hampstead, Kensington, St. John's Wood, or Chelsea. London was, after all, burgeoning in all directions. Fortunately each borough's special attributes can still be powerfully felt simply by spending part of a warm summer's day in the secluded peacefulness of the Leighton House Museum lawn or by taking a leisurely walking tour of any of these artists' communities. It then becomes immediately obvious that artists were undoubtedly among the first wave of urban dwellers powerfully drawn to the finest of the still relatively unsettled areas of outlying London. For artists' residences are time and again located on some of London's finest and most attractive real estate, from prominent hills to heavily wooded, secluded, and generously-sized lots which today continue to indicate that artists were drawn to those sites which most completely appealed to their aesthetic sensibilities. All four of their favored regions remain among London's most desirable real estate.[6] The architect Richard Norman Shaw's comment to Luke Fildes in 1875 concerning his newly leased lot in Holland Park, "I do most heartily congratulate you on having got that bit – and I feel quite certain you will *never* regret it," accurately summarizes the enthusiasm numerous artists felt after finally discovering and obtaining their small piece of personal paradise.[7]

Each of these four areas newly favored by artists possessed its own special physical charms. Hampstead beckoned those like P.F. Poole and Henry Holiday who loved higher elevations, beautiful vistas, and walks on a heath. St. John's Wood was discovered by the St. John's Wood Clique (including John Hodgson and H.S. Marks) and others to be unusually picturesque and notably free of pollution, while in Kensington artists such as George Frederic Watts and Luke Fildes were much attracted to the heavily wooded grounds of the former Little Holland House. All three of these neighborhoods offered artists assets very difficult to acquire in central London, particularly generous lots, fresh air, and the peace and quiet artists needed to fully concentrate upon their latest projects.

Of the four regions we are considering, Chelsea differed considerably from the others. Despite the fact that it, too, was located some distance from central London, its history and landscape contrasted greatly with that of the still sparcely populated Hampstead, Kensington, and St. John's Wood. With its illustrious past associated with the likes of Sir Thomas More, the Royal Hospital, J.M.W. Turner, Thomas Carlyle, and the Rossettis, Chelsea had long been heavily populated and was already associated in the minds of many with the arts. Beyond the mystique of its history, its unique attractions included those picturesque and sometimes seedy charms gained by its proximity to the Thames, and so magically captured by Whistler. That Chelsea became newly fashionable in the 1870s-80s is due to its transformation from a poor and working-class into a middle-class borough thanks to such sweeping changes as the construction of the Thames Embankment and the building of new avenues including Tite Street, the favorite address of such renowned Chelsea artists as John Collier, Anna Lea Merritt, John Singer Sargent, Whistler, and, of course, the writer Oscar Wilde. While the studio-houses of Chelsea were as grand as those found elsewhere, limited space meant that they were for the most part narrower, taller, and lacked large, lush gardens. Many of the observations which follow relate specifically to the suburbs of Hampstead, Kensington, and St. John's

Wood; however, as I note, several remarks do include
Chelsea, which rightfully enjoyed a fame equal to that of
any of the other artists' colonies.

This creation of a "new" Chelsea resembled in its
growing pains the changes taking place in the three
more rural regions, for in all cases one result of this
rapidly increasing population was the inevitable destruction of homes which had long housed London's poor, and
ways of life which had existed for centuries. Thus in
Kensington, Sir Frederic Leighton's house was located
adjacent to an old farm and was just a few doors from a
dairy and seedy public house. The encroaching new inhabitants were not always comfortable with neighborhoods so clearly in transition. For example, after Oscar
Wilde's move to Tite Street he found that he so disliked
living with a rear view of Paradise Walk, one of London's
poorest streets, that he was "forced" to hide this unpalat-
able rear view of this street with a Persian screen while
avoiding walks in that area (Holme 154). Such conflicts
are not obvious today because these tenements have long
since disappeared. Yet, before their inevitable destruction, such older, run-down structures played an important
role in the growth of artists' colonies, for they provided
make-shift housing and studios for many a poor artist who
wished to live as near as possible to more fortunate members of their profession. Many are the comments, such as
that written by Edwin Austin Abbey concerning the ancient Chelsea buildings Cally Bloomer and R.A.M. Stevenson (cousin of Robert Louis Stevenson) had just rented,
which were "a hole of a place . . . with two desperate
studios in the back yard . . . The studio was the most awful
place you can think of, in a nasty backyard, with a
dripping spout and a large puddle under it. I remember
that I wanted to lean my head against the wall and cry"
(Lucas 1:84).

While the memoirs and correspondence of more fortunate artists make it clear that they chose their particular
suburb due to specific physical charms, this was by no
means the only or even primary reason many artists
moved to one of these four sites. As the term "artists'
community" suggests, the desire for comradeship, to be

physically near other members of one's chosen profession, was a major force. While English artists had for generations lived in close proximity of one another, the new suburbs made this far simpler to accomplish due to the wealth of wide open spaces and readily available plots of land. For the first time artists could decide with ease to live directly beside one another or upon the same street. For example, Leighton could be found at Holland Park during the 1860s building a new studio-house next door to that of his young friend Valentine Prinsep, who, in turn, would lease part of his vast back lawn to G.F. Watts, Prinsep's former teacher and Leighton's closest companion. This arrangement thus enabled Sir Frederic to visit both Val and "the Signor" daily for some thirty years. St. John's Wood, the first fully established late Victorian artists' colony, seems to have grown almost overnight during this same decade into a tightly linked group of intimate companions, including P.H. Calderon, J. Hodgson, G.D. Leslie, H.S. Marks, and W.F. Yeames, collectively called the St. John's Wood Clique. These artists and their families' social and professional worlds were consequently closely linked for some two decades, with lawn tennis, plays performed in studios, evenings spent discussing art, and weekend sketching tours constant aspects of their daily lives.[8] In Hampstead, Frank Holl bought property in part to allow him the opportunity to live within one door of his longtime close confrere John Pettie (Reynolds 207). In Chelsea, Frank Miles could walk out his door and within moments enjoy the champagne of his caustic neighbor Whistler. Back in Kensington, Luke Fildes was able to look out his studio window at the elegant Queen Anne Revival style residence of his sometimes closest friend – and eventual favorite enemy – Marcus Stone, just a few hundred feet away from his.

Close friendships would not alone have turned these four regions into genuine artists' colonies. The politically ambitious and astute generation of the 1870s-80s was fully aware that social and professional benefits could be derived by living within ready hailing distance of the most powerful of the Royal Academy's rising stars who were only slightly older than they were. The most famous proof of this conviction was found at Holland Park. By the mid-1870s it was obvious to all that Leighton would be the Royal Academy's next president. Thus from that point we find Fildes, Stone, Colin Hunter, and others setting up shop as close as they could get to the shadow of his home. This simple idea of power or gain by association was readily grasped by writers; Joseph Hatton observed with a touch of humor that "Sir Frederick (sic) Leighton's house and studio are notable not only in themselves, but as the centre of an art colony which has been somewhere strikingly described as a red group of artists' houses, like soldiers or clansmen loyally closing round their chief" (Hatton 829).

If we are to fully understand the rapid growth and widespread fame of London's four artists' colonies, it is imperative that we specifically consider the artist houses in Hatton's reference. Among those first artists who settled in these four communities during the 1860s and 1870s we find at the central core what was fast becoming the power base of the late Victorian art world. Several were artists who only recently assumed the mantle as the Royal Academy's – and thus Britain's – greatest younger artists, including Lawrence Alma-Tadema, Leighton, Edwin Long, John Everett Millais, and much of the St. John's Wood Clique. Several others were just on the verge of being elected an Associate of the Royal Academy (A.R.A.), the surest pathway to fame and fortune, such as Fildes, Holl, John MacWhirter, John Pettie, Stone and many others. These artists were making incredible financial gains due to the astronomical prices contemporary art was then fetching, and all were willing to invest considerable portions of their real or imagined excess guineas in ways most likely to advance, promote, and maintain their popularity with patrons, the admiring public, and the popular press. Most visible and most commented upon was that widespread, middle-class later Victorian symbol of professional success and worth: a new house.

Inspired by Leighton's and Prinsep's examples of the mid-1860s, dozens of artists who could afford to – and many who could not – hired newly fashionable architects with a penchant for working for artists, including Edward

Godwin, Richard Norman Shaw, and Philip Webb, to design and custom-build residences for their peculiar professional, personal, and social needs. As a large central
studio measuring 40-50 feet long with huge light-seeking
north windows dominated most of these homes, these
several dozen private residences are now generically called
studio-houses.[9] After construction, shocking sums were
then spent on antique and custom-designed furniture and
Old Master and contemporary art, transforming each
home into that tenant's version of a "House Beautiful."
Rossetti and Whistler enthusiastically decorated their
residences with beautiful Oriental blue and white china,
Leighton's home included rare Middle Eastern carpets and
an impressive art collection with works by Constable,
Corot, Delacroix, Ingres, Reynolds, and many others, and
the most sumptuous artist house of all, Alma-Tadema's,
included hand-crafted and painted pianos and a custom-
designed gallery of contemporary British art. Such care
ensured that while these fair sized studio-houses might be
smaller than those of their more wealthy patrons and
visitors, they were inevitably far more exotic. After visiting
a few of these impressive structures, how could a prospec-
tive patron doubt that artists were urbane, educated, well
traveled, and above all, aesthetically and artistically superior beings? Viewing these houses collectively as well as
individually, how could one help but conclude that contemporary art was a "rock solid" investment already obviously made by many other wise businessmen?

The impact such houses had upon the general public
was unquestionably immense, and as a result the popular
press churned out many laudatory articles concerning
their attributes until the end of the century. Even as late
as 1893 we can find the artist Henry Woods, brother-in-
law of Luke Fildes, writing that while staying at a hotel in
Switzerland, the August 1893 issue of *Strand Magazine*
appeared with an illustrated article on the latter's residence. Among the hotel guests, "The rapture was general
concerning your house. Such a place could scarcely have
been imagined in London" (Fildes 132). Such consistently
positive press regarding studio-houses and the art created
within their walls assured that the hero-worshipping late

Victorian public would always associate the age's greatest art and artists specifically with Chelsea, Hampstead, Kensington, and St. John's Wood.

Studio-houses were best suited for the new suburbs. Indeed, they would have been not only very difficult but prohibitively expensive to build in inner London. Only the suburbs (or the freshly available plots in Chelsea) could provide artists with the large lots needed for these substantial habitations. Space was also a coveted commodity for other reasons. Many of these artists also desired generous gardens, which provided beauty and a place to escape. And these gardens could be utilized for social purposes. For example, many socially ambitious artists held open houses or "At Homes" on Sunday afternoons; during warm weather these were held in the rear gardens. There one could lounge around J.J.J. Tissot's (later Alma-Tadema's) colonnaded reflecting pool,[10] watch newly fashionable tennis stars playing on J.E. Hodgkin's or other Clique members' lawns in St. John's Wood (Morris 11-12), sip tea on Prinsep's lawn in Holland Park, or hear Gladstone give speeches supporting Home Rule in back of Henry Holiday's studio home in Hampstead (Holiday 320). These types of social activities were absolutely essential to worldly success. Visitors, including anyone from art critics to celebrity guests such as Robert Browning, Benjamin Disraeli, the Prince of Wales, Alfred Tennyson, Ellen Terry, and Oscar Wilde, helped to attract and convince potential buyers or patrons, who would then hopefully be favorably enough impressed with the artist's personality, social graces, good taste, and physical surroundings, to part with several hundred pounds for the artist's latest creation still wet and on display in the main atelier.

Living in suburbia also provided artists of the 1870s with much they desired from a professional standpoint. For the artist at work, generous green spaces served as a buffer from one's neighbors, providing the necessary quiet for contemplation. More importantly, these regions were still relatively pollution-free. This is an important point, as one can argue that the principal reason for this move to the suburbs was a craving for adequate sunlight, the principal and universal preoccupation of many late nineteenth-century artists. Artists at this time widely refused to work under artificial lighting conditions, making adequate natural lighting essential to their livelihood.[11] As London was world famous for its black fogs which turned day into hellish night, more densely populated and thus polluted central London was less than ideal for painters. The suburbs, then, provided artists with that vital "ingredient" more necessary on a daily basis than even inspiration: clean air. It is ironic that in this sense some of these suburbs would eventually fail the artist, for as London continued to expand, some of these increasingly inter-suburban artists' communities were themselves engulfed by the dreaded black fogs. Kensington especially suffered in this respect. By 1880 Luke Fildes was constantly complaining that he could paint just a few hours weekly, while Frederic Leighton found himself giving a public lecture at the Lord Mayor's dinner of 1882 on the unlikely topic of pollution abatement ("An Artist's View" 367). Nevertheless, artists living in suburbia gained dozens of additional work days each year simply by escaping inner London.

Despite what the public widely believed, artists living in studio-houses did not in themselves make an artists' colony. But once these highly visible artists with significant or promising careers settled in their favored locales, countless other artists followed. As I have indicated earlier, promising, mediocre, and unsuccessful artists all moved to these regions, living in whatever arrangements they could afford, from newly constructed studio flats to converted stables and other old and humble structures that had managed to survive destruction amidst the urban sprawl.[12] However depressing these arrangements might have been, they had the decided attraction of being near the residences of the most successful artists of their profession, and one never knew when this might work in one's favor. After all, older and more established artists saw it as their professional duty to assure the continued success of their chosen field by aiding the next generation as much as possible. The advantages of proximity are readily grasped simply by reading the diaries of the promising young sculptor Hamo Thornycroft or the memoirs of

Henrietta Rae after each moved to Holland Park. Professional critiques of their art work, patrons suddenly appearing with a commission, and the opportunity to aid
these famous, established artists were but a few of the
"perks" which came their way. For example, Rae and her
painter husband Ernest Normand were "adopted as the
proteges of the older artists among whom they lived. Their
studio was constantly visited by Leighton, Millais, Prinsep,
Watts and others" (Fish 47). Such concern meant a great
deal to the careers of struggling artists but could occasionally become too much of a good thing; one day, after
listening to some particularly annoying criticism from
Prinsep, Rae seized his hat and heaved it into her studio
stove (MacKinlay 581).

With the arrival throughout the 1880s of these younger
and lesser talents, the late Victorian artists' colonies were
fully established, functioning for the most part very effectively indeed. Artists visited one another on a daily basis,
sharing many thoughts related to their profession and
aiding one another when difficulties arose. Models went
from door to door within each community seeking employment, and were often sent to a neighbor's studio-house
because she or he was precisely another artist's "type."
Props and costumes were frequently borrowed. Potential
patrons were sent to a nearby artist better suited for or
more needy of a commission. Frame makers and color-
men set up shops conveniently nearby. All, for a brief
time, seemed blissful for the successful contemporary
artist.

Despite this vitality, which lasted some two decades,
by the late 1890s late Victorian art colonies were already
being viewed as a thing of the past.Time played its inevitable role, as much of the luster of these communities was
lost with the death of its most famous inhabitants, especially Leighton and Millais. Money, too, was a key issue.
Contemporary art had from the late 1880s fallen from
favor, and as a result the golden years of this profession
had clearly ended. By the Edwardian era the favored
neighborhoods of the Victorians were long since the bas-
tions of respectability, far too costly for the purses of most
young artists.[13] Artistically, too, much of the younger

generation *preferred* to find new inspiration elsewhere in London, especially in areas like Camden Town with its gritty reality. Despite these four areas' eventual loss of fame as artists' quarters, however, they had served the later Victorians well. In these regions artists had been able to establish roots and then create a public identity which was world renowned and to function on professional and social levels which were very much in harmony with the needs and desires of their time. For those able to look out comfortable studio-house windows and watch the daily activities of artistic life unfold, it was a fine time indeed for artists to be living in suburbia.

Notes

1. While the Victorians loved reading about many types of popular public figures, from politicians to actresses, it was the visual artists who received the late nineteenth-century equivalent of the media hype and attention now reserved for movie stars. For a discussion of Victorian artists, their residences and the popular press, see J. Lamb, "The Way We Live Now: Late Victorian Studios and the Popular Press," *Visual Resources*, 9 (1993): 107-25. To take this comparison with the movie industry a step further, the degree of attention devoted to artists was wholly appropriate, for they were the greatest creators of the most popular form of visual entertainment of their day, the annual Royal Academy and dealer exhibitions and related engravings.
2. See the Hamo Thornycroft Archives, Henry Moore Centre for the Study of Sculpture, Leeds City Art Gallery, journal entry, 6 October 1893.
3. See chapters 1-3 of Gile Walkley's *Artists' Houses in London 1764-1914* (London: Scolar Press, 1994), which thoroughly and entertainingly traces artists' movements about London. Also see M. Jacobs and M. Warner, *The Phaidon Companion to Art and Artists in the British Isles* (London: Phaidon, 1980).
4. These early and mid-Victorian residents included E. Cooke, A.H. Corbould, A. Elmore, J.C. Hook, A. Hunt, W.H. Hunt, and many more. Many histories of Kensington list specific artists and addresses.
5. Less popular areas of London which attracted their proponents included Bedford Park and Hammersmith. Some artists, including T. Sidney Cooper, Frederick Goodall, J.C. Hook, and J. C. Horsley opted to abandon London for the English countryside. As London was Great Britain's artistic capital, this decision meant having to keep in constant touch with the London art world. Some artists, such as Cooper, kept a London residence, while others such as Goodall, eventually returned to London.
6. While artists were well aware of the beauties of their chosen neighborhood and undoubtedly played a role in determining which community they eventually settled in, the immediate landscape in itself had little effect upon their art. From the 1870s, few ventured beyond their studio walls to sketch or paint the natural beauty of their surroundings. Even

landscape painters tended to find their subjects during summer sketching tours.

7. L.V. Fildes, *Luke Fildes R.A.: A Victorian Painter* (London, Michael Joseph, 1968): 36. Other examples of artists early on discovering prime real estate would be Leighton and Prinsep's purchase during the 1860s of generous plots in Holland Park and Frank Holl, P.F. Poole, and John Pettie's purchase of plots with wonderful vistas cut through beautiful green fields in Hampstead (Fitzjohn's Avenue).

8. Their links are intimately described in H.S. Marks, *Pen and Pencil Sketches*, 2 vols. (London: Chatto & Windus 1894).

9. The three most famous London studio-houses were those of Alma-Tadema, Leighton, and Millais. There were, however, dozens more; these are best illustrated and described in G. Walkley, *Artists' Houses in London 1764-1914* (London: Scolar Press, 1994).

10. This colonnade was built for Tissot and used as the setting for such works as *Holyday (The Picnic*; c. 1876) Tate Gallery, London. Alma-Tadema purchased this residence and much altered all but this reflecting pool.

11. Millais was a notable exception, sometimes working by artificial lighting.

12. For several examples of mass produced artists' studio flats, see chapter 8 of G. Walkley, *Artists' Houses In London, 1764-1914.*

13. There were a few artists who built notable homes in the 1890s, including Mortimer Menpes's Japanese fantasy in Chelsea and J.J. Shannon's remodelled home next to Leighton.

Works Cited

"An Artist's View of the Smoke Question," *Builder* 42 (1882): 367.

Cooper, T. Sidney. *My Life.* 2 vols. London: Richard Bentley and Son, 1890.

Fildes, L. V. *Luke Fildes, R.A.: A Victorian Painter.* London: Michael Joseph, 1968.

Fish, Arthur. *Henrietta Rae.* London: Cassell, 1905.

Furniss, Harry. *My Bohemian Days.* London: Hurst and Blackett, 1919.

Hatton, Joseph. "Some Glimpses of Artistic London." *Harper's New Monthly Magazine* 67 (November 1883): 828-50.

Holiday, Henry. *Reminiscences of My Life.* London: William Heinemann, 1914.

Holme, Thea. *Chelsea.* New York: Taplinger, 1971.

Lucas, E. V. *Edwin Austin Abbey, Royal Academician: The Record of His Life and Work.* 2 vols. London: Methuen, 1921.

MacKinlay, M. Sterling. "Random Recollections of a Bohemian." *Strand Magazine* 29 (1905): 576-83.

Morris, Edward and Frank Milner. *'And When Did You Last See Your Father?'* Liverpool: Walker Art Gallery, 1992.

Reynolds, A. M. *The Life and Work of Frank Holl.* London: Methuen, 1912.

Smith, M. H. Stephen. *Art and Anecdote: Recollections of William Frederick Yeames, R.A, His Life and His Friends.* London: Hutchinson, 1927.

4

London, Dickens, & the Theatre of Homelessness

Murray Baumgarten

*U*rban life in the Dickens universe is a theatrical code. Historians note his accuracy: Nineteenth-century industrial capitalism helped to define the modern city in theatrical terms (Gay passim, Schwarzbach ch. 10). Not only was this a function of the reconstruction of the cities and massive new investment in plazas, parks, and squares, it was also the result of capital accumulation and the increasing democratization of everyday life. Crowds now gathered, not only on ritualized occasions and events – executions, coronations, royal weddings, progresses, parades, and the like – they also congregated in the course of daily business, including commuting to work. The new spaces created by the urban reconstruction of London served as impromptu theatres for street performers who could now take their activities from local side-streets and neighborhood building courts to the potentially larger audiences congregating in these public arenas. Such urban theatrical phenomena punctuate Dickens's novels: Pip and Wemmick in *Great Expectations*, to take only one example, meet on the street amid the crowds going to and from work. Their encounters bear witness to these new experiential conditions, which shape their lives. As Wemmick changes into Jaggers's law-clerk on the way into the City and back into the benevolent son of the Aged P. on his return journey to Little Britain, Pip, standing-in for the Dickensian reader, discovers the transformative theatrical experience that defines this urban world.

Creating the infrastructure that made the modern city possible, the monumental building projects also provided a window into the easier pace of the past in the informal street performances they made possible by the new dramatic staging of the city. At the same time, they made everyone a performer. Lewis Mumford underlines the function of the modern city as encouraging and inciting "the greatest potential number of meetings, encounters, challenges between all persons, classes and groups, providing, as it were, a stage upon which the drama of social life may be enacted, and with the actors taking their turns as spectators and the spectators as actors" (184).

In spite of the new power-relations which maximized competition and which Noddy Boffin defines in *Our Mutual Friend* as "scrunch or be scrunched" (bk. III, ch. 5), nineteenth-century London was also the place of "playful self-making" for all, especially for the working and lower classes. "Through their convivial laughter, their sympathy, their nonhegemonic speech, and their imaginative exuberance" they asserted that "life is not warfare against sin, nor is it only competitive struggle." Without "wealth or status" they yet became "imaginatively adept at exploiting language, gesture, and common reality to transform, with a sense of ceremony, existences which would otherwise be overwhelmed by necessity and utility" (Morris 34-35). From the Artful Dodger in *Oliver Twist* to Rogue Riderhood in *Our Mutual Friend*, Dickens's novels offer a portrait gallery of such figures of transformation.

While the impact of capitalism on Dickens's world has been noted by many scholars, the social economy of theatrical self-presentation which I explore in this essay, following the important work of Robert Garis, has not received similar attention. My discussion traces this motif through several of his novels, focusing on how the city functions to reinforce the theatricalization of appearance and everyday life; I also elaborate its connection to aspects of the picturesque. Furthermore, the ways in which theatrical experience is deployed in the marketplace for economic gain has not been central to current discussions of Dickens's art which also tend to elide the urban experience. In his writings as in his world, the opportunities of London are available to all, including the homeless. The city as marketplace, labyrinth, and stage is the central scene of his work – a measure of his encompassing democratic art.

While Dickens's representations of lower-class life echo those of Mayhew, they also provide a dynamic sense of character and possibility. Where Mayhew's are static and reinforce conventional stereotypes of the poor that, reinforced by an anthropology developing spurious racial distinctions which would make class division a seeming fact of nature (as Thomas Prasch points out in his essay in this volume, "Photography and the Image of the London Poor") Dickens's characters dramatize their situations as part of a strategy of overcoming such barriers. While Silas Wegg is poor and a rogue, the way in which he accepts Boffin's offer to read to him – "No, sir. I never did 'aggle and I never will 'aggle. Consequently, I meet you at once, free and fair, with – Done, for double the money!" (bk. I, ch. 5) – is but one of many instances in *Our Mutual Friend* in which theatrical self-presentation functions to bridge class and social divisions as well as further economic gain.

Nineteenth-century urban reconstruction not only defined the theatre of everyday life, it also helped to create the homeless as a distinct and visible group: a class of people with access to this city stage but without personal location. Like other characters in Dickens's urban comedy, Silas Wegg has no home of his own yet he takes center stage throughout much of *Our Mutual Friend* by setting up his stand on a street corner. At almost the polar opposite of the social scale, Nicholas Nickleby discovers that he too can rely only on his self-presentation and role-playing as levers by which to attain a domicile of his own, in a manner of which Wegg is the undisputed master.

Nicholas Nickleby and *Our Mutual Friend*, among the Dickens novels most concerned with the theater, both focus on clothes-making. In *Our Mutual Friend* Jenny Wren models her dolls' clothing on that of society, while much of *Nicholas Nickleby* takes place in the Mantalini's dressmaking establishment. In both novels, appearances count for so much that clothing is put at its metaphoric center. In both, what a character wears is part of the modern industry of image-making and self-production. Not only his sister Kate but Nicholas as well will discover the power of the projected image, and the temptation to trade upon it for subsistence and possible wealth. Like dressmaking, the production of the self in this world is not a "natural" phenomenon but a technical – and technological – event that articulates the central values of this culture. Here, personality, like Miss LaCreevy's miniatures in *Nicholas Nickleby*, is composed. It is an image framed by the portrait painter's equivalent of a "Claude Glass" which functions to define a picturesque image.[1] Whatever the moral differences among characters, all are arrayed along the same ladder of self-making. Life for Boffin, Bella, Rokesmith, as for Nicholas, Kate, and Crummles, embodies the dressmaking idea, as Carlyle emphasizes in *Sartor Resartus:* we are in a world of cutting out shapes, stitching seams, and sewing on ruffles and borders, and thereby assembling a striking appearance out of the abstract, impersonal materials furnished by the industrial revolution, which began in England with the mass-production of cloth.

Just as appearance is an abstraction in this world, so personal relationships are here mediated by the abstractions of print and money. Thus it is entirely appropriate that Nicholas first learns of the job of tutor to Squeers through the abstract medium of a newspaper advertisement, which his uncle Ralph shows him. This is the beginning of Nicholas's education in the ways of the world. It is part of his introduction to the power available to those who can manipulate print and numbers; it is the beginning of his lessons that social appearance in this world is constructed appearance.

It is his appearance that leads Nicholas to employment throughout the novel. What he must learn in this *bildungsroman* is how to live up to his projected social role of gentleman. To be a knight and hero in this world is to fulfill the expectations of (aristocratic) appearance – and it is only through Nicholas's apprenticeship to the theatre of Crummles, a troupe that lives out the comic dramas they put on the provincial stage, that he discovers what it means to act his part. After that apprenticeship, he is ready for the fateful encounter with the Brothers Cheery-ble, which frees him from the financial grasp of his uncle.

Though we never quite learn what their business con-sists of, Dickens makes quite clear that the Cheerybles do not engage in the kind of financial sleight-of-hand that characterizes Ralph's activities. Their offices do not de-pend on the illusion-creating staging of which Ralph is so fond, in which he makes certain that the seedy Newman Noggs plays the role of gatekeeper to intimidate his clients. Nor are the Cheerybles, who are committed to an older style of business, engaged in setting up phony stock ventures which depend on false advertising, as is Ralph Nickleby at the beginning of the novel; and his orchestra-tion of the effort to drive local muffin makers out of business and replace them with a monopoly is the target of Dickens's satire in a scene that not only has the bite of Brechtian satire but functions by synecdoche to condemn all the instances of this morally shabby process.

The two firms are spatially counterposed in the novel; together they suggest the possibilities of urban life. The city thus becomes emblematic of the space between the old and new activities, between an older investment in a stable identity and a modern embrace of opportunity and dy-namic self-making. And their intermediary is the market that, while invisible, projects possibilities which in terms of their past histories, impresses the newcomers to the city not just as opportunities but as seemingly malevolent situations.

Like their more privileged contemporaries these new city-dwellers had to learn how to negotiate the city by learning to read its new alphabet and syntax. Among the novelists who took as their task that of deciphering city life, Dickens is primary, teaching his contemporaries what "city-knowing" and "city-thinking" is. The problem he faced is that, as Mary Ann Caws has phrased it, "there is no easy reading of the city or its texts, no simple shuffling about of ironies as covers of the situation." While Dickens informs us "about city misery, physical and mental, about loneliness and loss and powerlessness" in an act of the literary imagination that "we must not lose," it is also not in his work, nor can it be in ours, "an excuse for yet more city-despair, for yet less use of the imagination, political, textual, and personal" (Caws 2; 6).

By contrast with Mayhew and other social observers, even in his darker novels Dickens does not speak for the class divisions so evident in the city or accept them as natural or a social given. Rather, his plots enforce the possibility that the urban world is the site of moral self-making precisely because it brings people together across class and social lines. His is not Mayhew's static image-building but an art of dynamic and evolving situations and figures. The serial format of Dickens's novels enforces this transformational context, as does the city – the central site of his fictional project and personal life – with its ephemeral, transitory, changing experiences of repetition with variation. In his work, the content of the form crosses over like one of Carlyle's metaphors to insinuate change as the form of the content. Whether characters are cannibalistic or altruistic, it defines them whatever their place as part of the same universe of discourse. They speak to and for each other, as evidenced in the impact the Cheeryble Brothers make, even in adversarial confrontation, on Ralph Nickleby. Here Dickens's fictions articulate, as do Carlyle's essays and Marx's critiques, the radical modern notion of species-being. Though their examples are often negative ones like the Irish widow in *Past and Present* who, spurned by Edinburgh charities, dies in the city and infects it with typhus, they reveal the ways in which it is not possible to escape from our common humanity (Marcus 97-99). And while Marx emphasizes the lure of the market and Carlyle the snaring of personality in the labyrinth, Dickens foregrounds the theatrical power of the stage in connecting classes and individuals.

The repeal of English sumptuary laws in the 1820s and 1830s codified the greater freedom to rise and to fall of everyday life. Linkages that had seemed part of the order of things were broken. When characters change their clothes in Dickens – Bella leaving the Boffins, her benefactors, and returning to her family home in the simple dress with which she left; Bradley putting on his schoolmaster's teaching style along with his vest; Twemlow inserting himself into his silk stockings for dinner at the Veneerings – they define their person in terms of the theatrical effect they seek to create and in terms of which they expect to be read. Values which had previously gone without saying now had to be discussed, clarified, and articulated, as John Stuart Mill emphasizes in "The Spirit of the Age," making a distinction between manifest and latent social functions. "For, the obvious and universal facts, which every one sees and no one is astonished at, it seldom occurs to any one to place upon record; and posterity, if it learn the rule, learns it, generally from the notice bestowed by contemporaries on some accidental exception" (226-27). Change has made what seemed familiar strange. Now clothes were no longer directly connected to social class but, as Carlyle reminds us in *Sartor Resartus*, have become costumes to be donned as part of identity-games and role-playing rather than natural concomitants of place and position. As markers of conventions, which remained strong, clothes were now part of the manipulable furniture of self-presentation. Rather than being tied to place, competence, and craftsmanship as measures of value, clothing was one way of indicating the realm of desired identity. Perhaps that is why the sketch of Monmouth Street Dickens provides in *Sketches by Boz* is so vivid, the clothes turning into the lives of the people who wore them in a dreamer's dance of the imagination.

> We love to walk among these . . . and to indulge in the speculations to which they give rise; now fitting a deceased coat, then a dead pair of trousers, and endeavouring, from the shape and fashion of the garment itself, to bring its former owner before our mind's eye. We have gone on speculating in this way, until whole rows of coats have started from their pegs, and buttoned up of their own accord, round the waists of imaginary wearers; lines of trousers have jumped down to meet them; waistcoats have almost burst with anxiety to put themselves on; and half an acre of shoes have suddenly found feet to fit them, and gone stumping down the street with a noise which has fairly awakened us from our pleasant reverie, and driven us

slowly away, with a bewildered stare, an object of astonishment to the good people of Monmouth Street, and of no slight suspicion to the policemen at the opposite street corner. ("Old Clothes" 75)

Against that sense of possibility and renewed, reconstructed identity in and of the city, we have Carlyle's recurring image of the Jewish peddler, the Old Clothes man whom Mayhew also describes and Dickens evokes, as part of the nightmare possibility of this new world defined not by ascribed status but by the ready money earned through commerce and industry.

In Dickens's world the opportunities for self-presentation are manifold. They take place in the Victorian parlor, in which Mr Podsnap dismisses everything "not English" and Mr Bounderby reiterates his rise from birth-in-a-ditch to industrial and financial eminence in *Hard Times*, as well as Edith Dombey's and Bella Wilfer's self-definition before the bedroom mirror. It is not accidental then, or merely a taste for sociological completeness that brings the poor and the homeless to the center of Dickens's stage; rather, it is in their relations to the hegemonic middle-class that Dickens explores the range of possibilities offered by the urban theatre of modern life.

His exploration focuses on the public world as well as the private realm; he takes us into Chancery and the Inn, and the places in between. In his world, the homeless, whether Silas Wegg or Nicholas Nickleby, perform their self-making in the new public arena articulated by and in nineteenth-century European culture, in and along the modern street. Given its public status and accessibility, the throngs passing through it, and its availability for many purposes, the street superseded all other venues. *Little Dorrit* concludes with Arthur Clennam and Little Dorrit, freed of the imprisonments of the past, leaving the Marshalsea prison, and going out of the church where they have been married into "the roaring streets."

They paused for a moment on the steps of the portico, looking at the fresh perspective of the street in the autumn morning sun's bright rays, and then went down.

Went down into a modest life of usefulness and happiness. Went down to give a mother's care, in the fulness of

time, to Fanny's neglected children no less than to their
own, and to leave that lady going into Society for ever and
a day. Went down to give a tender nurse and friend to Tip
for some few years, who was never vexed by the great
exactions he made of her, in return for the riches he might
have given her if he had ever had them, and who lovingly
closed his eyes upon the Marshalsea and all its blighted
fruits. They went quietly down into the roaring streets,
inseparable and blessed; and as they passed along in
sunshine and shade, the noisy and the eager, and the
arrogant and the froward, and the vain, fretted, and chafed,
and made their usual uproar. (826)

Now the homeless and dispossessed individual is part not
of the picturesque pastoral or rural Wordsworthian landscape but the stage of urban life. He is not the leech-gath-
erer emerging from the rocky earth who serves as a moral
teacher in "Resolution & Independence" but a figure whose
moral value develops in the course of social interactions in
an epic tale rather than a lyric meditation. He is not the
figure who, as Wordsworth described his experience,
emerges from a crowded, indistinct landscape and awak-
ens the poet's mind from his "dreamy indifference" to
focus his attention on "a poetical object" (Wordsworth to
Lady Beaumont, 21 May 1807, in Wordsworth 145-51).
Dickens's characters are part of the panorama of the street
– of crowds and action and constant movement – a characteristic feature of Dickens's art. The picturesque individual has been turned into the unusual, eccentric performer
on the stage of urban life. Now he is part not of the
personal witnessing of the artist who has sought out the
picturesque for inspiration but the objective condition of
urban spectacle (Nord passim).

Capital city and commercial center, London in Dickens's fiction is the theatrical realm in which everyone,
including the homeless, make their entrance. They encounter economic possibility, despair as well as political
empowerment, and moral destiny in its streets. One can
also trace the connection of the interest in the picturesque
with the Victorian habit of "slumming"; the notion that
these people are the ruins of urban humanity encouraged
the development of social welfare and the rise of the social
worker as a profession.

Dickens generalized the pursuit of the rural ruin (modeled on the Gilpinian and Wordsworthian reading of, for

example, "Tintern Abbey"), and extended it to London, treated now as if the city were a ruin, its docks and shipyards, its monuments and housing warrens demanding a complex personal decoding. When Kate and her mother follow Newman Noggs to the rooms provided by Uncle Ralph on the ironically named Golden Square, when Kate walks to Madame Mantalini's or Nicholas negotiates the streets leading to the Cheerybles' place of business, they must deploy city habits only to be gained in their exercise. Nothing in their earlier experience prepares them for the confrontations with power and money that await them, and only their newly acquired street smarts will help them in the struggle to overcome them.

To follow the transformation of the picturesque into the Dickensian picaresque also charts the Wordsworthian presence in Dickens's art. *Nicholas Nickleby*, published in 1838 when Wordsworth was poet laureate, is not only a city novel but a travelogue whose main characters journey almost the entire length of England from London northward. It is also a portrait of London as an inhospitable place which echoes Wordsworth's view of the city in Book VII of *The Prelude*. When the Cheerybles talk of their entry into the city, it is "the wilderness of London" they refer to. This is the city of Hungerford Stairs with its Warrens' Blacking factory; it is a place of misery and despair where Oliver Twist will need great luck and much help to survive, and Nicholas Nickleby will be "reduced to the necessity" almost of begging (1:340, 339). And yet, it is only in London that Nicholas and Kate will be able to succeed. Like Oliver they have left the more settled and organized countryside with its orderly villages, for the chaos, anarchy, and opportunity of the city. Yet it is more than economic hope which brings these representative figures to London. The city beckons as a political and moral phenomenon: in a time of great change, it is the site of the story of success, for it is the theatre of possibility. And it is this theatrical trope which defines Dickens's chosen city.

H.M. Daleski has noted that in *Oliver Twist*, "the idea of homelessness is concretized in the image of the street . . . the central image of the novel." Daleski further notes that in looking "back on his work and seeking, in an 1841 Preface, to dissociate it from the genre of the Newgate novel," Dickens claimed that in *Oliver Twist* there were "no canterings upon moonlit heaths, no merry-makings in the snuggest of all possible caverns;" instead, what he had offered were "the cold, wet, shelterless midnight streets of London; the foul and frowsy dens, where vice is closely packed and lacks the room to turn." Those streets would seem "to have taken precedence in his imagination over the foul dens as the habitat of his criminals. But of course it is not only the criminals (and prostitutes) who walk the streets; they are also the wet and shelterless recourse of the law-abiding poor. Oliver is one of these, and when he makes his way to London, he reflects that it is 'the very place for a homeless boy, who must die in the streets, unless someone [helps] him.'" Dickens thus uses "the image of the street to insist on the connection between poverty and crime. Receiving the efflux of the poor, the streets engender criminals." It is precisely when Oliver "finds himself in the streets, homeless and starving," that he is approached by the Dodger, who takes him to the "'spectable old genelman' who will give him 'lodgings for nothink'" (Daleski "Introduction").

In addition to Oliver's victimization, Dickens also represented another aspect of the world of the London streets in his depiction of Wegg. Early in *Our Mutual Friend* this itinerant ballad-salesman sets up his peddler's stand on a corner. Within a matter of hours, Wegg has appropriated his environs, turning them into an ecological niche favorable to his existence by the exercise of his prodigious imagination (Fulweiler 60-61). "He had established his right to the corner by imperceptible prescription. He had never varied his ground an inch, but had in the beginning diffidently taken the corner upon which the side of the house gave." Echoing the habits of his betters, Wegg hangs out his own shingle. "On the front of his sale-board hung a little placard, like a kettle-holder, bearing the inscription in his own small text:

Errands gone
On with fi
Delity By

Ladies and Gentlemen
I remain
Your humble Servt
Silas Wegg.

Wegg carries his role further: "He had not only settled it with himself in the course of time, that he was errand-goer by appointment to the house at the corner (though he received such commissions not half-a-dozen times in a year, and then only as some servant's deputy), but also that he was one of the house's retainers and owed vassalage to it and was bound to leal and loyal interest in it." Like a consummate actor, his role-playing defines the roles of his counterparts, ignorance not standing in the way of his theatrical trajectory. Though he knows nothing of the house's inhabitants, "he gave them names of his own invention: as 'Miss Elizabeth,' 'Master George,' 'Aunt Jane,' 'Uncle Parker' – having no authority whatever for any such designations, but particularly the last – to which as a natural consequence, he stuck with great obstinacy." Of particular interest is his sense of the house as habitat:

> Over the house itself, he exercised the same imaginary power as over its inhabitants and their affairs. He had never been in it . . . but this was no impediment to his arranging it according to a plan of his own. It was a great dingy house with a quantity of dim side window and blank back premises, and it cost his mind a world of trouble so to lay it out as to account for everything in its external appearance. But, this once done, was quite satisfactory, and he rested persuaded that he knew his way about the house blindfold: from the barred garrets in the high roof, to the two iron extinguishers before the main door – which seemed to request all lively visitors to have the kindness to put themselves out, before entering. (*Our Mutual Friend*, ch. 5)

It is no accident that when opportunity knocks for Wegg in the person of Boffin, the homeless actor is ready for the role offered him. Reading "The Decline and fall of the Rooshian Empire" to Boffin, Wegg discovers his place in the social order, and once ensconced in the Bower, he quickly defines a place and home for himself, in fact so thoroughly that it is only subterfuge – the performance of Sloppy in the theatrical play devised by Rokesmith and Boffin – that makes it possible to remove this engaging scoundrel from the premises. After all, he has had the impudence to charge extra for poetry. "'For when a person comes to grind off poetry night after night, it is but right he should be paid for its weakening effect on his mind" (bk. I, ch. 5).

As his fortunes improve Wegg's canny negotiating style is revealed as part of his public self. His private person, however, is consumed by desperate mood swings, paranoia, and consuming anger: the more prosperity the less he can comprehend it. In him Dickens represents a central aspect of the psychology of homelessness. The same process ignites the outbursts of Betty Higden who responds to the offer to take her sick grandson to the hospital with terror. "'Stand away from me every one of ye!' she cried out wildly. 'I see what ye mean now. Let me go my way, all of ye. I'd sooner kill the Pretty, and kill myself!'" What is at stake here is not a misplaced attack on the Poor Laws and the Workhouses, which, by the time of the writing of *Our Mutual Friend* (1864-65) had been changed, but the response of the working and serving classes to the paternalism of their betters. "'Stay, stay!' said Rokesmith, soothing her. 'You don't understand.'" Betty Higden's response elaborates her and our current city experience. "'I understand too well. I know too much about it, sir. I've run from it too many a year. No! Never for me, nor for the child, while there's water enough in England to cover us!'" Dickens's narrator elaborates her comment, generalizing it in the voice of a fate-defining Greek chorus: "The terror, the shame, the passion of horror and repugnance, firing the worn face and perfectly maddening it, would have been a quite terrible sight, if embodied in one old fellow-creature alone. Yet it 'crops up' – as our slang goes – my lords and gentlemen and honourable boards, in other fellow-creatures, rather frequently!" (bk. II, ch. 9)

In "Night Walks," originally published in 1860 in *All the Year Round* and then reprinted in *The Uncommercial Traveller,* Dickens gives a personal account of what it is like to leave home and be in the streets. He begins "by declaring that an inability to sleep made him walk about the streets all night for a number of nights, and that this afforded him the opportunity of finishing his 'education in a fair amateur experience of houselessness.'" Quickly, he becomes

"one of the houseless," and takes us along on his wander-
ings, "'the restlessness of a great city' forming 'one of the
first entertainments offered to the contemplation of us
houseless people.'" Then follow numerous references to
"those houseless nights," and "the sights that are revealed
to his 'houseless eyes,' and the sounds that fall on 'houseless ears.'" But then, as Daleski notes, "Dickens suddenly
flashes into the thing itself, becoming Houselessness, like
the shade of the Analytical Chemist: 'Houselessness even
observed,' we are told, 'that intoxicated people appeared to
be magnetically attracted towards each other;' and 'walking the streets under the pattering rain, Houselessness
would walk and walk and walk, seeing nothing but the
interminable tangle of streets'" (Daleski "Introduction").
Dickens thus brings his reader to a realization of the
fundamental impact of homelessness on the human being.

His novels elaborate the theatrical repertory of the
modern urban world: from Gothic effect to Romantic surprise, from bourgeois tenacity to paranoid lashing out,
from philosophic resignation to schizophrenia, from bore-
dom to the fresh vision of innocence. It is the site of the
wonderful and the dreadful possibilities of modern city
life, which we, the reader, stalk as part of the progress not
only of Oliver and Nicholas but Eugene Wrayburn and
Bradley Headstone in *Our Mutual Friend*:

> Having made sure of his watching me, I tempt him on, all
> over London. One night I go east, another night north, in a
> few nights I go all round the compass. Sometimes, I walk;
> sometimes, I proceed in cabs . . . I study and get up
> abstruse No Thoroughfares in the course of the day. With
> Venetian mystery I seek those No Thoroughfares at night,
> glide in them by means of dark courts, tempt the school-
> master to follow, turn suddenly, and catch him before he
> can retreat. Then we face one another, and I pass him as
> unaware of his existence, and he undergoes grinding tor-
> ments. Similarly, I walk at a great pace down a short street,
> rapidly turn the corner, and, getting out of his view, as
> rapidly turn back. . . . Night after night his disappointment
> is acute, but hope springs eternal . . . and he follows me
> again to-morrow. Thus I enjoy the pleasures of the chase.
> (bk. III, ch. 10)

The first great practitioner of the detective novel, Dickens
creates a linguistic universe that in the energy, deftness,
and surprise of its syntax thereby simulates the theatrical

experience of life in the modern city. As we read his writing we participate in the modern theatrical project of urban life: modern identity has become staged identity.

Notes

1. "Claude Glass" — "Claude Lorraine Glass, also Claude Glass: a somewhat convex dark or colored hand mirror used to concentrate the features of a landscape in subdued tones. Sometimes applied to colored glasses through which a landscape etc., is viewed. Named from Claude of Lorraine 1600-1682, the French landscape painter." *Oxford English Dictionary*, Second edition. Oxford: Clarendon Press, 1989. 3: 285.

Works Cited

Caws, Mary Ann. *City Images: Perspectives from Literature, Philosophy, and Film*, New York: Gordon and Breach, 1991.

Daleski, H.M. *Homes and Homelessness in the Victorian Imagination*. Ed. M. Baumgarten and H. M. Daleski, New York: AMS Press, in press.

Dickens, Charles. *The Life and Adventures of Nicholas Nickleby*, London: Oxford, 1987.

Dickens, Charles. *Little Dorrit*, Oxford: Oxford Illustrated Dickens, 1987.

Dickens, Charles. *Our Mutual Friend*, Oxford: Oxford Illustrated Dickens, 1987.

Dickens, Charles. *Sketches by Boz*, Oxford: Oxford Illustrated Dickens, 1987.

Fulweiler, Howard W. "'A Dismal Swamp': Darwin, Design, and Evolution in *Our Mutual Friend*," *Nineteenth Century Literature* 49:1 (June 1994): 50-76.

Garis, Robert. *The Dickens Theatre*, Oxford: Clarendon, 1965.

Gay, Peter. *The Education of the Senses*, volume one of *The Bourgeois Experience: Victoria to Freud*, New York: Oxford University Press, 1984, 1986.

Marcus, Steven. *Engels, Manchester, and the Working Classes*, New York: Random House, 1974.

Mill, John Stuart. "The Spirit of the Age," in *Newspaper Writings, Collected Edition of the Works of John Stuart Mill*. 33 vols. Toronto: University of Toronto Press, 1986, 22: 227-316.

Morris, Pam. *Dickens's Class Consciousness. A Marginal View*, London: Macmillan, 1991.

Mumford, Lewis. *The Urban Prospect*, New York: Harcourt, Brace, 1968.

Nord, Deborah. "The City as Theatre: From Georgian to Early Victorian London," *Victorian Studies* 31:2 (Winter 1988): 159-188.

Schwarzbach, F. S. *Dickens and the City*, London: University of London, 1979.

Wordsworth, William. *The Letters of William and Dorothy Wordsworth*, ed. Ernest de Selincourt. Oxford: Clarendon, 1967.

5

Disvaluing the Popular: London Street Culture, "Industrial Literacy," and the Emergence of Mass Culture in Victorian England[1]

Edward Jacobs

For Victorian social critics and reformers, the "penny gaff" theatricals put on in impromptu theatres from the 1830s to the 1870s and the serialized penny fiction "bloods" pioneered by Edward Lloyd and George Reynolds during the 1830s were parts of the same problem: urban street culture. This street culture was a problem because its autonomy prevented "paternalistic" institutions like *The Society for the Diffusion of Useful Knowledge* from incorporating the lower classes into the hegemony of literate, Christian, middle-class culture. Reforming Victorians were especially appalled by the degree to which vagrants, costermongers, and other members of the London poor had appropriated literacy and the cheap literature made possible by iron presses and machine presses into a residually festive, vernacular sub-culture that competed both economically and "morally" with mainstream Victorian culture.[2] For at least since Lord Henry Brougham's *Practical Observations upon the Education of the People*, most reformers had glorified literacy and widely-circulating, cheap periodicals as the most efficient means of controlling "the lower orders." Thus Charles Knight's bitter 1846 resignation of *Knight's Penny Magazine* admitted that his and Brougham's "paternalistic" penny literature could not succeed unless someone eradicated the unfair vernacular competition being produced by vagrant boys and semi-literate hacks (Dalziel 47). Similarly, Hepworth Dixon's 1847 attacks on Lloyd and Reynolds in the *Daily News* warned of the proliferation of an autonomous "people's literature" that, by promulgating "its own system of morals and merits," was interfering with the values disseminated by "the higher and better known offsprings of the press" (quoted in Dalziel 47-8). And in moralizing upon his discovery that among vagrant boys, "bad books" were customarily "read aloud in the low lodging-houses in the evening by those who have a little education, to their companions who have none" (3:370), Henry Mayhew declared:

> We teach a lad reading, writing, and arithmetic, and believe that in so doing we are developing the moral functions of his nature; whereas it is often this ability to read *merely* – that is to say, to read without the least moral perception – which becomes the instrument of the youth's moral depravity. (3:370)

Yet while social critics saw street culture's "depraved" use of literacy as a major threat, they targeted penny gaffs as the institutional base that fostered this depravity. Thus, like most commentators on gaffs, Mayhew complains that they competed with such "rational" modes of leisure as the licensed theaters (Springhall 103-5), but he actually calls for legislation against them on the grounds that

> Here the stage, instead of being the means for illustrating a moral precept, is turned into a platform to teach the cruelest debauchery. The audience is usually composed of children so young, that these dens become the schoolrooms where the guiding morals of a life are picked up. (1:40)

Discussing the problem of vagrant youths, Mayhew later specifies gaffs as "school-rooms" where "the scenes and characters described in bad books are represented in a still more attractive form" (3:378). Nearly every other extant record of gaff performances similarly notes how substantially their material and audiences articulated with those of street literature (Springhall 113-4).

Just how literally early-Victorian social critics and politicians targeted penny gaffs as the "school-rooms" sustaining "bad books" is shown by the fact that, despite considerable criticism of Lloyd and Reynolds for obscenity and plagiarism (Hoggart, "Travesties" and "Edward"; James, "View"; Dalziel 47-9), their publishing activities faced no real legal or economic sanctions, while police and legislators undertook a twenty-year campaign to eradicate gaffs. This campaign began in 1839, when The Metropolitan Police Act (2 & 3 Vict., cap. 47) presumed guilt from attendance at gaffs (Stephens, "Thespis's" 123). The measure criminalized the leisure of an enormous population, for according to James Grant, in 1838 nightly attendance at London gaffs totaled about 24,000 (162). Despite the Act, gaffs continued to draw larger total audiences than the licensed West End theaters until roughly 1854, when the intensified police action inspired by the *Report of the Select Committee on Public Houses and Places of Public Entertainment* finally began to cripple gaffs' economic and cultural viability (Springhall 102, 111; Cunningham 164-76).

Murray Baumgarten argues elsewhere in this volume that many emergent aspects of early-Victorian urban life incited and depended upon theatricality,[3] and his argument for the broad cultural valences of theatre and theatricality makes even more significant the fact that Victorian social critics implicated penny gaffs in a sub-cultural theft of literacy and machine-printed literature. By analyzing the texts and contexts of gaff theatricals and the enormously popular blood, *Varney the Vampyre* (1840-48), this essay presents evidence that early-Victorian gaffs and bloods were indeed structured by the same "festive" misuse of literacy and print culture. Specifically, the comparison made here of slangs, gaff theatricals, and *Varney the*

Vampyre shows that each of these practices conventionally equated literacy with industrial work-disciplines, and subjected this "industrial literacy" to traditional forms of "festive misrule." Such a "misuse" of literacy was fostered, I contend, by the historical coincidence in England between industrialism and "popular education," and it was centered in the streets of London because of the peculiar supports that the capital had for centuries offered to alternative lifestyles for the poor.

Perhaps more provocatively, this essay argues that the destruction of the street culture centered on gaffs constituted a pre-condition for the take-over of the penny literature market by middle-class, paternalistic capitalists during the 1850s. By contrast, most accounts of this take-over perceive a continuity between the "popular" broadside and chapbook traditions and "mass" literature such as Sunday newspapers, and hence interpret the change from popular literature to mass literature in Victorian England as an instance of "incorporation." According to such accounts, the advent of the Hoe rotary steam press and other machine presses during the 1850s enabled highly-capitalized, middle-class publishers to establish a virtual monopoly over the booming newspaper and street literature markets, which they developed into a co-opting "culture industry." Specifically, such accounts argue that the widespread industrialization during the 1850s of periodical printing overwhelmed radical and popular publishing because this industrialization increased the initial capital investment required for genuinely mass publishing, made mass literature a longer-term profit venture by reducing profit margins in exchange for a wider circulation, and inaugurated a fundamental dependence upon advertising finance. In this climate, both the old unstamped press and popular publishers of such traditional genres as crime broadsides and chapbook literature simply did not have the money to compete in terms of price, circulation, or patronage by advertisers.[4]

As descriptions of how the proliferation of machine presses changed the business of penny publishing, such analyses are compelling. However, in arguing from this evidence that the middle-class "incorporated" popular lit-

erature, most accounts of the emergence of mass literature in England ultimately blame popular culture's festive
orientation toward pleasure for the co-opting forms and
contents of modern mass literature. Virginia Berridge, for
instance, describes mid-Victorian Sunday papers as a
"commercial synthesis" (256) "between the old non-political traditions of the chap-book and last dying speech and
the political radicalism of the unstamped and the Chartist
papers" (247). Yet, she maintains, "with the example of
chap-book and last dying speeches before them," Lloyd
and Reynolds in particular "expanded the sensation side
as never before," so that "the papers were the effective
means of social control which the establishment had always hoped the popular press might be" (256). In a similar
vein, Peter Mountjoy claims that the development of "the
entertainment" or "pleasure press" made the working
classes "adept at taking whatever amusement was offered
and rejecting calls for commitment, anxiety, or effort," and
thus helped to create as "the predominant working-class
attitude . . . that myopia and resistance to outside influence which leads to real conservatism" (268). Related
assumptions implicitly structure Louis James's ground-
breaking study, *Fiction for the Working Man*, where James
concludes that a "crucial opportunity offered during a
formative period of industrial urban life by the confluence
of cheap publications and increasing readership was lost"
by attempts "to reproduce the formulae of the past" (170),
which James equates with "superficial, immediately excit-
ing culture" and specifically associates with the "titillating
but worthless fiction" produced by Lloyd and Reynolds
during the 1830s and 40s (22; see also 112-3; 165-7).

Rather ironically, in view of how often such arguments
specify melodrama as the predominant ideological tool
that mass literature took from popular literature (Vicinus,
"'Helpless"; Humphreys, "Popular"; and James, "View"),
their construction of England's titillating popular culture
as the source of political and social corruption itself narrates the emergence of mass literature in England as a
tragic melodrama: the radical, political press is a mis-
prized hero, while the popular street tradition fulfills the
role of a prurient, "old non-political" villain fatally empow-

ered by capitalists with machine presses. However, the history of early-Victorian London street culture problematizes this melodrama by suggesting that hegemonic culture destroyed and replaced rather than incorporated the highly political form of festivity practiced within London's traditional popular culture. In turn, this evidence suggests that Ivan Illich's theory of "disvalue" may provide a more accurate frame for analyses of the emergence of mass literature in England than the notion of "incorporation." For this theory would maintain that capitalists with their Hoe presses could never have taken over the penny literature market, if the street culture surrounding penny gaffs had not already been quite literally muted and impoverished.

* * * * *

Like other customs, street culture's mockery of industrial literacy grew out of the historical experience of the people who performed it. The demographics of early-Victorian London street culture have been the subject of much controversy (Himmelfarb), but for the purposes of this analysis let us define that culture simply as the people who participated in penny gaff theatricals. Thus defined, it seems reasonable to accept Mayhew's specification of autodidacticism and "an impatience of steady labour" (3:369) as the prevailing characteristics of this culture. There are two peculiarities of English history that explain why London in particular was the center of a street culture which practiced literacy as a festive disruption of and alternative to rational schooling and industrial disciplines.

First and most broadly, the historical coincidence in England between industrialism and popular education gave the English poor good reason by the 1830s to perceive industrial work and school knowledge as two parts of an inhumane culture that was being forced on them from above. As E. P. Thompson (among many others) has shown, during the latter decades of the eighteenth century and the early decades of the nineteenth century, the growing implementation of steam-powered factories imposed time- and behavioral discipline upon workers who had for centuries been used to more casual, self-determined work rhythms and to easier articulations between work culture and festive traditions ("Time"). During roughly the same decades, many of the same poor people were subjected to a "monitorial" regime of popular education that constructed literacy as a mechanical discipline very much like factory production. Whether under the aegis of Andrew Bell's *National School Society* or Joseph Lancaster's *British and Foreign School Society*, all of the early schools which undertook to educate the poor relied pedagogically upon rote imitation and memorization, imposed time-discipline upon students with factory-like rigor, and rewarded acceptable reproduction of the models with power over other students. What little real content these lessons had was almost always ludicrously remote from the the students' culture, offering them such "useful" facts as the sub-classes of tropical birds. To students who came from an oral, festive culture, and who were likely to have had either personal or second-hand knowledge of factory work, these pedagogic methods surely associated literacy with the absurd strictures imposed by factories and by other "disciplinary" institutions such as workhouse or court.[5]

During the same decades, various groups within working-class culture also imposed literacy upon the English poor as a discipline. English workers had traditionally used festive customs like Saint Monday, mumming, or effigy-burning to "negotiate" about working conditions in oral, non-contractual ways that, in Clive Behagg's phrase, rendered worker culture strategically "opaque" to employers. However, by the Regency period, the skilled, literate workers who led the way into labor politics were qualifying themselves for contractual negotiation with factory owners precisely by championing literacy, and by sanctioning the time and behavioral disciplines needed by factory owners in order to exploit steam-power (Behagg; Reid; Thompson, "Time" and "Moral"). Simultaneously, as Paul Murphy and others have shown, the radical press prescribed literacy as part of the discipline of radicalism, and attacked penny fiction and the old, festive culture as related lies.[6]

This conjunction of upper-class and working-class disciplines did attenuate the allegiance of many English poor people to oral, festive culture. However, because

these disciplines used literacy and disciplined work behavior to prefer some workers over others, they also constructed an underclass whose experiences had taught
them to resent and mistrust the culture represented by
industrial work and schooled literacy. Inevitably, some
workers became unemployed because they either could
not or would not submit to industrial work disciplines, and
as Thomas Laquer emphasizes, the absurdities of popular
education motivated many people to become literate outside of its institutions, or to avoid literacy altogether
("Working" 198-202; "Cultural" 269-70).

The second and more specific reason why London
became the center of a street culture that flouted both
industrial work and schooled literacy involves two peculiarities of London's economy. In comparison to northern
industrial metropoli such as Manchester, London had
never had an industrial economy, *per se.* On the contrary,
London had for at least a century been the center of
alternative professions for the poor. Crime was pre-eminent among these alternative professions, but there were
also many legal forms of subsistence that did not impose
industrial time and behavior disciplines, and that were not
available in the provinces (because of more dispersed
population) or in the northern industrial cities (because of
the dominance of industrial wage labor). Costermongering
(the itinerant selling of greens, fish, and other food) was
one such occupation, and in more mediated ways, so was
service. But significantly, at least since the beginning of
the eighteenth-century, London had also offered an as-
tounding variety of careers centered on the production
and distribution of vernacular literature such as broadside criminal biographies. Because the publishing industry was substantially based in London, and because London was one of the first metropoli to develop a "public
sphere" (Habermas 57-67), both the passion for news and
the institutions for producing it developed earlier and
more extensively in London than in any other British city.
By the beginning of Victoria's reign this aspect of London
was so pronounced that several visitors, both British and
foreign, characterized London as "a City of Print" (Webb
23-4). Mayhew, significantly, devotes as many pages to the

various kinds of "paper workers" as he does to all "Sellers of Manufactured Articles," and moreover traces the history of London paper-working back to the Restoration, stressing it as a traditional alternative to "steady labour" (1:215-17). Even more significantly, in emphasizing that paper workers were more literate than most other street professions, Mayhew implicates them in creating the "ability to read merely" that in his view perpetuated vagrancy (1:213-14). Given that paper-working in London constituted such a thriving, variegated, and traditional way for poor people to subsist outside of industrial disciplines, it is only logical that when industrialism, popular education, labor politics, and radicalism combined manufacturing work and language into a juggernaut of discipline, those who could not or would not tolerate such a life style took refuge in London's festive street culture.[7]

A genealogy of London street culture specifying how many people actually immigrated to London street culture in search of non-industrial work would be far beyond the scope of this paper. However, if the arguments just presented at least suggest how and why London street culture became what it was, then almost all of the actual texts we have from early-Victorian London street culture demonstrate how consistently it did equate and defy industrial work and schooled language. As I mentioned above, and as Mayhew emphasizes at the opening of *London Labour and the London Poor*, costermongering was one of the major non-industrial professions besides paper-working that London street culture offered. And even though costermongers' work did not directly participate in the paper-working economy, their slang submits industrial literacy to festive misrule. Slangs were so pervasive among London street people in the 1840s that Mayhew identifies their use as one of the four distinguishing characteristics of "nomadic races" such as street people or the African and Native American tribes to whom he compares them. Such nomadic races, Mayhew generalizes, "vary their speech designedly, and adopt new words, with the intent of rendering their ideas unintelligible to all but the members of their own community" (1:2). And indeed, one costermonger told Mayhew, "The police don't understand us at all. It

would be a pity if they did" (1:23), and accounts by
Mayhew and his informants of police harassment confirm
this judgment (1:10; 1:16; 1:20; 1:29).

Significantly, costermonger slang thus protected its
users from surveillance by imposing a peculiar kind of
festive misrule upon normal, literate language. As Mayhew
explains,

> The *root* of the costermonger tongue, so to speak, is to give
> the words spelt backward, or rather pronounced rudely
> backward, – for in my present chapter the language has, I
> believe, been reduced to orthography for the first time. With
> this backward pronunciation, which is very arbitrary, are
> mixed words reducible to no rule and seldom referrable to
> any origin, thus complicating the mystery of this unwritten
> tongue; while any syllable is added to a proper slang word,
> at the discretion of the speaker. (1:23)

Beyond inverting normal pronunciation, coster slang vio-
lated its own grammar of inversion "at the discretion of the
speaker." It thus practiced language not as a contractual
discipline, but rather as a festive power game that incited
speakers to intrude "arbitrary" volition upon the rules of
language, just as traditions like Saint Monday in festive
work culture had intruded worker volition and play upon
employers and their means of production (Reid; Behagg).

Plagiarism was another practice shared by penny gaffs,
bloods, and other forms of street culture. As Paul Hoggart
and Louis James show with respect to Reynolds's and
Lloyd's plagiarisms of Dickens, these "plagiarisms" did not
simply reproduce mainstream literature. Rather, they engaged in a political struggle over the social meaning of
literary representations, and thus confronted mainstream
literature with the cultural fact of "heteroglossia" (Hoggart,
"Travesties" 32-6; James, "View"; cp. Bakhtin 275-6). As
such, these plagiarisms again underscore London street
culture's articulations with England's traditional festive
culture, since "heteroglossia" or "dialogic" form is both
structurally and historically connected to festive or "carni-
valesque" culture (Bakhtin 26-7).

James Grant's account of a gaff plagiarism of *Othello*
vividly illustrates how London street culture's plagiarisms
specifically subjected industrial literacy to festive misrule.
Before describing the actual show, Grant complains that

gaff performers "mangled" Shakespeare because their abridgements of the Bard were "guided by no fixed rules" of aesthetics (176). On the contrary, he bemoans, "Time is the only counsellor to whose directions they will conde-scend to lend an ear," because, "at most of these places the lessee is in the habit of standing on one side of the stage watching the time, and . . . when it is within a minute or two of that which he has in his own mind allotted for that particular piece, he exclaims, 'Time up! – finish the piece! – down with the curtain!' and it is all done as he desires." Thus, Grant reports, the performers of this *Othello* dwell on "some of the more interesting scenes in the first act," but when the "lessee" declares, "The time is up – commit the murder, and down with the curtain," the gaffers leap to the end and "enact that scene with an expedition with which it were in vain for any steam power to attempt to compete. . . . Desdemona is then strangled in a moment, down goes the curtain, and out go the audience" (176). As is emphasized by Grant's images of the gaff theatrical as a steam-powered affair directed by a capitalist's clock-time, this gaff *Othello* is a parody of the disjunctions between industrial time-discipline and human volition. Admittedly, its absurdly irregular pace might at first seem to be a parody of the irregular schedules sanctioned by pre-in-dustrial work customs. But because, as Grant indicates, the "lessee" *publicly* enforces time-discipline, the gaff per-formance *dramatizes* time-discipline being imposed upon artists by capitalists, and indeed satirically juxtaposes this imposition with Othello's senseless murder of Desde-mona.

Mayhew's transcripts of the tales two street boys alleg-edly told "out of" William Harrison Ainsworth's *Jack Shep-pard* in a related way demonstrate how aggressively street culture transformed printed literature into a mockery of industrial literacy. Mayhew repeatedly excoriated Ains-worth's criminal romance *Jack Sheppard* (1839) because it allegedly encouraged people who could "read merely" to become thieves (3:370; 3:378), and as John Stephens shows, the novel was in fact one of the pre-eminent sub-jects for gaff plagiarisms ("*Jack*"). However, both of the tales recorded by Mayhew transform *Jack Sheppard* into mockery of industrial literacy, rather than accepting it as a romanticization of crime, per se. Indeed, despite the narrators' claims that their tales are "out of" Ainsworth's novel, both tales draw on festive, oral tradition far more than on *Jack Sheppard.*

In the shorter of these tales, Jack is "hired" by a farmer who threatens to cut off Jack's head if he violates the master's rules, which require Jack to call familiar objects by mercantile and aristocratic phrases, such as "Tom Per Cent" for his master and "He's of Degree" for his bed (3:391). When the cat catches fire and sets the barn ablaze, Jack goes to his master and recites seven absurd lines of verse recounting the event in his master's language. "So Jack learned his lesson, and saved his head," concludes the narrator. "That's the end."

Clearly this tale mocks industrial literacy using the same tropes that we have seen in penny gaff theatricals. In the first place, the tale subjects Jack to an absurd and brutal linguistic discipline that parodies popular education. And while the narrator's conclusion may seem to recommend pragmatic compliance with this discipline, this tale *caricatures* that discipline, dramatizing how the master's lesson mangles "natural" human communication, just as the gaff *Othello* dramatizes the ways the lessee's time-discipline mangles art and Desdemona's body. Jack ostensibly learns his lesson, but his performance of it exposes how its innovations alienate communication in the name of capitalist ("Tom Per Cent") and hierarchic ("He's of Degree") ideology.[8]

The other tale also represents Jack as a trickster against industrial literacy, but it affords Jack more glory, since here his trickery both ruins the local parson and aristocrat and redistributes their money to the poor. This tale, told by another vagrant boy, begins according to the formula described by the first boy: "You see, mates, there was once upon a time, and a very good time it was, a young man, and he runned away, and got along with a gang of thieves" (3:389-90). Beyond this, however, Jack's adventures are not related to Ainsworth's novel. The plot begins when Jack robs a gentleman's house of one thousand pounds. The gentleman then lets a horse loose in a field and offers a reward for the recovery of the horse, "for he thought the man that got the 1000 [pounds] was sure to try to catch that there horse, because he was so bold and clever, and then the two men hid would nab him" (3:390). However, Jack sees through this trick, diverts the two men with rabbits, and takes the horse to the gentleman for his reward. "D–n it," exclaims the gentleman, "Jack's done me this time. . . . I'll give you another 100 [pounds] if you'll do something to the parson as bad as you've done to me'" (3:390). Jack agrees and "was standing in one of the pews like an angel, when the parson got to the church. Jack said, 'Go put your plate in a bag; I'm an angel come to take you up to heaven'" (3:390). Subsequently putting the parson in a bag in order to "take [him] up to heaven," Jack drags him through field and stream to the gentleman's estate, where the gentleman horsewhips the parson. However, the parson then prosecutes the gentlemen, ruining them both, while Jack absconds with the loot and distributes it to the poor.

Though Jack is a criminal in this tale, the tale celebrates him not because he is adept at stealing, but rather because his theatrical trickery subverts literate, upper-class society. For here Jack magically tricks the parson – surely a representative of literacy – by means of theatrical fiat: the parson takes Jack for an angel merely because Jack stands and speaks "like an angel." Jack's monopoly of trickery in this tale moreover disrupts the local capitalist economy and aristocratic society. When the gentleman hires Jack to trick the parson, Jack's trick reverts upon its buyer, replacing the capitalist-aristocratic order in which the gentleman and the parson compete, with Jack's communal-criminal order. Hence, despite some structural differences from the first tale, like it this one ridicules literate culture as dysfunctional and even more directly glorifies festive orality as a challenge to the literate, master culture.

While these tales focus on speech as the site of struggle between industrial and festive literacy, within the vernacular paper-working economy and culture, machine presses obviously constituted the most material sign of industrial literacy. In general, the English poor experienced machine presses and their products as part of industrial literacy simply because these machines came into common use at roughly the same time and to some extent in conjunction with both the "paternalistic" penny literature of Knight and Brougham and the development of popular education as a means for incorporating the poor into middle-class culture. Within the London paper-working economy specifically, machine presses made industrial literacy seem monstrous precisely to the generation of street people who participated in gaffs. Machine presses first developed in response to the needs of London newspaper publishers and printers, and when these machines came into use during the 1820s and 30s, many publishers discovered that they could largely replace the adult hand pressmen who for centuries had been protected as much by their expert skills as by their membership in the Stationers Company with young boys (called "flies") who simply fed paper into the machine at one end and removed it at the other (Gaskell 131; see also Dalziel 47). Given the long hours and dreadful conditions of such work, the advent of machine printing in London surely motivated the "flies" employed in it not only to indulge in the misrule offered by festive culture such as gaff theatricals, but moreover to perceive and resent the enormous disjunction between words formed by machine presses and words formed by gaff theatricals, criminal broadsides, and other festive modes of paper-working. This awareness of the cultural difference between festive, vernacular paper-working and industrial literacy among the juvenile audience of gaff theatricals was presumably reinforced to some extent by the adult pressmen whose skilled labor had been displaced by the flies' industrial servicing of machines.

Significantly, in context of the ways that machine presses trained London street boys to practice industrial literacy and festive literacy as radical opposites, several nineteenth-century witnesses describe the physical production of bloods intruding festive misrule upon machine presses. For example, Edward Lloyd issued reliable "hacks" a special lined paper that, when filled, corresponded to penny installments. Yet as several of Lloyd's authors related, this special paper encouraged them to fill up lines with short sentences – e.g., dialog – rather than to follow narrative logic (James, *Fiction* 33). Thus, much as the penny gaffers described by Grant plagiarized *Othello* by submitting it to industrial time-discipline, Lloyd's authors travestied authorship by letting printing-press technology "mangle" narrative logic in ways that street culture's festive modes of consumption (Mayhew 1:24-5) transformed into a satire on industrial literacy itself. Charles Manby Smith, a journeyman printer who allegedly worked for Lloyd, describes another way that hack writing mocked the time- and space-disciplines of machine presses. In this case, the author, fortified with spirits, arrived at the press several hours before the printing deadline, and wrote in the press building itself, first producing a basic narrative, which was laid out in rough, whereupon the author added dialog and digressions until the original matter sufficed for a penny number (221-28; cp. James, *Fiction* 34). By thus writing in immediate interaction with the processes of composition, imposition, and printing, this author immediately disrupted the work of compositors more than the industrial efficiency of machine printing, since this mode of authorship necessitated repeating composition, imposition, and printing in response to copy that gradually evolved, whereas typically these tasks could be done once, since the copy was finished before the production process began (Gaskell 5-8).[9] Yet in disrupting the skilled labor of compositors, this festive mode of authorship only foregrounded the political fact that machine printing depended substantively upon both festive authorship and the highly-skilled work of compositors. Hence, much as the gaff plagiarism of *Othello* caricatured the disjunction between human craft and industrial, capitalist time-discipline, the festive, interactive mode of authorship described by Smith threw into pointed relief the basis of cultural production in interactions between festive play and skilled craft.

Admittedly, inconsistencies in Smith's dates and addresses make the accuracy of this description questionable.[10] And certainly as a journeyman printer who repeatedly rails against his inability to find work, Smith had good reasons to exaggerate or invent instances of his trade's displacement. Still, such a festive parody of industrial authorship and publishing seems plausible, especially given the manifest ways in which the entry of machine presses into the London publishing trades foregrounded and politicized the difference between traditional modes of paper-work and industrial literacy. And significantly, what we know about the authorship of the most popular bloods of the 1830s and 1840s manifests a related collision between disciplined skill and festive play. Neither George W. M. Reynolds nor James Malcolm Rymer, the probable author of *Varney the Vampyre* (Bleiler xvii-iii), actually lived within the festive street culture surrounding penny gaffs. Rymer met Lloyd at a London Mechanics Institute (Hoggart, "Edward" 33), but Mechanics Institutes were sites of the industrial literacy advocated by radicals like Carlile and Wooler (Murphy), rather than of festive street culture, and in other contexts Rymer ridiculed the hack writers and vulgar readers of penny literature (James *Fiction* 36). Similarly, Reynolds learned the ropes of journalism and publishing in revolutionary France of the 1830s (Bleiler viii-ix), and afterwards consistently advocated industrial literacy as part of the discipline of Chartism. Nonetheless, Mayhew's account of costers reading *The Mysteries of the Court* (1:24-5) documents Reynolds flirting with some of the most customary tropes of street people's festivity, and Rymer consistently does so in *Varney the Vampyre*. The fact that authors who advocated industrial literacy actually succeeded by imitating street culture's mockery of it underscores the extent to which London street culture had by 1840 made this mockery a traditional part of the game demanded by London's poorest, most numerous, and hardest-to-please readers.

Published in parts between 1840 and 1848 (Bleiler viii), *Varney the Vampyre* is essentially a thousand-page long gaff, during which Sir Francis Varney uses his vampiric powers to ridicule industrial literacy. In pointed contrast to previous and subsequent literary vampires, Varney is an irrepressible wag; indeed, according to one of his accounts of his origin, immediately upon becoming a vampire, "The idea came across me of doing some mischief" (866). Not all of Varney's mischief directly targets industrial literacy, but he does *regularly* mock literate culture and its disciplines in ways that echo slangs, penny gaffs, and other street culture traditions. For example, at one point during the first and longest episode in Varney's career, he is courting the blood and affection of Flora Bannerworth, while simultaneously trying to dupe her ultra-rational brothers out of the family estates. Charles Holland, Flora's beloved, challenges Varney to a midnight duel, but insists on secrecy about it, because he knows that Flora and his friends will try to stop him if he declares his bold intention. However, his uncle, Admiral Bell, and Flora's brother Henry see Charles slipping out his window at night, and upon entering his room to investigate, they find letters, in which Charles says he is abandoning Flora, because "'I cannot make my wife one who is subject to the visitations of a vampyre'" (124). "An occurrence so utterly and entirely unexpected by both of them," says the narrator, "was enough to make them doubt the evidence of their own senses. But there were the letters, as a damning evidence of the outrageous fact, and Charles Holland was gone" (124). Of course, these "letters" are forgeries by Varney, and when Flora calls them such, Henry staggers back, "as if some one had struck him a blow," and declares, "'Good God! . . . I did not think of that'" (130).

As a con, Varney's prank here depends specifically upon its victims' unquestioning confidence in the authority of "letters," and directs laughter at that submission to literacy. The text indeed stresses this point, since Flora later explains to the men that they they fell for Varney's con because they impiously trusted writing more than their social experience of Charles (130-31). Elsewhere the text even more explicitly promotes the literate, aristocratic Varney as a member of festive street culture. For the text both structurally and thematically establishes a community between Varney and an illiterate prankster named – significantly – Jack. Jack Pringle originally appears in the romance as the servant-companion of Admiral Bell, one of the men duped by Varney's fraudulent letter, and his attitude toward literacy is summed up by his comment about a lawyer to whom he and Admiral Bell are summoned by another of Varney's forgeries: "'Quite ekal to a book, he talks . . . I never could read one myself, on account o' not knowing how, but I've heard 'em read, and that's just the sort o' incomprehensible gammon'" (71).

Structurally, the second longest series of episodes in *Varney the Vampyre* replaces Varney with Jack. After Varney's initial dealings with the Bannerworths, his characteristics are mysteriously dispersed into several new characters, among whom are a Baron Stolmuyer and a vampire physically unlike Varney. Obviously, this dispersion of Varney's characteristics into multiple characters transforms the text on one level into a game of detecting Varney. As these scenes unwind, the Baron appears more and more likely to be Varney in disguise. But in this disguise his trickstering is muted; instead of puns and pranks, he produces lyricism, such as the statement that a dream of his was so real that it will itself be dreamt of as reality (453). Consequently, despite the interest of this detective plot, half of the scenes in the new coastal locale occupied by the Baron focus on Jack, who is there sharing drinking stories with his old navy mates. A very practical textual logic seems to determine this split emphasis: given the previous success of Varney as a trickster, when the new mystery plot requires him to surrender his festive characteristics, the author of *Varney* compensates by relocating these traits in Jack, who indeed easily blooms into the kind of "Jack" celebrated by the two tales that vagrant boys told Mayhew "out of" *Jack Sheppard.*

When Jack later celebrates Varney as a king of misrule, the text makes this functional parallel between vampiric and festive culture explicit. During Jack's coastal adventures, he befriends James Anderson, the lover of Helen Williams, whose greedy mother is forcing her to marry Varney, disguised as the Baron. James asks Jack to smuggle him into the wedding so that he can see if Helen regrets marrying the Baron. Jack agrees, though the narrator remarks that, "As for the scheme of James Anderson to be present at the wedding, the more Jack thought of it, the more he liked it, because he considered that it afforded a chance, at all events, if not a good prospect, of as general a disturbance as any that had ever existed" (532). As it turns out, the wedding is transformed into a grand disturbance not by Jack's trick, but by the exposure of Varney's trick. The Bannerworth clan are invited to the wedding, and when the Baron appears, they identify him as Varney, who makes his escape amidst wholesale chaos (538). Intoxicated by this "disturbance," Jack leaps upon a chair and commends Varney for producing festive misrule: "'Hurra, hurra, hurra! Three cheers for old Varney!'" says Jack.

> I'll tell you what it is, mess-mates, he is the meanest fellow as ever you see; and as for you ladies who have been disappointed of the marriage, I'll come and kiss you all in a minute, and we'll drink up old Varney's wine, and eat up his dinner like bricks. My eye, what a game we will have, to be sure. I am coming – .

Just as Jack says this, "the admiral gave such a kick to one of the hind legs of the chair, that down came Jack as quickly as if he had disappeared through some trap-door" (538). This metaphor overtly connects Varney's and Jack's game of disturbance to theatrical farce, as do several woodcuts bordered with footlight and/or theatrical curtains (James, *Fiction* 150), and Jack's pratfall hence further advertises *Varney the Vampyre* as something that happens inside of gaff culture.

But Jack's fall here also initiates his abrupt and violent disappearance from *Varney the Vampyre*. Jack's only subsequent appearance immediately follows this marriage scene, when he tells Mrs. Williams (the parodically social-climbing mother who was going to sell her daughter to Varney in his disguise as the Baron) that Admiral Bell is madly in love with her. When Mrs. Williams accosts the Admiral in his bedroom, Admiral Bell declares: "'It's all that infernal scoundrel Jack Pringle's doings, I find. It's one of that lubberly, mutinous thief's tricks, and it's the last one he shall ever play me'" (557). And within *Varney the Vampyre*, so it is. After Mrs. Williams beats Jack in the streets to the "delight" of Admiral Bell (558), Jack vanishes from the text; the Admiral subsequently exposes Varney several times, but he is now "gouty" and unaccompanied by Jack (613-4; 677). The fact that Jack is drubbed out of *Varney the Vampyre* for his "mutinous thief's tricks" (557) instead of being (re)incorporated into the culture of hierarchy and discipline represented by Mrs. Williams and Admiral Bell ironically caricatures the history of London street culture as sketched by this essay. For if, as the evidence presented here suggests, early-Victorian street culture *challenged* the people, institutions, and technologies that during the 1850s replaced London's 150-year-old paper-working economy with mass literature, then it may be that the sustained, brutal attack by the police and government on gaffs during the 1840s and '50s *destroyed* rather than incorporated the particular bag of "mutinous thief's tricks" that was shared by gaffs, bloods, and other festive modes of paper-work.

Theoretically, such evidence for London street culture as a vernacular *alternative* to mass culture suggests that Ivan Illich's notion of "disvalue" accounts for more of the demonstrable facts about the emergence of mass literature in England than does the notion of "incorporation." For the theory of "disvalue" maintains that "mass" commodities gain economic value by establishing a "radical monopoly," in the sense of basic physical conditions that make vernacular alternatives to commodities impossible or at least unviable. Thus, in twentieth-century developed countries, urban road systems have established a radical monopoly for the automotive industry in so far as these roads make it impossible to perform the locomotion required for subsistence by walking or bicycling (Illich, "Beauty"). With respect to the advent of mass literature in nineteenth-century England, the shift to machine presses and the "sanitation" of urban streets established a radical monopoly for commodified periodical literature. For these machines circumscribed the market share attainable by more vernacular and less capital-intensive modes of producing and distributing cheap literature, while the disciplining of urban streets reduced the physical viability of festive modes of production and distribution. Notably, such an application of the theory of disvalue to changes in the Victorian penny press articulates historically with the analyses offered by Illich and by Michel Foucault of the ways that modern schooling and medicine eradicated people's cognitive and economic autonomy from centralized institutions (Illich, *Medical* and *Deschooling*; Foucault,

Birth and *Discipline*). Indicating these connections is not to claim that the theory of disvalue is the definitive answer to our analysis of this complex period of English history. But since the theory of disvalue has been almost entirely ignored by students of this period, some consideration of it may help to re-frame the questions that remain despite our increasingly detailed and material understanding of how mass literature emerged and was consolidated in mid-Victorian England. Certainly the theory of disvalue brings into focus one of the basic historiographical problems demonstrated by this essay: that our explanations of mass literature have too often blamed it on precisely the people who were brutalized for offering an alternative to it, and who thus continue to suffer from "the enormous condescension of posterity" (Thompson, *Making* 12).

Notes

1. A more developed version of this essay, entitled "Bloods in the Street: London Street Culture, 'Industrial Literacy,' and the Emergence of Mass Culture in Victorian England" appears in *Nineteenth-Century Contexts* 19 (1995): 321-47, whose editors I would like to thank for permission to publish the present essay.
2. See Gaskell 251-65 for a technical description, dating, and assessment of degree of distribution of the various new kinds of presses that emerged in the early decades of the nineteenth century. For the sake of simplicity, in this essay I have followed Gaskell in using "machine" presses to designate in general the various designs of presses (with both flat and cylindrical platens and both flat and rotary formes) that depended on steam power or other forms of power, as opposed to presses (made of both wood and iron, with both flat and cylindrical platens) that continued to be operated by hand. I use "festive" culture here in the sense of one whose customs harkened back to the traditional festive calendar. See Burke for a history of festive culture in the early modern period.
3. See chapter 4, page 74.
4. See Asquith, Bennett, "Revolution," Curran, and Williams for critical summaries of this argument; Spufford on the tradition of broadsides and chapbooks; and Arato and Gebhardt 207-19 on Adorno and Benjamin's concept of a "culture industry."
5. Sturt remains the most detailed, documentary study of the procedures and history of popular education. On the disjunction between popular education and popular culture, see Laquer, "Cultural" and "Working-Class." See Bennett, "Revolution" 248-52 and "Editorial", and James, *Fiction* 115-7 on the ways "paternalistic" penny literature mirrored the ludicrously "useful" content of popular education.
6. Besides Murphy, see also Laquer, "Cultural" 269-70, and Williams, esp. 49. However, see also Fox, who shows how the political caricatures

produced during the "war of the unstamped" by William Hone and Cruikshank articulated the "festive" tradition of broadside caricature with a radical critique of upper-class ideology.

7. In reviewing Dyos and Wolff's *The Victorian City*, Welsh says, "implicit in all these essays is the contrast with London provided by the industrial cities of Great Britain" (422). However, scholars have given surprisingly little overt attention to the ways London offered an alternative to industrial-style work, and even less to the ways its traditional "paper-working" economy did so. George scarcely mentions the peculiarly non-industrial character of much London labor and curiously excludes publishing from her survey of London trades. However, for documentation of the "street literature" economy see (besides Mayhew) Spufford, Sheppard, and Neuburg; and Chibnall on the specific tradition centered around criminality and policing.

8. Astonishingly, this tale is a version of a trickster tale recorded by Zora Neale Hurston among south-Florida African-Americans during the 1930s (85-6). Moreover, it is far from being the only instance of cultural commerce between early-Victorian London street culture and African-American culture. Several commentators report the popularity of "nigger tunes" at London gaffs (Springhall 108), and James Schlesinger records one gaff plagiarism of *Uncle Tom's Cabin* (Springhall 116).

9. Technically, "composition" is the process of setting type into lines and pages. "Imposition" is the process of arranging pages of composed type into "formes" that, when printed on two sides of a sheet and folded in the proper ways, will result in a "gathering" of textually sequential pages. "Printing" is the process of inking the formes of type and impressing them onto sheets of paper. Significantly, composition and imposition (both performed by "compositors") were not commonly or effectively mechanized until the later nineteenth century, whereas machine presses were in prototype by the early 1800s, and quite commonly used (especially in newspaper publishing) by the 1820s. See Gaskell 5-8; 251-96.

10. I am grateful to Michael Turner of the Bodleian Library for pointing out to me the dubiousness of Smith's testimony.

Works Cited

Adorno, Theodore. *Negative Dialectics*. New York: Seabury, 1973.

Arato, Andrew, and Eike Gebhardt. "Esthetic Theory and Cultural Criticism." *The Essential Frankfurt School Reader*. Ed. Andrew Arato and Eike Gebhardt. New York: Continuum, 1990.

Asquith, Ivon. "The Structure, Ownership and Control of the Press, 1780-1855." *Newspaper History: from the Seventeenth Century to the Present Day*. Ed. George Boyce, James Curran, and Pauline Wingate. London: Constable, 1978.

Bakhtin, Mikhail. *The Dialogic Imagination*. Tr. Emerson and Holquist. Austin: University of Texas Press, 1981.

Behagg, Clive. "Secrecy, Ritual and Folk Violence: The Opacity of the Workplace in the First Half of the Nineteenth Century." *Popular Culture and Custom in Nineteenth-Century England*. Ed. Robert Storch. London: Croom Helm, 1982.

Bennett, Scott. "Revolution in Thought: Serial Publication and the Mass Market for Reading." *The Victorian Periodical Press: Samplings and Soundings.* Ed. Joanne Shattock and Michael Wolff. Leicester: University Press, 1982.

_____. "The Editorial Character and Readership of *The Penny Magazine*: An Analysis." *Victorian Periodicals Review* 17 (1984): 127-41.

Berridge, Virginia. "Popular Sunday Papers and mid-Victorian Society." *Newspaper History: from the Seventeenth Century to the Present Day.* Ed. George Boyce, James Curran, and Pauline Wingate. London: Constable, 1978.

Bleiler, E. F. "Introduction." *Wagner the Wehr-wolf.* By George W. M. Reynolds. Ed. E. F. Bleiler. New York: Dover, 1975.

Brougham, Henry. *Practical Observations upon the Education of the People, Addressed to the Working Classes and Their Employers.* London: Richard Taylor, 1825.

Burke, Peter. *Popular Culture in Early Modern Europe.* New York: Harper & Row, 1978.

Chibnall, Steve. "Chronicles of the Gallows: The Social History of Crime Reporting." *Sociological Review Monograph* #29 (University of Keele) (October 1980): 179-217.

Cunnigham, Hugh. *Leisure in the Industrial Revolution, c. 1780-1880.* London: Croom Helm, 1980.

Curran, James. "The Press as an Agency of Social Control: an Historical Perspective." *Newspaper History: from the Seventeenth Century to the Present Day.* Ed. George Boyce, James Curran, and Pauline Wingate. London: Constable, 1978.

Dalziel, Margaret. *Popular Fiction 100 Years Ago.* London: Cohen & West, 1957.

Dyos, H. J. and Michael Wolff, eds. *The Victorian City.* 2 vols. Boston: Routledge & Kegan Paul, 1973.

Foucault, Michel. *The Birth of the Clinic.* Tr. Alan Sheridan. New York: Pantheon, 1973.

_____. *Discipline and Punish.* Tr. Alan Sheridan. New York: Pantheon, 1977.

Fox, Celina. "Political Caricature and the Freedom of the Press in Early Nineteenth-century England." *Newspaper History: from the Seventeenth Century to the Present Day.* Ed. George Boyce, James Curran, and Pauline Wingate. London: Constable, 1978.

Gaskell, Philip. *A New Introduction to Bibliography.* Oxford: Oxford University Press, 1972.

George, M. Dorothy. *London Life in the Eighteenth Century.* New York: Penguin, 1992.

Grant, James. *Sketches in London.* London: W. S. Orr & Co., 1838.

Habermas, Jurgen. *The Structural Transformation of the Public Sphere.* Tr. Thomas Burger with Frederick Lawrence. Cambridge: MIT Press, 1989.

Himmelfarb, Gertrude. "The Culture of Poverty." *The Victorian City.* Ed. H. J. Dyos and Michaeol Wolff, vol. 2. London: Routledge and Kegan Paul, 1973.

Hoggart, P. R. "Edward Lloyd, 'The Father of the Cheap Press.'" *The Dickensian* 80 (1984): 33-8.

_____. "Travesties of Dickens." *Essays and Studies* 40 (1987): 32-44.

Humphreys, Anne. "Popular Narrative and Political Discourse in Reynolds's Weekly Newspaper." *Investigating Victorian Journalism.* Ed L. Brake, A. Jones, and L. Madden. New York: St. Martin's, 1990.

Hurston, Zora Neale. *Mules and Men.* Bloomington: Indiana University Press, 1963.

Illich, Ivan. "Beauty and The Junkyard." *Whole Earth Review* (Winter 1991): 64-8.

_____. *Deschooling Society.* New York: Penguin, 1973.

_____. *Medical Nemesis.* Harmondsworth: Penguin, 1975.

James, Louis. "The View from Brick Lane: Contrasting Perspectives in Working-Class and Middle-Class Fiction of the Early Victorian Period." *Yearbook of English Studies* 11 (1981): 87-101.

_____. *Fiction for the Working Man 1830-1850.* London: Oxford University Press, 1963.

Jauss, Hans Robert. *Aesthetic Experience and Literary Hermeneutics.* Tr. Michael Shaw. Minneapolis: University of Minnesota Press, 1982.

Laquer, Thomas. "The Cultural Origins of Popular Literacy in England 1500-1850." *Oxford Review of Education* 2 (1976): 255-75.

_____. "Working-Class Demand and the Growth of English Elementary Education, 1750-1850." *Schooling and Society.* Ed. Lawrence Stone. Baltimore: Johns Hopkins University Press, 1976.

Mayhew, Henry. *London Labour and the London Poor.* 4 vols. New York: Dover, 1968.

Mountjoy, Peter Roger. "The Working Class Press and Working Class Conservatism." *Newspaper History: from the Seventeenth Century to the Present Day.* Ed. George Boyce, James Curran, and Pauline Wingate. London: Constable, 1978.

Murphy, Paul Thomas. "'Imagination Flaps its Sportive Wings': Views of Fiction in British Working-Class Periodicals, 1816-58." *Victorian Studies* 32 (1989): 339-64.

Neuburg, Victor. "The Literature of the Streets." *The Victorian City.* 2 vols. Ed. H. J. Dyos and Michael Wolff. Boston: Routledge & Kegan Paul, 1973.

Reid, Douglas. "The Decline of Saint Monday 1766-1876." *Past and Present* 71 (1976): 77-101.

Rymer, James Malcolm. "Popular Writing." *The Queen's Magazine* 1 (1842): 99-103.

_____. *Varney the Vampyre.* Ed. E. F. Bleiler. New York: Dover, 1972.

Shepard, Leslie. *The History of Street Literature.* Detroit: Singing Tree Press, 1973.

Smith, Charles Manby. *The Working-Man's Way in the World, being the Autobiography of a Journeyman Printer.* New York: Redfield, 1854.

Springhall, John. "Leisure and Victorian Youth: The Penny Theatre in London, 1830-1890." *Childhood, Youth and Education in the Late Nineteenth Century: Proceedings of the 1980 Annual Conference of the History of Education Society of Great Britain.* Ed. John Hurt. London: History of Education Society, 1981.

Spufford, Margaret. *Small Books and Pleasant Histories.* Athens: University of Georgia Press, 1982.

Stephens, John Russell. "*Jack Sheppard* and the Licensers: The Case Against Newgate Plays." *Nineteenth-Century Theatre Research* 1 (1973): 1-13.

_____. "Thespis's Poorest Children: Penny Theatres and the Law in the 1830's." *Theatre Notebook* 40 (1986): 123-30.

Storch, Robert. "Introduction." *Popular Culture and Custom in Nineteenth-Century England.* Ed. Robert Storch. London: Croom Helm, 1982.

Sturt, Mary. *The Education of the People.* London: Routledge and Kegan Paul, 1967.

Thompson, E. P. "The Moral Economy of the English Crowd in the Eighteenth Century." *Past and Present* 50 (1971): 76-136.

_____. "Time, Work-Discipline, and Industrial Capitalism." *Past and Present* 38 (1967): 56-97.

_____. *The Making of the English Working Class.* New York: Vintage, 1963.

Vicinus, Martha. "'Helpless and Unfriended': Nineteenth-Century Domestic Melodrama." *New Literary History* 13 (1981): 127-43.

_____. *The Industrial Muse.* New York: Barnes and Noble, 1974.

Webb, R. K. *The British Working Class Reader, 1790-1848: Literacy and Social Tension.* London: Allen and Unwin, 1955.

Welsh, Alexander. "The Victorian City." *Victorian Studies* 17 (1974): 419-29.

Williams, Raymond. "The Press and Popular Culture: an Historical Perspective." *Newspaper History: from the Seventeenth Century to the Present Day.* Ed. George Boyce, James Curran, and Pauline Wingate. London: Constable, 1978.

6

The City, the Country, and Communities of Singing Women: Music in the Novels of Elizabeth Gaskell

Alisa M. Clapp

> Margaret . . . had a repugnance to the idea of a manufac-
> turing town, and believed that her mother was receiving
> benefit from Heston air, so she would willingly have de-
> ferred the expedition to Milton. —Gaskell, *North and South*

> "I don't know about fine music myself, but folks say Marget
> is a rare singer, and I know she can make me cry at any
> time by singing 'Th' Owdham Weaver.'"—Gaskell, *Mary
> Barton*[1]

*L*ike Margaret in her novel *North and South*, Elizabeth Gaskell (1810-65) had "a repugnance to the idea of a manufacturing town." Like so many of her contemporaries, she attributed many of Victorian England's social ills to its growing urbanization. As the very title of *North and South* suggests, Gaskell depicted England as rigidly severed into urban, "northern" life and rural, "southern" life. In fact, this city-country dichotomy becomes an oft-discussed theme of Gaskell's novels.[2] In *Mary Barton* (1848) and *North and South*

(1854-5), Gaskell focuses on city life, depicting rural immigrants' rude awakening to urban conflicts. In *Cranford* (1853), *Ruth* (1853), *Sylvia's Lovers* (1863), and *Wives and Daughters* (1864-6), Gaskell depicts urban lifestyles encroaching on small rural towns.

Although the second quotation from *Mary Barton* seems initially unrelated to a discussion of social environment, I argue that one way Gaskell helps her characters to resign themselves to environmental change is to gather the women together to lament the changes around them through music like "The Oldham Weaver." Indeed, Gaskell's approach to locale is distinct from that of other Victorian writers because she so often focuses on the problems encountered by women: for example, domestic tensions of unemployed workers, women courting across class lines, and rural women resisting the encroachment of city ways. Just as Scottish women poets were sensitive to the changing way of life in the rural Highlands and depict it in their poetry, as Florence Boos' article in this volume describes, so too were Gaskell's women sensitive to their altered lifestyles. One way Gaskell's women cope is by forming women's communities, as scholars such as Pauline Nestor and Nina Auerbach have discussed. One prominent activity within these communities which is often not examined, however, is that of music. Gaskell's women sing together, play the piano for each other, and incorporate song lyrics into their dialogue.

The debate concerning art's relation to society endured throughout the nineteenth century. On one extreme, Matthew Arnold argued for art's rehabilitating qualities in reforming a corrupt society while, on the other, Walter Pater, with his "art for art's sake" doctrine, resisted such utilitarian uses of art. But to Gaskell's mind, aestheticism had everything to do with real life, as evidenced simply by the fact that she believed her novel writing contributed to social reform. Likewise, the musical situations in her novels—which I term aesthetic encounters—comment specifically on the struggle between urban and rural ways of life. Music-making, we must remember, relied on live performances in Gaskell's day, and the consequent exhibition of the human body—especially a woman's—complicated music performance for Victorian audiences and authors alike. I define aesthetic encounters, then, as literary portrayals of musical performances which actually comprise *three* aesthetics: the visual "picture" of the performers; the musical sounds heard by the characters; and the literary text of the lyrics being transmitted. In Gaskell's mind, not only is music sung by suffering women but its three components become paradigmatic of the city-country binary of her works.

First, the visibility of female performers incites vanity in the women themselves and sexual interest in their male voyeurs. The egotism, individualism, consumerism, and class divisions thus engendered reflect ramifications of urbanization and industrialization. For these reasons Gaskell casts both showy music and, by extension, cities negatively. Second and in contrast, the musical *sounds* of a performance provide spiritual comfort, develop emotional sensibilities, and encourage a communal spirit for the listeners, especially in the case of folk songs and hymns. Such music thus binds Gaskell's female communities together. Women who lack communities of singing women—such as Sylvia and Ruth—lack the supportive community necessary to protect them against the worldly encroachments of the city.

Sights and sounds of musical performance come to be paradigms of the city and the country, respectively. However, the third element of Gaskell's aesthetic encounter— musical *texts*—greatly complicates this neat dichotomy. Gaskell highlights song lyrics in the text and incorporates them into her women's dialogue so that they become a secret language among her women, much like African-American slaves' coded spirituals. Appearing to be trivial parlor entertainment to the outsider, music becomes a subtext as women consciously and unconsciously comment on the ills outside their parlor walls: specifically, the tumultuous change from agrarian past to urban present. This coding empowers Gaskell's communities of women by giving them a voice.

Despite such empowerment, Gaskell actually denies her women more power. She alludes to songs which depict women vigorously rebelling against the status quo, in both political and domestic situations. However, due to her middle-class sensibilities, Gaskell excludes the actual lyrics which suggest these socially rebellious or narcissistic actions of women and, instead, highlights the lighter, albeit vital, lyrics detailing women's communal experiences. Unlike nineteenth-century Scottish women whose poetry often contained political statements of resistance, Gaskell edits her literary songs so as to stifle any political undercurrents. Gaskell's women are accorded sympathetic reactions but denied social-reforming *actions*, actions which could change society. Though many scholars extol the agency of Gaskell's women, I argue that a close reading of the musical encounters suggests containment and conservatism.[3]

In short, Gaskell's heroines are taught the dangers of the city by the egotistical, singing urbanites, the communal spirit of the country from folk-singing communities of women, and, from the texts of songs, the passive endurance—not aggression—required to be a woman living in a changing landscape.

To think in terms of a city-country binary was quite common in the nineteenth-century. By 1887 Ferdinand Tönnies had formulated the terms *Gesellschaft* and *Gemeinschaft* to represent the city and country ideologies, respectively. *Gesellschaft* referred to "urban, heterogeneous, industrial societies" that were "culturally sophisticated and shaped by the rational pursuit of self-interest in a capitalistic and secular environment" while *Gemeinschaft* suggested "local, organic, agricultural" communities that were "modeled on the family and rooted in the traditional and the sacred" (Graver 14). Gaskell experienced the *Gesellschaft* and *Gemeinschaft* ideologies in her own lifetime and, notably, vilified the former, capitalistic system fairly consistently in her fiction.

Elizabeth Gaskell's early life was shaped by country living. Because her mother died when she was a year old, and her father felt unable to raise her, she was sent to live with her two aunts in the small town of Knutsford, Cheshire. This serene country village came to be a haven to which she would look for comfort throughout her life. However, her marriage to Unitarian minister William

Gaskell in 1832 took her to the industrial city of Manchester where she lived the rest of her life. As she writes:

> I was brought up in a country town, and my lot is now to live in or rather on the borders of a great manufacturing town, but when spring days first come and the bursting leaves and sweet earthly smells tell me that "Somer is ycomen in," I feel a stirring instinct and long to be off into the deep grassy solitudes of the country. (*Letters* 14)

Her abhorrence of city filth is probably best described in her evocation of Milton-Northern in *North and South*:

> Nearer to the town, the air had a faint taste and smell of smoke; perhaps, after all, more a loss of the fragrance of grass and herbage than any positive taste or smell . . . .Here and there a great oblong many-windowed factory stood up, like a hen among her chickens, puffing out black 'unparliamentary' smoke. (59)

Here, Gaskell defines the city against the country ("a loss of the fragrance of grass and herbage") but still with rural metaphors ("like a hen"). Winifred Gérin contends that this "great sensitivity towards her surroundings, whether beautiful like her Knutsford countryside, or crushing like the Manchester slums of her day" filled both Gaskell's experience and her literary imagination (xiv). For example, in *Mary Barton* and *North and South*, Gaskell explores the rural immigrants' initial, disturbing experience in the industrial city of Manchester. In *Sylvia's Lovers* and *Ruth*, Gaskell suggests the invasion of worldly forces into the remote, rural communities of Monkshaven (actually the port town of Whitby) and Fordham, respectively. In the former, this invasion comes in the form of a press gang which carries off one of Sylvia's lovers, while in the latter the worldly Bellingham seduces and carries off the innocent Ruth. In *Cranford* and *Wives and Daughters*, Gaskell portrays isolated communities that attempt to deal with pressures from the outside world, such as foreign arrivals, economic uncertainties, and scientific progress.

Though these urban-rural tensions affect men—from John Barton to Daniel Robson to John Thornton—clearly Gaskell's sympathies lie mainly with the wives, daughters, and sweethearts. They struggle to feed their starving families, support their men when they are in trouble with the law, keep the peace when classes clash, and maintain stability in an ever-changing world.

Gaskell contended that art could improve society, that her novels could enlighten the middle classes about the social ills surrounding them. In *Mary Barton*, this constituted giving "utterance to the agony which, from time to time, convulses this dumb people" (xxxvi). The didactic nature of her novels would then inspire her readers to work toward reform. By contrast, many women, including friends of Gaskell, were active in suffrage and social-reform movements (Nestor 9-11, Rubenius 1-18; 38-56). Though she did charity work which stemmed from her role as a minister's wife, Gaskell engaged in nothing on a large scale or on a political level. Gérin feels that through story-telling Gaskell found her own means of social reform "that would be distinct from her husband's educational programme" (60).

It is no wonder that music should also be an aesthetic form intricately tied with the social world around her. Gaskell mentions concerts with friends and lessons for her daughters frequently in her letters.[4] Her desire to have her daughters trained musically reflects an entire social convention that "respectable" young women should be able to boast musical competence. But Gaskell defined music against such focus on the self; rather, in her experience, music acted as a social adhesive. Concert-going bound together her circle of friends just as music discussions solidified mother-daughter relationships. For Gaskell, music was not to be a vehicle for vain display but for emotive expression. For example, she enjoyed "listening with both my ears, and half my heart to something so exquisite of Seb. Bach's" (*Letters* 681). Likewise, she urged her daughters to "listen with the heart" when playing their music lessons, with their feelings contingent upon the fictional context of the songs: "You ought to try and imagine the expression with which songs ought to be sung, according to their *words*, and meaning" (*Letters* 143). For Gaskell, then, music was socially valuable in its ability to create communities, express emotions, and convey meaning. Specifically as a woman's domestic art, it had the capacity to bring women together if the emotions and words of songs were highlighted. Yet it also had the potential to fragment women's communities due to vanity and jealousy which she depicts almost exclusively as an urban phenomenon.

Throughout her novels, Gaskell consistently equates superior musical skill with middle-class pretentiousness and love of display. To play well is to *look* good; this is most true of her city women. For instance, in *North and South*, Fanny Thornton flaunts her piano-playing (77) and points out Margaret Hale's lack of ability: "she's not accomplished, mamma. She can't play" (142). Such class snobbery and superficiality as Fanny's are also condemned in Mrs. Gibson in *Wives and Daughters*. Although Mrs. Gibson habitually sings Italian airs and speaks of Italian operas in front of fashionable company, Molly notes that her comments about the opera stars are mainly borrowed from critics' reviews (187). Further, to keep up appearances, Mrs. Gibson makes sure that Cynthia and Molly have musical training and exposure to fashionable concerts (614). Mrs. Gibson then looks for opportunities to exhibit her daughters. When the Hamley brothers come to visit, Mrs. Gibson insists on the young girls performing: Cynthia's playing, though "anything but correct" is still "charming" while Molly "was very shy of playing in company; and . . . went through her performance heavily . . ." (283). She completes "eighteen dreary pages" by Friedrich Kalkbrenner (1785-1849), only to find Mrs. Gibson sleeping and Roger flirting with Cynthia (284). This aesthetic encounter emphasizes social propriety and sexual caprice over any musical appreciation.

In *Mary Barton*, Job Legh initiates gendered commodification of the singing woman: when Will visits, he thinks, "What could he do for him? He could ask Margaret to sing" (180). Will is captivated by sight of the performer: "His very lids refused to wink, as if afraid in that brief proverbial interval to lose a particle of the rich music that floated through the room" (180). Margaret, who earns her money by singing for the Mechanics' Society, eventually becomes Will's wife and (apparently) never sings in public again. The professional singer is rescued from this conspicuous life and made into a respectable housewife. Ironically, though, this happens as a result of her conspicuousness before a stranger whom her grandfather hoped to entertain. Male audience members, like the Hamley brothers and Will Wilson, add another dimension to musical encounters since they see the sexual woman more than the musician. Troubled by this, Gaskell restricts most of her encounters to same-sex gatherings. Likewise, male musicians are usually vilified. In *Ruth*, not only is music associated with pretentious, upper-class balls (14) but also insensitive men: the urban Mr. *Bell*ingham "whose deadly music yet rang in [Ruth's] ears . . . tempting her" (100) as well as Mr. Bradshaw, Ruth's employer, a pompous, inaccurate singer "like an organ very badly played" (153) who fires her because of her illegitimate child. Male musicians thus seem especially dangerous to Gaskell's scheme and, perhaps as a consequence, she deals with very few of them in her novels.

Fashionable musical trends, bourgeois buying-power, and the commodification of music performance cause snobbery, superficiality, attention to self, consumerism, and unfeeling capitalism: in short, an urbanization of music. In condemning superficial music, then, Gaskell criticizes the *Gesellschaft* ideology associated with it.

If rural music avoids such problems it is because of its focus on the community (*Gemeinschaft*), not on the individual. Folk songs and traditional hymns formed the heart of rural music-making. Cecil Sharp, the noted nineteenth-century collector of folk songs, theorized that folk songs were most representative of a community since what was purely personal in them would be eliminated after several generations. Sharp writes that while "Art music . . . is the work of the individual," the folk-song is not only "communal in authorship" but it "reflects feelings and tastes that are communal" (15). Further, Sharp contends that though the words of folk songs were corrupted by being inaccurately recorded on paper, the music itself was usually not recorded and therefore "has been more faithfully preserved than its text" (102). Gaskell herself seemed charmed with Scottish ballads, several of which she recorded in her journal (e.g. "Jess McFarlane" and

"Weel May the Keel Row"). Gaskell's female communities find great comfort in coming together to sing folk songs, and the tunes especially represent emotional comfort, simplicity, and stability in times of conflict and change.

For instance, *Mary Barton*'s Alice Wilson, like many of her real-life counterparts in both England and Scotland, has been forced to emigrate from the country to the city. So she relies on the folk songs and hymns of her childhood to reunite her with the pastoral, utopian world of her past. On her deathbed she sings "old scraps of ballads, or old snatches of primitive versions of the Psalms" which are associated with "country churches half draperied over with ivy" (316). Evoking memories of the past, the utopian countryside, and her Christian faith, these ballads and vocal Psalms provide the spiritual basis for Alice to endure her existence.

Communities of women come together to share such comfort. Alice, Margaret, and Mary share an emotionally charged moment when Margaret sings "The Oldham Weaver," also known as "The Poor Cotton Weaver" (39), which communicates the pain of others which might very soon be theirs as women attached to similarly circumstanced men. Music is also integral to the female community at Cranford. When ruffled by Miss Jessie's tactless discussion of her relatives, the women of Cranford are soothed by music: "It was to take the taste of this [confession] out of our mouths, and the sound of this out of our ears, that Miss Jenkyns proposed music; so I say again, it was very good of her to beat time to the song" (8). Miss Jessie plays on "an old cracked piano, which I think had been a spinnet in its youth" and sings "a little out of tune" (7-8); both details show the antiquity and lack of sophistication of this rural community. Yet this time lack of culture does not divide women, as in Milton-Northern, but brings them together, for "we were none of us musical" (8). Likewise, in *Wives and Daughters*, Molly prefers the old Scots airs which Mr. Gibson often whistles to the annoyance of his wife who thinks them neither refined nor artistic (414). By so doing, Gaskell privileges native, rustic music over fashionable French songs and showy piano pieces.

Thus, songs have the potential to provide community and support for the heroines, accomplished primarily through the emotional sympathies engendered through the *music*. When the heroines lack such a community, however, trouble arises. Ignoring or missing the support of singing women, Sylvia and Ruth face heartbreak alone, heartbreak caused by outside, "city" forces—press gangs and rich seducers—which invade the rural havens in which they live.

Sylvia Robson, for instance, walks right past a group of women standing along Monkshaven's harbor who "held each other by the hand, and swayed from side to side . . . [singing] 'Weel may the keel row . . . that my laddie's in!'" (19), a song which speaks of losing one's man to the press gangs. Neither is she in communion with Dolly Reid, the Robsons' maid, who sings ballads and hymns. Dolly's singing the funeral psalm, "Our God, our help in ages past" (composed by Isaac Watts and based on Psalm 90:1-5) foreshadows the grief of losing a loved one (as in the line "our shelter from the stormy blast, and our eternal home"). Robson is executed only a few scenes later (315). Sylvia lacks this sensitivity to music and can never join in with these women. She thus is not forewarned or comforted by them when her lover disappears and her father is hung.

Ruth, too, is isolated from any nurturing, musical women early in the novel, despite living in a young girls' boarding school. Musical communities of women might have warned her of male seduction and helped to prevent her fall. Unlike Sylvia, however, Ruth later comes into contact with nurturing, "singing" women and listens to them: the kindly Mrs. Hughes has a "musical" voice (99); Miss Benson, the sister of the good, dissenting minister Mr. Benson, whistles (112); and Sally the maid sings "The Derby Ram" off key (191). As part of her eventual healing, Ruth is able to hear the rural church bells pealing "Life let us Cherish" (191) and also able to remember the songs her mother used to sing (316). Gaskell ends Ruth's life with music, symbolic of maternal bonds:

> They had never heard her sing; indeed the simple art which her mother had taught her, had died, with her early joyous-

ness, at that dear mother's death. But now she sang
continually, very soft and low. She went from one childish
ditty to another without pause. (448)

Reawakening this repressed art reunites Ruth spiritually
with her mother and the countryside of her childhood.

If the sights and sounds of music symbolically suggest
the city-country condition, the words have the potential to
point to some sort of action in response to this condition.
Gaskell alludes to over 15 songs in her novels (Rubenius
338-42; 364-70).   Many of the song lyrics invoked are
powerful female codes vividly depicting women's experiences in a society where rural life is changing to a modern
one. However, none of the songs is given in its entirety and
in so editing these songs, Gaskell manipulates the words
to conceal rebellious actions. Indeed, many of these folk-
songs and ballads chronicle lower- or middle-class women
cursing the political system and defying the marriage
system in an effort to forge their way in a society caught
up in urban-rural tensions. The rebelliousness of these
balladic characters parallels that of Gaskell's own male
characters: John Barton demonstrates in London for fair
workers' wages, Daniel Robson leads a rebellion against
the press gangs, and even Roger Hamley goes against
parental desires in pursuing personal interests. Gaskell's
women thus see men reacting against society's oppression
and also sing songs about female protagonists rebelling
against society. Yet such blatant subversion as well as
individualism troubled Gaskell by invoking the problem-
atic qualities of self-interested *Gesellschaft*. She therefore
conspicuously avoids quoting any of these subversive
lines, retaining only those lyrics about innocuous female
experiences so that her musical heroines are soothed into
social complacency.   Ultimately, she avoids any lyrics
depicting social defiance. Though Gaskell's progressivism
is constantly debated, her use of song lyrics clearly points
to a woman who, because of her middle-class conservatism, could ultimately not endorse the liberal, even lower-
class, rebelliousness chronicled in the very songs her
women sing.

One of the strengths of Gaskell's musical selections is
the number of songs which detail women's experience

within the context of rural-urban tensions. For instance, "Country Commissions to my Cousin in Town" alluded to in *Cranford* (12), depicts the urban luxuries now available to a rural housewife in providing for her family, for example, "A pair of shoe-buckles for pa . . . some silk of the latest new tint" (*Universal Songster* 239). "Leezie Lindsay," found in *North and South* (166), depicts an urban woman carried away to the Highlands by her rural lover; the line Gaskell highlights puts this landscape change in terms of the woman's wardrobe change, of "[kilting] her coats o' green silk" as she moves to the Highlands (found in only one of seven versions collected by Frances Child, 259). "The Oldham Weaver" describes urban poverty in a domestic setting, as both a man *and* his wife are affected.

A second strength of Gaskell's use of music is that song lyrics become codes within women's communities. Feeling defenseless in a world becoming more urban, individualized, and progressive, these women codify their worries within song lyrics and thus speak to one another through women's art. For instance, the women of Cranford have merely to mention "Tibbie Fowler" (114) and all understand the reference to a flaunting woman, much as they see Mrs. Glenmire. In *Wives and Daughters*, Miss Phoebe mentions aloud that Molly is becoming "'As tall and as straight as a poplar-tree' as the old song says" (466), but her sister realizes the significance of the remark: that, like the heroine of Shield's opera *Rosina*, from which the song comes, Molly has a lover. Though old-fashioned and prone to gossip, the sisters also have more serious concerns: that the old rules of etiquette are changing so that it is becoming more acceptable for young women to be out with young men. Through heavily coded song lyrics, the sisters thus show their concern for the larger social changes about them.

Men fail to understand these song codes. In *Wives and Daughters*, when Cynthia sings a French ditty—"Tu t'en repentiras, Colin . . . si tu prends une femme, Colin" ("You'll regret it, Colin . . . if you take a wife, Colin")—she is suggesting that her auditors, the Hamley brothers, may regret marrying her (466). However, Roger does not understand Cynthia's character as Molly does, and continues his advances until her disregard of their engagement enlightens him.

Women thus pour out inner turmoil about their changing world, and male-female relations within it, through songs. But Gaskell's sense of refinement cannot allow this advantage to everyone. Gaskell gives *Mary Barton*'s Esther a song as an epigraph to Chapter 21: "My rest is gone,/ My heart is sore/ Peace find I never,/ And never more" (273). These four lines from Goethe's *Faust* here relate to Esther's past love and present isolation. However, because of her outcast status as a prostitute, Esther cannot join the community of singing women in the novel. Further, her own song is marginalized by the text, given merely as an epigraph and not within the text itself.

In most cases, Gaskell mitigates the political power of songs not by their placement but by using only certain verses. For instance, the popular "Weel May the Keel Row" possesses political overtones in its curse upon the press gangs who snatch a woman's "laddie": "May all the press gangs perish, each lass her laddie cherish" (Dallas, verse 5). However, these lyrics are never given in the text of *Sylvia's Lovers*. The song is used only as foreshadowing of Kinraid, and not an instigation for the Monkshaven women to rebel, though Daniel Robson does.[5]

Mary Barton's "The Oldham Weaver," a popular Lancashire ballad set to the "Jone O'Grinfilt" tune, also involves biased authorial editing. Martha Vicinus describes the song as "the summation of all protest against the new conditions brought by industrialization" (49) as it depicts the poverty of hand-loom weavers replaced by machines. Gaskell includes those verses concerning Jone and Margit's tattered clothes (v.1), starvation (v.3), and abuse (v.5) which depict general, poignant suffering, yet chooses to omit drier, more specific details of the bailiffs' recompense and the individual, verbal retaliation of Jone: "They wouldn't have cared had they broken our necks . . . Then I come out of th' house and left him to chew that" (v.6). Further, none of Gaskell's listeners focus on the vital concluding stanza in which Margit denounces the system and threatens to go straight to the king:

Our Margit declared if hoo'd [she'd] clothes to put on
Hoo'd go up to London to see the great man
And if things were not altered when there hoo had been
Hoo swears hoo would fight with blood up to the een.
Hoo's nowt against th' king but hoo likes a fair thing
And hoo says hoo can tell when hoo can hurt.
(Quoted in Dallas 127-28)

Neither Alice, nor Margaret, nor Mary comments at all on the potential for social defiance found in this ballad, as Jone condemns his master and Margit, a *woman*, condemns the king. Rather, Gaskell highlights their emotional reaction to such suffering:

But Margaret, with fixed eye, and earnest, dreamy look, seemed to become more and more absorbed in realising to herself the woe she had been describing, and which she felt might at that very moment be suffering and hopeless within a short distance of their comparative comfort. (39)

As Amanda Anderson notes, the actual destitute people become lost in this reverie: "A grammatical problem in Gaskell's sentence tellingly reflects the eclipsing of the actual sufferers: no subject attaches to the phrase 'might . . . be suffering and hopeless' ('woe' can serve as the subject of 'hopeless' but not of 'suffering')" (121-22). The listeners are caught up in the general sorrow of the situation, not any particular people or sorrows. Absorbed in the sentiment but not the reality of the situation, Gaskell's women fail to become indignant. Thus, unlike Scottish poets such as Mary MacPherson, whose poetry became political to protest the lost way of life, Gaskell's women *retreat* into their singing without taking any political action.

Many songs deal with politics on a domestic level, discussing women who confront class or sexual politics with vigor. Often balladic heroines defy the conservative gender or marriage codes of the countryside; other times, they engage in unconventional marriages between urban and rural partners of different classes. For instance, Sally's "Derby Ram," in *Ruth* (191), depicts a class system where a servant goes to market and returns with far-fetched stories of enormous rams to confound the master ("The wool that was on its back, Sir,/ Made fifty packs of cloth,/ And for to tell a lie, Sir,/ I'm sure I'm very loth," v.

4). However, only the lines about "going to Derby . . . Upon a market-day" are given within the text of *Ruth*. The theme of worker defiance is dropped since Ruth never dreams of "confounding" her employer, Mr. Bradshaw, but accepts his dismissal when her past comes to light.

Similarly, the ballad "Barbara Allen" mentioned in *Mary Barton* (164) chronicles a rural woman who adamantly refuses to marry her wooer.[6] Gaskell's Mary Barton, on the other hand, quickly reverses her decision to reject Jem and asserts herself, ultimately, only in defending him in court. Likewise, the traditional Scottish ballad "Leezie Lindsay" (or "Lizie Lindsay") is quoted in *North and South* in reference to Margaret's "gown o' green satin" like Leezie's (166). Yet the ballad itself contains the subversive story of a woman who rejects rich lovers *and* her parents' wishes in order to run off with a man of her own choosing. This is something Margaret Hale, as a dutiful daughter, would never dream of doing.

The Scottish ballad, "Jock of Hazeldean" in *Cranford* (8), presents a woman who flees convention and a wealthy marriage match to run off with her lover, Jock: "They sought her baith by bower and ha',/ The ladie was not seen!/ She's o'er the Border, and awa'/ Wi' Jock of Hazeldean" (Rogers 82). *Cranford*'s "Tibbie Fowler" (114) even depicts a woman who exploits both her money and sexual attractiveness in luring dozens of men: "She's got pendles [earrings] in her lugs . . . High-heel'd shoon [shoes] and siller [silver] tags,/ And a' the lads are wooin at her" (v. 4, Johnson 452). In these two ballads, then, women actively assert themselves in gaining what they desire. Yet sexuality and wealth are worldly concepts foreign to the women of Cranford, and, in resisting them, Gaskell's rustic heroines can only criticize those other women—specifically, Miss Jessie and Mrs. Glenmire—who, like the ballad heroines, aggressively take the men they desire. Indeed, Miss Matty has passed up several chances to marry Mr. Holbrook simply for propriety's sake.

Elizabeth Gaskell's use of music, then, is complex. First, the individualism of musical performance is aligned with urban life, egoism, and consumerism, all of which Gaskell saw as leading to social strife. The antithesis of musical display is communal music which Gaskell consistently aligns with cathartic emotional release and—through her emphasis on folk-songs and ballads—the utopian, nurturing countryside. Women's musical communities express their common grievances about a society plagued by change, poverty, and injustice; women without communities, like Sylvia and Ruth, suffer great tragedies.

The sights and sounds of music represent, respectively, the battling forces of *Gesellshaft* and *Gemeinshaft* ideologies. However, the song texts are tense sites of struggle since both rural, communal experiences *and* progressive, individual rebellion exist in the original songs. The power behind Gaskell's use of song lyrics comes in her highlighting pivotal experiences of women through her textual choices. Indeed, most of these songs are "women's songs." They give a woman's perspective on changing society, highlighting topics that reflect the shift from an agrarian to a modern world: clothing styles of the country and the city ("Leezie Lindsay"), going to town to shop ("Country Commissions" and "Derby Ram"), romance between country and city people ("Leezie Lindsay"), poverty of families in the city ("Oldham Weaver"), longing for the country life of the past (Alice's ballad and the Shield song), and loss of lovers to social injustice ("Weel May the Keel Row"). Communal sympathy grows out of these musical dialogues and codings.

Communal sympathy is so rigorously extolled in these novels, however, that it precludes social *action*, action which, as with Daniel Robson and others, begins with one individual's revolt against the status quo. Yet so many of the songs in her novels describe a more aggressive fight by an individual. "The Oldham Weaver" describes a wife going to London to speak to the king, something Mary never considers doing though her father protests in London. "Weel May the Keel Row" curses the press gangs, which Sylvia never does. "The Derby Ram" describes tricking the upper classes, yet Ruth never dreams of aggressive deceit. Barbara Allen does not yield to a lover even when he is lying on his deathbed. "Leezie Lindsay" and the narrator of "Jock of Hazeldean" choose their husbands despite family and social pressure. And Tibbie

Fowler uses her sexuality to control men, much to the disgust of the Cranford women. Gaskell's women are too modest and proper to attempt such rebellions, so their music only takes them to the first step of their struggle—acquiescence—when it had the capacity to suggest more rigorous actions. Music is the key to human sympathy and emotions, but if its words suggest anything more unacceptable, Gaskell fails to acknowledge it.

For Gaskell, then, communities of singing women could appease the tension between country and city which bewildered the Victorian population and, significantly, keep women happily in their homes.

Notes

I wish to thank Nicholas Temperley, Amanda Anderson, Eric Gardner, Michael Goldberg, Tom Hove, and Sibylle Gruber for their helpful comments on various drafts of this article.

1. *North and South*, 59, and *Mary Barton*, 37; both from the Oxford Edition. All subsequent references will be to these editions of Gaskell's novels.
2. See, for example, Enid Duthie, *The Themes of Elizabeth Gaskell*, especially chapters 2-4; W.A. Craik, *Elizabeth Gaskell and the Provincial Novel*, throughout; and Edgar Wright, *Mrs. Gaskell: The Basis for Reassessment*, in particular chapters 5-7.
3. I am self-consciously reading Gaskell against such prominent works as Patsy Stoneman's *Elizabeth Gaskell*, Margaret Homans' *Bearing the Word* 223-76, and Felicia Bonaparte's *The Gypsy-Bachelor of Manchester* which emphasize the feminine power to be found in Gaskell's fiction. I argue that despite Gaskell's feminine symbolism (such as clothing, as Homans argues, or coded song lyrics, as I suggest) Gaskell is still conservatively denying feminine action. Further, the feminine agency that Stoneman roots in the domestic sphere and that Bonaparte roots in male characters (who become women's demonic double) is still not as powerful as the feminine action delineated in the song lyrics and denied to Gaskell's heroines.
4. See *Letters* 162-63, 169, 219, 305 for Gaskell's concert experiences; and 143-44, 160-61, 210, 215-17, 224, 267, 375, 774, concerning her daughters' lessons.
5. In "The Keel Row," a sailor's beloved brags about his blithe nature, his skill at dancing, his sweet kisses, his lack of learning, and his distinctive blue bonnet. Interestingly, these several attributes foreshadow the character of Charley Kinraid who will attract Sylvia's attention because of his blitheness (in contrast to her serious cousin Philip), woo Sylvia at a dance, swipe a kiss from Sylvia there, create an unfavorable contrast to the learned Philip, and be thought to be drowned when his distinctive bonnet with Sylvia's ribbon attached drifts to shore.

6. Alan Lomax, in a study of folk songs, explains the ballad's enormous popularity in both America and England since Barbara Allen rejects marriage, a woman's only socially recognized means toward self-fulfillment: "Barbara Allen . . . [humbles] and [destroys] the man whom she sees as her enemy and antagonist. That she dies at once of remorse, immediately frees her and her sisters of the guilt of hard-heartedness. No other supposition can, I feel, explain the unique position that this ballad occupies in our tradition" (171).

Works Cited

Anderson, Amanda. *Tainted Souls and Painted Faces: The Rhetoric of Fallenness in Victorian Culture.* Ithaca and London: Cornell University Press, 1993.

Auerbach, Nina. *Communities of Women: An Idea in Fiction.* Cambridge: Harvard University Press, 1978.

Bantock, Granville, ed. "The Derby Ram," in *One Hundred Songs of England for High Voice.* Bryn Maur: Oliver Ditson, 1914, 57-8.

Bonaparte, Felicia. *The Gypsy-Bachelor of Manchester: The Life of Mrs. Gaskell's Demon.* Charlottesville and London: University Press of Virginia, 1992.

Child, Frances James, ed. "Lizie Lindsay," in *The English and Scottish Popular Ballads.* 5 vols. New York: Folklore, 1956, 4:255-266.

Craik, W.A. *Elizabeth Gaskell and the English Provincial Novel.* London: Methuen, 1975.

Dallas, Karl, ed. "The Poor Cotton Weaver" and "The Keel Row," in *One Hundred Songs of Toil: 450 Years of Workers' Songs.* London: Wolfe, 1974, 125-28; 175-77.

Duthie, Enid. *The Themes of Elizabeth Gaskell.* London: Macmillan, 1980.

Gaskell, Elizabeth. *Cranford.* Ed. Elizabeth Porges Watson. Oxford: Oxford University Press, 1972.

_____. *The Letters of Mrs Gaskell.* Ed. J.A.V. Chapple and Arthur Pollard. Cambridge: Harvard University Press, 1967.

_____. *Mary Barton.* Ed. Edgar Wright. Oxford: Oxford University Press, 1987.

_____. *North and South.* Ed. Angus Easson. Oxford: Oxford University Press, 1982.

_____. *Ruth.* Ed. Alan Shalston. Oxford: Oxford University Press, 1985.

_____. *Sylvia's Lovers.* Ed. Andrew Sanders. Oxford: Oxford University Press, 1982.

_____. *Wives and Daughters.* Ed. Angus Easson. Oxford: Oxford University Press, 1987.

Gérin, Winifred. *Elizabeth Gaskell: A Biography.* Oxford: Clarendon Press, 1976.

Graver, Suzanne. *George Eliot and Community: A Study in Social Theory and Fictional Form.* Berkeley: University of California Press, 1984.

Hatton, J.L. and Eaton Faning, eds. "Barbara Allen," in *Songs of England.* 3 vols. London: Boosey and Hawkes, [1873], 1:111.

Homans, Margaret. *Bearing the Word: Language and Female Experience in Nineteenth-Century Women's Fiction.* Chicago and London: University of Chicago Press, 1986.

Johnson, James, ed. "Tibbie Fowler," in *The Scots Musical Museum.* 5 vols. Edinburgh & England: Folklore Assoc., 1962, 5:452.

Lomax, Alan. *The Folk Songs of North America in the English Language.* Garden City, NY: Doubleday, 1975.

Nestor, Pauline. *Female Friendships and Communities: Charlotte Brontë, George Eliot, and Elizabeth Gaskell.* New York: Oxford University Press, 1985.

Rubenius, Aina. *The Woman Question in Mrs. Gaskell's Life and Works.* Upsala: Lundequistka Bokhandeln and Cambridge: Harvard University Press, 1950.

Rogers, Charles, ed. "Jock of Hazeldean," in *The Scottish Minstrel: The Songs of Scotland Subsequent to Burns.* Edinburgh: William P. Nimmo, 1872, 82.

Sharp, Cecil. *English Folk Song: Some Conclusions.* 3rd ed. London: Methuen, 1954.

Stoneman, Patsy. *Elizabeth Gaskell.* Bloomington: Indiana University Press, 1987.

"Country Commissions to My Cousin in Town," in *The Universal Songster.* 2 vols. London: Jones, 1828, 1:239.

Vicinus, Martha. *The Industrial Muse: A Study of Nineteenth Century British Working-Class Literature.* New York: Barnes & Noble, 1974.

Wright, Edgar. *Mrs. Gaskell: The Basis for Reassessment.* London: Oxford University Press, 1965.

7

"Oor Location": Scotswomen Poets and the Transition from Rural to Urban Culture

Florence S. Boos

> Noo the bodies are gane an' their dwallin's awa'
> An' the place whaur they stood I scarce ken noo ava,
> For there's roarin' o' steam an' there's reengin' o' wheels,
> Men workin', an' sweatin', an' swearin' like deils.
>
> An' the flame-tappit furnaces staun' in a raw,
> A' bleezin' an' blawin' an' smeekin' awa',
> Their eerie licht brichtenin' the laigh hingin' cluds,
> Gleamin' far ower the loc an' the mirk lanely wuds.
> —"Gartsherrie," Janet Hamilton

The distinctive contribution of Mary MacPherson, Bell Robertson, Janet Hamilton, Mathilde Blind, and Violet Jacob to the literary culture of late-nineteenth and early twentieth-century Scotland has been largely forgotten, as their less-than-instant name-recognition might suggest. Like their fictional English counterparts present in the writings of Elizabeth Gaskell, studied in this volume by Alisa Clapp, these women gave gender-inflected expression to a culture marked by constant toil and material anxiety amid great natural beauty, but their attachment to their "mither tongue" also resonated with varying degrees of nationalist and anti-landlordist sentiments and a clear sympathetic identification with the hardships of fellow women.[1] To give a sense for some of the political themes that attracted these women, I will first examine three Victorian Scottish women poets – Mary MacPherson, Bell Robertson, and Janet Hamilton – who consciously tried to record some of the effects of agrarian immiseration, rural blight, and the disintegrating forces of urban conditions. I will then compare their work with that of Mathilde Blind's narration of violent evictions as formal tragedy and consider briefly an attempt by a post-Victorian "internal outsider," Violet Jacob – an educated and sophisticated member of East Angus society – to recover some of the language-patterns and values she projected onto Scottish peasants. All along this spectrum of growing distance from agrarian life women sought to defend, then to preserve and recover social and linguistic patterns of agrarian life that steadily receded from view, and bridge the growing distance between an unreachable past and an ineluctable present.

In my readings from the work of about a hundred Scottish women poets, I have, of course, noticed many parallels with such English Victorians as Elizabeth Barrett Browning, Augusta Webster, Christina Rossetti, Jean Ingelow, Amy Levy, or Mary Coleridge, but there are distinctive traits as well. These Scottish women's poems characteristically mix sympathy, plaint, and satire with occasional calls for resistance, and they often share a strong social and political focus, a preoccupation with issues of poverty and labor, and an intense identification with Scottish regional landscapes and the Scots language. Women in the Scotswomen's writings are more likely to be mothers and workers, whose courageous efforts to sustain families the poems commemorate. Many poems also mourn the death of children, and grieve the loss and disruptions of forced exile to the United States or elsewhere; for most of these women, immigration was a source of familial pain and regret, not hope. A separate subgenre of historical and religious poems celebrates Covenantors and other Presbyterian heroes, and still another pleads in impassioned rimes for temperance. Several of these poems also refract particular social and demographic shifts of nineteenth-century Scotland: depopulation of the Highlands and consequent movement of farmpeople from the countryside to the overcrowded slums of Glasgow and Edinburgh.

The most obvious marker of Scottish women poets, of course, is their use of the Scots (or Anglo-Scots) language. There are several registers of Scots linguistic usage, from Gaelic, to Central Scots, to Standard English shaded with a few Scottish elisions or vowel changes, and most of these writers wrote "English" as well as Scots poems. But the latter are usually among their best work.

Only a few poets of those I have read – Jessie Russell, Marion Bernstein, Joanna Picken, and Bessie Craigmyle, among them – express support for women's suffrage or women's rights to nondomestic work. Most of these writers, however, seem to assume that women should freely state their views on public and private affairs, as they condemn wife-beaters, sympathize with poor workers, and focus more generally on the economic problems of women's lives. They seemed to expect an audience that would appreciate nuances of speech-patterns that reflected regional and class differences, take seriously issues of contemporary Scottish politics and religion, and accept philanthropic sentiment and portrayals of daily life as natural features of poetic topography.

Late eighteenth and early nineteenth-century literary circles fostered Romantic attempts to appreciate distinctive and geographically specific aspects of poetic expression in the language of the rural, regional "folk." Ballads and broadsides had always replicated some features of everyday speech, but the poems of Robert Burns ("What can a young lassie do wi' an old man"; "I hae a wife o' my ain"; "Galloway Tam") and the Scottish novels of Walter Scott facilitated an assumption that certain dialect and regional usages were especially appropriate to emotions of national identity, as well as familial warmth.

As Martha Vicinus noted years ago in *The Industrial Muse*, however, the nineteenth-century dialect poetry of northern industrial England faced inherent limitations: "Dialect had originally been written out of a strong sense of place and class, but a writer who attempted to appeal to a mass audience diluted whatever made his writing unacceptable to his potential audience. . . . Only by writing platitudes acceptable to everybody could such a problem be avoided" (229). The extensive home audience for Scots language writing, by contrast, diminished the need for such accommodation and "dilution," for English laws, customs, and language usages were still felt as inimical colonial impositions more than a century after the Act of Union. The language in which Scottish poets naturally sang and spoke may have been a provincial argot to London bookbuyers, but the Scots prized its lilting rhythms and melodies for their blunt satire and unaffected lyricism.[2]

During the nineteenth century, population shifts and the rise of Scottish industrial centers produced significant changes in the country's social and linguistic patterns. In the fifty years between 1851 and 1901, the proportion of males employed in agriculture dropped from 30 to 14 percent, and the population of the Highlands declined steadily as the population of Scotland continued to grow (Smout 58). More precisely, the population of Scotland grew 12 to 14 percent each decade between 1861 and 1911, but a declining birth rate and heavy emigration depleted the population of the Highland counties in every decade after 1841. About 20 percent of the population lived in the Far Northern and Highland Counties in 1801, 15.7 percent in 1841, and 8.3 in 1901 (Flinn 38). Much of this emigration from the Highlands was forced in "clearances" effected by violence and accompanied by great suffering. Lowland agrarian regions were also depopulated in the same period, but their emigration was for the most part voluntary, and unattended by comparable forms of cultural resistance and disintegration.

Historians agree that the Highland landscape was unable to support a large population, for the soil was thin and poor, grazing was feasible only in summer, and the area's valleys supported potato crops that were small at best. The Gaelic-speaking inhabitants of this region were intensely reluctant to leave their traditional land, however, for they believed passionately (in the words of one historian) that "occupation of a traditional area of land, and not acquisition of new wealth, was the greatest good that life had to offer" (Smout 64). Strongly motivated by the desire to preserve their language and the cohesion of their families, crofters and even more marginal cotters (or sub-tenants), divided and subdivided their small holdings among their children rather than emigrate from their wildly beautiful ancestral lands, drawing small supplementary incomes from kelp-gathering, fishing, and migrant farm labor.

A few quotations may illustrate the limited resources available to these subsistence Highland crofters. One of the region's most enlightened landlords was James Matheson, who bought the Isle of Lewis in 1844 and invested much of his income derived from other sources to support the local economy in ways that enabled his tenants to remain. Even under these ideal conditions, however, a visitor to the Outer Hebrides in the 1880s described a typical Lewis croft:

> The typical Lewis crofter's house was built by the crofter himself; it had double low thick walls of loose stone united by a packing of earth or clay . . . There was no chimney and often no window. . . only one door, used by the cattle and family alike. Inside, the house usually contained three compartments. In the middle was the living room with a blazing peat-fire filling the house with smoke. Rough stones covered with clay made a cold and damp floor. On the one side of this middle compartment was the sleeping room, on the other the byre. The byre had no paving, and the manure liquids percolated into the ground. (Day 296)

Lowland laws interpreted landlords' traditional rights to dues from hereditary tenants as full ownership rights with the privilege of alienation,[3] and most Highland landlords in the mid-and late-nineteenth century tried to consolidate small plots into larger ones, replaced crofts with sheep pasturage and then with tourist deer-parks, and encouraged former tenants to rely on marginal industries, such as kelp-gathering, which proved to be unprofitable in the long run (Mitchinson, ch. 21, Smout, ch. 3). Even in the 1820s, Sir Walter Scott wrote that

> . . . the Highlands have been drained, not of their super-fluity of population, but of the whole mass of the inhabitants, dispossessed by an unrelenting avarice, which will be one day found to have been as short-sighted as it is unjust and selfish. Meantime, the Highlands may become the fairy-ground for romance and poetry, or the subject of experiment for the professors of speculation, political and economical. But if the hour of need should come – and it may not, perhaps, be far distant – the pibroch may sound through the deserted region, but the summons will not be answered. (Blind 116)

During the Sutherland Clearances of 1811-20, the Ross-shire Clearance of 1855, and a later series of forced evictions in the Outer Hebrides, Skye, and Tiree that led to the Highland Land War of 1881-86, landlords' agents torched crofters' homes, and forced the inhabitants onto emigrant ships.[4] Archibald Geikie, a geologist, visited the Isle of Skye during the eviction of tenants from the Macdonald lands in the 1880s, and later described a scene like that of Richard Redgrave's painting, *The Emigrant's Last Sight of Home* (1858).

> As I was returning from my ramble, a strange wailing sound reached my ears at intervals on the breeze from the west. On gaining the top of one of the hills on the south side of the valley, I could see a long and motley procession winding along the road. . . It halted at the point of the road opposite Kilbride, and there the lamentation became loud and long. . . . It was a miscellaneous gathering of at least three generations of crofters. There were old men and women, too feeble to walk, who were placed in carts; the younger members of the community on foot were carrying their bundles of clothes and household effects, while the children, with looks of alarm, walked alongside. . . . When they set forth once more, a cry of grief went up to heaven, the long plaintive wail, like a funeral coronarch, was resumed, and after the last of the emigrants had disappeared behind the hill, the sound seemed to re-echo through the whole wide valley of Strath in one prolonged note of desolation. The people were on their way to be shipped to Canada. (Geikie, 226-27)

Resistance to these evictions especially inspired two of the poets we will consider, Mary MacPherson and Mathilde

Blind. Fierce expressions of outrage informed the powerful Gaelic poems of the Inverness and Glasgow poet Mary MacPherson (Màiri Nic A' Phearsain, "Big Mary of the Songs," 1821-98). Her Gaelic songs forcefully lament in sometimes formulaic descriptors the decline of an ancient rural culture, and place clear blame on landowners and their hired militia. In "Nuair Bha Mi Og" ("When I Was Young"), the speaker returns to the depopulated country-side of her youth, then bitterly joins other forced emi-grants at the ballad's end:

> . . . Ach dh'fhalbh an t-àm sin 's tha 'n gleann fo bhròn;
> Bha 'n tobht aig Anndra 's e làn de fheanntaig,
>   Toirt 'na mo chuimhne nuair bha mi òg. . .
> 'S nam faicinn sluagh agus tighean suas annt',
>   Gum fàsainn suaimhneach mar bha mi òg.
>
> Nuair chuir mi cùl ris an eilean chùbhraidh,
>   'S a ghabh mi iùbhrach na smùid gun seòl,
> Nuair shéid i 'n dùdach 's a shìn an ùspairt,
>   'S a thog i cùrsa of Thìr a Cheò;
> Mo chridhe brùite 's na deòir le m' shùilean,
>   A' falbh gu dùthaich gun sùrd, gun cheòl,
> Far nach faic mi cluaran no neòinean guanach,
>   No fraoch no luachair air bruaich no lòn.
>
> [. . . but that time's past and the glen's in gloom;
> Andrew's croft, overgrown with nettles,
>   reminding me of when I was young. . .
> had I seen houses and people there still
>   I'd be happy as I was when young.
>
> When I turned my back on the fragrant island,
>   and boarded the steam-ship which has no jib,
> when she blew her horn and began her churning,
>   and made her way from the Isle of Mist,
> my heart was broken, my eyes tear-filled,
>   leaving for a land without cheer or song,
> where I see no thistle nor joyful daisy,
>   no heather nor rushes on brae or lawn.] (88-91)

Even in the English rendering of Meg Bateman, the heavily stressed, chantlike alliterative and assonantal patterns of the poem resonate mournfully with a sense of the dignity of a lost way of life.

In her 1885 "Incitement of the Gaels," MacPherson urged election of the candidates of the Highland Land Law

Reform Association, who supported the crofters' right to retain their holdings. She reviews for her audience the bloody suppression and forced emigration of the inhabitants of the Isle of Skye, the scene of Geikie's reminiscence quoted above. In the instance she records, local landowners, their Sheriff "Ivory" and his troops crushed a rent-strike, called by crofters to protest the theft of their traditional grazing rights.

> Dh'ainmichinn iad air an cinn,
>   Bha seinn air ainneart luchd an fhearainn,
> A thionndaidh 'n còta air an druim,
>   'S a dh'ith na rainn dhe'n d'rinn iad ealain.
>
> Falbh le leabhraichen 's 'gan seinn
>   Dha na suinn a bh'aig a'bhaile –
> "Gheibh sibh mil air bàrr an fheòir
>   Am Manitòba, is na fanaibh."
>
> Phàidh na h-uachdarain dhaibh duais
>   Mas do ghluais iad o'n a' bhaile,
> Ach 's e'n gad air an robh 'n t-iasg
>   A fhuair na siòchairean, 's iad falamh.
>
> [I could name them one by one,
>   who sang against the owners of the land
> and turned their coats upon their backs
>   and ate the words which had been their art.
>
> Who went with books, declaiming loudly
>   to the young men working the homelands,
> "Why stay here when you can reap honey
>   from the top of the grass in Manitoba?"
>
> The landowners offered to pay a reward
>   to the young men if they'd leave the township,
> but it was only the withe where the fish had hung
>   the wretches got when they were starving.]

The Crofters' Holdings Act of 1886 finally legalized the crofters' right to fixed rents determined by an independent commission, conferred tenure to those who paid these rents, and granted tenants the right to will their land to their heirs. Sadly, however, the population continued to decline throughout the next century. First World War casualties, mechanized farming, contraction of the merchant fleets that provided supplementary fishing income, and a complex series of other economic changes made more gradual and "voluntary" the dislocation (most) Highland landlords had forcibly begun.

Another voice of lament and protest was that of the Grampian poet Bell Robertson, as recorded in her ballads in the *Greig-Duncan Book of Ballads*, vol. II, *Lays of Buchan and Other Poems*. Robertson's language seems normalized towards Standard Central Scots, but her lilting rhythms grieve the impoverishment of land-reconversion, and attack the landowner who has seized common grazing land.

> I hae seen the lambs bleating their careful dams weeping,
> To guard them frae Lowrie that made them his prey,
> Now Lowrie is starvin', it's what he's deservin'
> Since the beauty of Buchan is banished away. . . .
>
> Woe to our gentry, they've ruined a' our country,
> And brought our fine pasture so deep in decay
> Mong hedges and ditches they've spent a' our riches,
> And banished our beauty entirely away.
>
> Lament all ye shepherds for want o' your clipherds,
> Wi' sighing and sobbing and sorrow for aye;
> Let my song be respected since sheep is rejected,
> And they from their pastures are banished away.

Although the focus of her work was different, one of the most striking of the Scottish women poets was Janet Thompson Hamilton (1795-1873), a Lanarkshire spinner and weaver, and mother of ten, who learned to write at fifty-four, and composed two volumes of poetry and several prose sketches of rural life.[5] A resident of the village of Langloan near Coatbridge (outside of Glasgow), she died before the most violent and publicized of the late-century Highland clearances, but witnessed many shades of the transition from agrarian to urban life. Her political poems and satires, in her native "Doric" and a separate Glaswegian-influenced dialect, memorialized the tales told by her country grandmother, attacked city life and misuse of science and wealth, and noted the hazards of coal-mining and the oppression of women seamstresses. "Oor Location," for example, canvasses a grittily detailed cityscape of toiling workers and tavern-frequenters:

A hunner funnels bleezin', reekin',
Coal an' ironstane, charrin', smeekin';
Navvies, miners, keepers, fillers,
Puddlers, rollers, iron millers;
Reestit, reekit, raggit laddies,
Firemen, enginement, an' Paddies;
Boatmen, banksmen, rough and rattlin',
'Bout the wecht wi' colliers battlin',   [weight]
Sweatin', searin', fechtin', drinkin',
Changehouse bells an' gill-stoups clinkin',   [drinking cups]
Police-ready men and willin' –
Aye at han' when stoups are fillin',
Clerks, an' counter-loupers plenty,
Wi' trim moustache and whiskers dainty,
Chaps that winna staun at trifles,
Min' ye they can han'le rifles. . . .
Frae whence cums misery, want, an' wo,
The ruin, crime, disgrace an' shame,
That quenches a' the lichts o' hame,
Ye needna speer, the feck ot's drawn   [ask;bulk]
Out o' the change-house and the pawn.

The industrial Glasgow whose overcrowding Hamilton decried in the 1860s had been a place of rapid change since the early 1800s, when its sudden growth of population herded its new inhabitants into squalid tenements. Augmented by newcomers from the countryside, between 1830 and 1870 the population surged from 200,000 to 500,000, with an increase of 70,000 between 1840 and 1850 alone, and the suburbs grew faster than the inner city (Cage 9). Ninety-four percent of the population was working class, according to the census of 1841, and these people labored to make Glasgow a leading center for all the engineering and mechanized trades (1-7). In 1842, Edwin Chadwick's *Sanitary Condition of the Labouring Population of Great Britain* called the city "possibly the filthiest and unhealthiest of all the British towns of this period . . . in the courts of Argyle Street there were no privies or drains, and the dung heaps received all the filth which the swarms of wretched inhabitants could give." Some sections of Glasgow had a population density of 500 to 1000 per acre by 1860, but not before the 1866 City Improvement Act was any attempt made to control the excesses of tenement housing or to provide new dwellings. The mortality rate surged from epidemics of cholera and typhus, and by 1850 one half of all children born in Glasgow died before their fifth birthday. Although epidemics became less prevalent after the 1850s, only in the 1870s did the death-rate begin to decline (Cope 43-47; 75).

Against this background, it is hardly surprising that thoughtful observers such as Hamilton commented with satiric bitterness at the industrial "progress" that had disrupted an entire way of life.

> It's Mannon we worship, wi' raspin' and' greed,
> Wi' sailin' an' railin' at telegraph speed,
> Get gowd oot the ironstane, an' siller frae coal,
> An' thoosan's on thoosan's draw oot o' ae hole.
> Wi' oil shale aneath us, an' fire-warks abune,
> I think we'll tak' lowe, an' bleeze up to the mune.
> "Rhymes for the Times: IV. 1865"

In other poems, she denounces the ravaging of once-peaceful areas such as Gartsherrie and "sweet Simmer-lee".

> Oot-ower the aud brig, up to sweet Simmerlee,
> Sweet, said ye? – hech, whaur? – for nae sweetness I
>   see;
> Big lums spewin' reek an' red lowe on the air,
> Steam snorin' an' squeelin', and shiles muckle mair!
>
> Explodin' an' smashin' an' crashin', an' then
> The wailin' o' women an' goranin' o' men,
> A' scowther't an' mangle't, ase painfu' to see –
> The sweetness is gane, noo it's black Simmerlee.
> "A Wheen Aul' Memories": III. "Simmerlee"
>
> Noo, mark ye, the ashes, the dross, an' the slag –
> Wad ye think it was they put the win' i' the bag
> O' the big millionaires; that 'mang danners an' cinners,
> The Co. should ha'e gather't sic millions o' shiners?
> "A Wheen Aul' Memories": IV. "Gartsherrie"

The growth of the Glaswegian alcoholic subculture was an obvious reaction to the unbearable stress of these changes, and one response in turn was one of the British Isle's more vigorous temperance movements, with a large radical wing that promoted many forms of worker self-help and non-alcoholic entertainments. Keir Hardie was among many labor leaders who began their political lives in a Good Templar Lodge (Cage 163). Quite a bit of poetry was composed for temperance recitation and singing, and many of Janet Hamilton's poems, such as "The Drunkard's Wife," "The Contrast," "Neebor Johnnie's Complaint," and "The Plague of Our Isle," are spirited or moving examples of this genre. In "The Three Golden Balls," for example, she attacks the owner of the local pawnshop as a profiteer in human weakness:

> Vampire-like, the blood he drains
> From the drunkard's burning veins.
> The whisky-shop absorbs his cash,
> The pawn-shop swallows down the trash
> Of household gear and wretched clothing.
> Ah! my soul is sick to loathing
> Of the sights, and sounds, and crimes
> Of these murder-tainted times,
> When a bath of blood has charms,
> And power to set a world in arms;
> And the bather may be bolder
> If a forty-ticket holder.   [eligible voter]

Hamilton does not sentimentalize rural life, either. One of her "Doric" poems, for example – "Grannie's Crack aboot the Famine in Auld Scotlan' 1739-40" – brings the same passion for telling detail to the ravages of an eighteenth-century famine in the countryside.

More remarkable, perhaps, are Hamilton's self-reflective observations on her own language usage, in two poems, "A Plea for the Doric," and "Auld Mither Scotland." In the first, she laments the passing of her "mither" speech:

> Nae, mither! nae; we maunna pairt!
>   E'en tho' they say thou's deein';
> That speech is gaun, they say thy face
>   We'll sune nae mair be seein'.
> But oh! I fear the Doric's gaun,
>   For, mang baith auld an' young,
> There's mony noo that canna read
>   Their printit mither tongue.

At one point, she even makes a rare direct reference to English economic imperialism and linguistic dominance:

> I like the English tongue fu' well
>   In writin' an' in readin';
> But 'tween the English an' the Scotch

> There's lack o' truth an' breedin'.
> It's England's meteor flag that burns
> > Abune oor battle plains;
> Oor victories, baith by sea an' lan',
> > It's England aye that gains.

Her sense that linguistic assimilation is one of the deepest forms of personal loss and cultural betrayal – a sense shared by many members of subordinated cultures – resonates in her "Plea for the Doric":[6]

> Forgi'e, oh, forgi'e me, auld Scotlan', my mither!
> Like an ill-deedie bairn, I've ta'en up wi' anither;
> And aft thy dear Doric aside I hae flung,
> To busk oot my sang wi' the prood Southron tongue. . . .

> Juist think gif the "Cottar's ain Saturday Nicht"
> War stripped o' the Doric, wi' English bedicht –
> To the leal Scottish heart it wad ne'er be the same;
> Wi' sic truth and sic feelin' it wadna strike hame. . . .

> I'm wae for Auld Reekie; her big men o' print
> To Lunnon ha'e gane, to be nearer the mint;
> But the coinage o' brain looks no a'e haet better,
> Though Doric is banish'd frae sang, tale, and letter.

> But there's a'e thing I'm sure o – ere lang I maun gang,
> Yet aye whan I dow I maun lilt a bit sang;
> And sae soun' shall I sleep 'neath the auld mossy stane,
> That I'll never hear tell whan the Doric is gane.

The "big men o' print" to whom she refers probably included Norman MacLeod of *Good Words*, which had a circulation of 110,000 before it moved from Edinburgh to London in 1862. The first editors of the *Spectator* and the *Saturday Review* were also Scots (James Rintoul and J. Dutton Cook, respectively), and after Hamilton's time the *Scots Observer* moved southward to become the *National Observer* in 1890.[7]

The Glasgow region's many women and children handweavers earned less-than-subsistence wages, and in "The Lay of the Tambour Frame," Hamilton described the common plight of embroiderers and other needleworkers in rhythms which replicate the heavy monotony of their labor. In stark contrast to the delicately weaving "Lady of Shalott," the tambour worker (embroiderer) is:

> There, with colourless cheek;
>   There, with her tangling hair;
> Still bending low o'er the rickety frame,
>   Seek, ye will find her there.
> Tambour, ever tambour,
>   With fingers cramped and chill; –
> The panes are shattered, and cold the wind
>   Blows over the eastern hill.

Notice Hamilton's use here of standard English, perhaps in an effort to appeal to a wider audience. In the tradition of Thomas Hood's "The Song of the Shirt" (1843), she exhorts men to support their working sisters:

> Selfish, unfeeling men!
>   Have ye not had your will?
> High pay, short hours; yet your cry, like the leech,
>   Is, Give us, give us still.
> She who tambours – tambours
>   For fifteen hours a day
> Would have shoes on her feet, and dress for church,
>   Had she a third of your pay. . . .
>
> Raise ye a fund to aid
>   In times of deep distress;
> While man helps man, to their sisters in need
>   Brothers can do no less.
> Still the tambourer bends
>   Wearily o'er the frame.
> Patterns oft vary, for fashions will change –
>   She is ever the same.

Hamilton's poems and reminiscences effectively memorialized the transition from weaving to coal-mining and factory work, from village to city outskirts and urban slum, and cautioned her fellow workers to care for the well-being of their neighbors and families. MacPherson and Robertson reworked traditional materials to celebrate cultural and human loss, but Hamilton struggled in her complex exhortations to accommodate the vanishing Scottish language and way of life of the urban industrial environment which engulfed her.

One of the century's more remarkable narrative poems about rural Scotland is "The Heather on Fire," Mathilde Blind's saga of the members of a Skye family who are evicted from their home, forced onto an emigrant ship, and die when the ship wrecks on a nearby coast. Published the year of the passage of the Crofters' Act of 1886, it was written by the German-born and English-educated poet and biographer Mathilde Blind, daughter of a political exile and lifelong supporter of progressive causes, who had spent several summers in Scotland. Before she published "The Heather on Fire" at the age of 45, Blind had written biographies of George Eliot and Madame Roland, translated Strauss's *The Old Faith and the New*, and published *The Prophecy of St. Oran and Other Poems*.[8]

"The Heather on Fire" is the most ambitious historical poem I have found by a Victorian woman on a Scots subject, and it presents the forced evictions of the Highlands – the likely backgrounds of the members of the Skye family, their histories of attachment for each other, and the nature of their daily work – in carefully elaborated social and physical detail. Blind writes in high English diction whose similes and formal versification are sometimes stilted, but events and set-pieces borrowed from Greek or Senecan tragedy are rendered more poignant and believable by Blind's detailed treatment and careful historical setting.

In her preface, Blind recorded her 1884 visit to the site of a ruined village:

> All that remained of the once flourishing community was a solitary old Scotchwoman, who well remembered her banished countrymen. Her simple story had a thrilling pathos, told as it was on the melancholy slopes of North Glen Sannox, looking across to the wild broken mountain ridges called "The Old Wife's Steps." Here, she said, and as far as one could see, had dwelt the Glen Sannox people, the largest population then collected in any one spot of the island, and evicted by the Duke of Hamilton in the year 1832. The lives of these crofters became an idyll in her mouth. She dwelt proudly on their patient labour, their simple joys, and the kind, helpful ways of them; and her brown eyes filled with tears as she recalled the day of their expulsion, when the people gathered from all parts of the island to see the last of the Glen Sannox folk ere they went on board the brig that was bound for New Brunswick, in Canada. "Ah, it was a sore day that," she sighed, "when the old people cast themselves down on the sea-shore and wept." . . . the once happy people were all gone – gone, too, their dwelling-places, and, to use the touching words of a Highland minister, "There was not a smoke there now." (3-4)

Blind's endnotes describe the firing of crofts and the pain and deaths of those evicted, events which she conflated in the climax of her plot.

> Timber, furniture, and every other article that could not be instantly removed was consumed by fire, or otherwise utterly destroyed. . . Some old men took to the woods and the rocks, wandering about in a state approaching to or of absolute insanity; and several of them in this situation lived only a few days. Pregnant women were taken in premature labour, and several children did not long survive their sufferings. . . . In such a scene of devastation it is almost useless to particularise the cases of individuals: the suffering was great and universal. I shall, however, notice a very few of the extreme cases, of which I was myself an eye-witness. John Mackay's wife, Ravigall, in attempting to pull down her house, in the absence of her husband, to preserve the timber, fell through the roof. She was in consequence taken in premature labour, and in that state was exposed to the open air and to the view of all the bystanders. . . . I was present at the pulling down and burning of the house of William Chisholme, Badinloskin, in which was lying his wife's mother, an old bedridden woman of nearly one hundred years of age, none of the family being present. . . . Fire was set to the house, and the blankets in which she was carried out were in flames before she could be got out. She was placed in a little shed, and it was with great difficulty they were prevented from firing it also. Within five days she was a corpse.[9]

Blind's tale is arranged into four cantos, or "duan," which trace three generations in the life of a doomed Highland family. The old grandfather Rory, crippled during the Napoleonic Wars, has since been unable to farm, and his wife has done field-labor as well as raised their children. Their son Michael marries the poem's heroine, Mary, orphaned daughter of Rory's comrade Donald, and they have four children by the time the evictions begin, in "Duan Third".[10] "Duan First" describes the crofters' long-standing love for their island home, the laborious life of Michael's parents, the young lovers' response to nature, and their happy but serious courtship. In lines reminiscent of Keats' "Isabella, or the Pot of Basil," Blind also marks the exploitive dominion of "the lord of all that land":

> XLVI
> To him belonged the glens with all their grain;
> To him the pastures spreading in the plain; . . .
> To him the forests desolately drear,
> With all their antlered herds of fleet-foot deer;

To him the league-long rolling moorland bare,
With all the feathered fowl that wing the autumn air.

XLVII
For him the hind's interminable toil:
For him he ploughed and sowed and broke the soil,
For him the golden harvests would he reap,
For him would tend the flocks of woolly sheep, . . .
For him the back was bent, and hard the hand,
For was he not his lord, and lord of all that land?[11]

"Duan Second" briefly describes the couple's wedding celebration, during which Michael's father Rory recalls the virtues of his lost comrade Donald, Mary's father. In "Duan Third," Michael and Mary are happily married, but their years together have been filled with hardship, anxiety, and toil. They and the other crofters continue to love the land, however:

. . .   – as mothers oft are fain
To love those best who cost them sorest pain;
So do these men, matched with wild wind and weather,
Cling to their tumbling burns, bleak moors, and mountain heather. (Stanza III)

In stanzas VII-XVII, Mary, who is heavily pregnant, sings and tends to a sick child in Michael's absence. Michael's mother knits socks, and the couple's eldest daughter Ranza carefully milks her dearly-loved cow. This idyll is disturbed when neighbors report that the landlord's men have begun a series of evictions, and Mary anxiously watches flames rise from several adjacent farms.

XXIV
And through the rolling smoke a troop of men
Tramped swiftly nearer from the upper glen;
Fierce, sullen, black with soot, some carrying picks,
Axes, and crowbars, others armed with sticks,
Or shouldering piles of faggots – to the fore
A little limping man, who cursed and swore
Between each word, came on post-haste; his hand,
Stretched like a vulture's claw, seemed grabbing at the
land. . . .

When the evictors arrive at their own cot, Mary shields her younger daughter Maisie, as

XLII

. . . the men fell to their work and broke
The rough-cast walls with many a hammer stroke;
Pulled down strong beams, set the mossed thatch on
    fire,
While Ranza, quivering, flew towards the byre
To save their cow and calf; and the young son
Of seven seized what he could lay hands upon,
And dragged it in the roadway, for the lad
Knew well 'twas all the wealth his hard-worked father
    had.

Old Rory helps his now-aged and palsied wife escape
and finds blankets to cover her, but she subsides into
shock and dies soon afterward. When Michael's fishing
boat returns, he encounters a scene of mass turmoil, with
burning crofts and terrified kinspeople everywhere:

XLVIII

And through the dire confusion and the smoke
From burning byres, the cattle roaring broke,
And made with terror, rushed down from the fells;
Whole flocks tore bleating onwards, with the yells
Of furious dogs behind them; whins and trees
Caught fire, and boughs fell crackling on the leas,
And smouldering rafters crashed, and roofs fell in,
And showers of wind-blown sparks high up in air did
    spin.

XLIX

Distracted, stunned, amazed, the hurrying folk
Sway to and fro; some harness to the yoke
The loudly whinnying horses, and on van
Or cart, in desperate haste, toss what they can
Of their scant household goods: clothes, bedding,
    chairs,
Spades, hoes, and herring-nets, and such like wares;
And high atop of all, well nigh despairing,
Wives, mothers, children – howling, weeping, swearing.

When Michael reaches his now-homeless family at the
beginning of "Duan Fourth," he bears Mary to a nearby
ruin and attends to her as she groans in the agony of
childbirth, delivers a stillborn daughter, bids Michael
goodbye, and dies. He manages at least to bury his dead
before the "great Lord's hireling men" drag the surviving
family members to the emigration ship Koh-i-noor. The
crippled Rory somehow manages to escape to land before

the ship makes its way through a storm out into the open sea, but freezes in horror as he sees the ship suddenly break apart in the distance.   Rory imagines Michael holding the children to him as they drown, and a tragic chorus ends the poem.

> XLVII
> . . . Safe in the deep,
> With their own seas to rock their hearts to sleep,
> The crofters lay: but faithful Rory gave
> His body to the land that had begrudged a grave.

In the course of her narrative, Blind employs several dramatic vignettes and set-pieces which resemble genre paintings of Highland life – a girl standing in the fields (Jules Breton, *The Song of the Lark*, 1884), a Highland wedding (David Wilkie, *The Penny Wedding* 1818), women awaiting absent fishermen (Frank Bramley, *Hopeless Dawn*, 1888). Some of her descriptions, however – of Mary defying the invaders, and Michael clutching the children to his body in the sinking ship – are more individuated, and the smoke rising from the burning of crofter homes in the glens, and forced embarkation and shipwreck are grounded in reality. A final Turneresque description of the departing Koh-i-Noor obliquely recalls Ruskin's commentary on *The Slave Ship* in the first volume of *Modern Painters* (1: part 2, sect. 5, ch. 3):

> XXXIX
> Therewith it seemed as if their Scottish land
> Bled for its children, yea, as though some hand –
> Stretching from where on the horizon's verge
> The rayless sun hung on the reddening surge –
> Incarnadined the sweep of perilous coast
> And the embattled storm-clouds' swarthy host,
> With such wild hues of mingling blood and fire
> As though the heavens themselves flashed in celestial
>   ire. (Stanza xx)

"The Heather on Fire" achieved only one printing, perhaps because much of its London audience found it melodramatic, or cared little about dispossessed crofters, but Blind's epic poem remains a noteworthy example of politically committed Victorian narrative verse.[12] Blind's determination to treat the fate of Highland cotters with the full palette of classical Roman tragedy also anticipates some aspects of a somewhat later Scottish vernacular revival, a self-conscious fin de siècle and early-modernist effort to fashion psychologically charged symbolic landscapes and haunting refrains from legendary folk-motifs.

In the Scottish dialect poetry of Violet Jacob, sophisticated distance and empathy merge in the poetic representations of idealized rural consciousness. Jacob (1863-1946, born Violet Kennedy-Erskine) was born in Montrose, north of Dundee and south of Aberdeen, as the daughter of the eighteenth Laird of Dun. She lived in India for several years before she returned to Scotland, where she wrote *Verses* (1905), *Songs of Angus* (1915), *More Songs of Angus* (1918), and the works collected in *The Scottish Poems of Violet Jacob* (1944). I will conclude this essay with some brief comments on "Craigo Woods," one of a line of rustic/pastoral monologues exemplified by Tennyson's Lincolnshire poems ("Northern Farmer Old Style") or the work of Charlotte Mew ("The Farmer's Bride").

The anonymous speaker in "Craigo Woods" is an old man, who has lived all his life near the Woods. He believes these Woods are inhabited by a wraith (the sort of spirit whose misdeeds formed the subject of Janet Hamilton's poem "Spunkie"), and their outer bounds provide a somewhat nebulous symbolic image of the rural heaven to which he aspires. Nothing in the speaker's remarks suggests unusual social awareness, but his childlike, mystical response to the material world confers symbolic significance on the commonplace objects and places around him. The poem's slow and mournfully syncopated rhythms convey the speaker's love for the plants, weather, and indwelling spirits of his locale:

> Crago Woods, i' the licht o' September sleepin'
>   And the saft mist o' the morn,
> When the hairst climbs to yer feet, an' the sound o'
>   reapin' [harvest]
>   Comes up frae the stookit corn,   [bundled in sheaves]
> And the braw reid puddock-stules are like jewels
>   blinkin' [red toadstools]
>   And the bramble happs ye baith,
> O what do I see, i the lang nicht, lyin' an' thinkin'
>   As I see yer wraith – yer wraith?

The old farmer's identification with the Woods culminates in a touching faith that the puddock-stules (toadstools) he loves will travel with him to the Wood beyond death.

> There's a road to a far-aff land, an' the land is yonder
> Whaur a' men's hopes are set;
> We dinna ken foo lang we maun hae to wander,
> But we'll a' win to it yett;
> An' gin there's woods o' fir an' the licht atween them,
> I winna speir its hname, [ask]
> But I'll lay me doon by the puddock-stules when I've
> seen them,
> An' I'll cry 'I'm hame – I'm hame.'

The old man of Craigo Woods is a poetic projection of an old man by a middle-aged woman, of course, and Jacob's syntax and diction, unlike that of Hamilton's "Oor Location" and "Auld Mither Scotland," often seems artful and archaising rather than colloquial. There is something evocatively displaced as well as mournfully precious about the psychological ambiance of this forest, however, an idealized Wood beyond the World of bitter disputes about enclosures and deer forests.

More than stereotypes about the conceptual concerns of Victorian women might suggest, then, the writers I have surveyed took clear political and economic positions in their verse. As a loose confederation of regional social orders became urbanized and industrialized, Robertson, MacPherson, Hamilton and others deplored the human misery caused by economic change, and sought to retain cohesive values of family and culture. A few reformist outsiders such as Blind wrote poetry about the Highlands, but their expressions of solidarity with the victims found little resonance in England. Modernist Scottish poets such as Violet Jacob self-consciously sought to preserve regional character and language as ethnographic artifacts, and pay tribute to the historical qualities of regional poetic languages threatened with dissolution in a twentieth-century sub/urban argot, and the partial successes of such "revivalists" depended heavily on prior traditions preserved in great part by nineteenth-century Scotswomen poets.

Janet Hamilton, we will remember, feared to rise from her grave, lest she should fail to hear the accents of her native "Doric," and see that much of the vigorous village-and-town-life she recorded is now gone. Perhaps Blind's passionate efforts at tragic empathy or the highly crafted work of Violet Jacob and her fellow vernacular revivalists might have provided some consolation to her. If not, the vigorous wraith of Hamilton might still be sighted, as she walks the cityscapes and countryside of "Auld Mither Scotland," and hovers for a few moments to blend with the lights and shadows of Craigo Woods.

Notes

1. About 130 of the more than 6000 works listed in a recent bibliography of nineteenth-century British and American women's poetry compiled by Gwen Davis and Beverly Joyce were printed in Scotland, or bear titles which suggest Scottish themes. A canvass of Catherine Kerrigan's *Anthology of Scottish Women Poets* and other collections would raise this total to nearly two hundred volumes. Such lists have fuzzy edges, of course: some of these authors were not Scottish, and some Scottish women poets published outside Scotland. But the ratio of English to Scottish women writers as represented in standard bibliographies would seem to stand at about 40 to 1. The collections of the Mitchell Library in Glasgow contain more than a hundred more volumes of poetry by Victorian Scotswomen.
2. Linguists commonly recognize language subdivisions of Scotland that have existed since the Middle Ages. (Scottish) Gaelic is one of two separate languages spoken in the Highlands (the region of Mary MacPherson), though most Gaelic speakers also speak "Highland English." The "Insular Scots" English of the Orkneys and Shetlands is heavily influenced by Norse usage, and "Northern Scots" is the language of the Grampians and the rest of eastern Scotland north of the Dee (the region of Bell Robertson). "Southern Scots" or "Border Scots" is the language of many ballads, and "Ulster Scots" is the language of the Scots-Irish immigrants who have returned to Scotland.

    Most Scots, however, speak one of the varieties of "Central Scots," subdivided into "East Central" (the language of Edinburgh), "West Central" (the language of Glasgow, region of Janet Hamilton), and "South Central" (Dumfries and Galloway) Scots (Kay, "The Dialects of Scots," ch. 10). Central Scots serves as a partially assimilated standard language, sometimes called Anglo-Scots, whose usages are for the most part common to all regions. Most nineteenth-century readers probably considered Central Scots a kind of "national" language, one that Janet Hamilton and some others called "the Doric."
3. In "Storm-Clouds [of Anarchy] in the Highlands," *Nineteenth Century*, 16 (September 1884): 379-95, J. A. Cameron pointedly describes the evolution in the law as "a great wrong, amounting to a national crime":

"Until 1745, the year of Culloden, the clan system of land tenure prevailed in the Highlands, under which the ground belonged not to the chief alone, but to the community. A clansman could not be dispossessed of his holding by his chief. After 1745, however, the English system was introduced. The clans that had remained loyal to the Crown, as well as those that had thrown in their lot with Prince Charles, had their lands practically confiscated. The Highland chiefs, in short, were assimilated in position to English landlords. They were by the central government invested with the fee-simple of the land which was once held by the laird and the clansmen in common, and so a great wrong, amounting to a national crime, was done to the Highland population."

4. Hugh Miller argued forcefully that such forced evictions occurred on a wide scale, much more than many observers wanted to admit: "Men talk of the Sutherland clearings as if they stood alone amidst the atrocities of the system; but those who know fully the facts of the case can speak with as much truth of Ross-shire clearings, the Inverness-shire clearings, the Perthshire clearings, and, to some extent, the Argyleshire clearings. . . Crossing to the south of the great glen, we may begin with Glencoe. How much of its romantic interest does the glen owe to its desolation? . . . While the law is banishing its tens for terms of seven or fourteen years, as the penalty of deep-dyed crimes, irresponsible and infatuated power is banishing its thousands for life for no crime whatever," *The Witness*, cited by Mathilde Blind, *The Heather on Fire* 117. Hugh Miller was a journalist whose writings on social issues appeared in his *Essays*, 7th ed. (London: Nimmo, 1875).

5. This edition of Hamilton's poems reprints the contents of two previous volumes, *Poems and Ballads* with Introductory Papers by the Rev. George Gilfillan and the Rev. Alexander Wallace, D. D., 1863; and *Poems of Purpose and Sketches in Prose of Scottish Peasant Life and Character in Auld Langsyne, Sketches of Local Scenes and Characters* (with a Glossary), 1865.

6. For example, see passages from Gordon Williams, *Scenes Like These*, William McIlvanney, *Docherty*, Lewis Grassic Gibbon, *Sunset Song*, cited in Kay, 126-29; 170-71.

7. *The Scots Observer: A Record and Review* was published in Edinburgh from 1888 to November 1890, and reappeared in London as T*he National Observer* from 1890-1897.

8. *George Eliot*, 1883; *Madame Roland*, 1886; David Strauss, *The Old Faith and the New*, 1873 and 1874; *The Prophecy of St. Oran and Other Poems*, 1881. The title work of the latter narrates the ill-fated love of one of St. Columba's monks, Oran, for the daughter of a Pictish Chieftain Mona, and the ensuing murder of this pair by the puritanically zealous monks.

9. "Gloomy Memories," by Donald MacLeod, cited in Blind, 109-110. Another account is given of inhabitants' attempts to escape their evictors, as Rory escapes the Koh-i-noor. In response to a Royal Commissioner, a crofter gave evidence that, "I saw a man who lay down on his face and knees on a little island to hide himself from the policeman, who had dogs searching for him in order to get him aboard the emigrant ship. . . . There was another case of a man named Angus Johnson. He had a dead child in the house, and his wife gave birth to three children, all of whom died.

Not withstanding this he was seized and tied on the pier at Lock Boisdale, and kicked on board. The old priest interfered and said, 'What are you doing to this man? liet him alone, it is against the law!' The wife of the man who was tied and put aboard afterwards went to the vessel. The four dead children would be buried by that time. . . . The people were hiding themselves in caves and dens for fear of being sent away from the island. . . . There were many such cases at the time. It was about forty years ago" (cited in Blind 113-14).

10. Blind's descriptions of Mary in stanzas 35-37, for example, read like an attempt to render into poetry the emblematic scene of Jules Breton's painting *The Song of the Lark*, in which a peasant girl pauses enraptured to listen to the bird's song.

11. See also "Isabella," stanza xv, "For them the Ceylon diver held his breath. . . ."

12. Blind's later volumes of poetry on more general subjects – *The Ascent of Man* (1888); *Dramas in Miniature* (1891), *Songs and Sonnets* (1893), and *Birds of Passage* (1895) – were more favorably received.

Works Cited

Blind, Mathilde. *The Heather on Fire*. London: Walter Scott, n.d.

Cage, R. A. *The Working Class in Glasgow: 1750-1914*. London: Croom Helm, 1987.

Day, J. P. *Public Administration in the Highlands and Islands of Scotland*. London, 1918.

Davis, Gwen and Beverly Joyce. *Poetry by Women to 1900*. London and New York: Mansell, 1990.

Geikie, Archibald. *Scottish Reminiscences*. Glasgow: Maclehose, 1904.

Glasgow. *Insight City Guides, APA Publications*. New York: Prentice Hall, 1991.

Flinn, Michael. *Scottish Population History from the 17th Century to the 1930s*. Cambridge University Press, 1977.

Hamilton, Janet. *Poems: Sketches and Essays*. New edition. Glasgow: Maclehose and Sons, 1885.

Kay, Billie. *Scots: The Mither Tongue*. Edinburgh: Mainstream, 1986.

Kerrigan, Catherine. *An Anthology of Scotish Women Poets*. Edinburgh University Press, 1991.

Mitchinson, Rosalind. *A History of Scotland*. London: Methuen, 1870.

Robertson, Bell. *Lays of Buchan and Other Ballads*. Peterhead: Printed at the Buchan Observer Works, 1906.

Ruskin, John. *The Works of John Ruskin*, ed. E. T. Cook and A. Wedderburn. 39 vols. London: George Allen, 1903-12. (*Modern Painters* I, part 2, section 5, chapter 3).

Smout, T. C. *A Century of the Scottish People 1830-1950*. London: Collins, 1986.

Vicinus, Martha. *The Industrial Muse*. New York: Barnes and Noble, 1974.

8

Re-forming London: George Cruikshank and the Victorian Age

Anne L. Helmreich

Over his lifetime, the English artist George Cruikshank (1792-1878) witnessed the rapid industrialization and growth of his native London. The city and its environs more than tripled in population between 1800 and 1871: from 1,265,000 to 3,931,000 (Evans 405). Cruikshank observed London's developments closely and responded with both wit and vitriol in his depictions of the city's varied neighborhoods and inhabitants. Through his art, Cruikshank alerted viewers to many of the issues which were to define the Victorian age, particularly, the emergence and gradual acceptance of the middle class and its values of morality, ideal femininity, and domesticity.

The city became a major focus in Cruikshank's art in the 1820s and 1830s when the artist put aside his caricatures of politicians and the aristocracy, especially the royal family, in favor of social commentaries which slyly poked fun at the foibles of London's classes, whose distinct characteristics became more pronounced as the decades advanced. By the close of his career, Cruikshank was regarded as an apostle of moral reform, best known for his didactic temperance narratives rather than his anti-monarchical jibes of the late-Georgian period.

Cruikshank's metamorphosis was intimately linked to changes in the city of London as its citizenry sought to manage the profound social change accompanying the city's rapid industrialization. The artist's increasing preoccupation with the mores and habits of his fellow Londoners was matched by changes in his personal life, art, and politics. In the 1820s the artist adopted the trappings of a moderate, middle-class existence, marrying and taking up residence at 25 Myddleton Terrace in the suburban district of Pentonville. He tempered his dissolute behavior, staying relatively close to home and foregoing his late-night rambles through London's night-spots (Patten, *Life* 216-17).

Around the same time, many of the political-broadsheet publishers with whom Cruikshank had worked faced financial difficulties due to the changing political atmosphere. Spurred by a pledge "not to caricature His Majesty in any immoral situation," the indebted artist turned his attention to book illustration and comic albums suitable for middle-class consumption while retaining a modicum of lower-class appeal.[1] With this shift in venue and audience, Cruikshank earned the approbation of conservative art critics; indeed, the Tory journal *Fraser's* (1833) insisted that Cruikshank had

> quitted ere long the shabby crew who wished to make him
> their property, and has settled down, if not into the genuine
> faith of a Tory, at least into that approach to orthodoxy
> which consists in the detestation of a Whig. ("Gallery of
> Literary Characters" 190)

While *Fraser's* interpreted Cruikshank's cessation of caricature as evidence of his Tory sympathies, other critics suggested that Cruikshank's shift away from caricature stemmed from his admiration for "political liberality" and the more enlightened ministers who came to power in the 1820s and 1830s (Clark 146). Perhaps the best explanation for Cruikshank's seemingly Janus-faced politics is that supplied by Marc Baer, who rightly argues that Cruikshank, "like most of his contemporaries," "was terrorized by the possibilities of democracy," and his fear of the mob linked "his anti-Jacobin work in the first decade of the nineteenth century with his Whiggishness of the 1830s" (296).

In choosing to portray the social classes of London, Cruikshank was not renouncing politics per se as many biographers have maintained, but instead changing tactics in his ever-evolving project to reform London society.[2] As Cruikshank's target shifted from the government and the aristocracy to the lower classes, his art became increasingly didactic and moralistic. Cruikshank's rejection of scurrilous caricatures of ruling elites in favor of subjects of family, ethics, and self-reform paralleled and, indeed helped to shape, larger changes taking place in British culture during the first half of the nineteenth century when middle-class commentators turned from criticizing the upper classes to reforming their own class and those below them.

The perception that London was in need of social reform arose largely from the changes wrought by industrialization which had caused a radical reordering of urban spaces and social relations. With a population of over two million people by 1861 (as compared with over 250,000 in Manchester, Liverpool, and Birmingham), nineteenth-century London was "the largest center of industry, the largest port, the largest provider of services, [and] the largest concentration of consumers" (Himmelfarb 308).

Under this facade of productivity, however, lurked a den of sin, at least according to the Tory writer Robert Southey, who articulated the growing fear that crime, violence, and immorality were rending the fabric of the city:

> London is the heart of your commercial system but it is also the hot-bed of corruption. It is at once the centre of wealth and the sink of misery; the seat of intellect and empire, . . . and yet a wilderness wherein they, who live like wild beasts upon their fellow creatures, find prey and cover. . . . Ignorance and misery and vice are allowed to grow, and blossom and seed, not on the waste alone, but in the very garden and pleasure ground of society and civilisation. (1:108)

Faced with such disturbing descriptions of the city, Londoners found increasing need to order the potential chaos of the public sphere to meet the new demands of industrial capitalism and to ensure the desired respect for individualism and property. The reorganization of the public sphere occurred through both overtly political processes, such as the institution of the Metropolitan Police in 1829, the expansion of the criminal code, and the imposition of the New Poor Law in 1834, and less obviously political maneuvers, namely, redefining the role of the domestic sphere.

With the desire for stability and order in the public sphere, the private sphere came under increasing scrutiny as the family was reconceptualized as the most effective site for instruction in self-regulation and control. The new ideology of domesticity – "a code of rules and regulations for the governing of individual lives" – was broadly disseminated (Weeks 27). Since unacceptable public behavior was believed to stem from immoral conditions in the home, nineteenth-century reformers turned their attention to the living conditions of the poor in seeking to stem the supposed tide of crime and violence engulfing Victorian London. Cruikshank's images of London, in their focus on the degeneracy of London's upper and lower classes, were directly involved in the numerous inquiries into the living conditions of London's urban populace conducted throughout the nineteenth century.

The social investigations conducted by artists and reformers were vital for both stimulating social attitudes and political legislation, such as the Public Health Act of 1848, and enabling the middle classes to create and to justify their role as moral leaders of English society. Thus, much nineteenth-century literature and art, including George Cruikshank's depictions of London, helped to shape and express the middle-class's vision of the ideal society, based on entrepreneurship and domesticity and cleansed of aristocratic corruption and working-class resistance.

Cruikshank's gradual acceptance of middle-class values was intimately bound up in his portrayal of London and the social contrasts that the growing city provided. As London expanded, the formerly heterogeneous city became increasingly segregated into homogeneous neighborhoods: according to the historian Donald Olsen, "strict social segregation became a prerequisite for success in any new development" (18). The wealthy and middle classes took up residence along the outskirts of London, leaving the interior to businesses and the poor. The West End, close to the business firms of central London and far from the noxious fumes of the docks and manufacturing districts of East London, became the fashionable district. The improved public spaces of the West End – parks, shopping boulevards, and tea gardens – became backdrops for the display of fashion and wealth by London elites. In his early prints of London, Cruikshank turned his critical eye to these practices, continuing his earlier strategy of ridiculing the flaws, vices, and excesses of the well-to-do and powerful.

In such works as his *Monstrosities Series*, Cruikshank satirized the upper class's fascination with dress and status, implicitly condemning its vapid lifestyle. His print *Monstrosities of 1821*, for example, shows the fashionable social gatherings that took place in Hyde Park. Fashion, in this print, does not indicate England's healthy economy as some writers argued; instead, clothing helps to reveal the inadequacies of England's wealthy elite. The luxuriant fur coat and tightened stays worn by a man on the left signifies that he is a dandy who spends his days in idle consumption rather than industrious production. The ridiculously oversized hat and tight boots of a soldier, whose profile mirrors that of a toy poodle in the foreground, suggests that he is a frivolous figure incapable of guarding or guiding anything. This numeration of the excesses of the aristocracy and those who wished to emulate them fed directly into the middle class's desire to differentiate itself from the upper classes and to promote its ideology of the moral responsibility of wealth (Perkin 277).

Cruikshank's satirical renderings of the elite neighborhoods of west London also reflected his dissatisfaction with the rhetoric of growth and improvement which characterized early nineteenth-century London. With the increased availability of stagecoaches after 1810 and the development of the omnibus in 1829 and the railways in the 1830s, middle-class suburbs sprang up outside the city. An 1811 French-American visitor to London was struck by the city's incessant growth:

> London extends its great polypus-arms over the country around. The population is not increased by any means in proportion to these appearances,– only transferred from the centre to the extremities . . . People live in the outskirts of the town in better air, – larger houses, – and at a smaller rent, – and stages passing every half hour facilitate communications. (Simond 2: 199)

Although numerous Georgian architects, city officials and reformers promoted London's growth and rebuilding, a number of skeptical critics, Cruikshank among them, lamented the vast, grandiose building schemes, especially given England's weakened economy following the Napoleonic wars. Cruikshank's representations of London from the 1820s and '30s differ greatly from contemporary topographical depictions, such as those by Thomas Shepherd published in James Elmes's laudatory book *Metropolitan Improvements* (1829). Shepherd focused on the monumental architecture erected in recent decades, such as the architect John Nash's reconstruction of Regent Street. His images depict polished classical facades flanking broad streets populated by orderly citizens going about their daily business. Shepherd's prints supported Elmes's claims that London was being rapidly improved from "dirty alleys, dingy courts and squalid dens of misery and crime" into "stately streets" and "squares that court the breeze" (Elmes 2).

Cruikshank completely rejected this convention. His images of London repeatedly expressed doubts about the rhetoric of improvement touted by writers, artists, and architects. Cruikshank's print *London Going Out of Town*, (1829), for example, decried the onslaught of suburbanization (Plate 6). Cruikshank animated the various building elements–brick kilns, pickaxes, mortars, and shovels–so they appear as an autonomous army invading the countryside. The result is unending rows of jerry-built terrace houses that belch smoke and decay immediately after they are built, a marked contrast to the open squares and clean Palladian architecture of Sheperd's London.

In his print *Salus Populi Suprema Rex* from 1831-2, Cruikshank turned his attention to the uneven application of sanitary improvements. Following the 1828 Report of the Commission on the London Water Supply, the five companies supplying water to the districts north of the Thames sought remedies to ensure the distribution of clear water. However, John Edwards, the owner of the Southwark waterworks which supplied water to the area south of the Thames, refused to discontinue drawing water from a sewage dispersal point on the Thames. Cruikshank's image graphically illustrated the need for reform. The Thames, typically shown in topographical views as a placid, blue foreground, is portrayed as muddy and choked with sewage pouring forth unchecked from drains lining the river banks. Edwards, crowned by a chamber pot and seated on a closet stool, allows the sewage to mix with the river water while he imperiously ignores borough residents' cries for clean water.

Even Cruikshank's images of the Great Exhibition of 1851, regarded as a symbol of England's industrial and technological prowess, subverted current descriptions of London as a magnificent spectacle (Gibbs-Smith 7). In the print *London in 1851* Cruikshank showed Regent's Circus swollen and engorged with the vast throngs flocking to London to see the exhibition. The spectacle is not the Exhibition, but the crowds who overwhelm Nash's architecture and prevent his streets from performing their circulatory functions. The serene nobility of Regent's Circus suggested in earlier topographical views is undercut by Cruikshank's rowdy mobs who appropriate Nash's classical facades for their own uses. Improving London, Cruikshank would come to argue, could not be achieved by rebuilding the city, but necessitated addressing the moral condition of London's vast lower-class populace.

Cruikshank's artistic exploration of lower-class London had begun in the 1820s, when the metropolis emerged as a subject of fascination for artists and writers tapping into Londoners' and outsiders' curiosity about the vast city (Fox 188, Patten, *Life* 222, Potts 29). One of the most popular accounts of the city's contrasting neighborhoods was Pierce Egan's *Life in London* (1820-21), illustrated by George and Robert Cruikshank.

Life in London describes the adventures of three well-to-do, young "swells" – Jerry Hawthorn, Corinthian Tom, and Bob Logic, the Oxonian – who explore London's high and low life in a series of adventuresome "sprees." The ribald tone of the text and images invited readers to enjoy vicariously the youths' flouting of convention as they ventured into spaces unfamiliar to middle-class readers. The three characters around which Egan and the Cruikshanks wove their tongue-in-cheek narrative were highly suitable vehicles for examining London's different neighborhoods: wealthy and unencumbered by familial supervision, the three youths engaged in both respectable pursuits, such as attending art exhibitions, and disruptive behavior, such as tipping over a watchman's box, represented in the vignette titled *Getting the Best of Charley*. In this print, Corinthian Tom is shown knocking over a watchman's box above which hangs a sign warning that "whoever sticks bills or commits any other nuisance will be prosecuted." The ensuing hilarity ridicules the city's attempts to control the behavior of its citizens.

While this image encouraged readers to laugh at the pathetic and seemingly useless watchmen, Cruikshank had hit upon an issue troubling many Londoners: the fear that local patrols were unable to stem the increasing tide of crime and disorder. By 1829, London officials overcame their reluctance to infringe upon the traditional liberties of English citizens and created the Metropolitan Police Force (Emsley 22-25). In *Getting the Best of Charley*, Cruikshank, in the time-honored tradition of the comic, used the representation of a transgression to offer up a social criticism and to reinforce a socially agreed-upon law (Eco 6; 8).

Other images from *Life in London*, particularly those depicting lower-class haunts, more directly reflected middle- and upper-class Londoners' disdain for the poor, who were believed to be the source of much of London's violence and crime (Wiener 16; 24-25; 67-69). When the young men visit a lower-class coffee shop near the Olympic, their classical profiles, smooth skin, and condescending gestures immediately set them apart from the crowd of beggars and prostitutes, whose coarse facial features, unruly behavior and preoccupation with food, drink, and sex supposedly reveal them as inferior, impure types (Cowling 124-130). The lower-class women, in particular, with their thickened features, grotesque expressions, and heavy-set bodies that refuse to remain clothed, are in marked contrast to their betters. The obscured and shattered portraits of Innocence and Virtue hanging over the fireplace reinforce Egan's claim that the coffee shop revealed the "drunkenness, beggary, lewdness, and carelessness" characteristic of London "'LOWLIFE'" (181).

The rambunctious atmosphere of this Strand coffee shop, while presented as a plausibly humorous subject for cloistered middle-class readers, corresponded to Londoners' anxieties regarding the supposed links between immorality and revolution. Accounts blaming the French Revolution on the degeneracy of the lower classes – such as *The Public Ledger*'s 1816 description "that the French Revolution, with all its constant horrors, was preceded by a total revolution of decency and morality" – led middle-class reformers to argue that the most effective way to thwart the mob and ensuing threats to political and economic stability was to promote domesticity and its values of morality and respectability (Weeks 27).

Cruikshank's illustrations to *Life in London*, although executed in a spirit of humor, provided excellent evidence for the supposed disparity between the middle-class ideal and the lower-class predilection for unbridled sexual expression and violence. In the ensuing decades, fears concerning the lower-classes' lack of stability and reliability mounted. Artists, writers, and other sorts of social investigators turned their attention to the streets of England's major cities, particularly London, to study the impoverished lower classes.

A key feature of the urban investigations conducted around the mid-century was their focus on typing urban dwellers, a practice at which Cruikshank was particularly adept. In fact, much of Cruikshank's imagery, in making differences in class readily visible through differentiated physiognomy and behavior, anticipated the work of such social reformers as Henry Mayhew, who argued that each class "has its peculiar and distinctive physical as well as moral characteristics" (1).[3] As Thomas Prasch explains in his essay on mid-Victorian photography in this volume, the conceptualization of the poor as "a race apart" shaped much mid-century art production, particularly images accompanying journalistic accounts of urban life.

In *London Characters* (1827-9), a reworking of the tradition of representing street cries, Cruikshank made even more explicit his earlier connections between physiognomy, race, and behavior. He employed prevalent stereotypes linking class and intellectual inferiority to physical traits in his individual portraits of different occupations. For example, the large hooked nose of the Old Clothes Man supposedly rendered him recognizable as a Jew, and the blank stare, sloping forehead, and out-thrust jaw of the heavy-set Parish Beadle signaled his limited intellect according to the phrenological discourses of the time (Cowling 59).[4]

Viewers easily grasped Cruikshank's visual language of class and behavior. According to the art critic William Clark, Cruikshank's images carried so much information that on "the brow" of his

> population a condensed memoir is graven; they are ticketed and labelled; we see at a glance what line of conduct they adopted – in which society they have moved- whether or not they are in their usual station – "how they are off" in the world. (143)

"Ticketing and labelling" the poor was an important first step in reformers' attempts to solve the problem of poverty. Constructing the poor as a separate race created a sense of distance between the lower classes and their middle-class observers. The middle classes, endowed with a notion of superiority and difference, thus felt justified in imposing their values on the lower classes, who lived in a state of unenlightenment. In particular, middle-class reformers, such as Edwin Chadwick, John Hoggs, Henry Mayhew, and James Kay-Shuttleworth, pointed to the immorality of the poor as the cause of their squalid living conditions. Moral reform was thus promoted as the answer to poverty (Himmelfarb 323-332; 356-370).

Social investigations, while broadening the influence of the middle classes, were also implicit in disempowering and depoliticizing the working classes, whose collective activities had achieved public validation through the tragedy of the Peterloo Massacre in 1819. As Nancy Armstrong has shown in her history of the novel, texts by social investigators and images of urban life worked together to transform working-class activities such as gathering in pubs from "signs of an opposing political organization" into "those of a degenerate culture" (170). Repeatedly the working classes were shown to lack a "stable and sustaining domestic life" (162). By pointing out the flaws in working-class culture, these images and texts produced norms of sexuality and family which the working classes eventually adopted in order to participate fully in the "new moral world based on the ideal of labour" (Perkin 290).

The process of reinscribing working-class culture can be detected in such works as George Cruikshank's and Charles Dickens's collaborative texts *Sketches by Boz* (1836-7) and *Oliver Twist* (1837-8). In *Sketches by Boz*, the writer and artist provided limited glimpses of life in London. The book was sharply different, however, from *Life in London*. Instead of the tongue-in-cheek, quasi-scandalous tone of Pierce Egan, Dickens employed gentle humor tinged with moralism and didacticism. The vignettes describing different London neighborhoods carefully highlighted acceptable and unacceptable behavior. For example, Monmouth Street, in the poor, used-clothing district, was favorably compared with the adjacent area of Seven Dials because of its greater degree of domesticity. Dickens informed readers that although the Monmouth street inhabitants were "dirty" and their "habitations . . . distinguished by disregard of outward appearance and neglect of personal comfort," on whole they were "a peaceable and retiring race" (50; 54). Cruikshank conveyed the dirty yet domesticated existence of Monmouth street by portraying the proprietors of the used-clothing shops complacently smoking pipes while their wives care for their infants and their older children play in the gutter. The region of Seven Dials, on the other hand, is absent of any sign of domesticity. Dickens instructed his readers that although on any given summer evening relations may appear "harmonious," in actuality:

> A more primitive set of people than the native Diallers could not be imagined. Alas! the man in the shop illtreats his family; the carpet-beater extends his professional pursuits to his wife . . . [and] the Irishman comes home drunk every other night and attacks everybody. (50)

In Cruikshank's print, the savage qualities of the Diallers are embodied by the women, depicted as grotesque shrews who fight on the streets while the neglected, tattered children look on in amazement and the men laugh (Plate 7). These boisterous working-class women, more masculine than the men, have failed to be fully socialized according to prevailing conventions of femininity and cannot provide proper homes for their families. They are neither symbols of working-class resistance nor colorful accouterments to a picturesque scene; they are uncaring mothers and thus, the apparent source of working-class degeneracy.

Oliver Twist still more fully described the effects of immorality on lower-class London. The narrative focuses on poor orphans who are easily led into a life of crime without the moral guidance of a proper home. In his rendering of Oliver's abduction, Cruikshank captured the wretched conditions of inner-city London which Dickens described at the outset of the novel:

> Covered ways and yards, which here and there diverged from the main street, disclosed little knots of houses, where drunken men and women were positively wallowing in filth; and from several of the door-ways, great ill-looking fellows were cautiously emerging, bound, to all appearance, on no very well-disposed or harmless errands. (49)

Oliver's abduction takes place in a narrow, building-lined street, against the backdrop of a beer-shop (Plate 8). The small group of onlookers gathered around Nancy and Oliver are characterized by down-turned mouths and sunken chins, signifying their ignorance. The prominence of the beer shop, only briefly mentioned in the text, explicitly linked lower-class poverty and crime to drink, an argument echoed by many social commentators (Himmelfarb 385; Wiener 79).

In this print, Cruikshank linked together two of the key elements identified by reformers as the chief causes of disorderliness in lower-class urban districts: chaotic crowds of people, which allowed criminals to remain anonymous, and the easy availability of alcohol, which enhanced the ill-effects of the crowd. In the early nineteenth century, public drinking establishments, particularly ginshops and beershops such as the one depicted by Cruikshank, were increasingly associated with the supposed degeneracy of the lower classes. This was in part because middle- and upper-class consumers had relocated their drinking practices to the private sphere as "a mark of respectability," leaving public establishments to the lower classes (Harrison 45). Middle-class fears of drunken urban mobs, such as those popularly imagined to have ravaged Paris, as well as spurious statistics relating crime to alcohol consumption rendered these public drinking places into targets of reform (Harrison 69).

London – the seat of government and the largest gathering of British citizenry – was a key site in the campaign against public drunkenness. This campaign was waged largely against gin, thought to be more conducive to violence than beer, which the powerful free-trade lobby and London brewing industry promoted as a temperance beverage over the protests of evangelicals and magistrates.

In the late 1820s and '30s, Cruikshank was increasingly associated with the campaign against spirits. His images, set in London establishments and streets, naturalized the supposed link between drunkenness and the spaces of the urban lower classes.

As early as 1829, in a print published in his series *Scraps and Sketches*, Cruikshank attacked the gin shops, or palaces, which swept London after the reduction of the spirit duty in 1825. These shops employed the new commodification techniques developed in other retail enterprises, luring customers in with elaborate facades and glittering interiors (Girouard 21). Cruikshank, always eager to reveal the deception underlying the display of wealth, depicted the gin shop as a death-trap presided over by a skeleton barmaid masquerading behind a mask and fashionable dress. Scattered throughout the room are other signs of death, such as cask labels stating "Deady's Cordial" and "Kill Devil." The impoverished patrons eagerly drink the spirits which have already taken a toll on them: the man is in rags, the mother's face is twisted into a grotesque grimace, and the child in her arms is skin and bones.

This work–Cruikshank's first anti-drink print–provides a glimpse into Cruikshank's own thoughts on the subject of alcohol. Produced for his own comic album, without guidance or interference from another author, Cruikshank was clearly condemnatory of both the gin shop owners, who profited by selling death, and the lower-class patrons who wilfully ignored the signs of death around them.

While reformers generally agreed that measures preventing the lower classes from drinking gin were necessary since excessive drinking of spirits was considered one of the major causes of lower-class violence and crime, they could not agree on the means by which alcohol consumption should be limited. John Wight's *Sunday in London* (1833), illustrated by Cruikshank, indicates the various positions taken on the subject.

The object of Wight's text was to critique a recent bill "to promote the better observance of the Lord's day" by, among other measures, banning the sale of alcohol on Sundays.[5] Wight was outraged at the disparities of the bill, which primarily affected the lower classes since they often shopped on Sundays after being paid on Saturday evenings. In order to reveal the disingenousness of the bill, Wight devoted his text to illustrating how all three classes of London spent their Sundays in immoral pursuits. In his accompanying illustrations, Cruikshank revealed the moral failings of each class. The poor, for example, are depicted as an inebriated, fighting, and ill-dressed mob, while the wealthy, although shown sitting in church, are represented as overweight, overdressed, and bored. The rich are no more moral than the poor. To combat these problems, Wight proposed that "the Higher Orders" "set a better example to those below them . . . [and] to inculcate and patronize rational and healthful recreations" instead of brutalizing sports, gambling, and cheap gin (85-86). *Sunday in London* allowed Wight and Cruikshank to expound on two favorite themes: the upper class's failure to execute its paternalistic duties and the bawdy, debauched character of lower-class life.

In the print *A-gin-court* of 1838, produced for *The Comic Almanack*, Cruikshank reiterated the link between lower-class degeneracy and the availability of gin. The scene takes place in a dark, enclosed court untouched by urban improvements and presided over by a gin shop (Plate 9). The easy accessibility of alcohol has resulted in complete chaos, instigated by masculinized women who take up their domestic implements to fight.[6]

Although Cruikshank and his audience presumably found humor in this upending of gender stereotypes, the image raises several key questions troubling many reformers: Was mob behavior due to gin, to the underlying moral degeneracy of the working classes, to poverty and its accompanying decrepit living conditions, or a combination of these three factors?[7]

Cruikshank's image implicitly suggested that the confining living conditions of the urban poor, in combination with the availability of spirits, were a breeding ground for disruptive behavior. Such a critique of the urban environment was foreclosed in the succeeding decade, however, when Cruikshank more firmly located the source of intemperance and immorality within the individual and the family.

By the 1840s, the tone and manner of Cruikshank's art dramatically changed and the humor of his earlier anti-drink subjects disappeared. This shift was in keeping with the growing legitimacy and popularity of the temperance movement. Originally a narrow evangelical movement, temperance gained recognition in the 1830s as politicians and other reformers took up the cause. In 1831, the London-based British and Foreign Temperance Society, best known for preaching moderation, was founded. In 1834 James S. Buckingham organized the Select Committee of the House of Commons on the Prevailing Vice of Drunkenness; also, in the early 1830s, a number of teetotal societies were founded in northern towns. Teetotalism (as opposed to moderation) slowly gained influence in London and in 1835 the New British and Foreign Society for the Suppression of Intemperance, "the first London-based national teetotal society," was established (Harrison 90-146).

Many of these societies targeted the working classes in the belief that England's future industrial progress hinged on their sobriety and adherence to the new work-place discipline associated with manufacturing enterprises. For the working classes, the close links between abstinence and "respectability" insisted upon by middle-class reformers provided clear incentives for moderation or abstinence.[8] While early temperance advocates focused on curbing the sale of alcohol, mid-century efforts, acting upon the accepted belief that drunkenness stemmed from the individual's lack of moral fiber, focused on converting drinkers to temperance, or better yet, teetotalism.

Although Cruikshank had apportioned some blame for drinking to the purveyors of cheap alcohol in his anti-drink work of the 1830s, his temperance works of the 1840s came down resolutely on the side of the individual. His two key temperance series, *The Bottle* (1847) and *The Drunkard's Children* (1848), were intended to spark a moral conversion leading to the renunciation of alcohol.

The Bottle is a sentimental narrative describing the decline of a working-class family due to drink. Cruikshank later claimed that he intentionally published the series as cheaply as possible (it sold for a shilling) so that it could be purchased by the working classes (Jerrold 132). The first plate of the series portrays a small, comfortably furnished home; a ceramic cottage on the mantelpiece signals domestic bliss. It is within this home, rather than the public streets, that the cycle of decline begins when the father tempts the mother with a drink. She is soon addicted and without her moral guidance her husband drinks uncontrollably. He is subsequently fired and the family then loses its home. They are forced to take up begging in order to pay for drink (Plate 10). In this image, drinking is no longer a humorous part of working-class culture as in Cruikshank's earlier prints. Instead, it is a threat to the family and to an ordered, industrious urban society. The drunken family, standing in front of a spirits shop, contrasts vividly with the well-do-do family on the left: they are careworn, ill-dressed, and the graveyard in the background portends their future. The differences in the two families coalesce around the women. The higher morals of the well-dressed family are represented by the charitable, caring mother whereas the degeneracy of the impoverished family is conveyed by the drunken mother's disregard for her family's well-being. The conclusion to the story is predictable. The father kills the mother in a drunken rage and dies in jail while his children take to the streets.

The Bottle was extremely successful, selling over 100,000 copies, and its clear-cut moral narrative enabled its easy transition into other media. Critics, while voicing a fear that the series evidenced a "contraction" in Cruikshank's artistic abilities, generally agreed that the extreme legibility of the images rendered them highly effective, especially in "deterring sober people from drinking" (Bates 56; J. H. F. 112). The art critics' enthusiasm over Cruikshank's achievement was undermined, however, by reports, such as the one recorded in Mayhew's *Life and Labour in London*, that the initial impetus for abstinence caused by the prints wore away within hours (25). More trenchant criticism of the print series was levied by Charles Dickens, who chastised Cruikshank for blaming drinking on moral weakness rather than environmental or cultural factors:

> The philosophy of the thing, as a great lesson, I think all wrong; because, to be striking and original too, the drinking should have begun in sorrow, or poverty, or ignorance – the three things in which, in its awful aspect, it does begin. The design would thus have been a double-handed sword – but too 'radical' for good old George, I suppose. (Jerrold 95-96)

Dickens's opinion was a minority one, however. Cruikshank's biographer Blanchard Jerrold, in keeping with the general belief that drinking stemmed from moral failure, argued that Cruikshank's "drama is only too true to life" and, moreover, that ascribing drinking to the "excuses" of sorrow, poverty, or ignorance would have "weakened the tremendous force of his moral" (97).

Cruikshank's narrative converted at least one drinker: George himself. Jerrold reported that after executing *The*

Bottle, Cruikshank took "the plates to Mr. William Cash, then chairman of the National Temperance Society, for his approval." Upon viewing the plates, Cash turned to the artist and "asked him how he himself could ever have anything to do with using 'The Bottle,' which, by his own showing, was the means of such dreadful evil" (98). After some reflection, Cruikshank signed the pledge and re-solved "to give his example as well as his art to the total abstainers" (99).

The next year Cruikshank produced a sequel to *The Bottle*, *The Drunkard's Children*, which follows the moral decline and eventual demise of the children of the earlier series. The son becomes a criminal and the daughter a prostitute, consequences which many Victorians regarded as the inevitable result of excess drinking (Wiener 24-25; 79). The final plate portrays the daughter taking her life by flinging herself off one of London's new high level bridges (Plate 11). The lesson is clear: a lack of moral guidance leads to drinking and eventually to death, and no improv-ing of London's architecture can prevent an individual's moral failure. Improvement must occur within the home and especially within the figure of the mother, who is the moral bulwark of her family.

The final plate of *The Drunkard's Children* became one of Cruikshank's most well-known images. As a result of his temperance prints, Cruikshank was much in demand for speeches on temperance. His public talks harped on many of the themes expressed in his art: abstinence was necessary to end crime, particularly murder, and mothers must serve as moral exemplars for their families (Jerrold 109; 119). Recognition of Cruikshank's work on behalf of the new moral order of the Victorian age came in 1873 when the Grampion Club nominated him for a knight-hood, observing that "For upwards of fifty years, Mr. Cruikshank has enjoyed the highest celebrity as an Artist, while his artistic powers have uniformly been put forth in support of sound morals and government" (Memorial from the Grampion Club to the Secretary of State for the Home Department, Gladstone Papers, #80, vol. xviii). The Crown, however, refused to endorse knighthood on the grounds that no artist since Sir Edwin Landseer had been so rewarded (Memo, Verso of Letter from Duke of Argyll to Clement Colvin, 16 December 1873, Gladstone Papers, #78, vol. xviii). Despite this setback, upon Cruikshank's death in 1878, numerous art critics praised him as a staunch supporter of middle-class values (Bates 87; Thompson 251).

Although Cruikshank's nomination for knighthood may not have been predicted in 1820, there was a logical progression to his career. His prints reveal that as he turned his attention from the faults of the ruling classes to the changes shaping his native London, he continued to preach on behalf of social order and reform, using humor and didacticism to reprimand the upper and lower classes. The increasing segregation of the city, the uneven application of metropolitan improvements, and the degeneracy of working and lower-class culture incited Cruikshank and led him to espouse middle-class values. Through first criticizing aristocratic waste and then portraying lower-class spaces and women as degenerate and immoral, Cruikshank helped promote the middle-class values of moderation, domesticity, and ideal femininity. It was through the depiction of London's varied neighborhoods and classes, a seemingly apolitical subject, that a very political goal was attained: the widespread acceptance of middle-class values and power.

Notes

Much of the research for this essay was conducted through the auspices of the UCLA Art Council Curatorial Fellowship. I would like to thank Cynthia Burlingham and David Rodes of the Grunwald Center for the Graphic Arts, UCLA, for their encouragement and support during my tenure, which resulted in the exhibition "Life in London, Prints and Book Illustrations from the Richard Vogler George Cruikshank Collection" (1992). I would also like to thank Chris Bell and J.E. Helmreich for their comments on various drafts of this essay.

1. For an elucidation of Cruikshank's financial difficulties, see Patten, *Life* 209-214. According to Mary Dorothy George this pledge "contributed to his [Cruikshank's] renunciation of political caricatures," but as Robert Patten has correctly pointed out Cruikshank continued to issue "the odd [political] plate up through 1871" (George xli, Patten, *Life* 176).
2. The recent process of re-evaluating Cruikshank's career began with the 1974 collection of essays edited by Robert Patten. This collection has recently been reissued in light of the continuing interest in Cruikshank's

art demonstrated by Patten's 1992 biography and various exhibitions organized to celebrate the bicentenary of Cruikshank's birth, such as John Wardropper's *Cruikshank 200* (Museum of the Order of St. John, 1992).

3. George Cruikshank and Henry Mayhew were friends and they collaborated on a number of publications, including *1851, or, the Adventures of Mr. and Mrs. Sandboys and Family, who came up to London to "Enjoy Themselves" and to see the Great Exhibition.*

4. Cruikshank was quite familiar with the practice of phrenology, publishing his own text on the subject entitled *Phrenological Illustrations, or, an Artist's Views of the Cranological System of Doctors Gall and Spurzham* (1826).

5. As Brian Harrison has explained, "Apart from closing during Sunday morning service, many drinking-places – especially in London – opened almost continuously throughout the week" (58-59).

6. An undated inscription, written in Cruikshank's hand and appended to an early version of this image, explicitly links violence and alcohol: "The social glass[,] more fighting – Brutality and Bloodshed has arisen from the social glass than any other cause." Box I-97, #10034-S. Department of Prints and Drawings, Victoria and Albert Museum, London, England.

7. The text accompanying the print, a mock letter written by an illiterate country yeoman to his sweetheart, supports a comic reading of the image: ". . . [we've] allso Bean pressant at a Dredfull drunken row in a coart in pety france wich master and me Geting into the Coart end we was quite jamd in & in Devvaring to cut our Lukky receevd sevral Unlukky blos but at last the noo polease Arivd & every Sole tuk to his Eels & as master laffubly sed insted off the Batl of a Gin court turnt out the Batle of Runnymede." "Joe Cose in London to Phoebe Buttercup in the Country," *The Comic Almanack for 1838* (London: Charles Tilt, 1838): 41.

8. See, for example, John O'Neill, *The Drunkard* (London: Tilt and Bogue, 1842), for an account of "a poor mechanic" who was "encouraged to pursue his taste for poetry in preference to debasing enjoyments – to cultivate the bay and not the vine." He thus "outlived many sad examples of intemperance and misery; to behold happier prospects for the poor; to see the noblest in the land exerting themselves for the salvation and improvement of their fellow-man in humble life" (v).

Works Cited

Armstrong, Nancy. *Desire and Domestic Fiction.* New York: Oxford University Press, 1987.

Baer, Marc. "Cruikshank." *Print Quarterly.* 10 (September 1993): 295-296.

Bates, William. *George Cruikshank.* London: Houlston, 1879.

[Clark, William]. "Life and Genius of George Cruikshank," *The Monthly Magazine* 15 (February 1833): 129-147.

Cowling, Mary. *The Artist as Anthropologist: the Representation of Type and Character in Victorian Art.* New York: Cambridge University Press, 1989.

Dickens, Charles. *Oliver Twist.* Ed. Kathleen Tillotson. Oxford: Clarendon, 1966.

Dickens, Charles. *Sketches by Boz*. Philadelphia: Lea and Blanchard, 1839.

Eco, Umberto. "The Frames of Comic 'Freedom'" in *Carnival!* New York: Mouton Publishers, 1984, 1-9.

Egan, Pierce. *Life in London*. London: Sherwood, Neely, and Jones, 1821.

Elmes, James. *Metropolitan Improvements or London in the Nineteenth Century*. New York: Benjamin Blom, 1968.

Emsley, Clive. *The English Police, A Political and Social History*. New York: St. Martin's Press, 1991.

Evans, Eric J. *The Forging of the Modern State, Early Industrial Britain, 1783-1879*. New York: Longman, 1983.

Fox, Celina, ed. *London – World City 1800-1840*. New Haven and London: Yale University Press, 1992.

"Gallery of Literary Characters, No. XXXIX, George Cruikshank, Esq.," *Fraser's Magazine* 8 (August 1833): 190.

George, Mary Dorothy. *Catalogue of Political and Personal Satires . . . Vol. X, 1820-1827*. London: British Museum, 1952.

Gibbs-Smith, C.H. *The Great Exhibition of 1851, A Commemorative Album*. London: HMSO, 1950.

Girouard, Mark. *Victorian Pubs*. New Haven: Yale University Press, 1984.

Gladstone Papers, Vol. xviii, British Museum Additional MS 44,103. Department of Manuscripts, British Museum, London, England.

H.F., Jas. "George Cruikshank," *Biographical Magazine* 3 (May 1852): 107-114.

Harrison, Brian. *Drink and the Victorians*. Pittsburgh: University of Pittsburgh Press, 1971.

Himmelfarb, Gertrude. *The Idea of Poverty: England in the Early Industrial Age*. New York: Knopf, 1984.

Jerrold, Blanchard. *The Life of George Cruikshank*. London: Chatto and Windus, 1882.

Mayhew, Henry. *London Labour and the London Poor*. Harmondsworth: Penguin, 1985.

Olsen, Donald. *The Growth of Victorian London*. New York: Holmes and Meier, 1976.

Patten, Robert. *George Cruikshank's Life, Times, and Art, Volume 1: 1792-1835*. New Brunswick, NJ: Rutgers University Press, 1992.

_____, ed. *George Cruikshank: A Revaluation*. Princeton: Princeton University Press, 1992.

Perkin, Harold. *Origins of Modern English Society*. New York: Ark Publications, 1969.

Potts, Alex. "Picturing the Modern Metropolis: Images of London in the Nineteenth Century." *History Workshop* 26 (Autumn 1989): 28-56.

[Simond, Louis]. *Journal of a Tour and Residence in Great Britain, during the years of 1810 and 1811*. Edinburgh: George Ramsay and Co., 1815.

Southey, Robert. *Sir Thomas More; or Colloquies on the Progress and Prospects of Society*. London: John Murray, 1829.

Thompson, Alice. "A Bundle of Rue: Being Memorials of Artists Recently Deceased, George Cruikshank," *The Magazine of Art* 3 (1880): 247-251.

Weeks, Jeffrey. *Sex, Politics, and Society*. New York: Longman, 1989.

Weiner, Martin. *Reconstructing the Criminal, Culture, Law, and Policy in England, 1830-1914*. Cambridge: Cambridge University Press, 1990.

[Wight, John]. *Sunday in London by George Cruikshank.* London: Effing-
     ham, 1833.

9

Photography and the Image of the London Poor

Thomas Prasch

*T*he poor in their midst were a race apart, Henry Mayhew assured his readers at the outset of his revelations about *London Labour and the Labouring Poor* (1861-62). Tribes of atavistic nomads, he explained, thrived at the center of civilization:

> There are – socially, morally, and perhaps even physically considered – but two distinct and broadly marked races, viz., the wanderers and the settlers – the vagabond and the citizen – the nomadic and the civilized tribes.[1]

Mayhew credited to this racial difference many of the "moral characteristics" of the English poor, including "repugnance to regular and continuous labour," improvidence, "inability to perceive consequences," drunkenness, "insensibility to pain," gambling, dancing, and much else. John Thomson, recapitulating this discovery of the poor a quarter century later, similarly opened his photographic collection *Street Life in London* (1876-77) with the image of "London Nomades" (Plate 12). Crediting Mayhew's work, Thomson reiterated the argument:

In his savage state . . . man is fain to wander. . . . On the
other hand, in the most civilized communities the wanderers become distributors of food and of industrial products
to those who spend their days in the ceaseless toil of city
life. Hence it is that in London there are a number of what
may be termed, owing to their wandering, unsettled habits,
nomadic tribes.[2]

Racial difference had for Thomson, as for Mayhew, behavioral consequences. Thomson attributed to his wanderers
many of the same traits Mayhew had earlier described,
including improvidence, inability to plan ahead, resistance to "settled labour," and contempt for law.

In both Mayhew and Thomson, the argument for
nomadism among the "tribes" of London was reinforced by
the selection of London labor their works explored. They
limited their view exclusively to marginal labor, what Mayhew termed London's "street-folk" and Thomson its "street
life." In both cases, the emphasis on the marginal was
employed not only to reinforce the argument for the racial
difference of the working poor, but to assert strict limits to
the possibilities of ameliorative reform. It also served to
elide the dramatic changes in the character of the working
class and working-class culture in the period. This was a
period of dramatically changing labor and labor relations,
resulting from the consolidation of industrialism, new
forms of labor specialization, and newly energized efforts
at unionization. It was the era E. J. Hobsbawm and others
have identified with the formation of a distinctive working-
class culture in England, defined by dress and recreation
as well as behavior and politics (see, for example,
Hobsbawm, "Formation" and "Making"). Yet such a picture
of industrial transformation has no place in Mayhew's or
Thomson's accounts.

The focus on marginal labor in Mayhew and Thomson
is thus also an emphasis on static forms of labor, largely
unchanged by the forces of industrial society. In Thomson's work, which often deliberately updates Mayhew's
account, the form of labor is changed only in details, not
in its structure. Thus, for example, "Street Advertising"
(*Street Life* 37), showing workers plastering the walls of
London, reflects the advances of the advertising industry,
but the form of the labor remains not much different than

that of Mayhew's "London Boardman" (*London Labour* 1: 301) walking the streets with sandwich-board advertisements (and still retained by Thomson; *Street Life* 101). The technology of photography had changed between Mayhew's illustration of "Interior of a Photographer's Travelling Caravan" (*London Labour* 3: facing 191) and Thompson's picture of "Photography on the Common" (*Street Life* 40), but not the trade itself. And in many other cases (sweeps, caners, flower women, shoeblacks, etc.) there is no evidence of change at all.

The centrality of Mayhew's work to the construction of Victorian conceptions of a "culture of poverty" has been widely recognized (Himmelfarb ch. 14, Thompson and Yeo, Thompson). Thomson's place in the forefront of the history of documentary photography has also been widely recognized, although his direct debt to Mayhew has been less noted.[3] The common visual territory of the two works, however – the dependence of both *London Labour* and *Street Life of London* on photographic evidence, employed as a guarantee of the accuracy of the accounts – has been little explored. Himmelfarb, for example, despite her critical attention to Mayhew's text in *The Idea of Poverty*, offers no critical evaluation whatever of the images that accompany it. Himmelfarb misses Thomson's work entirely, but then so does E. P. Thompson, who notes no one following Mayhew's trail until Charles Booth commenced his *Life and Labour* project forty years later (Thompson 43).

Nor have the dynamics of that deployment of photography as evidenced in Mayhew and Thomson been adequately examined. Victorian ideas about the truth value of photographs have received some attention in recent scholarship (see, for example, Sekula, "Invention," Tagg ch. 2), but not the specific use of photographs in these particular texts. For photographic images never stood alone, but were always seen in relation to previous visual representations and accompanied by explanatory texts that determined the range of their meaning. The images thus depended on existing visual conventions and were linked by their textual accompaniment to contemporary anthropological discourses on race and class.

Thus photographic images (or, in Mayhew's case, drawings derived from photographs) were employed to reinforce the truth claims of the journalistic accounts of Mayhew and Thomson, following period conventions of accepting photographs as simple transcripts of reality. What in fact got transcribed, however, was a pre-existing set of assumptions imbedded in the already established pictorial genres and compositional conventions upon which Victorian photographers drew. Understanding the meaning of such photographs as evidence, knowing what precisely they can be taken as evidence of, requires an examination of the rules of genre and composition the photographers followed and the relation of those rules to the assumptions underlying the texts, especially about the poor as a separate race.

Mayhew accompanied his text with both "sketches" (usually group scenes, fitting fairly clearly into the conventions of sketches of London life[4]) and "sketches based on daguerreotypes" (usually portraits of individual street sellers). For the latter he employed the services of Richard Beard, the daguerreotypist who opened London's first photography studio (Newhall 29). All the photographic images on which sketches were based were posed studio portraits. The three-step process by which Beard's daguerreotypes were translated into sketched images allowed, it should be noted, several steps for distorting intervention (Fox, "Social Reportage" 105). Thomson's work was first of all a photographic exploration, accompanied by texts.

Photography never operates outside existing visual conventions; the aesthetics of mid-Victorian photography were, in fact, decidedly non-innovatory in character, drawing on traditional aesthetic authorities as part of a strategy to justify photography's status as an art. H. P. Robinson's popular guidebook *Pictorial Effect in Photography* (1869), for example, relied heavily on Joshua Reynolds (Taylor). Thomson himself grounded his aesthetic on Ruskin's ideas about unity of subject (White 40). Rather than inventing new ways to see, then, photography replicated existing visual conventions, operating within the same range as established painting and graphic arts. In the case of the photographs of images of London's street life, a clear set of conventions already existed, in the "Cries of London" genre.

In the typical "Cries of London" sequence, isolated street types are shown selling their wares, with individual plates devoted to specific types of street vendors (for instance, fruit vendors or flower girls). The emphasis was on the vendors' marginality, underlined by their formal isolation: they exist in the street, they sell their wares, but we usually see neither transactions nor interactions with others in the street. The figures appear as types, not individuals, as representatives of their particular trade, with an emphasis on their wares, their accessories, and their cries. Their identity thus consists entirely of their labor. The genre can be traced as far back as Elizabethan times, but was revived in a proliferating range of reprints and piratings, especially in children's books, after 1760. Around the turn of the century, new versions were being produced, revised to fit the reshaping of London as a metropolis. Royal Academy painter Francis Wheatley produced a painted series of "Cries" in the 1790s that became a model for a range of imitations and parodies (Shesgreen, Roberts, Fox, *Londoners* ch. 7).

By the early nineteenth century, the genre had become a standard for most of the major graphic artists of the day, including George Cruikshank, John Thomas Smith, Thomas Rowlandson, and Thomas Busby.[5] The circulation of images from the genre figured in the creation of London urban spectatorship in the Georgian period; they were thus a part of a way of seeing the city specifically organized around spectacle (Nord, Baumgarten, this volume). The proliferation of examples continued through mid-century, when Beard posed his street-life types for Mayhew; Mayhew made his own direct contribution to the genre with his *London Characters* (1874). The genre became, in a sense, a natural source to draw on for the process of extending urban spectatorship into the territory of the London poor, the journey Mayhew promised and Thomson echoed. They continued to be echoed to the end of the century, when Paul Martin produced his images of street types, originally printing them as "cut outs" in which the street life around the figures was erased entirely (Flukinger, Schaaf, and Meacham 43).

The Beard images, in their final form as "sketches based on photographs," functionally reproduced the main characteristics of the "Cries of London" genre: the association of figure and wares, the emphasis on accessories, and the isolation of the figure. In an image like "London Costermonger" (Plate 13), for example, the "Cries" genre is reproduced down to the "Cry" itself of "Here Pertaters! Kearots and Turnups! fine Brockello-o-o!" (Mayhew 1: facing 13). Parallel images, minus the cries, continue to appear in Thomson, in pictures like "Black Jack" (84) and "The Water-Cart" (104). At the same time, the studio origins of the photographs used by Mayhew were disguised by the process of remaking Beard's daguerreotypes into engravings, in which the backgrounds were no longer obviously studio backdrops. As a result of the sketched-in backgrounds, the viewer imaginatively repositions the subject into the street. And sometimes the results could be even more decidedly deceptive, as in "The Rat-Catcher of the Sewers" (Plate 14), which suggests that the camera captured live action rather than a static studio pose with elaborately sketched backgrounds (Fox, "Social Reportage" 111).

Beard's images added to the "Cries of London" genre, however, a new claim for veracity derived from their being based on photographs. In this sense, the images from photographs drew new power from the contemporary discourse about photographs being a "transcript of nature," a discourse that led Henry Fox Talbot to title his pioneering 1844 book on photography *The Pencil of Nature*. The mechanical character of the photographic medium was almost universally taken in the Victorian period as the basis for a new sort of truth claim.[6] Thus Samuel Morse wrote that photographs "cannot be called copies of nature, but portions of nature herself" (quoted in Sekula, "Invention" 86). The *Photographic Art-Journal* insisted in its debut issue that "if twenty photographers in succession were to take a view of the same object . . . the resulting pictures would be identical in every feature" ("What Is Photography" 12). Ruskin, in a rather grumpier tone, noted in

Cestus of Aglaia (1865) that "photography can do against line engraving just what Madame Tussaud's wax-works can do against sculpture. That, and no more" (*Works* 19: 120). Even while denying the artistic claims of photography, Ruskin accepts the medium's representational claims.

Such language masked the intervention of the photographer in the process. The photographer had a role in the selection, composition, and manipulation of the image in the darkroom, all carried out with an agenda grounded on culture, not nature. In Beard's case, the claim to transcriptive truth masked not only the studio as site, but the dependence on the pre-existing graphic tradition of the "Cries of London." The transcriptive truth claim was further reinforced by the affiliation between images and text: by the appearance of Beard's posed images in Mayhew's journalistic exploration of the London underworld.

Beard's photographs thus grafted an existing set of aesthetic conventions for the visual portrayal of the urban poor onto a newer set of discursive claims about the naturalistic meaning of the photographic image. This served to bolster a similar fusion of discourses in Mayhew's accompanying text. The already conventional mode of urban spectatorship was combined with a new, ostensibly scientific discourse on race, in which, as in the opening argument of *London Labour*, class division was read as racial difference.

Mayhew anchored his discussion of "wandering tribes" on the contemporary ethnography of J. C. Pritchard (comparative cranial measurements of different races) and Andrew Smith (racial distinctions between South African tribes). Gertrude Himmelfarb suggests a slippage in Mayhew between a biological conception of race and a "typical, loose Victorian sense of the term" that lacks roots in biology" (324), but George Stocking, Jr., more correctly sees only the former evident in Mayhew (213-219; see also Cowling 59). Mayhew opens his argument with an extended quotation from Pritchard on the differing head-shapes among "the rudest tribes of men" and "the most civilized races" (1:1). He reasserts the argument by recurrent references to those "bred" to the street, repeated

allusions to miscegenation, and regular comparisons between English street people and "savage" groups.[7] For
Mayhew, clearly, race was rooted in biology and linked to
class difference.

The slippage between categories of race and class
underpinned many of Mayhew's arguments against the
efficacy of philanthropy and reform. If the London underclass was racially distinct, and that racial difference had
behavioral attributes, after all, there was not much point
in trying to change them. The emphasis on difference in
Mayhew was underscored by Beard through his isolating
compositional strategies. Most often, he photographs a
single subject posed with the tools and wares of his or her
trade, the sketched-in street backdrop empty. The selection of subjects for photographic portraits also further
underlined Mayhew's physiognomic characterizations of
the poor's difference, a characteristic also evident, as Ann
Helmreich demonstrates, in Cruikshank's caricatures of
London's lower orders (see in this volume 157–78).

Thus, images accompanying Mayhew's text regularly
underline physical deformity or racial otherness. For example, "The Lucifer Match Girl" (1: facing 429) appears
physically misshapen, her head in particular beetle-
browed, her eyes small and dull, her expression blank.
"The Street-Seller of Nutmeg-Graters" (1: facing 330) features distorted legs and arms, a blank expression, and a
sign reading "I Was Born A Cripple," and the "Crippled
Street Bird-Seller" (2: facing 55) is similarly distorted in
limb and dull in expression. "The Irish Street-Seller" (1:
facing 96) is racially marked by facial features as well as
her pipe. "Doctor Bokanky, The Street Herbalist" (1: facing
197) is turbanned and dark-skinned, the "Hindoo Tract
Seller" (1: facing 239) also turbanned, darker still, and
shifty-eyed as well. "The Jew Old-Clothes Man" (2: facing
73) is racially distinguishable by his hook nose as well as
his hair and beard. The repeated illustration of such
extremely evident racial and physical difference works by
association to suggest the difference of the street people
as a whole.

Such a strategic manipulation of images, again em-
ploying both the discourses of photography's "transcrip-

tive" character and anthropology's racial "science," figured even more clearly in Thomson's work. Given the advantages of further technological development, the photograph itself replaced sketches based on it in Thomson's work and the camera could move from the studio to the street, making the argument for his images' naturalism even more powerful (Newhall 249-257; White 21; 38; 41). His strategies of selection and composition, however, like the accompanying texts about the "nomadic tribes" in our midst, remained unchanged.

Thomson honed his photographic techniques in East Asia, using his camera to promote the opening of the East to Western influence and commerce. The opening of the East to Western commerce was an explicit justification Thomson made for his work (see, for example, *Illustrations*, "Introductions" and *Straits* v-vi; 8). In his writings on East Asia, Thomson showed a clear familiarity with the ongoing debates on racial categorization in anthropology in the 1870s. For example, he praised the Papuan ("Pepohoan," as he calls them) people for their racial purity, linking that purity to their physical beauty (*Straits* 315-338; *Illustrations*, "Natives of Formosa"). The evidence of miscegenation he found on Macao, in contrast, he equated with racial degeneration (*Straits* 277, *Illustrations*, "Macao"). His photographs of racial types in Asia correspond, with their concern for measurement, to the call by T. H. Huxley for standards of anthropological photography that allowed for easier comparison of racial types in 1869.[8] Thomson made his own contribution to the debate sparked by Alfred Russell Wallace on Pacific racial typology, commenting on Cambodian racial types and carefully distinguishing them from neighboring groups, and illustrating his essay with sketches based on photographs, for the Ethnological Society of London (G. [sic] Thomson). He thus was fully cognizant of contemporary anthropological racial theory.

While developing his sense of racial difference, Thomson was also creating a photographic method to support arguments about racial distinction. His aesthetics were founded on the principle of pictorial unity, derived from Ruskin (White 40), wedded to the notion of human "types." The notion of the social type as photographic subject thus united Thomson's aesthetic practice and the typological notions then current in anthropology as well as in social investigation (Edwards; Cowling 125-129; 332-333).

Social types, rendered in images that isolate them from their surroundings and reinforce their identity through an emphasis on tools or wares, become conflated with distinctive racial types. That distinction was furthered by the different treatment accorded the Chinese ruling class, accompanied by the textual claim for their racial difference from the masses (see, for example, Thomson, *Straits* 277). That his focus was on types, not individuals, justified his compositional intervention. A similar argument about "types" was offered by Dr. Barnardo in defense of his photographs of London street urchins; intervention – extending from careful posing to deliberately shredding the clothes and dirtying the faces of his subjects – was justified as a means of capturing the truth of types, not individuals (Lloyd; Rosen 29-30; Prasch 293-302).

Thomson's Asian photographs feature characteristic "types" portrayed in a mode familiar to us already. They are wedded to their tools or wares and isolated from the street life of which they were a part. He reinforced this isolation through a variety of compositional strategies. He especially favored pyramidal arrangements as a means of reinforcing pictorial unity; this had been one of the central tenets of Robinson's compositional handbook (*Pictorial Effect* 67-70) and was already evident in Beard's work (as in, for example, the arrangement of figures in "London Costermonger" Plate 13). Against the common practice of the period, Thomson often took the background out of focus instead of presenting clear focus throughout the depth of field, a focusing strategy that looked forward to P. H. Emerson's photographic "naturalism." Thomson extensively employed framing devices (background doorways, for instance) to outline his figures. His most "exotic" images were also his most isolated subjects, as is most evident in his images of prisoners punished in the caque (a form of stocks) and in a cage, both appearing absolutely isolated on empty plains.

Returning to London in 1875, Thomson turned the same compositional strategies – and similar assumptions about racial difference – toward the street life of the city. In his preface to *Street Life*, he defended photography as a transcriptive tool for the accurate portrayal of street types: "The unquestionable accuracy of this technique will enable us to present true types of the London Poor and shield us from the accusation of either underrating or exaggerating individual peculiarities" (*Street Life*, "Preface"). Note that Thomson saw no contradiction in his commitment to accuracy and his search for "true types."

The accompanying texts reinforce not only the truth claims of the photograph, but also the argument that the marginal laborers of London constituted racially distinct tribes.[9] Of the men employed carrying sandwich-board advertisements, for instance, the text notes: "Unlike many street trades, the business is not followed by a special tribe. Costermongers, for instance, are almost a race apart, and different both in their habits and their physique from the rest of the population" (70). The argument was further reinforced by recurrent comparisons between the working class of London and the races of Asia. Thus, for example, the London nomad "reminded me of the Nomades who wander over the Mongolian steppe" (2). Some of the comparisons – of flood control and garbage removal, for instance – contrasted the Chinese laborer's conditions favorably with those of his English counterparts (12; 95).

The emphasis on type in Thomson's photographs again led him to draw on the visual language of the "Cries of London" genre, featuring many of the same marginal trades (flower and fruit sellers, caners, market workers) while updating others, and marked by the same visual iconography. As in earlier versions of the form and as in Beard's images, the figures usually appear in isolation, identified by wares and accessories. As in his Asian photography, Thomson used a range of photographic techniques to underline the isolation. Compositionally, he continued to depend on pyramids to suggest unity of type; note, for example, the arrangement of figures in "London Nomades" (Plate 12) or "Covent Garden Labourers" (Plate 15). This unity was reinforced by diagonals and framing doorways in the background. Even more than in his Chinese photographs, Thomson employed a tight foreground focus and a blurring of background detail, seen perhaps most clearly in his picture of Thames River boatmen, "Workers on the 'Silent Highway.'" In at least two of the images, "Black Jack" and "Flying Dustmen," Jeff Rosen has noted that background material is removed entirely (29). And again, his most startling images were also his most isolated, as in "The Crawlers" (Plate 16), a picture of one of the "old women reduced by vice and poverty to that degree of wretchedness which destroys even the energy to beg" (80), her solitary figure shown against a dark empty doorway and beside a dirty blank wall. The overall effect was thus to update the "Cries of London" genre, remaking the conventions to fit the terms of a photography that has moved into the street.

As with Mayhew, it should be noted, the effect of this fusion of new technology, up-to-date racial thinking, and old aesthetics was to restrict the possibility of ameliorating the condition of the London poor.[10] The texts of *Street Life of London* do advocate a range of paternalistic reforms, but they also suggest the limits of reform. The poor were a part of a natural order, as with the flower women of Covent Garden: "By the side of the wealthy salesmen . . . there are innumerable hangers-on, parasites of the flower world, who seek to pick up the few crumbs that must inevitably fall" (7). The situation of the sandwichboard men was explicitly dismissed as hopeless: "Taken as a body, it would be difficult to help these men to a better condition" (71). For Thomson as for Mayhew, social types were fixed, as race was, and to a large degree unalterable.

If class is race and race is character, the condition of the poor becomes their nature. As photography created in images of "types" the terms through which these racial characteristics are fixed, it contributed to that "natural" condition. The "naturalism" of the photographic medium, established by the discourse about the photograph as "transcript of nature," reinforced this conclusion. The emphasis in accompanying texts on the racial distinctiveness of the London "nomads" further underlined the point.

Thus the positioning of the mid-Victorian London poor as a subject of the new "documentary" photography and the new social-scientific exploration was, to a large extent, nothing new at all. The iconography of the images presented preserved the existing visual traditions associated with the "Cries of London" genre, maintaining that genre's focus on marginal street trades and those images' isolation of their subjects from street interaction. What *was* new was the authority the photographic images gained through the claims of truth that came with the "transcriptive" art of photography and the racial "science" of anthropology. These new truth claims served to justify something else quite old: the conviction that poverty was natural, as "natural" and unremediable as race itself.

Notes

I have benefitted from comments on this work at several different stages, and I would like in particular to acknowledge the contributions of M. Jeanne Peterson, Patrick Brantlinger, William Cagle, K. Dian Kriz, and Marcia Cebulska.

1. Mayhew, *London Labour* 1: 3-4. The date given in the text is of the final book version. A pamphlet edition, in which drawings based on Richard Beard's daguerreotypes first appeared, was published from 1850 to 1852. The pamphlet edition, in turn, drew upon and expanded from the original articles published in the *Morning Chronicle* in 1849-50. The book version collected most of the pamphlet material, incorporated portions of the earlier newspaper articles, and added some additional, more recent, material. For a brief publishing history, see Himmelfarb 322-323 and 566 n. 35; a more detailed discussion of the work's evolution appears in Humphreys 16-28. For alternative readings of nomadism in Mayhew's *London Labour*, see Brantlinger and Ulin, an account that underlines the lapses in Mayhew's attempts to impose a system of scientific categories, and Gallagher, an analysis that treats Mayhew's ambivalence about the role of his nomads in the circulation of goods. Mayhew's emphasis on racial difference, however, is tangential in these accounts. And both are concerned with Mayhew's text, not the accompanying images.

2. Thomson and Smith, *Street Life in London*, preface; see also 61. *Street Life* originally appeared in periodical form in 1875-76, with photographs by Thomson and texts by Thomson and temperance reformer Smith. For background on Thomson and *Street Life* see White; Rosen.

3. On Thomson's innovations in photography, see White 28; 41, Rothstein 7, Thomas 146. An exception to the neglect of Mayhew's influence on Thomson is Rosen, who discusses the link in detail.

4. Such London sketches were a form developed by George Cruikshank, "Phiz.," and other graphic illustrators. The conventions associated with the genre, especially as developed in Cruikshank's work, are examined in detail by Ann Helmreich in this volume.

5. George Cruikshank, *Cries of London* (1815); John Thomas Smith, *Vaga-bondia* (1820); Thomas Rowlandson, *Rowlandson's Characteristic Sketches of the Lower Orders* (c. 1820); Thomas Busby, *Cries of London* (1823). Of Cruikshank's street characters, Louis James has noted the central role of type over individuals; James argues that he "does not really see *people*" (110). Cruikshank's significant contribution to the reshaping of the genre in the nineteenth century is dealt with in more detail in Ann Helmreich's contribution to this volume.

6. For a general discussion of this point, see Sekula, "Invention," and Tagg ch. 2. Although the notion of photography as a "transcription of the real" dominates discussion in Victorian photography – the phrase itself recurring with mechanical regularity – it was not uncontested in the period. For disputes about photographic realism, specifically involving Thomson and the contemporaneous dispute over Dr. Barnardo's fundraising photographs, see Rosen esp. 9; 29-30; 34; Prasch 289-302. On the rancorous debate in the later 1880s about photographic "naturalism," pitting H. P. Robinson against P. H. Emerson, see Prasch ch. 4.

7. On street breeding, see, for example, Mayhew 1:7; 158; 340, 2:208, 3:304; 351). On miscegenation, see Mayhew 1:6; 289, 2:11; 506, 3:88; 186; 384-485, 4:231-233; 229; 421; 424. For comparisons between English street people and "savage" groups, see Mayhew 1:1-3; 213, 3:233-234; 317.

8. On Huxley's suggested methodology, see Edwards. For Thomson's method, see his "Geographical Photography." On typology and anthropology more generally, see Cowling; Sekula, "The Body and the Archive" 343-388.

9. The texts were penned by Thomson and by Adolphe Smith, a temperance activist. All Smith's texts were initialled. Only two of Thomson's own contributions were, but internal evidence (Thomson's preference for direct reporting of dialogue, more detailed description of the circumstance of the photographs, and comparisons with China) suggest uninitialled contributions were Thomson's own.

10. For an interpretation more sympathetic to Thomson as a reformer (contrasting his agenda with Mayhew's), see Rosen.

Works Cited

Brantlinger, Patrick, and Ulin, Donald. "Policing Nomads: Discourse and Social Control in Early Victorian England," *Cultural Critique* 25 (1993): 33-63.

Busby, Thomas. *Cries of London: Drawn from Life.* London: L. Harrison, 1823.

Cowling, Mary. *The Artist as Anthropologist: The Representation of Type and Character in Victorian Art.* Cambridge University Press, 1989.

Cruikshank, George. *Cries of London: As They Are Heard Daily; with Character Cuts of Those Who Traverse the Streets of London with Articles to Sell.* London: J. Chappel, 1815?

Edwards, Elizabeth. "Photographic 'Types': The Pursuit of a Method," *Visual Anthropology* 3: 2-3 (1990): 241-247.

Fox, Celina. "The Development of Social Reportage in English Illustrated Periodicals during the 1840s and early 1850s," *Past and Present* 74 (February 1977): 90-111.

_____. *Londoners.* London: Thames and Hudson, 1987.

Flukinger, Roy, Aaron Schaaf, and Standish Meacham. *Paul Martin: Victorian Photographer.* Austin: University of Texas Press, 1977.

Gallagher, Catherine. "The Body Versus the Social Body in the Works of Thomas Malthus and Henry Mayhew," in Gallagher and Thomas Laqueur (eds.), *The Making of the Modern Body: Sexuality and Society in the Nineteenth Century.* Berkeley: University of California Press, 1987, 86-106.

Himmelfarb, Gertrude. *The Idea of Poverty.* New York: Knopf, 1984.

Hobsbawm, Eric. "The Formation of British Working-Class Culture" and "The Making of the Working Class 1870-1914," in *Workers: Worlds of Labor.* New York: Pantheon, 1984, 176-193; 194-213 respectively.

Humphreys, Anne. *Travels into the Poor Man's Country.* Athens: University of Georgia Press, 1977.

James, Louis. "Cruikshank and Early Victorian Caricature," *History Workshop* 6 (1978): 107-120.

Lloyd, Valerie. *The Camera and Dr. Barnardo.* Hartford: Barnardo School of Printing, 1974.

Mayhew, Henry. *London Characters: Illustrations of the Humour, Pathos, and Peculiarities of London Life.* London: Chatto and Windus, 1874.

_____. *London Labour and the Labouring Poor.* 4 vols., 1861-62; rpt. New York: Dover Press, 1968.

Newhall, Beaumont. *History of Photography.* New York: Museum of Modern Art, 1982.

Nord, Deborah Epstein. "The City as Theater: From Georgian to Early Victorian London," *Victorian Studies* 31:2 (1988): 159-188.

Prasch, Thomas. "Fixed Positions: Working-Class Subjects and Photographic Hegemony in Victorian Britain." Ph.D. diss. Indiana University, 1994.

Roberts, W. *The Cries of London.* London: Connoisseur, 1924.

Robinson, H. P. *Pictorial Effect in Photography: Being Hints on Composition and Chiaroscuro for Photographers.* London: Piper and Carter, 1869.

Rosen, Jeff. "Posed as Rogues: The Crisis of Photographic Realism in John Thomson's *Street Life in London,*" *Image* 36:3/4 (1993): 9-39.

Rothstein, Arthur. *Documentary Photography.* Boston: Focal Press, 1986.

Rowlandson, Thomas. *Rowlandson's Characteristic Sketches of the Lower Orders, Intended as a Companion to the New Picture of London.* London: Samuel Leigh, 1820-22?

Ruskin, John. *Library Edition of the Works of John Ruskin.* E. T. Cook and Alexander Wedderburn, eds. 39 vols. New York: George Allen, 1903-1912.

Sekula, Allan. "The Body and the Archive," in Richard Bolton, ed., *The Contest of Meaning: Critical Histories of Photography.* Cambridge: MIT Press, 1989, 343-389.

_____. "The Invention of Photographic Meaning," in Victor Burgin, ed., *Thinking Photography.* London: Macmillan, 1982, 84-109.

Shesgreen, Sean. *The Criers and Hawkers of London: Engravings and Drawings.* Aldershot: Scolar Press, 1990.

Smith, John Thomas. *Vagabondia*. London: J. and A. Arch, 1820.

Stocking, George, Jr. *Victorian Anthropology*. New York: Free Press, 1987.

Tagg, John. *The Burden of Representation: Essays on Photographies and Histories*. London: Macmillan, 1988.

Taylor, John. "Henry Peach Robinson and Victorian Theory." *History of Photography* 3:4 (1979): 295-303.

Thomas, Alan. *Time in a Frame: Photography and the Nineteenth Century Imagination*. New York: Schocken, 1977.

Thompson, E. P. "The Political Education of Henry Mayhew." *Victorian Studies* 11:1 (1967): 41-62.

Thomson, G. [*sic*]. "Notes of Cambodia and its Races," *Transactions of the Ethnological Society of London*, n.s. 6 (1869): 246-252.

Thomson, John. "Geographical Photography." *Scottish Geographical Magazine* 23:1 (1907): 17-27.

_____. *Illustrations of China and Its People: A Series of 200 Photographs, with Letterpress Descriptive of the Places and People Represented*. 4 vols., London: Sampson Low, Marston, Low and Searle, 1873.

_____. *Straits of Malacca, Indo-China, and China, or Ten Years' Travels, Adventures, and Residence Abroad*. New York: Harper and Brothers, 1875.

_____ and Adolphe Smith. *Street Life in London*. London: Sampson Low, Marston, Searle and Rivington, [1877].

"What Is Photography?" *Photographic Art-Journal* 1 (1858): 12.

White, Stephen. *John Thomson: Life and Photographs*. London: Thames and Hudson, 1985.

Yeo, Eileen and Thompson, E. P. *The Unknown Mayhew*. New York: Pantheon, 1971.

10

Midnight Scenes and Social Photographs: Thomas Annan's Glasgow

Ian Spring

*T*homas Annan's celebrated photographs of Victorian Glasgow are often compared to other photographic representations of nineteenth-century urban poverty: for example, Jacob Riis's photographs of the east side of New York. The particular nature of Annan's work, however, is best understood in the context of, first, the development of early Scottish photography and, second, ethnographic representational practice in the British Victorian city. In light of recent discoveries of new work by David Octavius Hill and Robert Adamson (detailed in a major exhibition at the Scottish National Portrait Gallery and a subsequent book by Sara Stevenson in 1991) Annan's work can be seen as a kind of mirror-image of what is now regarded as the explicitly ideological mission of the Edinburgh photographers. Previous work on Annan and ethnographic images of Glasgow, however, has tended to impute a spurious intentionality to the work of writers and reformers. Thus, in social histories, the complexity of the ideological discourses of improvement and charity are neglected in favor of a simplistic opposition between working and middle class or capitalism and social reform. Partly because of this, Thomas Annan's photographs of urban Glasgow have proved an enigma for most commentators because of Annan's absolute silence regarding the political or social consequences of the project. Instead of struggling, ineffectually, to probe Annan's intentions, we should instead look at his work in a Foucaultian sense as a particular ethnographic practice brought to bear upon its subjects.[1] Strangely, in this context, Annan's *Old Streets and Closes*, first published in book form in 1878, can be seen not as a progenitor of social reform, but as a result of it. The photographs themselves, taken immediately before the demolition of the High Street slums, were constructed by an intense Victorian curiosity about the inhabitants of the inner city. In ethnographic terms, the "other," or the foreign, marginalized element of their own people. In one way, then, the Annan photographs, almost from their inception, are interpolated through a powerful nostalgic gaze.

In order to contextualize this body of work, it is necessary to emphasize the preeminence of early Scottish photography. William Henry Fox Talbot announced the invention of a negative/positive process of photography in 1839. In 1843, Robert Adamson, of St Andrews, Fife, who had been taught Talbot's calotype process by his elder brother, John Adamson, set up a calotype studio on Calton Hill in Edinburgh. In June of that year, Adamson met and joined in partnership with David Octavius Hill, an Edinburgh painter, who was interested in using photography as an aid to portrait painting.[2] This proved to be a very fertile partnership indeed and the results of their collaboration over the next few years (mostly portrait photographs of Edinburgh worthies and studies of local architecture) are among the most important photographs of this early period.

There have been several studies of the photographs of Hill and Adamson, but the recent discovery of some previously lost photographs by them and, consequently, the reconstruction, mostly by Sara Stevenson, of a documentary body of photographs of Newhaven, a fishing port on the fringes of Edinburgh, has revealed not only important pioneering work by Hill and Adamson but also a significant ideological underpinning of their enterprise. In fact, according to Stevenson in *Hill and Adamson's "The Fishermen and Women of the Firth of Forth,"* the Newhaven photographs can be viewed explicitly as their answer to the contemporary debate about the nature of Victorian urban communities:

> The Newhaven photographs can be looked at as D. O. Hill's response and contribution to the debate. The Rock House studio faced the Old Town which was constantly in his view, and the contrast between the desolation of the slums and the lively health of the village was naturally dramatic. Hill's admiration for Newhaven is undoubted and the photographs may be read as an analysis of praise as effective as the reports condemning the slums. . . . Hill had a passion for light and the physical breadth and freedom behind the idea of aerial perspective . The horrors of city confinement and darkness would have struck him forcibly. . . . The reason Hill did not photograph the paupers was that he clearly did not consider it right to do so. (24-25)

The position of Hill and Adamson's Edinburgh studio in Rock House, a cottage-like dwelling built on the edge of Edinburgh's Calton Hill, is crucial to the understanding of this argument On Calton Hill itself were all the glories of Georgian New Town Edinburgh (often referred to as the "Athens of the North") including the aborted National Monument, an attempt to build an exact scale replica of the Parthenon on the top of the hill. Immediately facing the studio, however, was Calton Jail, a massive structure built on the popular panopticon model in 1815, and beyond, the squalor of the Old Town. In an important painting by Hill, *In Memoriam, The Calton 1862*, this contrast is obvious and both Adamson, as a photographer in the shadows of the hill, and Hill, indirectly (as one of his paintings is collected from the gate to Rock House) are portrayed as players in the wider Edinburgh scene that is suggested by the background. (Plate 17)

However, Adamson and Hill's decision, in light of the reality of the nineteenth-century Edinburgh that confronted them was, metaphorically, to turn their face away. There is not a single image in their work of working-class

inner Edinburgh. Instead, through their photographs of
the Newhaven fishermen, Hill and Adamson attempted to
document a purer, better style of working-class life with its
vision of simple pleasure, stern religion and the vagaries
of fate.

A few years later, however, some forty-five miles dis-
tant, in Glasgow, the larger and more industrial of Scotland's two great conurbations, there were middle-class
Scots willing to turn their attention to the inner-city poor.
In 1858, a small volume entitled *Midnight Scenes and
Social Photographs* by "Shadow" (a pseudonym for Alexander Brown, a small-time printer and would-be social reformer in Glasgow) appeared. The book consisted of some
general observations of the slum areas of the east end of
Glasgow and a revelation of the distress and widespread
depravity of its inhabitants. The ingenuous prose passages of which the work consists, however, are very carefully constructed. They form six days (Monday to Saturday) of perambulations through the "night-side" of the city
by Shadow and an acquaintance. The foreword to the
book states the intention: "The writer of the following
sketches does not wish the reader to imagine that their
appearance arises from any supposed literary excellence,
but rather because it is presumed they will be found to
contain facts and observations not without value on a
subject of great and increasing interest, viz., the condition
of the poor, and the classes generally inhabiting the lower
depths of society. Should the 'Photographs' present a tone
painfully dark and gloomy, it will be remembered that
most of them have been taken by moonlight, from the
'night-side' of the city" (7).

The point about Shadow's collection is that the book
does not employ photographic illustrations at all. In fact,
this mention of photography is employed simply as a
metaphor for his observations (in the form of what are
called 'sketches' – also metaphorically). This usage is
primarily intended to emphasize the truth value of the
contents – at a time when photography was inexorably
associated with a true unmediated representation of reality – literally "the pencil of nature." The metaphoric function of the art of photography is exemplified by the etching

by George Cruikshank that forms the frontispiece to the book[3] (Plate 18). In the center there are several scenes of depravity supposedly associated with the east end of the city and combined together in the same fashion as in popular etchings such as Hogarth's *Gin Lane*. There is a man lying on the ground with blood pouring from his head, a drunken couple, a man beating his wife with child in arm, a woman being restrained by policemen in large top hats while a child clings to her waist, some children huddling together in the foreground. In the background is the only source of redemption, a preacher addressing his congregation, and a couple of ragged figures turn away from the frenzy towards him. Also, in the extreme left foreground stands a camera on a tripod capturing these scenes. To further emphasize the efficacy of this instrument to mirror reality and strip away the veneer to expose the truth another ploy is introduced. In the left background bounded by a wall, directly in the path of the camera, a section of the stone apparently melts away to expose the extremely debauched clientele of a rather downbeat tavern. By the camera, the photographer himself, Shadow, is again only revealed in silhouette, half hidden behind part of a set of curtains that frame the scene.

This form of representation is developed not only in Shadow's prose sketches but also in popular fictional texts of the time. For example, in this extract from W. Naismith's sensationalist popular novel, *City Echoes: or, Bitter Cries from Glasgow* (1854):

> The localities where many of those Mission Halls are built are in most instances the very antipode of human civilization. . . . Glaring taverns, mysterious loan offices accessible only by stairs as dark and slippery as the lives and fortunes of those they aid with their momentum to misery and chaos, glare everywhere with their lurid witchery. Closes gaping, black and grim in the sickly gaslight, have at their entrances little knots of suspicious looking characters. Young men closely shaven, bearing the unmistakable prison crop, the greasy cap and muffler . . . barefooted girls and half-naked women with disfigured looks, ragged children and barking curs, all mingle in a horrid melee. (154)

Soon, however, a genuine photographic record of urban Glasgow was to emerge. Thomas Annan was the founder of a family firm of photographers that still exists in Glasgow today (still selling prints from their original plates). He was born in 1829 in Dairsie, Fife. In 1845 he began a seven-year apprenticeship as a lithographic engraver in Cupar, later moving to Glasgow to work with Joseph Swan, a well-known engraver of city views and maps. Around 1850, he became interested in photography and in 1855 set up business as a "collodion calotypist" in Woodlands Road, Glasgow.[4]

Between 1868 and 1871, Annan took photographs of the old closes of the east end of Glasgow, mostly around the High Street, which were built around the decaying buildings of the medieval town. Bound volumes of these prints were produced for the town council and framed copies were hung on the walls of Glasgow University and exhibited in the Kelvingrove museum. An edition of one hundred quarto-size copies was published by the Glasgow City Improvements Trust in 1878, and further editions, with additional plates, followed up to 1900.[5] Most of the photographs were taken within a small area around the High Street in the east end of Glasgow. This was an area of particularly dense population centered on a series of narrow closes or enclosures leading up the spine of the old town towards the medieval cathedral (Plates 19 & 20).

The way in which the inhabitants of these slum dwellings appear in Annan's photographs is especially interesting. Some photographs merely show the closes deserted, but these are the exception. Most feature people, usually posed and directly addressing the reader; usually these are individuals, leaning on a doorway, or small groups, huddled together, as, for example, in the photographs of 80 High Street or 29 Gallowgate. In one particularly effective study, of 118 High Street, the inhabitants are grouped and posed together, children sitting in front, women standing behind, with one solitary teenage boy breaking the exact symmetry of the group, as for a conventional group portrait. The distinctive difference is that, in the narrowest of alleyways, they are squeezed between the two gray walls that frame them and define the focus of the picture, between indefinite dark spaces of doorways in the foreground and a vague murky sky in the background. In one well-known study, 65 High Street, a young boy in a shiny bowler hat (lit from above), like a refugee from one of the Ragged School portraits popularized at the time, stands leaning on one wall. His double seems to appear in 37 High Street, carrying a water jug, slightly blurred. Characteristic of all the photographs are the children, or dogs, or occasional adults, who do *not* appear. Unwilling or unable to pose for the lengthy exposure time required, they appear as blurred ghosts, in various degrees of detail. Phantom inhabitants of the dingy underworld, they give Annan's photographs, more than anything else, their strange, unearthly quality and remind us of the representational nature of these images. Perhaps not surprisingly, attempts were made to erase these ghosts from later editions of the prints. On nearly all of the photographs, even those of deserted closes, the inhabitants are represented by their very vestments: the washing that is suspended from every possible window (washing tubs, jugs and other paraphernalia also appear frequently despite the supposed unsanitary nature of the slum dwellers). These often form fantastic shapes, occasionally blurred in the image by an infrequent gust of wind. They constitute much of the interesting texture and pattern of the individual images. Therefore, what we see is an illuminating but highly constructed view of these people, bereft of action, the top-lighting giving them Neanderthal brows and lost chins. They appear perhaps disinterested, posed in a fashion, and docile. Anita Mozley, in her commentary on the photographs, remarks: "Their presence in his photographs, while evidently not unwelcome to [Annan] does not seem, either, to have been especially sought, and was probably occasioned by the imposing presence of this tall man and his cumbersome photographic apparatus from the world outside the closes. Even sanitary workers, doctors and teachers feared to venture into these dens without protection" (vii). Nevertheless, these people, constructed by a discipline and technology beyond their immediate knowledge, constitute the most interesting aspect of this body of photographs. In fact, what has been constructed, through the texts themselves, is the exact antithesis of Cruikshank's engraving: no vice, no drunkenness, no crime, merely an orderly people, husbands, wives and children, all preoccupied with maintaining a degree of cleanliness.

Today, Annan's images are well known, but there is one common misconception that must be addressed. Although Annan's work was commissioned by the trustees of the Glasgow City Improvements Trust, their notable exposure of east-end slums was not, as many believe, instrumental in the plans for demolition and improvement of the area realized in the 1870s and '80s. Annan's work, therefore, cannot be compared to other photographic projects directly involved in the legal process of instigating slum clearance, for example, the contemporary photographs of the Quarry Hill area of Leeds, investigated by John Tagg. In fact, the Glasgow City Improvements Act of 1866 (derived from the City Improvement Bill introduced by the publisher Blackie in 1865) had already decided on these plans. The ancient slums around High Street were removed and replaced by new tenements (to degenerate into the slums of the late twentieth century) by the end of the 1880s. These plans were partly predicated by the benevolence of Victorian philanthropists, but were due, in no small part, to commercial concerns; with the increasing demand for city center space and rented housing, especially with the development of the railway centered at the top of the High Street.

Annan's work was purely documentary, and must be read in this light. This was an attempt to record a piece of vanishing social history and to satisfy the immense curiosity for the strange land of urban low-life which Shadow provokes. Annan belongs quite definitely to the same ethnographic tradition. His work was, quite literally, a curiosity, an exposé of the slum underworld for the Victorian middle-classes unwilling, unlike Shadow, to venture into the depths themselves. His readers were comfortable middle-class Victorians like himself. *The Painted Windows of Glasgow Cathedral* of 1868, one of Annan's earlier volumes of photographs, carries the epithet:

> For Christian merchants we make our plea,
> The pulse of the business world are we;
> With tenants and servants at our command,

And spending ever with liberal hand.
Yet e'en by us how much has been won,
For the cause of right. See what we have done!

And say, in view of facts like these,
Do we only live to take our ease?

In one respect, Annan's photographs are similar to Shadow's prose passages; they have no political dimension, they are mere representation. Yet in many ways they are totally different. First, they are not Shadow's social photographs "taken by moonlight," but require long exposures in daylight even in the least gloomy and oppressive closes and wynds. They have no access to the inner sanctum of the tenement dweller (thus giving the lie to Cruikshank's inordinate claims for the camera's power of revelation). Second, whereas Shadow had some familiarity with the comparatively new form of the sociological interview, Annan has no facility to let his subjects speak or to put his words in their mouths. Whereas in Shadow the plight of the masses is exemplified through the peculiar sufferings of chosen typical or stereotypical individuals, in Annan's photographs they remain the anonymous (and sometimes regimented) masses.

Both Shadow's work and Annan's can be classified as ethnography, a particular practice or representing and delineating people or cultures that really derives, in its accepted form, from the classificatory sciences born in the late eighteenth and early nineteenth century. Ethnographic representation implies, as scholars such as Foucault and Said have pointed out, a particular power relationship between the represented and the representer. The most common tool of this practice is to represent and define the subject of the inquiry as, literally, the "other," a people or race exhibiting characteristics that are structurally opposed to the characteristics of the culture or race of the observer which was generally the supposed dominant ideology and culture of the "civilized" world (in this case the Victorian middle classes). Thus, it is not surprising that would-be reformers of the time (including, for example, Henry Mayhew) should refer to their fellow citizens as "arabs" or "natives." Thomas Prasch also notes this particular terminology in respect of John Thomson's photographs of the London poor.[6] Similarly, Shadow notes: "No nautical explorer ever fell among savages who looked with greater wonder at his approach." In order for this distancing process to work, however, a certain form of representation may be implied. Perhaps Annan is at a disadvantage because his form of representation, photography, is more suited to representing his subjects metonymically, or partially, through examples of their demeanor or habitat. Shadow, on the other hand, represents his subjects metaphorically, and that is the precise value of the photographic analogy he employs. In both cases, there is clearly a bias towards a supposed verisimilitude. In Shadow's case, however, this is more directly constructed by the text. However, the clearly paradoxical nature of this representational metaphor is not obvious to some commentators on Shadow's work. John McCaffrey, a historian, comments in the introduction to the modern reprint of *Midnight Scenes and Social Photographs*:

> In his role as the Shadow he is keenly observing but unobserved (see how George Cruikshank brings out this aspect in his frontispiece illustration). He strives as far as possible to be present but not in such an obtrusive way, as would be the case today with a television camera and crew, as to affect the behavior of those whose circumstance he depicts. Like a social photographer [sic] he seeks to give the reader the true and exact image he sees through the senses of his own senses [sic] . . . the word pictures sometimes flash with vivid detail. (viii)

McCaffrey's confusion over the use of Shadow's informing metaphor (especially in the infelicitous comparison with the television crew) is unfortunate. The error is twofold: first, to accept Shadow's supposed objectivity at face value, rather than as a construction of the text itself. Second, to accept Shadow's compassion as a kind of authorial intent instead of, as we can see, a construction of the particular kind of institutional practice he brings to bear on his subjects. The same problem seems evident in a more recent commentary by Andrew Noble, a literary scholar who sees Shadow's collection as "where the realistic technology of the camera undermined the corrupt literary analogies derived from painting on which sentimental Scottish writing depended," and who notes, "the squalor, destitution, alcoholism and prostitution of the Glasgow slums seem near incredible. We have, of course, by this time the remarkable Annan photographs to corroborate Shadow's evidence. . . . His is a quite remarkable book in terms of its detail and compassion. The 'photographs' he takes are of a heart of darkness in slum Glasgow which needed only nocturnal exploration to reveal" (85). Noble's insistence on Shadow's comparative realism, his compounding of the photography metaphor, and his readiness to conjoin "squalor and destitution" with "alcoholism and prostitution" ("corroborated" by Annan, which they are not; Annan's characters being alcoholics or prostitutes only by implication!) show that his commentary only functions *within* the distinctive institutional discourse of the original text.

Ethnographic representations during this period were well established in Scotland, the primary impulse being, as Malcolm Chapman, among others, has shown, directed towards the Celtic fringe in the Highlands and islands and intent upon shaping the inhabitants, within an established romantic discourse, into the residue of an ancient, barbaric, but heroic race. Ethnographic investigation into the inner world of the city slums was, however, as carefully and fully constructed, but with distinct differences. George Stocking, an American anthropologist, notes:

> From the perspective of contemporary middle-class observers, the primitivism at the bottom of the social scale now had a dual character. On the one hand, there was the rural primitivism of the pre-industrial world, marginalized in England and still flourishing on the Celtic fringe; on the other, there was the urban primitivism of preindustrial London, metastasizing in every industrial town and city. The first, which was to be the subject matter of the science of folklore, could still be looked at through an elegiac filter of "soft" primitivism, the more so as the blood sports of the villages were outlawed and the raucous visitations of Plough Monday were transformed into Plough Sunday services. But there were no traces of "Merie England" to be found in the new city slums, which provided the subject matter of the urban reformer's science of social statistics. They remained, even in the process of reformation, a disturbing and alien phenomenon – so far removed from the amenities and the morality of civilized life that many observers, including Friedrich Engels and Henry Mayhew, were impelled to use racial analogies to capture the sense

of difference. Thus for Engels the working classes were "a
race apart" – physically degenerate, robbed of all humanity,
reduced morally and intellectually to near bestial condition,
not only by economic exploitation, but by competition and
association with the coarse, volatile, dissolute, drunken,
improvident Irish, who slept with their pigs in the stinking
slums of Manchester. And for Mayhew, the street folk of
London were a "nomad race" without "the least faculty of
prevision," flouting the middle-class ethic of sexual re-
straint and hard work, reduced to the terrible alternation
of "starvation and surfeit." (251)

In the investigation of Victorian "philanthropists" the
urban masses have no folklore, no customs, no lifestyle,
no *habiliment*. They are simply constructed, we could say,
under the double yoke of the need to work and the need to
worship (and in a superficial sense, the need not to of-
fend). All differences, all personality, all real life is subsumed under a label whose name, ever shifting, may be
vice, misery, vicissitude, destitution, immorality or (even)
misfortune. Shadow's *objectivity* and his *compassion* are
real in the sense that, in real life, Alexander Brown probably intended to be both objective and compassionate and
very possibly succeeded. But within the text they are both
constructed; objectivity, as we have seen, through the
metaphoric structure, and compassion within a specific
discourse of charity that has its roots in a peculiarly
Victorian ideology.

Victorian concerns with charity have been mapped out
in some details by various scholars. Axiomatic to the
popular model is the acceptance that industrial society at
this time required that a percentage of the population
accepted their own essential poverty and, consequently,
inner city squalor. Charitable institutions arose to serve
a twofold purpose: to salve the conscience of the middle
and upper-classes represented by the growing band of
philanthropists and reformers concerned at the immediate plight of the poor and to achieve at least the implied
consent of the masses to the social hierarchy. This was
achieved only partially through coercion, but predomi-
nantly through the process of hegemony. The two main
instruments of this process were the class system and
religious morality. Within this hegemonic discourse, the
same reformers were unable to see any cause for the

misery of the poor but their own vice and drunkenness. This is made especially clear by the work of the Mission movement of the time. For example, the Church of Scotland's *Commission on the Religious Condition of the People* of 1891:

> received from the superintendent of the Glasgow City Mission what it termed "interesting glimpses – some of them painfully interesting – of certain conditions of city life." These included references to the large number of brothels in the center of Glasgow, as well as to other houses which "cannot be designated as brothels" but to which "young women go . . . in the evening for prostitution." It also noted the activities of an organization which gave free breakfasts on Sundays to waifs and strays, including "many girls of that class who are just between losing and winning" and commented that there was "a sadder class still." The Commission clearly was aware that prostitution existed on a large scale in the cities, and wrote that "its victims are legion," but its intelligence was not good: it was not able "to estimate the full extent of the social evil; it walks in the dark, and in the city its paths are not known." (172)

It is also clear in these revealing examples of Stocking's "science of social statistics," from William Logan's *Moral Statistics of Glasgow in 1863*, which succinctly map out the absolute distinction between the day and night side of the city:

> The Moral Statistics of Glasgow:
>
> To cash yearly offered by professedly Christian Glasgow to Bacchus £1,184,412
>
> To cash yearly offered by professedly Christian Glasgow to Belial   £819,183
>
>   £2,003,595

> "Hear, O heavens; and give ear, O earth" – six parts given to the devil, and one part to Jesus Christ! – six times more for hell than for heaven! by the commercial capital of the most religious nation in the world, by the city whose glorious motto is, – "Let Glasgow flourish by the preaching of the Word," and at a time when one of her ministers, at the public meeting of the Benevolent Society, declared little children were to be seen gathering turnip skins with which to allay the pangs of their hunger. "O that our head were waters, and our eyes fountains of tears, that we might weep day and night" for the madness of our people! (75)

That the misfortunes of the poor could be commonly ascribed to drink, especially in the cities (sexual promiscuity was especially characteristic of the rural working class) and thus relatively easily prevented is, as here, the accepted nostrum of the times. The paradoxical nature of this type of textual evidence must be apparent to even the most hidebound historian. And it is exemplified in the fact that all these observations and statistics relate only to what might be termed the "leisure" or extramural interests of the community. What always remains hidden relates to production. It is the work available and the wages paid to the people through those institutions whose interests are also close to the hearts of the businessmen, philanthropists (and publicans whose own weekly portion derived from the generous offerings of those devotees of Bacchus) which, through its self-evident inadequacy, disabled the working classes and divorced them from the exercise of self-help so beloved of the city missionaries. Ethnographic photographs of rural communities often associate the people with objects of labor: ploughs, or spinning wheels. The urban masses are not even afforded that small favor. In fact, as they appear in the photographs of Annan, they are counterpointed with the wreckage of their own insufficient "leisure" environment, the tenement backcourts, yards and closes.

A similar confusion to that arising over Shadow's implied compassion has also arisen in regard to Annan's real intentions in constructing the *Old Streets and Closes.* Stevenson comments on this:

> The [Glasgow] photographs are not a soulless record of derelict buildings, they are a curiously moving account of the closes. They are not, however, directly appealing in a way that would make it clear that Annan was concerned about the people living there. . . . The strength of feeling is generalized rather than personal. . . . Is it the truth, is it our knowledge of the subject, that gives the photographs the feeling we read into them? The possibility that a photographer can be detached or cynical about his work has to be met because it is commonly raised. . . . The need to prove a photographer's sincerity means that we have to check the truth we can see in the photographs against the historical truth of the man's life and words. . . . Was he an insensible man who may have noticed the smell in passing but was otherwise unconcerned? From Annan's history and character, this is clearly not so. . . . By keeping his photographs unspecific, idealized rather than squalid, he gave the closes the weight of sorrow or tragedy. In the same way, Dickens' novels portraying the same kind of distress-

ing conditions are great art made from human depression.
(16-17)

Stevenson's view, as a biographer, is based on a particular interest in identifying the motivational impulse of the man as photographer/artist. However, the argument is further developed by Julie Lawson, who contextualizes the problem of the moral imperative of the "artist" in the following way:

> The apparent contradiction or moral questionableness of admiring photographs which have as part of their intrinsic subject matter the suffering of human beings is properly disturbing to us. The problem has been raised in several ways and with varying degrees of pertinence. At its most trivial level, it is raised by those who set up a straw man in the form of a hypothetical commentator who, epitome of decadence, stands admiring (in appropriately limp-wristed fashion) the textural beauty of decaying brickwork or beams of light dancing on a stream of fetid water running in a gutter. This somewhat unconvincing straw man is then knocked down by charges of the sin of insensitivity to the human or social reality. (40-46)

This argument has, in fact, a substantial pedigree and was expounded in an important seminal text on photography, Susan Sontag's *On Photography,* which deploys two terms that have since been assimilated into critical work with their own particular meanings: the "flaneur" and the "picturesque":

> For more than a century, photographers have been hovering about the oppressed, in attendance at scenes of violence – with a spectacularly good conscience. Social misery has inspired the comfortably-off with the urge to take pictures, the gentlest of predations, in order to document a hidden reality, that is, a reality hidden from them. Gazing on other people's reality with curiosity, with detachment, with professionalism, the ubiquitous photographer operates as if that activity transcends class interests, as if its perspective is universal. In fact, photography first comes into its own as an extension of the eye of the middle-class *flaneur,* whose sensibility was so accurately charted by Baudelaire. The photographer is an armed version of the solitary walker reconnoitering, stalking, cruising the urban inferno, the voyeuristic stroller who discovers the city as a landscape of voluptuous extremes. Adept of the joys of watching, connoisseur of empathy the *flaneur* finds the world "picturesque." (55)

It is undoubtedly the case that Annan's photographs have remained so popular due to their aesthetic as well as their documentary value. However, the uneasiness expressed by Stevenson and Lawson is not due to any confusion between these values but rather due to an absence of intentionality. Therefore, the "problem of the picturesque," while having wider ramifications for our reading of photographic texts in general, is not a particular problem in this reading of Annan's work. We can see that Shadow's intentions and the clear Victorian ideological basis for his work are obviously expressed through the hierarchy of discourse that frames his prose "sketches" with a degree of personal objectivity. John Thomson's images of the urban poor in London are contextualized by the prose descriptions penned by Adolphe Smith that accompanied their publication.[7] Annan himself remained resolutely silent about the photographs of the *Old Streets and Closes*. But to regard this silence as indicative of personal detachment is a mistake of the same order as the confusion over the comparison of Shadow's and Annan's work.[8] The intentionality behind these representations is, as scrutiny of the texts reveals, only inscribed in the texts themselves. If Annan's representations seem more objective, born of the more "modern" discourse of document or ethnography rather than Victorian concerns with morality, charity and social class, it is because of the technology that allows these texts to be constructed: the "all-seeing" eye of the camera which, as John Tagg points out in *The Burden of Representation*, constructs particular meaning because of strengths and limitations of its physical apparatus. The meaning of Annan's photographs depends on the interaction between the photographer's own skills, the generic traits of the photographic apparatus, and the particular historical, social and institutional context of the discourse he employs. David Bate identifies this relationship.

> The photographs are identified as evidence where, if the spaces that they represent were not open to the "great" purifying agencies of sun and wind, they were nevertheless sufficiently illuminated to register the *purifying light* of the photographic emulsion. *Purifying* in the sense that the bourgeois and middle-class anxieties about sexuality (in-

cest and prostitution), crime and disease contaminating the
"good" working classes and spreading wider – could be
alleviated by these images.... But where there *is* light, there
is investment of interests and ideologies. It is important
that we reject reflectionist questions of whether such images were positive (showed the "real" conditions) or negative
(objectified the working-class as victims), in favor of consideration of the kinds of world that this practice of photography constructed. (19-20)

It is, in fact, the "investment of interests and ideologies" in Victorian Glasgow, outlined above, that enable us
to more fully appreciate the importance of Annan's *Old
Streets and Closes* and their place in urban representations of the time. However, Thomas Annan's Glasgow
does not simply represent a frozen moment of the past. It
lives on in the realms of representation and is constantly
recontextualized and reinterpreted in new and surprising
ways. Today, in Glasgow shops you can purchase Annan's photograph of No. 65 High Street in postcard form.
Notably, the photograph is bleached and rendered in sepia
(unlike the straightforward black and white of the original
prints). As if to quell any doubts, the reverse gives some
details under the heading "Art Cards." Shop windows are
stocked with Annan prints framed for domestic consumption and countless city center pubs and restaurants
mount Glasgow's old streets and closes on their walls.
One generation's misery incarnate becomes another's con-
sumable style.[9]

Notes

1. For Foucaultian perspectives on photography, see David Green, "On
   Foucault: Disciplinary Power and Photography," *Camerawork* 32 (1985):
   6-9; David Green, "A Map of Depravity," *Ten-8* 18 (1985): 36-43; David
   Green, "Classified Subjects: Photography and Anthropology," *Ten-8* 14
   (1984): 30-37; Roberta McGrath, "Medical Police," *Ten-8* 18 (1984):
   13-18; David Bate, "Photography and the Colonial Vision," *Third Text*, 22
   (Spring, 1993): 81-91; Suren Lalvani, "Photography, Epistemology and
   the Body," *Cultural Studies* 7:3 (October 1993): 442-465.
2. On this relationship see Van Deren Coke. *The Painter and the Photograph: From Delacroix to Warhol.* Albuquerque: University of New
   Mexico Press, 1972.
3. Cruikshank, a reformed drinker, often addressed such issues in his later
   work. See Anne L. Helmreich, in this volume, 157–78.

4. Annan's career is summarised in Sara Stevenson's *Thomas Annan 1829-1887*.

   See also Margaret Harker, "Annans of Glasgow," *British Journal of Photography* (October 1973): 960-69. Margaret Harker, "From Mansion to Close: Thomas Annan, Master Photographer," *The Photographic Collector* 5:1 (1975): 81-95; J. A. Fisher, "Thomas Annan's 'Old Closes and Streets of Glasgow,'" *Scottish Photography Bulletin* (1987/1988). The business moved to Sauchiehall Street in 1859 and has remained in that vicinity ever since.

5. The currently available edition of Thomas Annan is published by Dover Press, New York. The various published editions of the collection are detailed in J. A. Fisher, *T. Annan's Old Closes & Streets of Glasgow: A Guide* (Glasgow: Glasgow City Libraries, 1977). The exact locations of the photographs have also been carefully detailed by Fisher.

6 . "The poor in their midst, Henry Mayhew assured his readers, were a race apart, tribes of atavistic nomads at the center of civilization: 'there are – socially, morally, and perhaps even physically considered – but two distinct and broadly marked races, viz., the wanderers and the settlers – the vagabond and the citizen – the nomadic and the civilized tribes." John Thomson, recapitulating this discovery of the poor a quarter century later, similarly opened his photographic collection *Street Life in London* with the image of "London Nomades": "hence it is that in London there is a number of what may be termed, owing to their wandering, unsettled habits, nomadic tribes.'" See Thomas Prasch in this volume, 179; 180.

7. For example, Adolphe Smith's commentary on one of Thomson's photographs – "Hookey Alf" of Whitechapel: "In the photograph before us we have the calm undisturbed face of the skilled artisan, who has spent a life of tranquil, useful labour, and can enjoy his pipe in peace, while under him sits a woman whose painful expression seems to indicate a troubled existence, and a past which even drink cannot obliterate By her side, a brawny, healthy 'woman of the people,' is not to be disturbed from her enjoyment of a 'drop of beer' by domestic cares; and early acclimatizes her infant to the fumes of tobacco and alcohol. But in the foreground the camera has chronicled the most touching episode. A little girl, not too young, however, to ignore the fatal consequences of drink, has penetrated boldly into the group, as if about to reclaim some relation in danger, and drag him away from evil companionship," John Thomson and Adolphe Smith, *Street Life in London* (London: n.p., 1877): 113.

8. Similarly, Shadow has been rediscovered and his work uncritically assimilated into recent social histories of Glasgow; for example, in Damer. A student magazine published in Glasgow has also taken the title *The Shadow*. The editorial explains: "The aim of the author was to ruthlessly expose the appalling housing conditions and poverty experienced by the working-class . . . the Shadow provided a relentless critique of glaring inequalities . . . he explodes the myths and misconceptions surrounding poverty. . . . Could this also be the Glasgow of 1990?" *The Shadow*, 1: 1 (Winter 1990) was published by Glasgow College Students Union. There was no subsequent issue.

9. For a more detailed and general account of representations of Glasgow, see Spring.

Works Cited

Annan, Thomas. *Photographs of the Old Streets and Closes of Glasgow 1868-1877*, Intro. by Anita Ventura Mozley. New York: Dover, 1977.

Bate, David. "Illuminating Annan," *Portfolio Magazine*, 3 (Spring/Summer 1989): 18-20

Chapman, Malcolm. *The Gaelic Vision in Scottish Culture*. Edinburgh: Blackwell, 1985.

Church of Scotland. *Commission on the Religious Condition of the People.* Edinburgh: n.p., 1891.

Damer, Sean. *Going for a Song*. London: Lawrence and Wishart, 1990.

Glasgow Corporation Housing Department. *Farewell to the Single End.* Glasgow: Glasgow Corporation Housing Department, 1976.

Lawson, Julie. "The Problem of Poverty and the Picturesque: Thomas Annan's *Old Closes and Streets of Glasgow* 1868-1871," *Scottish Photography Bulletin* 2 (1990): 40-46.

Naismith, W. *City Echoes; or, Bitter Cries from Glasgow*. Paisley: n.p., 1854.

Noble, Andrew. "Scottish Writing and the Nineteenth-Century City," in George Gordon ed. *Perspectives of the Scottish City*. Aberdeen University Press, 1985, 42-73.

A Sabbath School Teacher (William Logan). *The Moral Statistics of Glasgow in 1863*. Glasgow: n.p., 1864.

Shadow (Alexander Brown). *Midnight Scenes and Social Photographs, being descriptions of the streets, wynds and dens of the city*. 1858; rpt. intro. by John McCaffrey. University of Glasgow Press, 1976.

Sontag, Susan. *On Photography*. New York: Random House, 1973.

Spring, Ian. *Phantom Village: the Myth of the New Glasgow*. Edinburgh: Polygon, 1990.

Stevenson, Sara. *Thomas Annan 1829-1887*. Edinburgh: National Galleries of Scotland, 1990.

Stevenson, Sara. *Hill and Adamson's 'The Fishermen and Women of the Firth of Forth.'* Edinburgh: National Galleries of Scotland, 1991.

Stocking Jr., George W. *Victorian Anthropology* New York: Free Press; London: Collier Macmillan, 1987.

Tagg, John. "God's Sanitary Law: Slum Clearance and Photography," in *The Burden of Representation* (London: Macmillan, 1988).

11

Lessons in Stone: Architecture and Academic Ethos in an Urban Setting

Sarah V. Barnes

In 1851, a bequest from the wealthy cotton merchant John Owens enabled the civic-minded middle-class citizens of Manchester, England to establish an institution of higher education. The founders aimed to create a university of the highest caliber, devoted to serving the needs of one of Victorian England's most dynamic provincial cities. By the early years of the twentieth century, what began as Owens College had become the University of Manchester, first of the English civic universities, dedicated to providing a new model of higher education stressing scientific research, practical professional training, regional service, and more open access. As a product of the energy and determination of Manchester's middle class, the university constituted a monument to the Victorian age.

With its imposing block-long range of four-story stone buildings, erected between 1869 and 1902 and occupying a prime location along one of the city's busiest thoroughfares, the University of Manchester at the turn of the century was a monument in a literal as well as a figurative sense. Designed by the famous nineteenth-century architect Alfred Waterhouse, the structure housing the university was constructed in a style referred to at the time, and still known today, as "Collegiate Gothic." Characterized by such elements as narrow arched windows, a steep and varied roof line, strong vertical elements, and an asymmetrical façade punctuated by numerous gables and bays, the style is perhaps best exemplified by the two ancient English universities of Oxford and Cambridge. Indeed, many of the Oxbridge colleges' original stone buildings date from the Middle Ages. However, several of England's civic universities, beginning with Manchester, also adopted Gothic features in their architecture, despite the institutions' nineteenth-century origins and their use of modern materials and contruction techniques.

In Manchester's case, Waterhouse's buildings, erected in stages over the course of three decades, consist of four main blocks, arranged in the form of a quadrangle. Entry into this enclosed space is through a tall gateway tower which dominates the front range of buildings along Oxford Road. With the exception of the chemistry and physics laboratories housed in less elaborate structures at the back, Gothic elements, including high-pitched red slate roofs and numerous narrow arched windows separated by stone buttresses, predominate throughout (Plate 21).

The question is why: Why did the supporters of Owens College and their architect Alfred Waterhouse choose Gothic, a style usually associated in academic architecture with quiet domestic cloisters, for buildings meant to serve an urban, nonresidential purpose? What does the choice reveal about the institution's sense of identity and its relationship with the city of Manchester? The response is not as obvious as it might appear. Rather than reflecting a simple nostalgia for traditional forms, the choice of Gothic points to an element of ambiguity inherent not only in the style itself, but also in the English idea of the civic university.

In the nineteenth century, the issue of style often generated intense debate, not only among architects but also among the general public. In an endeavor original to the Victorians, theorists and practitioners alike sought consciously to define a mode of building which was characteristic of the age (Williams 130). At the same time, many found in architecture a means of reforming society's flaws or of reasserting the power of traditional sources of authority. Often, Victorian architects and their patrons, whatever their combination of motives, turned to medieval forms to accomplish their ends. As a result, although Gothic revivalism influenced other types of nineteenth-century English artistic expression, including literature and painting, in architecture, especially in public buildings, the Gothic style triumphed. Despite its pervasiveness, however, the phenomenon was far from monolithic in content. Replete with historicist implications, Gothic Revival architecture could also reflect nothing other than an effort to turn the natural adaptability of medieval forms to a variety of modern purposes, not all of which accorded with the style's historical connotations. As a result, the essential meaning of the Gothic Revival resists easy characterization (Archer 336-39, Mancoff 10-11; 73-75).

The same was true concerning the identity of England's civic universities, particularly as revealed in their architecture. In the late nineteenth century, as is still the case today, the English idea of the university in general was largely determined by the traditions of Oxford and Cambridge. The prestige possessed by the two oldest English universities gave them enormous cultural authority, even as they experienced criticism and pressure to reform their archaic ways and adapt more readily to the demands of a modern society. Although Owens College and the other nascent civic universities were established as alternatives with a different mission, nonetheless they could not escape entirely the influence of the nineteenth-century Oxbridge idea of the university, with its emphasis on liberal learning in a cloistered, domestic atmosphere. As evidence of this fact, some historians have suggested that the civic universities imitated the Oxbridge style of collegiate Gothic with the explicit intent of evoking the tradition and prestige associated with the ancient institutions, whose medieval origins were so plainly apparent in their architecture. Furthermore, these historians argue, the tendency to house the civic universities' science laboratories in plainer, more frankly utilitarian structures while reserving the more elaborate Gothic style for arts buildings reflected an "academic pecking order," dictated by the Oxbridge idea of a university and perpetuated by the civics, which accorded greater status to the humanities despite the new universities' supposed commitment to promoting scientific and technological subjects. In other words, for the civic universities, use of the Gothic style constituted a symbolic acknowledgment of the superiority of Oxbridge and its values (Lowe and Knight 87-91).

Certainly on the surface this seems a plausible argument. Why else erect what appeared to be an imitation of an Oxbridge college in the midst of the dirt and grime of an industrial city? Yet, in the case of Manchester at least, the link between architecture and academic ethos was neither so simple nor so straightforward. Although the university's buildings functioned as a means of defining the institution and its relationship to its urban setting, the message was more complex than the argument above would suggest. In the first place, from the beginning Manchester's leaders explicitly disavowed any intent to emulate the ancient universities. To the contrary, not only did they recognize such a goal as impossible, they scorned the effort, preferring instead to create a new model for higher education in England based on the university's identity as a civic institution, serving the needs of industry and the professions (Barnes 91-110; 156-171). Why, then, did they choose a Gothic design for the institution's architecture? Deciphering further the nature of Manchester's sense of identity as revealed by its public face requires first a more detailed understanding of Victorian Gothic architecture in general and of the university's architect Alfred Waterhouse in particular, followed by a closer examination of the financing, design, and use of the buildings themselves.

Much of nineteenth-century English architecture, both secular and religious, reflects the influence of the Gothic Revival and its two most noted proponents, A.W.N. Pugin and John Ruskin. In advocating a return to a medieval style, both theorists sought to recover the moral qualities associated with a past age as an antidote to the problems of modern society. Pugin, in particular, urged a restoration of the medieval era's social order, based on the central institution of the Christian church. Not surprisingly, his ideas proved especially congenial to representatives of England's established elite, including members of the Anglican clergy, who witnessed the erosion of their customary authority as the nineteenth century progressed. An architect himself, though not always consistent in following his own dictates, Pugin called for a strict adherence to original English models in buildings meant to evoke the social relations of the nation's medieval past. Ruskin, on the other hand, was more concerned with the medieval era as a source of values, both social and aesthetic, to serve as a remedy for the evils wrought by industrialization. A connoisseur of architecture rather than a practitioner, his treatises on the subject nonetheless commanded widespread influence throughout the second half of the nineteenth century. In such works as *The Seven Lamps of Architecture* (1849) and *Stones of Venice* (1851), Ruskin wove together social criticism and aesthetic judgment, producing a theory of truth and beauty in architecture which rested on the inherent organicism, the naturalness, the flexibility and the variety, along with the honest craftsmanship, apparent in Gothic forms. These elements, he argued, constituted the architectural signifiers of a morally superior civilization. Seeking to recapture such values for the modern age, many Victorian architects attempted to express Ruskin's idealized view of medieval society in their own Gothic Revival designs (Archer 336-40; Williams 130-48; Smith 92-121).

Yet not all architects who built in the Gothic style adhered to a strictly historicist use of Gothic elements any more than they accepted completely Pugin's emphasis on the centrality of the Christian church or Ruskin's radical critique of industrial England. These Victorian architects, among them Thomas Graham Jackson and Alfred Waterhouse, saw Gothic architecture less in terms of specific stylistic details to be meticulously reproduced than as the embodiment of an artistic approach to building which was particularly appropriate to the needs of late Victorian England. In Jackson's words:

> It was not the letter but the spirit of Gothic architecture which was of use to us; its frank conformity to circumstance, its glorious liberty from the fetters of dogma . . . , its ready response to the calls of construction, its unaffected naturalism, and its welcome acceptance of fresh ideas and principle. If we caught that spirit, I held that the revival would have served its turn; the outward forms of the old style would seem less and less essential and would naturally pass away, and leave us with something more directly expressive of ourselves. (Jackson 121)

Waterhouse espoused a similar philosophy. As one of his biographers notes, "He was interested in making buildings for use in the nineteenth century rather than recreating a medieval dream. Whatever their inspiration his designs were emphatically Victorian first and foremost . . . His basic attitude to sources [was] that they should be used as inspiration but subordinated to the functional and structural needs of the present." (Maltby, MacDonald, and Cunningham 18-21). Architectural historian Stuart Allen Smith agrees, noting that while Waterhouse "had perhaps as good a knowledge of historic styles as any architect of his day, yet he would not copy formulas from the past. His plans are a functional solution to problems presented. Having logically solved the needs of client and site in a plan, he then produced an elevation to suit it" (Smith 120-21). The rolled iron beam, Smith adds, not the pointed arch, "determined the exterior rhythm of his structures" (118-19; Crook 143). As a result, architectural historian Mark Girouard observes "Whatever their stylistic affiliations, [Waterhouse's] buildings always looked unmistakably Victorian. His Gothic . . . could never be mistaken for medieval Gothic . . . nor would he have wanted it to be" (35). To architects like Jackson and Waterhouse, then, the Gothic style represented less an imitation of the past than a useful vehicle for expressing the potential of new materials and methods of construction. Thoroughly modern in design, their buildings represented an attempt to define an authentically Victorian architecture.

Waterhouse's cavalier attitude toward sources notwithstanding, he was recognized by contemporaries as one of the foremost Gothic revivalists of the era (Parr 671; Girouard 64; Maltby, MacDonald, and Cunningham 18). "His practice was so prolific," writes a modern commentator, "that one could say, with justification, that he did more than almost any other individual to establish the standard architectural dress of the late nineteenth-century town" (Maltby, MacDonald, and Cunningham 6). Born to a family of prosperous Quakers in 1830, Waterhouse was raised outside of Liverpool and attended school in London. Although he showed early signs of artistic ability, Quaker sensibilities dictated that his talents be directed toward the more practical profession of architecture. Apprenticed to Richard Lane, a leading architect in Manchester (from whom he apparently learned very little), Waterhouse served his time before setting out to travel around Europe. Returning to Manchester in 1855, he set up practice on his own (Parr 671, Smith 102).

Initially, Waterhouse's projects consisted mainly of private homes, along with one or two commercial structures (Smith 102-8). Then, in 1859, his first significant commission came to him as the result of a winning entry in a competition for the design of the new Manchester Assize Courts. Hailed by one contemporary publication as an example of the "New Secular Gothic . . . the most important specimen of civic Gothic which the revival has yet produced," Waterhouse's Assize Courts building not only introduced the Gothic Revival style to Manchester but also established the architect's reputation as a leading Gothic revivalist (Crook 81). Influenced especially by the medieval town halls of Belgium and Holland, the building also combined stylistic elements from France, Italy, and England, producing an effect which could only be described as eclectic (Crook 81). Four stories tall and occupying approximately half a city block, the structure boasted numerous narrow, arched windows as well as several towers and turrets, including a steeple-like structure rising from the center. Overall, the effect was one of spiked verticality, interrupted by horizontal string-courses separating each floor and polychrome striping along the roof.

Although Ruskin, upon seeing the Assize Courts, remarked approvingly that the building was "much beyond everything yet done in England on my principles," the theorist could not take total credit for the inspiration (quoted in Crook 81). "In deciding on Gothic for the Assize Courts," writes Stuart Allen Smith, "Waterhouse was prompted not by anything he read but by actual examples of Gothic civic work sought out and studied. This search confirmed that Gothic architecture was applicable to modern requirements" (108). Once completed, the commission in turn demonstrated the success of Waterhouse's approach. The design possessed practical as well as aesthetic appeal, while the architect's handling of its execution proved his competence as a professional. As Smith goes on to remark "It would be difficult to overestimate the importance of the Manchester Assize Courts building in the future career of the young architect. Not only did it bring him national attention, it brought him almost universal praise. . . . It stood throughout Waterhouse's lifetime as evidence of his fidelity to his client, his thoroughness in design matters and his obvious ability to produce a workable and practical structure. In short, it stood as proof that here was a capable, reliable man able to deal confidently yet sympathetically with men of business singly or in groups" (108).

The qualities Waterhouse displayed in completing his first major commission served him well throughout his professional life. He developed a reputation for his willingness to work closely with clients, striving both to stay within budget and to incorporate their ideas into his plans (Parr 5: 671-2). Indeed, it was as an effective and innovative planner that Waterhouse became best known, mainly on the strength of his second major project in Manchester, the monumental Town Hall. As the biggest civic commission of its time, the contract for the Town Hall, like the Assize Courts, was awarded based on the results of a competition, held in 1867 (Smith 112). Wedged into an awkward triangular site, the new building had to be designed in a way to accommodate effectively the various functions of city government and at the same time make a grand statement reflecting the civic pride of Manchester's citizens.

As the judges of the competition made clear, although Waterhouse's elevations were suitably striking, his design won primarily on the basis of the convenience and practicality of its internal arrangements (Smith 112; Maltby, MacDonald, and Cunningham 23-25). Structured in the form of an isosceles triangle with a hollow core, the four-story building consists of three corridors, two long and one short, with meeting rooms and offices lining the exterior walls. In the center of the core is a large public hall, accessible at one end by means of a ceremonial staircase, and situated so as to create three internal courtyards at the three corners of the triangle which in turn allow light and ventilation to penetrate. Walkways link the central structure to the exterior corridors, providing a convenient method of crossing from one side of the building to the other without having to walk around the entire perimeter. Meanwhile, stairways located at each corner of the triangle allow access to the various levels of the building. Externally, the Town Hall presents a series of imposing stone façades. The main frontage, representing the short side of the triangle, faces one of the city's important public squares and boasts a tall clock tower which marks the central entrance to the building. The other two sides, although somewhat less dramatic (owing to the lack of perspective available from the sidewalks running immediately alongside), nonetheless present a varied surface of bays, pavilions and entryways, all executed in rich Gothic detail (Plate 22).

Manchester's Town Hall stands today as one of the foremost examples of Victorian civic architecture in the Gothic Revival style, noted not only for its ingenious layout, but also for its characteristic adaptation of historic forms to modern conditions, and its "bold use of new materials, notably iron, plate glass and terra-cotta" (Crook 81). Small wonder, then, that when the supporters of Owens College decided they needed someone to direct the construction of their new buildings, they approached the architect who was already at work on the city's most prominent public structure. By the late 1860s, the college itself, having struggled initially to gain support, had come to represent one of the city's most prized assets. Its original location, in an ill-adapted house situated in an unhealthy part of the city center, had become painfully inadequate. The proposed plan for new buildings on a new site, part of a larger effort to incorporate and expand the institution, reflected Owens's growing popularity and consequent need for larger and more suitable space. A meeting of the city's notables, held in February 1867, gave rise to the official "Owens College Extension Movement," whose object was to direct the proposed expansion and raise enough money to finance it. The city's most successful businessmen and professionals took part in the project and over 300 citizens, of all ranks, contributed to the general fund, making the Owens College Extension Movement a true civic endeavor.

By December, 1868, the Building and Site subcommittee had selected the institution's new location, just outside the city center, along a main thoroughfare which was convenient to public transportation. At the same time, the subcommittee recommended the appointment of Waterhouse, "a gentleman already well known in Manchester for the ingenuity of his plans and the elegance of his designs," to serve as college architect (Owens College Extension, "Minutes of Subcommittees," December 1868; *Second Report of the Extension Committee*, December 3, 1869). Waterhouse faced a difficult challenge. Members of the official Building Committee, made up of professors, trustees, and organizers of the extension movement, each had ideas about where the new buildings should be situated on the lot, how they should be arranged internally, the size of individual classrooms, and whether to have external stairways or internal corridors. As architect, Waterhouse had to listen carefully to his clients' often conflicting suggestions and produce a plan upon which all could agree. Achieving consensus required several months and five series of drawings, each painstakingly prepared and explained by Waterhouse himself (Owens College Extension, "Minutes of Subcommittees," 1868-1873).

The final master plan called for a quadrangle, to be built in stages. The first structure, set back 200 yards from the street so as eventually to form the western inside wall, was to contain classrooms, including a 380-seat lecture theater for the chemistry classes, workshops, a library, office space, and a student common room. Located directly behind the main building was the chemistry laboratory, containing more than 4,000 square feet of space. The central pile was to be in stone, with the laboratory built of less expensive brick (Plate 23). Construction began in 1869 and the first buildings were opened, with much fanfare, in time for the beginning of the fall term in 1873. In commenting on the occasion, the *Manchester Examiner* described the city's newest civic landmark in the following terms:

> The building opened yesterday is in the Gothic style, of a collegiate and early type. The walls are throughout faced with York stone. It is set back about 200 yards from Oxford Road, and presents an imposing front to the street. It is 300 feet in length, and varies in width, these variations being so arranged, however, as to add to, rather than detract from the architectural merits of the structure. Utility and ornament are also combined in a flèche arising from the centre roof. The block is divided into three floors, and contains the principle lecture rooms and classrooms. (8 Oct. 1873)

As for the structure's internal arrangements, college officials were well pleased with the architect's efforts. "Internally," remarked their report, "the College building and its fittings . . . reflect the greatest credit to Mr. Waterhouse's skill in working out in detail the multifarious requirements of the Committee and the Senate. The lecture halls, library, classrooms, and rooms for experiment and research, are airy and well lighted, commodious and easy of access. They have been finished throughout with a careful avoidance of all useless or meretricious ornament, but with such substantial fitness and elegance as will foster pride in the Professors and Students, and will convince the subscribers that the funds entrusted to the Extension Committee have been well and handsomely applied" (Owens College, *Report of Council* 4).

The second stage of the master plan, completed in 1887, added the northern and half the eastern sides of the quadrangle and included an imposing gateway tower intended to provide access to the inner courtyard now beginning to take shape. These new buildings housed the biological and geological laboratories, a natural history museum open to the public, and meeting rooms for the college's governing council. Commenting approvingly on the latest addition to the college's premises, the *British Architect* noted that:

> The main frontage to Oxford Road is finely dominated by a massive tower, and is admirably balanced and effective in its disposition and outline. . . . The façade of the rear range of buildings, which has been long completed, comes into touch with the newly-completed front part . . . in a very pleasing way. The two staircase projections flanking the clock gable in the centre break up this front into a very agreeable picturesqueness, and the early Gothic type adopted for the design is peculiarly appropriate to the buildings. Altogether, this modern University and its home reflect immense credit on the governing body and their architect. (26)

The final stages of construction saw the addition of the Christie Library (opened in 1898) and the ceremonial Whitworth Hall (1902), completing the quadrangle. Both buildings, bearing the names of the individual contributors whose gifts had financed the construction, displayed the same Gothic elements as Waterhouse's other designs for the college, although on a somewhat grander scale, as befitted the institution's increasing prominence. Meanwhile, laboratory space for engineering (1886) and accommodations for the medical school (1874) were added at the back, while a special physics building (1900) was constructed north of the main structure.

In examining the ground plan and elevations of the college's buildings, a number of features stand out. First, consider the choice of a quadrangular arrangement (Plate 24). Contrary to the assumption made by some historians, the evidence shows that the decision was not a reflexive imitation of the closed, academic cloisters of medieval Oxford and Cambridge but rather a solution, arrived at after prolonged argument, to particular problems of space, light, ventilation, noise, and cost. As envisioned by Waterhouse, the quadrangle plan had the merits of making maximum use of the lot, allowing sunlight and fresh air to circulate freely while minimizing the sound of

traffic along the main thoroughfare, and permitting construction to proceed in logical stages as the college's
finances permitted (Owens College Extension, *Second Report*). Next, consider the treatment of the sciences. While
the chemistry building located behind the main structure
was certainly less imposing from the outside, inside was
contained one of the most advanced laboratories in the
world at the time. As one of the most active members of
the Building Committee, chemistry professor Henry Roscoe explicitly requested a modest exterior for the structure
housing his department, in order that more money might
be available for apparatus and other internal fittings. The
same consideration held true for the engineering and
physics buildings added later. Biology, geology, and the
natural history museum, on the other hand, were all
housed in the main Gothic quadrangle. All in all, despite
the grand façade of the buildings housing the arts classrooms at Owens, far more space and money were devoted
to accommodating science subjects (Great Britain, *Reports
of the Commissioners* 500).

The emphasis given to housing the sciences in turn
reflected the evolving mission of the college. In its early
years, before the extension movement, Owens had sought
to   provide the citizens of Manchester with access to a
general liberal arts education, centered on the traditional
classical subjects, with the addition of some elementary
courses in chemistry and physics. Lack of demand for this
curriculum almost led the institution to shut its doors.
Only after Roscoe's arrival in 1857 and a subsequent
reorientation in the direction of advanced scientific teaching and research did the college's prospects begin to
improve. The extension movement, coinciding as it did
with the growth of public concern regarding England's
industrial competitiveness, took advantage of increasing
interest in scientific education to promote a new mission
for the college. Acknowledging that Owens could never
rival Oxford and Cambridge in teaching the humanities,
Roscoe and his colleagues advocated instead a focus on
science and technology as a means of distinguishing the
college and at the same time better serving the needs of
the city's industry. It was Roscoe who pitched the cam-

paign for an expanded institution to leading Manchester manufacturer Thomas Ashton, who in turn spearheaded the extension movement which enabled the college's new mission, and new buildings, to take shape (Barnes 90-110).

Yet the college never lost sight of its original objective of providing Manchester's middle class, excluded for socio-economic or religious reasons from the nation's elite institutions, with access to a traditional university education. In fact, until the last decade of the nineteenth century, the majority of Owens students continued to earn a Bachelor of Arts degree rather than the newer Bachelor of Science, and many graduates pursued careers in teaching or one of the other professions, rather than going into industry or business (Owens College, *Calendars*; Victoria University of Manchester, *Register of Graduates*). Moreover, although most students resided at home or in private lodgings, for the few who did live in college-sanctioned halls of residence, Owens sought to emulate the amenities offered by the residential Oxbridge colleges and foster a similar atmosphere and spirit. Thus, even as the institution endeavored to create a new model for higher education in England, stressing scientific research and training, along with more democratic access, it was never entirely free from the ideals associated with the traditional English idea of a university.

Waterhouse's buildings reflect this tension. The architect, already well-known to Manchester's leading public men, was chosen on the strength of his work on other important civic commissions and his reputation for well-planned designs that did not exceed his clients' budgets. These two areas, internal arrangements and cost, were clearly the greatest concerns of the college's Building Committee. No mention was ever made of the external design of the building and it is tempting to assume that the college's officials simply expected Waterhouse to use the same Gothic details that he employed in his other civic structures (Owens College Extension, "Minutes of Committees"; "Minutes of Subcommittees"; Waterhouse correspondence). At the time of his appointment, however, Waterhouse was also engaged in designing new

Gothic revival additions for Balliol College, Oxford and Gonville and Caius College, Cambridge, a fact which may not have gone unappreciated by the Owens Building Committee. To the architect, the style served as a means of expressing not only civic pride but the spirit of the modern age. In his view, Gothic was therefore appropriate for important public structures like Manchester's town hall or an expanded Owens College, both buildings representing monuments to voluntary civic effort. Yet, for passersby at least, as well as for those who taught and studied within, the college's new façade may well have evoked a sense of the tradition and prestige associated with England's most ancient and revered institutions of higher learning. Such was the ambiguity inherent within the Gothic Revival style, as within the ideal of the civic university itself.

The building that suggests this connection most directly is the ceremonial Whitworth Hall, the last and most ornate addition to the college quadrangle. Fronting the busy thoroughfare of Oxford Road, the Hall serves to gather the Owens community, in all its academic finery, to observe in public view the customary rituals of academic life (Plate 25). That the Gothic edifice, for years blackened by the coal-smoke of the Victorian industrial city, bears the name of Sir Joseph Whitworth, famous self-made Manchester engineer and staunch advocate of higher scientific and technical education, symbolizes the essentially ambiguous, often contradictory nature of the civic university's mission in an urban setting. For despite its pioneering aims, the University of Manchester was never entirely free from associations with the Oxbridge ethos, even when attempting to assert an independent identity in the form of civic architecture. Regardless of intent, its Gothic Revival buildings communicate a nostalgia for traditional forms and ideals, at the same time that they embody a modern spirit of innovation based on local initiative. The final interpretation is in the eye of the beholder.

Works Cited

Archer, John. Rev. of *The Dilemma of Style: Architectural Ideas from the Picturesque to the Post-Modern*, by J. Mordaunt Crook. *Journal of the Society of Architectural Historians* 49:3 (1990): 336-40.

Barnes, Sarah V. "Defining the University: A Comparative Perspective on the Process of Creating Institutional Identity at the University of Manchester and Northwestern University." Diss. Northwestern University, 1995.

British Architect. January 14, 1887. Documents Book #1. Uncatalogued. University of Manchester Archives.

Crook, J. Mordaunt. *The Dilemma of Style: Architectural Ideas from the Picturesque to the Post-Modern.* London: John Murray, 1987.

Girouard, Mark. *Alfred Waterhouse and the Natural History Museum.* New Haven: Yale University Press, 1981.

Great Britain. *Reports of the Commissioners . . . with regard to Scientific Instruction.* [Devonshire Commission], Minutes of Evidence. Vol. XXV, C. 536. March 31, 1871.

Jackson, Basil, ed. *Recollections of Thomas Graham Jackson.* London: Oxford University Press, 1950.

Lowe, R.A., and Rex Knight. "Building the Ivory Tower: The Social Functions of Late Nineteenth-Century Collegiate Architecture," *Studies in Higher Education* 7:2 (1982): 81-91.

Maltby, Sally, Sally MacDonald, and Colin Cunningham. *Alfred Waterhouse, 1830-1905.* London: Prudential Assurance Company, Ltd., 1983.

Manchester Examiner. October 8, 1873. Documents Book #1. Uncatalogued. Manchester University Archives.

Mancoff, Debra. *The Arthurian Revival in Victorian Art.* New York: Garland Publishing, 1990.

Owens College. *Report of the Council to the Court of Governors, October 6, 1873.* UA/22. University of Manchester Archives.

_____. *Calendars.* 1860-1907. UA/19. University of Manchester Archives.

Owens College Extension. "Minutes of Committees." 1868-1873. UA/1. University of Manchester Archives.

_____. "Minutes of Subcommittees." 1868-1873. UA/1. University of Manchester Archives.

_____. *Second Report of the Extension Committee, December 3, 1869.* UA/1/27. University of Manchester Archives.

Parr, Michael. "Waterhouse, Alfred," *Dictionary of Business Biography.* 5 vols. Ed. D.J. Jeremy. London: Butterworths, 1986.

Smith, Stuart Allen. "Alfred Waterhouse: Civic Grandeur" in *Seven Victorian Architects.* Ed. Jane Fawcett. London: Thames and Hudson, 1976, 92-121.

Victoria University of Manchester. *The Victoria University of Manchester Register of Graduates.* Manchester University Press, 1908.

Waterhouse, Alfred. "Letters to Owens College Officials." 1869-1873. Owens College Documents Book #1. Uncatalogued. University of Manchester Archives.

Williams, Raymond. *Culture and Society, 1780-1950.* New York: Columbia University Press, 1983.

Notes On Contributors

Sarah V. Barnes

Sarah V. Barnes earned a Ph.D. in comparative history from Northwestern University and is currently teaching at Southern Methodist University in Dallas, Texas. Her research focuses on the history of higher education in Britain and the United States. The material for the essay included in this collection was drawn from a larger study, supported in part by a fellowship from the Fulbright Commission, which deals with the University of Manchester and Northwestern University.

Murray Baumgarten

Murray Baumgarten, founding director of The Dickens Project, is Professor of English and Comparative Literature at the University of California, Santa Cruz. He is the editor-in-chief of the Strouse Carlyle Edition; the first volume, a critical edition of *On Heroes, Hero-Worship, and the Heroic in History* was published by the University of California Press in 1993.

Florence S. Boos

Florence S. Boos has been at the University of Iowa since 1973 where she is Professor of English. Previous works include *The Poetry of Dante G. Rossetti* (1963) and *The Design of William Morris's 'Earthly Paradise'* (1991). She has edited *The Juvenilia of William Morris* (1982), *A Bibliography of Women and Literature, 1975-1980* (1988), *Socialism and the Literary Artistry of William Morris* (1990) and *History and Community: Essays in Victorian Medieval-*

ism (1992). She is currently at work on a book on working-class women poets in Victorian Scotland.

Mary Burgan

Mary Burgan is currently General Secretary of the American Association of University Professors. She is on extended leave from a professorship in English at Indiana University-Bloomington. She has published essays on nineteenth- and twentieth-century fiction and on issues in higher education. Her most recent publication in literary studies is a book, *Illness, Gender, and Writing: The Case of Katherine Mansfield* (1994). She is now working on a study of twentieth-century American short stories written by southern women.

Alisa M. Clapp

Alisa M. Clapp is a Ph.D. candidate in Victorian literature at the University of Illinois. She has published on Gaskell in the *Michigan Academician* while her dissertation is titled "On Wings of Song: Music as Cultural Discourse in Victorian Literature and Society."

Anne L. Helmreich

Anne L. Helmreich is currently a Research Assistant at the Center for Advanced Study in the Visual Arts, National Gallery of Art, Washington, D.C. She was the recipient of the first Walter L. Arnstein award for dissertation research in Victorian studies, sponsored by the Midwest Victorian Studies Association, for her dissertation, "Contested Grounds: Garden Painting and the Invention of National Identity in England, 1880-1914" (Northwestern University, 1994). Her work on British prints results from a UCLA Art Council Graduate Curatorial Fellowship at The Grunwald Center for the Graphic Arts (1991) and an internship with the Department of Prints and drawings at the Art Institute of Chicago (1990).

Edward Jacobs

Edward Jacobs is Assistant Professor of English at Old Dominion University in Virginia where he teaches eighteenth- and nineteenth-century literature, literary theory and film studies. He has recently published several articles on British publishing history and the novel, and is finishing a book on the relations between literary and historiographical Gothicism.

Linda R. Krause

Linda R. Krause is an associate professor at the School of Architecture and Urban Planning, University of Wisconsin–Milwaukee. Her scholarly interests include nineteenth and twentieth-century architectural and urban design theory, criticism, and history. Her recent publications have included critiques of "imageability" in contemporary Milwaukee and neo-regionalist architectural theory.

Joseph F. Lamb

Joseph F. Lamb is Assistant Professor of Art History at Ohio University, where he teaches courses in the history of photography and nineteenth and twentieth-century art. Among his previous publications are articles on Victorian studios and the popular press, Victorian art periodicals, and the late work of G. F. Watts. He is currently president of the *Historians of British Art*.

Debra N. Mancoff

Debra N. Mancoff, Associate Professor of Art History at Beloit College, writes and lectures on Victorian art and the Arthurian Legend. Author of *The Arthur Revival in Victorian Art* (1990) and editor of *The Arthurian Revival: Essays in Form, Tradition, and Transformation* (1992), her most recent work is *The Return of King Arthur: The Legend Through Victorian Eyes* (1995).

Harold Perkin

Harold Perkin is Professor of History and Higher Education at Northwestern University. Educated at Cambridge University, he taught at Manchester and Lancaster Universities before coming to the United States in 1985. His books include *The Origins of Modern English Society, 1780-1880*, *The Rise of Professional Society: England since 1880*, and (forthcoming) *The Third Revolution: Professional Society in International Perspective*, which deals with post-industrial society in Britain, the United States, France, both Germanies, Soviet Russia, and Japan. He is the founder and Vice-President of the Social History Society of the U.K.

Thomas Prasch

Thomas Prasch, a contributing editor (for film) of the *American Historical Review* and past managing editor of *Victorian Studies*, received his Ph.D. in English history from Indiana University. His dissertation concerned working-class subjects and Victorian photography. He has published on Victorian responses to Islam, the 1862 London International Exhibition, photographers P.H. Emerson and H. P. Robinson, and the Victorian re-discovery of Gerrard Winstanley.

Ian Spring

Ian Spring is head of Cultural History at the Southampton Institute, Southampton, England. Previous publications include *Phantom Village: The Myth of the New Glasgow* (1990).

D. J. Trela

D. J. Trela has published *A History of Thomas Carlyle's "Oliver Cromwell's Letters and Speeches"* (1992) and edited *Margaret Oliphant: Critical Essays on a Gentle Subversive* (1995). Trela is Guest Editor of forthcoming special issues of *Victorian Periodicals Review* on "Women Editors and Critics." Other projects include a critical edition of Carlyle's *Past and Present* and a study of Oliphant's literary criticism. He works at Roosevelt University in Chicago where he is Associate Professor of English and Director of the School of Liberal Studies.

Index